Latin American Identity in Online Cultural Production

"This book is an original contribution to an exciting new field and provides a grounding for cybercultural studies in the historical framework of Latin American cultural studies as well as in Anglo-American cybercultural critical discourses."

—**Scott Weintraub**, The University of New Hampshire

"Taylor and Pitman, the leading scholars in this subject, have given a new epistemological look at Latin American culture and its lettered citizens— including USA Latinidad—by acknowledging and analyzing the (frequently contestatory) cybernetic turn in the region. No study like this has been attempted before and it is a long overdue approach within Latin American Cultural Studies. Scholars, students, and generalist readers will find extremely engaging each of the chapters covering the interplay between cultural products/practices and the cyber condition of our times. This superbly researched book is the necessary cartographical guide to navigate the re-imagined/remediated identity in Latin America."

—**Luis Correa-Díaz**, University of Georgia

This volume provides an innovative and timely approach to a fast growing— yet still under-studied—field in Latin American cultural production: online digital culture. It focuses on the transformations or continuations that cultural products and practices such as hypermedia fictions, net.art and online performance art, as well as blogs, films, databases, and other genre-defying web-based projects, perform with respect to Latin American(ist) discourses, as well as their often contestatory positioning with respect to Western hegemonic discourses as they circulate online. The intellectual rationale for the volume is located at the crossroads of two equally important theoretical strands: theorisations of digital culture, in their majority the product of the anglophone academy; and contemporary debates on Latin American identity and culture.

Claire Taylor is Senior Lecturer in Hispanic Studies at the University of Liverpool, UK.

Thea Pitman is Senior Lecturer in Latin American Studies at the University of Leeds, UK.

Routledge Studies in New Media and Cyberculture

1 **Cyberpop**
Digital Lifestyles and Commodity Culture
Sidney Eve Matrix

2 **The Internet in China**
Cyberspace and Civil Society
Zixue Tai

3 **Racing Cyberculture**
Minoritarian Art and Cultural Politics on the Internet
Christopher L. McGahan

4 **Decoding Liberation**
The Promise of Free and Open Source Software
Samir Chopra and Scott D. Dexter

5 **Gaming Cultures and Place in Asia-Pacific**
Edited by Larissa Hjorth and Dean Chan

6 **Virtual English**
Queer Internets and Digital Creolization
Jillana B. Enteen

7 **Disability and New Media**
Katie Ellis and Mike Kent

8 **Creating Second Lives**
Community, Identity and Spatiality as Constructions of the Virtual
Edited by Astrid Ensslin and Eben Muse

9 **Mobile Technology and Place**
Edited by Gerard Goggin and Rowan Wilken

10 **Wordplay and the Discourse of Video Games**
Analyzing Words, Design, and Play
Christopher A. Paul

11 **Latin American Identity in Online Cultural Production**
Claire Taylor and Thea Pitman

Latin American Identity in Online Cultural Production

Claire Taylor and Thea Pitman

Routledge
Taylor & Francis Group

NEW YORK AND LONDON

First published 2013
by Routledge
711 Third Avenue, New York, NY 10017

Simultaneously published in the UK
by Routledge
2 Park Square, Milton Park, Abingdon, Oxfordshire OX14 4RN

First issued in paperback 2016

Routledge is an imprint of the Taylor and Francis Group, an informa business

Library of Congress Cataloging in Publication Data

Pitman, Thea.
Latin American identity in online cultural production / Thea Pitman,
   Claire Taylor.
      p. cm. — (Routledge studies in new media and cyberculture)
   Includes bibliographical references and index.
   1. Information technology—Latin America.   2. Digital media—Latin
America.   I. Taylor, Claire, 1972–   II. Title.
   T58.5.P494 2012
   303.48'33098—dc23
   2012032777

ISBN 13: 978-1-138-24332-3 (pbk)
ISBN 13: 978-0-415-51744-7 (hbk)

Typeset in Sabon
by Apex CoVantage, LLC

We would like to dedicate this volume to Sylvia Taylor, John Taylor, Maureen Pitman and Leonard Pitman

Contents

List of Plates   ix
Acknowledgments   xi

Introduction: Approaches to Latin American Online Cultural
Production   1

1 Cartographic Imaginaries: Mapping Latin(o) America's Place
   in a World of Networked Digital Technologies   28

2 Reworking the 'Lettered City': The Resistant
   Reterritorialisation of Urban Place   57

3 From Macondo to Macon.doc: Contemporary Latin
   American Hypertext Fiction   84

4 Civilisation and Barbarism: New Frontiers and Barbarous
   Borders Online   115

5 *Mestiz@* Cyborgs: The Performance of Latin American-ness
   as (Critical) Racial Identity   141

6 *Revolución.com*? The Latin American Revolutionary Tradition
   in the Age of New Media (Revolutions)   169

Conclusion: Latin American Cultural Practice Online:
A Continuing Dialogue between Discourses   198

Notes   201
Bibliography   221
Index   243

Plates

1.1 Brian Mackern, *netart latino database*, opening screen.

1.2 Praba Pilar, 'Cyberlabia 2' digital print.

1.3 Praba Pilar, 'Cyberlabia 8' digital print.

2.1 Marina Zerbarini, *Tejido de memoria*, opening screen.

2.2 Marina Zerbarini, *Tejido de memoria*, cycle of images.

3.1 Jaime Alejandro Rodríguez, *Gabriella infinita*, opening screen.

3.2 Jaime Alejandro Rodríguez, *Gabriella infinita*, 'Mudanza'.

3.3 Belén Gache, *WordToys*, 'Southern Heavens'.

4.1 Guillermo Gómez-Peña, *The Chica-Iranian Project: Orientalism Gone Wrong in Aztlán*, 'Kurdish Llorona'.

4.2 Guillermo Gómez-Peña, *The New Barbarians*, 'En el hall del genocidio'.

4.3 Guillermo Gómez-Peña, *The New Barbarians*, 'Piedad Post-colonial'.

4.4 Martha Patricia Niño, *Relational Border Map*, opening screen.

5.1 Guillermo Gómez-Peña, 'Ethno-Techno: A Virtual Museum of Radical Latino Imagery and Fetishized Identities', photograph of El Ethnographic Loco.

5.2 Los Cybrids (René Garcia, John Jota Leaños and Praba Pilar) 'Webopticon: Sistema de vigilancia' digital mural.

5.3 Los Cybrids (René Garcia, John Jota Leaños and Praba Pilar), 'Humaquina: Manifest Tech-Destiny' digital mural.

5.4 Los Cybrids (René Garcia, John Jota Leaños and Praba Pilar), screen from opening sequence of website.

5.5 Alex Rivera, *Cybracero Systems*, opening screen.

5.6 Alex Rivera, *Cybracero Systems*, 'How to Node Up'.

6.1 Fran Ilich, *possibleworlds.org* logo, from opening screen.

Acknowledgments

Throughout the research and planning of this volume we have been fortunate to count on the support and advice of many friends and colleagues who have helped and inspired us along the way. We would like to thank all those who have helped us to access information, given us the benefit of their advice and knowledge of subjects far beyond our own disciplinary and area studies context, read early drafts of this work at various stages, or have inspired us with their comments and feedback on papers given pertaining to this project. These friends and colleagues include Victoria Barr, Debra Castillo, Luis Correa Díaz, Stephanie Dennison, Charles Forsdick, David Frier, Chris Harris, Kirsty Hooper, Geoffrey Kantaris, Par Kumaraswami, Héctor Perea, Lisa Shaw, Kim Stringer, Emma Tomalin, Carlos Uxó, Youxuan Wang, Frances Weightman, Scott Weintraub, and the anonymous readers at Routledge. We would also like to express our gratitude to the cultural producers whose work we have analysed in this volume, both for their time and patience in answering our queries and allowing us to cite them, and for their generosity in allowing us to reproduce images of their work; to Belén Gache, René Garcia, Guillermo Gómez-Peña, the *Hiperbarrio* team, Fran Ilich, John Jota Leaños, Brian Mackern, Eduardo Navas, Martha Patricia Niño, Praba Pilar, Alex Rivera, Jaime Alejandro Rodríguez, Yoani Sánchez and Marina Zerbarini, we are immensely grateful. Thanks are due to several scholars who have granted us permission to cite their work in draft form, including Debra Castillo and Raquel Recuero. Thanks are also due to the Modern Humanities Research Association, the Faculty of Arts, University of Leeds, and the University of Liverpool International Collaboration Fund for their financial support for this project. Likewise, we extend our thanks to our respective departments—the School of Cultures, Languages and Area Studies at Liverpool, and the School of Modern Languages and Cultures at Leeds—for their ongoing support. On a more personal note, Claire would like to thank Jairo, Lara and Catherine; Thea would like to thank Haynes, Noah, Louis and Alice.

All translations from the Spanish in the volume are our own, unless otherwise stated. It should be clarified that Thea is co-author of Chapter One and sole author of Chapters Five and Six. The credit for all other sections of the work is due to Claire. It goes without saying that any errors in this volume are our own.

Introduction
Approaches to Latin American Online Cultural Production

The rapid increase in connectivity across Latin America, alongside the equally rapid take-up of new technologies across the region, has brought with it growing and vibrant communities of online cultural practitioners, as well as the rise of new artistic and literary forms. This volume focuses on the transformations or continuations that cultural products and practices such as hypertext fictions, net.art, blogs and online performance art, as well as web-based projects that go beyond generic boundaries, perform with respect to a series of prominent Latin American(ist) discourses. These discourses all preexisted the internet and have long histories in Latin America: Here we focus on how they adapt, transmute, or perpetuate themselves in online practice. Given that we deal, therefore, with new media genres and with Latin American(ist) discourses, the intellectual rationale for the volume is thus located at the crossroads of two, equally important, theoretical strands: theorisations of digital culture, in their majority the product of the anglophone academy; and contemporary debates on Latin American identity and culture.

Bringing together recent theorisations in digital cultures with empirical research in the broader field of internet studies, we begin by setting out debates on new terminology and genres. We then address some of the central popular and scholarly concerns about globalisation, homogenisation, and cultural specificity on the internet. Here, we situate our own response within a growing trend in internet studies that has been marked by the focus on the local and the culturally specific, all the while taking into account the global reach of new media technologies. Subsequently, drawing together debates taking place within Latin American cultural studies on new forms of cultural expression, and on the problematisation of the concept of area studies, the volume proposes that Latin American online cultural production be approached via notions of the postnational, updated in our context as the 'postregional'. We adapt aspects of the postnational approach that has emerged in Hispanic studies during the last decade, refining it to argue for a 'postregional' approach that will enable us to understand the complex ways in which Latin American identity is articulated online. Here, and throughout the chapters of this volume, we explore how the online works we analyse force a rethinking of conventional conceptualisations of territoriality, agency, citizenship, and local and global affiliations, among others—many of which notions are central to conceptualisations of Latin America itself as a region, and to current debates in Latin Americanism. Our volume thus speaks to two disciplinary fields—namely, internet studies and Latin Americanism—and, working in negotiation between these two disciplines, we propose an innovative theoretical model for understanding how the defining discourses of Latin America are reconfigured online. Our contention is that Latin American digital culture, and the theoretical and analytical models we propose for it, engage with some of the central issues troubling both internet studies and Latin Americanism today. That is, if, as we discuss below, the issue of locatedness is one of the central contemporary dilemmas in both internet studies and Latin American studies, then our key argument is that it is in Latin American online cultural practice where we can find some of the most fruitful and critical engagements with this dilemma.

The scope and terminology of Latin American studies are currently subject to problematisation and debate. In this light, a clarification regarding our terminology is necessary: throughout this volume we follow in the footsteps of recent scholarship, such as that of Diana Taylor (2003) or Debra Castillo (2005), who envisage transnational cultural connections between Latin Americans and the estimated 40 million Latinas/os resident in the US, and argue that such works should be analysed within a framework of 'Latin/o American hemispheric studies' (Taylor 2003:xvii). Following these scholars, we approach the range of cultural products analysed in this volume as part of a continuum of identities, indicating how the concept of Latin American identity underpinning this volume is one that is not exclusively bound by accepted nation-state and/or regional borders. Where relevant, we distinguish clearly between the two communities. Elsewhere we employ the term 'Latin(o) American' to refer to discourses and issues that, given the shared heritage, affect or are pertinent to both equally. As we argue throughout this introduction and in the chapters that follow, Latin American identity often traverses nation-state/regional boundaries, can be composed of multiple and diasporic identities, and indeed, the growing opportunities to express these identities are often facilitated by new media technologies and their ability to cross borders.

This introduction is divided three main sections: firstly, we place our model of online cultural production within the context of some of the central debates that have taken place within digital culture studies in the past two decades, particularly as regards globalisation, embeddedness and (tactical) resistance. In so doing, we argue for an understanding of Latin American online cultural production as both engaging with global trends and technologies, and yet as speaking to local and regional concerns, providing for potentially localised and resistant forms of expression. Following on from this, we dialogue with Latin Americanism, with a particular focus on debates taking place in recent years over the potential demise of the area studies model. Here, in our revisiting of these debates, we propose that online cultural production provides an excellent location for exploring the potential of a postregionalist framework. Thirdly and finally, we plot out the emergent and transmuting discourses of Latin American-ness online, noting how contemporary online practices dialogue with predigital discourses, before going on to set out the trajectory that the subsequent chapters of our study take through these discourses.

THE STUDY OF LATIN AMERICAN ONLINE CULTURAL PRACTICE: NEGOTIATING A PATH BETWEEN DISCIPLINES AND GENRES

Given the rapid rise in the take-up of the internet over the last two decades, and the concomitant development of new cultural forms that often push the boundaries of existing conceptualisations of genres and generic conventions, debates over the exact terminology with which to approach these new phenomena are still being undertaken. For this reason, we set out here an overview of current debates, and then negotiate our own position within these. We start, first, with disciplinary concerns, and then subsequently discuss genre and generic conventions.

Regarding attempts to delineate the disciplinary boundaries and approaches, the transdisciplinary enterprise of internet studies—or, to borrow Silver's term, the 'interdiscipline' of internet studies (Silver 2006:4)—encompasses approaches that draw on politics, media studies, communications studies, ethnography, literary criticism and art history, among others, and has already begun to develop significant conceptual and methodological tools with which to approach new media technologies and practices. That said, and perhaps precisely due to its wide-ranging, interdisciplinary scope, internet studies is, in the words of Silver, the 'largest umbrella underneath which many of us would huddle' and thus constitutes a 'meta-field' (Silver 2004:55). Indeed, a cursory glance at some of the leading journals and institutes in internet studies confirms just how broad this umbrella is: the Oxford Internet Institute, for instance, engages in research stretching from governance to network integration, while leading journals such as *Convergence: The International Journal of Research into New Media Technologies* include articles ranging from gender and technology to copyright, educational technology and virtual reality, among many other topics. Our focus is on the cultural studies strands within this 'large umbrella' or interdiscipline, and as we explain now, our analyses of the works in this volume draw in particular on approaches arising from cybercultural theory, studies in digital cultures, and ethnographic approaches to internet use.

In regard to cybercultural theory, we acknowledge that the term itself—'cyberculture'—is a debated one, having come under scrutiny in recent years for its implicit reliance on utopian, patriarchal conceptualisations of online activity as encapsulated in cyberpunk visions of the 1980s in which the user is freed from the body and from material constraints, to navigate a purely virtual realm.[1] That said, what we do find useful in cybercultural perspectives is the emphasis on the cultural implications of online technologies, a stance neatly summed up by Pierre Lévy who has been careful to insist that 'cyberculture' encapsulates not only the infrastructure but also the 'practices, attitudes, modes of thought, and values' that are thereby enabled and developed (Lévy 2001:xvi). For our own purposes, where we employ terms such as 'cyberculture' or 'cyberspace' in this volume, we tend to do so particularly where works interrogate or problematise some of the assumptions underpinning these terms; we thus tend to employ it in inverted commas even if not explicitly so. What we draw from cybercultural studies, therefore, is the emphasis on cultural manifestations online, although, as our chapters show, we also trace the constant and complex interactions taking place as practitioners move back and forth across media—a feature that is predominant in the work of Latin American practitioners.

From research in digital cultures more broadly, we take the understanding that the online sphere is 'no longer a realm separate from the offline "real" world but fully integrated into offline life' (Miller 2011:1), and the rethinking of some of the assumptions underpinning older conceptualisations of cyberculture in the light of web 2.0 technologies (Creeber and Martin 2008). While we cannot pretend to cover each and every digital format, we do aim in this volume to adapt the ideas set forth by scholars of digital cultures for our specific purposes. In particular, we develop an understanding of the complex ways in which, to borrow Deuze's term, the 'praxis of digital culture' involves 'individualization, post-nationalism and globalization' (Deuze 2006:64), features which we explore in more depth in the course of our introduction.

Finally, we also take inspiration from developments in internet ethnography in recent decades. While our work is not internet ethnography, since we have not followed the content creators of the works we discuss, and have not engaged in sustained periods of participant observation, we adopt the insistence on embeddedness that has characterised recent work in the field. Debates on the localisation of the internet have been the focus of studies by Christine Hine (2000), Daniel Miller and Don Slater (2000) and John Postill (2011), and we take on board the insistence of these and other researchers on the necessity of exploring how embeddedness, locality and cultural specificity are negotiated and produced online.

In summary, our critical practice embraces the (somewhat unwieldy) term of 'networked digital culture studies'. Merging Silver's 'networked culture studies' with notions of 'digital cultures' as expounded by Miller, Deuze and others, 'networked digital culture studies' indicates our understanding of, on the one hand, how the networked and the offline combine, and, on the other, the underlying cultural studies approach to our case studies. Here, we understand the term 'networked' in all its rich (predigital) history, encompassing both on- and offline networks; as the chapters in this volume reveal, the cultural artefacts we explore in this volume frequently combine online and offline practice. Our approach, therefore, draws on the various debates we have noted above, while also taking into account the complex ways in which the Latin American practitioners we examine often deliberately resist the notion of a 'pure' online realm.

Just as debates over the broad disciplinary or transdisciplinary boundaries of research into online culture are still taking shape, so too, the emergence of new genres and cultural forms, and their associated nomenclature, has been the subject of much discussion in recent years. As noted above, our focus in this volume is on the cultural manifestations of Latin American(ist) discourses online; in other words, we explore how new media technologies are being put to innovative uses for cultural purposes, as well as exploring the continuities that these new cultural manifestations hold with older, predigital formats and the discourses they were instrumental in constructing and circulating. We now provide an overview of recent debates on new media genres, noting how our research of necessity draws on a variety of theorisations and analytical tools that have been developed to approach a range of genres—electronic literature in its varied forms, or net.art, for instance—while at the same time noting where there is significant overlap across cultural practices. We do not conceive of the boundaries between the various genres we explore to be impermeable; indeed, throughout this volume our approach is informed by the fact that many of the practitioners whose work we study operate across a variety of genres and create works which, in many cases, do not fit neatly into one generic model. Hence we negotiate here between different generic conventions, and in the chapters that follow, we pay attention to generic specificities as well as indicating where cultural practice in one genre speaks to, and is informed by, practices in another.

Broadly speaking, the genres covered in this volume include blogging, hypertext fiction, net.art and multimedia art more broadly, and online performance art. To take the first of these, we discuss blogs in Chapters Two and Six of this volume. The advent of the blog in the late 1990s, with the launch of Pyra's free weblogging software in 1999 (Mead 2002; Turnbull 2002) gave rise in the Hispanic world, as elsewhere, to the explosion of the blogosphere and of the blog as a form of expression in the early to mid-2000s. While the boom in blogging worldwide, and in many parts of Latin America, tended to be in the first half of the 2000s, with the rise since then of social media platforms such as Orkut, Facebook, and more latterly the micro-blogging site Twitter,[2] blogs still remain a major player in Latin American digital culture. According to estimates cited by Recuero, for instance, in 2007 over 9 million users in Brazil accessed and read blogs, representing almost half the population of internet-active users in that country (Recuero 2008). Indeed, as we note in Chapter Six, in certain countries, such as Cuba, blogging was growing significantly in importance throughout the latter half of the 2000s, as evidenced by the growing notoriety of Yoani Sánchez and the group of like-minded bloggers that she has helped to develop, while in other contexts, such as the blogging arm of the *hiperbarrio* project in Colombia analysed in Chapter Two of this volume, blogging still remains an important force for digital inclusion, albeit alongside the use of other more recent web 2.0 platforms such as Flickr and Open Street Map. In this regard, our research in these two chapters is informed by recent research on blogging which has highlighted aspects such as the significance of blogging for citizenship (Tremayne 2006), the use of blogs for activist purposes (Kahn and Kellner 2004) and the importance of users themselves in the creation of content (Russell and Echchaibi 2009). At the same time, our chapters also sit within the context of research into Latin American-specific uses of the blog format, including Paul Fallon's work on blogging in the US-Mexico border region (Fallon 2007), Elisabeth Jay Friedman's research into the use of blogs (among other tools) by Latin American lesbian networks (Friedman 2007), Hernando Rojas and Eulalia Puig-i-Abril's research into the use of blogs in Colombia (Rojas and Puig-i-Abril 2009), Cláudio Penteado, Marcelo dos Santos and Rafael Araújo's chapter on the use of blogs in Brazil's *Cansei* protest movement (Penteado, dos Santos and Araújo, 2009), Beatriz Peña Calvo and colleagues' work on the Cuban blogsphere (Calvo Peña 2010a) and Tori Holmes's research into the creation of local content in blogs in Brazilian *favelas* (Holmes 2012).[3]

Where blogging has associations with primarily factual written forms, such as the diary format, citizen journalism, or the *crónica* and *testimonio* genres in a Latin American context,[4] works which abide more closely by fictional literary conventions fall into the category of hypertext fiction. There is by now a relatively large corpus of theoretical and analytical works on what, broadly speaking, can be termed hypertext fiction, ranging from early works such as those of Landow (1992) and Bolter (1991), to more recent volumes such as those of Hayles (2008) or Ciccoricco (2007). The concepts set forth by these scholars, such as 'hypertext fiction' and other cognate terms such as 'network fiction' (Ciccoricco 2007), 'electronic literature' (Hayles 2008), or 'ergodic literature' (Aarseth 1997), imply an understanding of these works through a predominantly literary-textual paradigm. Our volume draws on the terminology developed by such theorists, particularly as regards the potential for nonlinearity, the creation of active readers, and collaborative authorship. In the light of these often heated debates, Chapter Three of this volume explores both the potentialities and the limitations of the medium, through its analysis of the hypertext novel, *Gabriella infinita* by Colombian author Jaime Alejandro Rodríguez, and the collection of short hypertext fictions, *WordToys*, by Argentine Belén Gache.

Those works which are cultural products making use of hyperlinking, but do not, essentially, contain a narrative arc nor invoke a character (features necessary to qualify as hypertext fiction), we here in this volume denominate under the category 'net.art' understood in the broadest terms.[5] Here, drawing on the now growing body of scholarly and practitioner work on this art form, we flag up as particular features the (revival of) avant-gardist tendencies (Stallabrass 2003:48; Corby 2006:6; Daniels 2009:29), the meta-discourse on the medium (Baumgärtel 2001:24; Stallabrass 2003:139), and the deliberate (re- and/or mis-) use of coding (Stallabrass 2003:36–39; Blais and Ippolito 2006:25). In Chapters One, Two and Four we explore features such as ASCII-art and browser art as a subset of net.art in the case of Mackern's *Netart latino database*, hyperlinking and remixing of web-based content in the case of Niño's *Relational Border Map*, and resistant recycling of images and other sources in Zerbarini's *Tejido de memoria*, Navas's animations and Praba Pilar's digital prints. This is not to say, of course, that the works of Mackern, Niño, Navas and Zerbarini, for instance, do not share features with more properly literary forms; there are undeniably elements of narrative within some of the files comprising Zerbarini's work, and there are elements of text (in the form of short lexia) in Niño's relational map. But, we argue here that while they may draw on literary heritage in some aspects, they cannot be analysed through a purely literary paradigm, and hence in these chapters we situate the work of these cultural producers in the broader context of net.art, and the particular place of net.art in Latin America.

A further genre with which we engage in this volume is that which can be broadly expressed as online performance art. Developments in new media technologies have led to debates in performance art circles from the last decade of the twentieth century and into the twenty-first, particularly as regards conventional understandings of performance art as site-specific and/or involving corporeal presence, and, conversely, the use of new media technologies offering distance and/or virtual participation. This has led to the redefining of the boundaries of performance art, with the coining of new terms and (sub)genres, such as Antoinette LaFarge and Robert Allen's notion of 'media conmedia performance works' which involve the 'melding [of] comedic performance traditions with new media technologies' (LaFarge and Allen 2005:213), Giges and Warburton's elaborations of 'telematic performance' involving real-time 'remote performance collaborations' (Giges and Warburton 2010:25), or Dixon's notion of 'digital performance' in which computer technologies play a key role in 'content, techniques, aesthetics or delivery form' (Dixon 2007:3, *passim*). Moreover, it has also led to complex understandings of performance art itself, and a reviewing of its historicity. Miroslaw Rogala has noted that participation in the same location *and* across dispersed locations stretches back at least to the Futurists' conception of audience collaboration in participatory art works (Rogala 2010:300), Boris Groys's genealogy of participatory art sets it within a continuum first started by the early Romantics (Groys 2008:19), while Steve Dixon has asserted that the legacy goes even further back, arguing that 'networked art and creative collaboration over a distance has an ancestry that can be traced back to the earliest hand-delivered messenger correspondences of antiquity' (Dixon 2007:420). It is within the context of these debates surrounding online performance that we discuss the works of Guillermo Gómez-Peña, Los Cybrids and Alex Rivera in Chapters Four and Five. Here, we consider the performative aspects of these online works, even when the works themselves are not strictly speaking, or solely, performance art, and, where relevant, we also explore how these works make reference to the offline performances with which they dialogue and investigate how these pieces speak to the delicate negotiations between offline corporeal presence and online virtuality.

It is, of course, the case that some of the cultural products that we study in this volume do not fit comfortably within any of the generic categorisations listed above. The overriding reason for this is because they function as *conceptual* art works that employ whatever means they chose—often several at once—to achieve their objectives; such works are defined by their approach more than by their genre. These works typically have clearly defined political agendas and thus also fit within a framework of hactivism/tactical media art (see below for more detailed coverage of this). While this is the case of Los Cybrids' and Alex Rivera's work studied in Chapter Five, it is even more clearly the case of a cultural producer such as Fran Ilich studied in Chapter Six, whose project to create his own server, complete with online bank, can be seen to employ aspects of all of the genres outlined above in its conceptual assault on the form and function of the internet and online culture as a whole.

If, as we have shown in our overview of the transdisciplinary and genre-specific approaches to new media arts, the negotiations between presence and absence, and between local specificities and new media technologies have been at the forefront of discussions by scholars and practitioners alike, these questions come together in one of the central concerns raised about the internet: the relationship between the internet (and new media technologies more broadly) and globalisation. One of the most frequently raised concerns about the internet in scholarly debates and the popular press is the connection between the internet and globalisation, and the perceived pernicious influence such a link may have. Globalisation is discussed in virtually all monographs and companions in the field of internet studies (see, for instance, Bell 2001; Lévy 2001; Creeber and Martin 2008; Nayar 2010; Miller 2011). Early scholarship tended to establish close links between the internet and globalisation; for Pierre Lévy, for instance, globalisation is 'the first fundamental aspect of cyberculture' (Lévy 2001:31), and indeed, this link is reflected in the image of the 'global village' as a widely recognised metaphor for the internet in the popular imagination.[6] For many scholars and activists, the task of interrogating the exact relationship between the internet as a communications infrastructure and globalisation as the systemic underpinning of neoliberalism has been the logical next step. In this regard, globalisation understood in its market-based sense—the removal of barriers between nation-states to facilitate the flow of goods, capital and labour—has given rise to two predominant concerns: firstly, concerns over the weakening of local cultures and the concomitant increase in cultural homogeneity; and secondly, concerns over the extent to which globalisation (and thus the internet as its tool) functions in the interests of late capitalism.

The changing shape of national cultures in the face of globalised cultures promoted by the internet is well documented in scholarship over the past two decades. Certainly, the fact that the internet as infrastructure leads to the weakening of the traditional role and meaning of the nation-state is undisputed, although scholars have debated the extent to which this waning of the nation-state necessarily results in the erosion of national cultural specificity. In an early work on the governance of cyberspace, Brian Loader succinctly summed up the prevailing discourses on globalisation and the internet:

> nation-state boundaries are said to be weakening both from the development of global economies where 'cyberspace' is where your money is, and also from the lack of control of national governments over communications in cyberspace.
>
> (Loader 1997:1)

Given the indisputable effect that the internet has had in weakening the role of the nation-state, fears regarding the loss of cultural specificity, and of increasing homogenisation—for which, read Americanisation—abound in popular discourses regarding the internet, and in some scholarly accounts. Here, what Robert Holton has called the 'homogenisation thesis' comes into play, in which it is proclaimed that 'global culture is becoming standardised around a Western or American pattern', and that this is predicated upon the 'development of information technology and global communications' (Holton 2000:140&142). In this regard, US sociologist Herbert Schiller's comments best sum up this approach: Schiller cautions that the free flow of information enabled by new media technologies means the 'ascendance of US cultural products worldwide' (Schiller 2001:161) and that, thus, the rapid development of information technologies has 'underpinned the capacity for [US] cultural domination' (Schiller 2001:161).

These concerns raised by Schiller are echoed in many different cultural contexts, and point to anxieties regarding the purported homogenising effects of the internet on local cultures. From a broadly postcolonial perspective, Bosah Ebo's edited volume of 2001 was an early example of responses to this question, providing a series of reflections on the extent to which globalisation of necessity means 'cyber-imperialism', and exploring the conditions of 'cyber-globalization', to use Marwan Kraidy's term (Kraidy 2001:28). Meanwhile, from a gendered perspective, scholars have raised concerns over the globalising tendencies of the internet with regard to the specificity of women's lives and the local spaces within which women are rooted. In this regard, Anne Scott, Lesley Semmens and Lynette Willoughby have argued that:

> Women are often identified with local identities and the particularities of place [. . .]. As these geographies of place and locality are subverted

by new geographies of information flow, women face a double challenge: they must defend their local spaces against the threat posed by a
disembodied globalization, and they must also create spaces within the
new electronic media for their own voices.

(Scott, Semmens and Willoughby 2001:13)

While Scott *et al.*'s argument here might seem potentially reductive in the tacit
assumption that women are, indeed, inextricably linked with local space, their
inveighing against a globalisation perceived as 'disembodied', as well as their
call for the formulation of alternative spaces for expression, prove useful in
summing up the potential dangers of a globalised, homogenised cultural space.
Indeed, their comments are reflective of broader trends in cyberfeminism which
aimed to counter utopian conceptualisations of the internet as a global, disembodied domain.[7] In all of these cases, as with many others characterising early
approaches to the relationship between the internet and cultural globalisation,
concerns are raised over the waning of the nation-state as arbiter of cultural
capital, and the loss of local places of resistance to homogenising global cultures, two issues which will be revisited in more depth below.

With respect to the second common concern raised regarding globalisation,
many scholars have drawn systemic links between new media technologies
and the interests of global corporatism. For many, economic globalisation
in its current formulation serves the interests not of a global community
of equals, but of the major multinational corporations who dominate late
capitalism today, giving rise to the shorthand term 'neoliberal globalization',
to indicate how this form of globalisation functions in the interests of neoliberalism (Fotopoulos 2001:241). As Kellner notes, globalisation for some is
seen as a 'cover concept for global capitalism' and accordingly is condemned
as 'another form of the imposition of the logic of capital and the market
on ever more regions of the world' (Kellner 2002:286). For many, thus,
globalisation, involving the economic and social restructuring of advanced
capitalist societies, is predicated upon the advances of information and
communication technologies. Here, Manuel Castells's famous formulation
of 'informational capitalism' (Castells 2001b), in which global capitalism
functions via a restructuring enabled by networked flows of information,
establishes a tight nexus of globalisation, new media technologies and late
capitalism. Similarly, Christian Fuchs's arguments regarding what he terms
'translational network capitalism' have posited that 'regimes of accumulation, regulation, and discipline [. . .] increasingly base the accumulation of economic, political, and cultural capital on transnational network
organizations that make use of cyberspace and other new technologies for
global coordination and communication' (Fuchs 2008:87). Luis Suárez-
Villa, meanwhile, has posited the term 'technocapitalism' to illustrate how
the 'rapid and unprecedented global flows of investment capital supported
by innovations in software, communications, and electronics' function to
'dynam[ise] the accumulation of capital' (Suárez-Villa 2009:19).

That said, while the contiguities between communications technologies and neoliberal globalisation have been forcefully argued by the likes of Castells, Fuchs and others, the equation internet = globalisation = neoliberalism is by no means so clear cut (and Castells and Fuchs themselves indicate this in their own works). As many scholars have argued, while there is a tendency towards polarisation in responses to globalisation, globalisation's effects are by no means so homogenising, and, indeed, most scholars reject the reductionism of globalisation to homogenisation. Holton finds that globalisation is conventionally understood through three major theses—homogenisation, polarisation, and hybridisation—and concludes that the simple assumptions that globalisation means homogenisation are unfounded. Kellner, meanwhile, urges that we 'avoid both technological and economic determinism and all one-sided optics of globalization in favor of a view that theorizes globalization as a highly complex, contradictory, and thus ambiguous set of institutions and social relations, as well as one involving flows of goods, services, ideas, technologies, cultural forms, and people' (Kellner 2002:286). Indeed, in one of the first in-depth approaches to the cultural effects of globalisation, Arjun Appadurai set down a timely reminder that 'the globalization of culture is not the same as its homogenization' (Appadurai 1996:42). Here, Appadurai argued, 'the critical point is that both sides of the coin of global cultural process today are products of the infinitely varied mutual contest of sameness and difference on a stage characterised by radical disjunctures between different sorts of global flows and the uncertain landscapes created in and through these disjunctures' (Appadurai 1996:43). Appadurai's assertions chime with our approach in this volume, in that we do not equate the global reach of new media technologies with cultural homogeneity, and indeed, we follow Appadurai's lead in exploring how global flows and new technologies may actually provide room for the expression of new identities.

Furthermore, and with particular relevance to the subject matter of this book, information and communication technologies as a motor for globalisation, can, as a great variety of studies have shown, provide greater room for expression of local identities, or for identities that negotiate between the local and the global, instead of always resulting in the imposition of a globalised, homogenised, Americanised, identity. Empirical research, particularly in nonmetropolitan contexts, has demonstrated the cultural specificity of internet use and internet practices, and has often revealed how internet-based forms of expression can provide a way of bolstering, rather than undermining, local cultural identity. Mark Warschauer's ethnographic study of online technologies in Hawaii in the late 1990s, for instance, revealed that interacting with ICTs allowed participants the opportunity to 'explore and strengthen their sense of individual and collective Hawaiian identity' (Warschauer 2000:161). Daniel Miller and Don Slater's research into Chat and ICQ use in Trinidad demonstrated that online exchanges were closely tied to local circumstances and may have 'strong continuities with earlier forms of kinship' (Miller and Slater 2002:208). Soraj Hongladarom's research into Thai uses of the internet has shown that it functions both as 'an embodiment of cosmopolitan culture' and yet also can be a 'tool for cultural preservation and propagation' and thus serves 'not [to] globalise, but localise' (Hongladarom 1999:397), while Hans Ibold's research on cultural identity and internet use in Kyrgzstan has revealed how this gives rise to 'emergent cultural identities' that are 'idiosyncratically local and uniquely in-between' global and local cultures (Ibold 2010:521). These and many other similar studies have indicated how the expression of local identities may actually be furthered, rather than erased, by the use of new media technologies. Indeed, as John Posthill has recently cautioned, we need to be wary of the 'misguided idea that our "local communities" are being impacted upon by a global Network Society [and] the internet' (Postill 2011:xi), and instead should be asking ourselves 'how variously positioned field agents and agencies [. . .] compete and cooperate over' local identity formation on the internet. This does not mean, of course, that all subaltern interventions online will of necessity be resistant or subversive; rather, that local identity formation on the internet is an act of negotiation, and these identities may at times be oppositional, but at other times in compliance with dominant state-sponsored or conservative conceptualisations of identity.

Just as we must be cautious regarding assumptions about cultural homogenisation and internet use, so, too, have theorists and practitioners challenged the purported conjunction of new media technologies with neoliberalism. As a variety of studies have demonstrated, the purported tools of globalisation—new media technologies—are frequently put to use by anti-globalisation movements precisely to challenge (from within) the neoliberal system. The reduction of barriers of place, the speeding up of communications, the rapid dissemination of information via multiple channels, and the opportunity to create temporary and multiple alliances, have all contributed to making internet-based activities central to the workings of many *anti*-globalisation movements. For instance, Ayer's research on early examples of such movements concluded that the internet can prove an 'efficient and accessible way for individuals and groups' to 'collectively contest [. . .] new and emerging global arrangements' (Ayers 1999:136). Tellingly, Ayers argues that the 'rise of global and regional trade pacts combined with the interdependence of communications technology has encouraged a transnationalisation of a variety of social forces, from multinational corporations to antinuclear activists' (Ayers 1999:136), indicating how the very same features—the potential for global reach and rapid communication offered by new media technologies—can function in the service of multinationals, *but also* in the service of oppositional, antiglobalisation movements. More recently, John Clark, researching the rise of the 'dotcauses' and the growth of transnational mass protest movements against perceived injustices of neoliberal globalisation, concludes that 'the rise of the Internet and dotcauses is transforming civil society advocacy' (Clark 2006:66). The words of one antiglobalisation activist, cited by Clark, are particularly revealing in this regard, in that the goals are stated as 'to build a resistance—both high-tech and grassroots, both focused and fragmented—that is as global, and as capable of coordinated action, as the multinational corporations it seeks to subvert' (Klein, quoted in Clark 2006:51). This sense in which the antiglobalisation movement mobilises the very same tools of (neoliberal) globalisation, but against the grain, indicates that globalisation is not always a hegemonic phenomenon and that, indeed, technologies with global reach do not, of necessity, entail the advancement of the globalisation model promoted by multinational corporatism.

Moreover, it is important to note that practitioners themselves often champion the use of new media technologies against the grain, a phenomenon which is most immediately obvious in the growing debates by, and practices of, tactical media activists. Having its origins in the Next Five Minutes (N5M) groupings and conferences, of which the first was held in Amsterdam in 1993, the notion of tactical media has been extensively developed by the Critical Art Ensemble, a collective of artists working at the intersections of new media, political activism and installation art. Drawing on Michel de Certeau's distinction between the strategic and the tactical, the Critical Art Ensemble define tactical media as a form of 'digital interventionism' that 'challenges the existing semiotic regime by replicating and redeploying it in a manner that offers participants in the projects a new way of seeing, understanding and [. . .] interacting with a given system' (Critical Art Ensemble 2001:8).[8] This notion, in which the tools of a regime are used to replicate and yet to redeploy (to parody, to challenge, to speak back to) that system, is one which indicates how (new) media technologies can (temporarily) be put to use against the grain and, as will be seen in the examples analysed in this volume, is central to the practice of many of the Latin American new media practitioners whose work we examine, most particulary the work of Fran Ilich as noted earlier. In the words of Geert Lovink, one of its most prominent exponents, tactical media thus are 'forced to operate within the parameters of global capitalism, despite their radical agendas' (Lovink 2002:257), and are inspired by a refusal to 'leave globalism to the investment houses and multinationals' (Lovink 2002:256). Tactical media projects, thus, exist of necessity within the parameters of global capitalism and employ its tools, presenting a tactical, temporary challenge. Not aiming to enact a revolutionary overthrow of the system—*pace* Fran Ilich's playful statements on the subject of revolution analysed in Chapter Six—, instead tactical media, in the words of Rita Raley, involve a 'micropolitics of disruption, intervention and education' (Raley 2009:1).

The notions of electronic civil disobedience as developed by the Critical Art Ensemble as a tactical media practice from the mid-1990s onwards have been widely influential in informing other activist projects worldwide, particularly those involving interrogations of US-Mexico relations. The Critical Art Ensemble defined electronic civil disobedience as involving a 'decentralized flow of particularized micro-organizations' that would 'produce multiple currents and trajectories to slow the velocity of capitalist political economy' (Critical Art Ensemble 2001:15). Such a concept informed, and continues to inform, the practice of the Electronic Disturbance Theater, a digital activist group founded in 1997 by Latino activist Ricardo Domínguez and whose activities included virtual sit-ins in solidarity with the Zapatistas which were effected by overloading servers using the group's FloodNet tool—these practices and the inspiration behind it are also neatly expressed in the term 'Digital Zapatismo', also coined by the group.[9] More recently the group has also developed the *Transborder Immigrant Tool* (2009), a mobile telephone tool developed using GPS to aid undocumented immigrants crossing the U.S.-Mexico border in finding water supplies. Domínguez describes the tactics of the EDT as 'not only using the latest technology' but also 'negat[ing] the dominant ideologies that surround this technology's politics, distribution, and "commodification"' (Domínguez, in interview with Fusco 2003:153). In this sense, the EDT's practices involve using globalised media infrastructures against the grain and to campaign against neoliberal globalisation.

With these factors in mind, our volume sets out a vision of new media technologies as both potentially resistant and (resistantly) local. We emphasise the importance, to borrow the words of Miller and Slater, of refusing to 'treat the internet independently of its embeddedness' (Miller and Slater 2000:8). Indeed, as our own edited volume of 2007 demonstrated, Latin American online practice is grounded within broader trends in Latin American culture, and cultural specificities are often reproduced or worked through online. As the various contributions to that volume demonstrated, from the use of blogging to create a sense of local identity in a poor *bairro* of São Paulo (Sá 2007), to the construction of local communities which transcend the nation-state as is the case in the Tijuana Bloguita Front (Fallon 2007), Latin American online practice is, indeed, multiply and complexly embedded. More recently, Tori Holmes's empirical research into blogging in a Brazilian *favela* has demonstrated that the work of online content creators is strongly embedded in their local specificity (Holmes 2012). Thus, as we argue in this volume, the online practitioners whose work we discuss speak to global movements, and also to Latin American-specific cultural and literary traditions and issues. Hence the works analysed in this volume exist in constant dialogue, both synchronic and diachronic, with other influences and movements: diachronic dialogue with prior existing literary, cultural and artistic forms, and synchronic dialogue with contemporary, offline and online concerns. We can see examples of the former, for instance, in the hypertext narratives of Argentine Belén Gache as analysed in Chapter Three, which resonate with a rich Latin American tradition of literary experimentation, or examples of the latter in the net.art of Marina Zerbarini as analysed in Chapter Two, which dialogues closely with the offline, place-based praxis of the Madres de Plaza de Mayo, all the while sketching out new territorialities online. In these works, as in other works by new media artists in Latin

America, there is a constant negotiation between off- and online space, and between existing genres and new, hybrid formats. Neither radically new, nor uncritical continuations of existing models, these online works dialogue with offline practices and predigital models. Similarly, our approach as scholars to these works involves negotiating a path through existing and new theorisations, and between potentially global theories of new media, and embedded theories of Latin American-ness.

LATIN AMERICAN (CULTURAL STUDIES): THE PROBLEMATISATION OF THE REGION?

If the debates around globalisation, the internet and local specificity are by no means straightforward, neither is the question of Latin American identity, and the shape and scope of Latin Americanism as a discipline have come under scrutiny in recent years. In the paragraphs that follow, we plot our fit with existing debates in Latin Americanism, and argue that, in order to develop insights into Latin American online practice, we must engage in a dialogue with Latin American (cultural) studies.

Firstly, our approaches to and analyses of Latin American cultural production online situate themselves within a wider tradition of (popular) cultural studies in Latin Americanism in recent decades. The wide range of research and publications on Latin American cultural products has brought important changes to Hispanism, in particular in its focus on the nonliterary, on the popular (in both sense of the folk and of the mass) and on the subaltern. John Beverley (1993), Debra Castillo and Edmundo Paz-Soldán (2001), Doris Sommer (2006), and Jean Franco (1987), to name but a few, have all pushed the boundaries of traditional, philology-based Latin American studies, and have studied, among other things, *testimonio*, popular narrative for women, film, mass media and melodrama. Moreover, scholars from Latin America itself, such as Beatriz Sarlo, Jesús Martín-Barbero or Néstor García Canclini, have engaged in studies of popular culture and mass media which have made significant contributions to the development of cultural studies, although not always explicitly framed as such. The works of these scholars have been defined by some as cultural studies *avant la lettre*; Ramón de la Campa, for instance, has described García Canclini's *Hybrid Cultures* as presenting 'a way of doing cultural studies in Latin America that begins by acknowledging the now prevalent nexus of cultural production under globalization and neoliberalism' (de la Campa 1999:72). For his own part, Néstor García Canclini has declared that 'comencé a hacer Estudios Culturales antes de darme cuenta que así se llamaban' ['I started doing cultural studies before I even realised that's what it was called'] (García Canclini 1996, quoted in Mato 2003:389), suggesting both an acceptance of the label, but also staking out a claim for his own critical practice as predating the development of the discipline. Jesús Martín-Barbero, meanwhile, has specifically framed his own theoretical approach in regard to the long-standing tradition of *ensayismo* in Latin America, affirming that 'yo no empecé a hablar de cultura porque me llegaron cosas de afuera. Fue leyendo a Martí, a Arguedas que yo la descubrí [. . .] Nosotros habíamos hecho estudios culturales mucho antes de que esa etiqueta apareciera' ['I didn't start talking about culture due to outside influences. It was through reading Martí and Arguedas that I discovered it. [. . .]. We had done cultural studies well before that label appeared'] (Martín-Barbero 1997, quoted in Mato 2003:389). Martín-Barbero's comments here suggest that so-called cultural studies approaches may be particularly fitting in a Latin American context, given that many of the prominent figures who have shaped notions of Latin American-ness—such as Martí and Arguedas—are forerunners of such an approach.

That said, Latin American cultural studies as a discipline—or perhaps a transdisciplinary enterprise[10]—has generated much debate. Nelly Richard, for instance, has noted that a common critique of cultural studies is that it 'propicia una mezcla desinhibida de técnicas, procedimientos, estilos, teorías y métodos' ['encourages an uncontrolled mix of techniques, procedures, styles, theories and methods'] (Richard 2003:441), and argues that 'podría decirse que, con los estudios culturales, el saber universitario ha ganado en progresismo pero [. . .] ha perdido en densidad teórica y también en sutileza intelectual' ['it could be said that, with cultural studies, academic knowledge has gained in progressiveness but [. . .] has lost in theoretical density and also in intellectual subtlety'] (Richard 2003:445). Santiago Castro-Gómez, meanwhile, notes how some scholars 'constat[an] con horror el crecimiento espectacular de los estudios culturales' ['have greeted the spectacular rise of cultural studies with horror'] (Castro-Gómez 2003:344), and view cultural studies as a 'presencia creciente de la metodología "light"' ['growing presence of 'lite' methodology'] (Castro-Gómez 2003:347). Nevertheless, a significant number of scholars—including Castro-Gómez himself—see in Latin American cultural studies an important development which can provide interpretative frameworks for the study of contemporary Latin American culture. For Castro-Gómez, cultural studies are important in the context of the waning of the nation-state as the space of 'concentración de la hegemonía política y cultural' ['the concentration of cultural and political hegemony'] and the concomitant rise of the culture industries (Castro-Gómez 2003:349). In this sense, cultural studies can play an important role in assessing new cultural products, above and beyond those legitimated by lettered culture, and this would include digital media and internet-based works, although Castro-Gómez does not mention these explicitly.

Abril Trigo, Ana del Sarto and Alicia Ríos, meanwhile, have been extensively involved in mapping out the contours of Latin American cultural studies, and, in their introduction to a special issue of the *Revista Iberoamericana*, they argue for an understanding of Latin American cultural studies as not simply a branch of 'unos estudios culturales supuestamente universales' ['purportedly universal cultural studies'] (Trigo, del Sarto and Ríos 2003:324). Instead, they argue that,

> aún cuando operan dentro de la globalización y en respuesta a ella, los estudios culturales latinoamericanos están imbuidos de un manojo de metodologías, paradigmas crítico-teóricos y constelaciones ideológico-políticas forjados en distintos momentos de la amplia trayectoria del pensamiento y la crítica cultural en y sobre América Latina.

> [Albeit operating within and as a response to globalisation, Latin American cultural studies are imbued with a range of methodologies, critical-theoretical paradigms, and political-ideological constellations that were forged in diverse moments of the broad trajectory of thought and cultural criticism in and about Latin America.]

> (Trigo, del Sarto and Ríos 2003:324)

Here, Trigo *et al.* stress that, contrary to some common criticisms, Latin American cultural studies is not an imposition of external models, nor the simple compliance with market forces and globalisation. Continuing in this vein, and echoing the words of Martín-Barbero and García Canclini, Trigo *et al.* then locate their praxis in the long-standing tradition of Latin American thought, arguing for a conception of Latin American cultural studies as involving dialogue between Western schools of thought such as structuralism, postmodernism, linguistics and anthropology on the one hand, and, on the other, the essayistic tradition stretching back as far as Bello and Sarmiento, as well as 'la crítica de la dependencia, la pedagogía del oprimido, la teología de la liberación o las teorías específicamente atinentes a la problemática cultural, como la transculturación o la heterogeneidad' ['dependency theory, the pedagogy of the oppressed, liberation theology, or theories specifically focused on the question of culture, such as transculturation or heterogeneity'] (Trigo, del Sarto and Ríos 2003:325). It is within Trigo *et al.*'s definition of Latin American cultural studies that we situate our own critical practice. Latin American cultural studies is, thus, a zone of reflection which includes on a theoretical level influences from both regional essayistic traditions and other, nonlocal discourses, and analyses, on a material level, both local cultures and their relationship to globalisation.

If debate surrounding Latin American cultural studies and the focus on popular cultural forms has increased, recent developments in the field have led to what we might term the problematisation of Latin American (cultural and area) studies. While the interventions mentioned above are starting to put Latin American cultural studies on the map, a parallel debate argues for what we might, conversely, term the 'undoing of the map.' This debate has been generated by scholars as diverse as Neil Larsen, Daniel Mato, Walter Mignolo and Jon Beasley-Murray who have all, in different ways, critiqued the notion of Latin American (area) studies. As early as 1995, Larsen, in his book *Reading North by South*, argued that the 'seemingly natural and spontaneous availability of Latin America as a subject for discourse' is in fact 'partly a holdover from the colonial past' (Larsen 1995:1), with the resultant implication that Latin American studies as a discipline may involve the (unwitting) perpetuation of colonial impositions. Larsen's timely warning serves as a critique of any reductive stance that would take 'Latin America' as a given or as a passive object of study, and highlights the potential neo-colonial implications of doing so. In a similar vein, Idelber Avelar has set down the urgency of interrogating the history of Latin Americanism, arguing that in its very constitution it is based on exclusionary practices. For Avelar, it is thus essential that Latin Americanism be interrogated via exploring 'how and through what process the postulate of a continental identity creates a field of inclusions and exclusions, assigns positions, interpellates and constitutes subjects' (Avelar 2000:122–123). In this respect, therefore, the project of Latin American studies itself is troubled, and cannot be taken as an unproblematic given; instead, the very postulate of a continental identity must be interrogated.

Walter Mignolo reminds us that area studies (which, of course, includes Latin American studies) emerged as a consequence of the 'hierarchical division into First, Second and Third worlds' in the second half of the twentieth century (Mignolo 2000:221). Mignolo's questioning of the geopolitics of area studies as a discipline again suggests a further, and problematic, hierarchical imposition at the heart of Latin American studies as a project. In a similar fashion, Mato has explored this concept further, arguing that Latin American cultural studies is 'epistemologically, ethically, and politically loaded with the history of the application of the US and Western European hegemonic concept of area studies to Latin America'. Area studies is, thus, for Mato, suspect, since it is 'historically marked by the interests of imperial and other forms of transnational and international dominance' (Mato 2003:793)—again rendering problematic the project of Latin American area studies. Beasley-Murray, meanwhile, takes a different tack and argues that the entire project of area studies has entered into a crisis in the era of globalisation since 'there is no absolutely external viewpoint from which to delineate the neatly compartmentalized global system that Area Studies represents' (Beasley-Murray 2003:227). Beasley-Murray's assertion suggests that globalisation renders invalid the very notion of area studies itself since there is no longer any clearly defined 'area' to be studied, and again serves to further undermine the basis of Latin American (area and/or cultural) studies. Similarly, Alberto Moreiras, delineating a historiography of Latin Americanism, argues that what he terms a 'first' or 'historical' Latin Americanism (that is, the conventional, area-studies-based Latin Americanism), is no longer valid. For Moreiras:

> the first, or historical, Latin Americanism has come to a productive end with the end of the disciplinary paradigm of rule that understood the progress of knowledge as the panoptic search and capture of 'positions, fixed points, identities'.

(Moreiras 2001:45)

Here, Moreiras argues that 'Latin America' is no longer defined by fixed points (if, indeed, it ever was), and hence the concept of 'Latin America', and of 'Latin American studies' is no longer valid in its traditional form.

The critiques raised by these scholars have direct relevance for Latin American (cultural) studies, since the troubling of the project of area studies and of Latin American studies specifically, represents a potential troubling of the very foundations on which, ostensibly, Latin Americanists base our research, demanding a reassessment of what it means to engage in Latin American studies in our contemporary, globalised world. This problematic—that is, the ways in which the project of area studies is troubled, and the fact that the notion of 'Latin America' is no longer closely mapped out onto discrete regional and geographical contours—is, we argue, central to Latin American cultural practice online, and to our own critical approach to it. This is because the issue of location—the extent to which the very objects of study themselves can be defined as *Latin American* in the first place—is central to the very nature of this emerging discipline. To talk of Latin American online cultural practice is, as we argue in this volume, not an outright paradox, but rather emblematic of new forms of Latin Americanism which are resonant with the critiques raised by the scholars above. Such works, involving the construction, performance and consumption of parts or the whole of the work online, trouble clear-cut notions of location, since a work may be produced by authors/creators from a variety of different geographical locations, hosted in another one, and consumed/recreated by users in yet other ones. That is not to say that location ceases to matter; rather, it means that Latin American online practice by its very nature requires a Latin American cultural studies that takes into account the problematisation of area studies. It is therefore at the intersection of these two developments—on the one hand, a rise in scholarly debates on Latin American (popular) culture and new media, and, on the other hand, the deconstruction of the term 'Latin America' in itself—where the study of Latin American online cultural production lies.

Indeed, our argument returns full circle to the question of new media technologies as we think through the problematisation of area studies in our particular context with reference to recent discourses on the postnational. Appadurai's notion of the postnational, which succinctly draws together globalisation, new media technologies, modes of global connection across localities and (national/postnational) identities, proves particularly useful for our argument. If nationalism, for Appadurai, is the 'ideological alibi of the territorial state' (Appadurai 1996:159), then, from the late twentieth century onwards, 'the nationalist genie, never perfectly contained within the bottle of the nation-state, is now diasporic. Carried in the repertoires of increasingly mobile populations of refugees, tourists, guest workers, transnational intellectuals, scientists and illegal aliens, it is increasingly unrestrained by ideas of spatial boundary and territorial sovereignty' (Appadurai 1996:160–61). Crucial in Appadurai's argument is the place and role of territory and territorial sovereignty in relation to founding national concepts of citizenship and national identity; in Appadurai's model it is the *territorial* state that comes under pressure from the forces of the postnational. This emphasis on territory, and on the progressive dissociation of territory from (national) identity, has particular relevance to our volume, as we explore the ways in which Latin American online cultural production makes productive and tactical use of new media technologies to rethink some of the central discourses of Latin American (territorial) identity. Indeed, particularly significant for the purposes of our volume is the fact that Appadurai's argument uses the creation of virtual neighbourhoods to exemplify the growth of the postnational; these, for Appadurai, have the potential to counteract some of the negative pressures of the nation-state (Appadurai 1996:197).

If such are the fundamentals of the postnational as expounded by Appadurai, it has also more recently been seen in Hispanic-specific contexts as a fruitful tool through which to interrogate prevailing assumptions of the nation-state. These interventions range from Silvia Bermúdez *et al.*'s edited volume which posits the contemporary configuration of Spain as postnational (Bermúdez, Cortijo Ocaña and McGovern 2002), through Kirsty Hooper's and Helena Miguélez-Carballeira's arguments for the formulation of Galician studies as necessarily postnational (Hooper 2007 and 2011; Miguélez-Carballeira 2009), to Román de la Campa's call for a postnational understanding of Hispanism and Latin Americanism (de la Campa 2005), and Alberto Moreiras's call for a critical regionalism, to name but a few. In the context of Hispanism elsewhere in the globe, the 'post' of 'postnational' for Hooper 'is predicated not on an apocalyptic vision of the end of the Galician nation, but on the need to relativize and move beyond that universalizing (and therefore anything but universal) national narrative' (Hooper 2007:133), while for Miguélez-Carballeira, the postnational means that the 'concept of the "classic nation" (not necessarily the concept of "nation" altogether) has been superseded' (Miguélez-Carballeira 2009:277). Thus, in our context, to borrow Miguélez-Carballeira's term, it is not the concept of the region *per se* that has been superseded, but the classic concept of the region in which identity, territory and citizenship were tightly bound together. Here, de la Campa's notions of the postnational are particularly relevant for us, since he posits in postnationalism a possible solution to the problem of attempting to sustain areas of study through 'single metasignifiers' such as Hispanism or Latin Americanism, particularly given the 'plethora of conflictive elements' contained by the latter term (de la Campa 2005:302). De la Campa, then, crucially, links emerging discourses of the postnational to precisely the crisis of Latin Americanism (and of Hispanism more broadly) of which we spoke above. In its place, de la Campa argues for a 'postnational understanding of Hispanism' which would mobilise 'post-Hispanist discourses' (de la Campa 2005:302&306); as he argues, this involves understanding that we are witnessing 'not, therefore, an end of the nation in a rigorous sense, as many have augured, but rather a symptom of its dispersal' (de la Campa 2005:306). In other words, the nation-state as arbiter of cultural capital may indeed be waning, but this does not render the notion of the national nor of Hispanic identity valueless; rather, the notion of Hispanic identity and discourse must be understood within the context of global flows, diasporic communities and the intricate crossings of nation-state borders. De la Campa's exhortations for a post-Hispanism echo those of Moreiras who has argued that if the 'classic' model of Latin Americanism is no longer valid, then a 'second Latin Americanism' is possible via the notion of 'critical regionalism'. While not here specifically citing the post-national, Moreiras's call for a critical regionalism which entails 'simultaneously thinking through the contradictory totality of global integration and fragmentation' (Moreiras 2001:75), and which would involve the study of the 'historical fissures [and] the aporias of identity formation' that are constitutive of Latin Americanism, shares many concerns with de la Campa's vision of post-Hispanist discourses. Moreiras's argument that Latin Americanism should involve a regionalism which must be critical is particularly fruitful, highlighting the importance of maintaining a critical stance towards the very notion of the unproblematic or 'classic' region itself.

What we take from these debates is the emphasis on the postnational, the post-Hispanist, and the post- or critical-regionalist. Where the interrogation of the classic nation-state is the central question of postnationalism, here, we extrapolate to argue that our practice must involve the interrogation of the 'classic' region, and the interrogation of the 'classic' model of Hispanism/Latin Americanism. We propose studying the fissures in, as well as the remobilisations of, certain 'Latin American' cultural values and discourses, thus positing a conception of Latin American online culture and critical practice as 'postregional'. If, in the formulations of Appadurai and others, the postnational relativises and moves beyond the national narrative, then 'postregional' Latin American practice relativises and moves beyond the master narratives of 'Latin American-ness', while simultaneously mobilising, reworking and critiquing those narratives. This, we argue, is the positionality *par excellence* of Latin American online cultural production: Arising precisely through the very contradictions and tensions of the medium itself—that is, from the problematic, and unresolved tensions in online interaction between the local and the global, between expression uncoupled from geographical specificity, and reterritorialisation—Latin American online culture plays upon these contradictions and tensions, and thus becomes a 'postregional' Latin American cultural practice. Latin American cultural practice online, as 'Latin American postregional practice' is thus a practice which works through the dismantling of the conventional conceptualisations of 'Latin America', all the while taking up, engaging with and reworking, tropes and discourses of 'Latin American-ness'. At the same time, this 'postregional' practice also allows for moving beyond the classic region without negating the value of regionalism altogether. In this way, Latin American online cultural practice plays with presence and absence enabled by new media technologies, and we can find within it a simultaneous tactical use of online fluidity and border-crossings, coupled with a tactics of reterritorialisation, reaffirmations of place, and reworkings of locality.

Therefore, to talk of *Latin American* online cultural practice is not as paradoxical as it sounds. As we have argued elsewhere (Taylor and Pitman 2007), in Latin American online cultural practice, from the harnessing of globalised technology in the interests of grass-roots organisations (as seen, for instance, in the tactics of the Zapatistas), to the expression of new collective identities which, while crossing national borders, nevertheless make explicit references to location and geographical space (as in the Tijuana Bloguita Front mentioned briefly above), new forms of negotiation between the local and the global, and between the virtual and the real, are constantly being elaborated. Such new forms do not render the notion of a *Latin American* online culture redundant; rather, they suggest new ways of forming and understanding local, regional and transnational affiliations which go beyond the conventional boundaries of their nation-state. Hence an understanding of, and approach to, Latin American online culture which is framed within the notion of 'critical regionalism' allows us to see online works as a 'Latin American postregional practice': a knowing, active and tactical regionalism. Latin American online works are frequently involved in the negotiations between on- and offline spaces, and between old and new cultural forms. Similarly, our approach to them must be located at the conjunction of theorisations in digital cultures, empirical studies located elsewhere around the globe, Latin American cultural studies, and theories developed by Latin American scholars and practitioners themselves. The recent problematisation of area studies need not be, we argue, an impediment to the study of online culture, but may, on the contrary, be an enabling concept through which to view Latin American online practice: as postregional practice, Latin American online works engage in resistant reterritorialisation, frequently 'blogging back' both to globalised conceptualisations of the internet, and to some of the leading tropes of Latin American-ness, creating hybrid and shifting identities and communities online.

THE CONSTRUCTION OF LATIN AMERICA

In terms of how this relationship of hybrid and shifting identities is thought out, our project concentrates on a particular phenomenon which has overshadowed Latin American thought from the outset. This phenomenon is the construction of 'Latin America' as a concept. It is perhaps a commonplace now to talk of Latin America as being as much a construct of discourses as a physical entity based on land and territory. If, to borrow Edmundo O'Gorman's now famous phrase, the Spanish conquistadores, far from describing America, were engaged in the 'invention of America' so that 'the historical appearance of America lay in considering the event as the result of an inspired invention of Western thought and not as the result of a purely physical discovery' (O'Gorman 1961:4), then nineteenth-century Latin American men of letters (and these were, predominantly, men), were engaged in 'the invention of (Latin) America'. Nineteenth-century men of letters were also typically statesmen, and their writings were constantly engaged in 'narrating the nation' to appropriate Homi Bhabha's term (1990). As Doris Sommer's seminal study *Foundational Fictions* (1991) has shown, even purportedly fictional works functioned to imagine the consolidation of the nation-state: For instance, nineteenth-century romantic novels could often be allegories for the wedding of different national factions. Other texts, as those by Martí, Rodó and others more specifically attempted to narrate, or discursively construct, the region as a whole.

All this demonstrates how writing and politics are mutually imbricated and, more specifically, how narrative and Latin America as concept are intertwined, returning us again to one of the fundamental questions of Latin Americanism. If, as we noted above, the foundations of Latin Americanism are coming under question in recent scholarship, so, too, are the discourses of Latin American identity itself. Here, we may remind ourselves of Larsen's insistence that we need to interrogate the 'seemingly natural and spontaneous availability of Latin America as a subject for discourse' (Larsen 1995:1), since Latin America is a construct, rather than an organic entity. Similarly, we need to take on board Mignolo's arguments that Latin America is a complex process related to changing configurations in the field of imperial forces; what he calls the 'making and unmaking [of] the Americas' is part of a larger project of the 'imperial allocation of cultures' (Mignolo 2000:127), and as such the discourses of the 'making of the Americas' must be put under scrutiny.

If Latin America has been constructed through discourses which purport to name it, then, we propose, this construction is no less prevalent in online discourses of Latin American-ness, which often hark back to those founding narratives. It is this prevalence of founding narratives which has provoked our interest in tracking down and analysing such narratives online. Our present volume explores a series of prominent Latin American(ist) cultural discourses that preexisted the internet, and traces their development, mutation and reworking when they are interpellated online. While there are many such discourses, we have, of necessity, confined our project to six broad discourses which, we feel, have been central to the 'invention of Latin America' over time. These discourses and conceptualisations of Latin American-ness are: the mapping of the entity called 'Latin America'; the Lettered City as defining the dissemination of power in the emergent Latin American nations; the magical real as encapsulated in the narration of the settlement of Macondo; the discourse of racial mixing or *mestizaje*; the dichotomy of civilisation versus barbarism; and the concept and practice of revolution. While not pretending to be exhaustive, the discourses selected are ones which, in their different ways, have shaped the discussions and representations of 'Latin American-ness' over the decades, and thus are central to the construction of Latin America as a concept.

Our first chapter starts with perhaps *the* founding discourse of Latin American identity: the 'mapping out' of Latin America itself as a geographical and conceptual entity. In 'Cartographic Imaginaries: Mapping Latin(o) America's Place in a World of Networked Digital Technologies' we engage with recent scholarship on the map as a naturalising representation and cartography as a geopolitical enterprise, and then proceed to explore the specific implications of these issues in relation to Latin America and to online space. Here, we explore scholarship that has revealed the colonial assumptions underpinning the mapping of the Americas as a continent (Mignolo 2000, Pratt 1992), as well as recent scholarship in internet studies which has focused on the neo-imperialist assumptions encoded within the very protocols which structure or 'map out' internet content, and within the conventions of the practice of internet geography *per se*. The chapter then goes on to examine work by three Latin(o) American cultural producers—Uruguayan net.artist Brian Mackern, Latino digital media artist Eduardo Navas and Latina performance and digital media artist Praba Pilar—to discern the extent to which they articulate resistance to hegemonic, neo-imperialist cartographic discourses, via the proposal of alternative cartographies and epistemologies of Latin America and its place in a globalised world.

Chapter Two follows on from the thread of the mapping out of identity along spatial lines as set out in Chapter One to now focus on one particular geographical-conceptual space: that of the city. In 'Reworking the "Lettered City": The Resistant Reterritorialisation of Urban Place', we explore one of the most influential discourses of Latin American studies as expounded in the mid-twentieth century, although stretching back to the colonial era in its conceptual reach: that of Ángel Rama's 'Lettered City' (1984). Rama's model identified power structures within the city which allied the colonial elites with written discourse; power within cities, and the discourses that emanate from them, are, according to Rama, the preserve of the colonial (and later, the creole) elite and function to the exclusion of nonelites (women, the indigenous populations, the lower classes and so on). This chapter proposes a rereading of Rama for the twenty-first century by way of an analysis of literary-cultural works such as the Colombian digital inclusion project, *Hiperbarrio* and the net.art work, *Tejido de memoria* by Argentine Marina Zerbarini, where the focus of expression shifts from the elites to the marginalised. The chapter analyses firstly the resignification of the urban political centre as manifested in *Tejido de memoria*, highlighting how the geographical specificity of the Madres de Plaza de Mayo movement is mapped onto online space. The chapter then focuses on the reformulations of the margins as exemplified in *Hiperbarrio*, and engages with the notion of the *barrio* as both space of segregation and locus of cultural resistance. As the analysis reveals, the geographical tropes upon which these websites rely can be seen to be both reinforced and transformed by their use in online space; if, as we noted above, recent empirical and theoretical work on place and online practices shows that this entails not the loss of locatedness, but its reworking, then these works make use of the potential of the internet to force a rethinking of place and territory. In both these works, the city as fundamental to the development of a national and pan-Latin American consciousness, and as the arbiter of state-sponsored, elite culture, comes into question.

Chapter Three, meanwhile, moves from the representation of physical locales to the consideration of a central mythical locale in the Latin American literary landscape—that of Macondo—although it then expands from this locale to models of literary creation *per se*. Here, Macondo is taken as emblematic of the mode of representation of Latin American-ness broadly defined as magical realism, and we then extrapolate from this to investigate how contemporary narrative online both continues and yet poses certain challenges to the Macondine model. In 'From Macondo to Macon.doc: Contemporary Latin American Hypertext Fiction', we explore the transformations taking place in contemporary hypertext fiction, taking as objects of study the works *Gabriella infinita* by the Colombian writer Jaime Alejandro Rodríguez, and *Wordtoys* by the Argentine writer Belén Gache. Focusing on the mythical locale, the potential for textual reconfigurations, and the function of the author-reader relationship, the chapter charts how contemporary hypertext fiction speaks to a rich Hispanic heritage of literary experimentation. At the same time, we investigate how these works explore the possibilities offered by digital technologies, all the while engaging in self-referential commentaries about both the enabling possibilities *and* the limitations of these technologies for literary practice in Latin America.

Following on from this, Chapter Four moves onto another founding discourse which maintains some elements of spatiality via the image of the frontier, but which more properly sets up conceptual rather than geographical borders: the well-established and much-debated dichotomy between civilisation and barbarism. In 'Civilisation and Barbarism: New Frontiers and Barbarous Borders Online', we explore this founding discourse, set up as early as the first chronicles of the *conquistadores* where the Americas figured as a zone in which the competing forces of civilisation and barbarism are played out, and popularised via Domingo Faustino Sarmiento's notion of *civilización y barbarie* as expounded in his *Facundo* of 1848. The chapter traces the remnants and recurrences of the key terms of Sarmiento's debate as they are taken up online, and focuses in particular on the works of two Latin(o) American cultural producers: Mexican/Chicano online performance artist Guillermo Gómez-Peña, and Colombian net.artist Martha Patricia Niño. Here, we explore how these two artists invoke the terms of barbarism in creative and challenging ways, and either challenge the dichotomy, or reread it in the light of globalisation and contemporary conflicts.

Where Chapter Four focused on a discourse predicated on a polarised understanding of races and cultures as expounded by Sarmiento, Chapter Five takes as its focus a discourse based on the mixing of races and cultures: that of *mestizaje*. Furthermore, in contrast with Chapter Four where we chose to focus more explicitly on the representation of cultural identities, Chapter Five focuses on the representation and performance of specifically (mixed-) racial identities in online cultural production. Thus in '*Mestiz@ Cyborgs: The Performance of Latin American-ness as (Critical) Racial Identity*', we start by analysing the relationship between the discourse of cyborgism and the discourse of *mestizaje* as necessary groundwork in order to be able to examine the reasons why three specifically Latino (groups of) cultural producers have chosen to create mixed-race cyborg figures that circulate in their online work and are used to voice their concerns regarding the relationship between new technologies and racial minority groups in the United States. The cultural producers and products analysed here include Guillermo Gómez-Peña's deployment of ever-mutating 'ethno-cyborgs' in his early online work, and the more tactical and disturbing web presence of a group of performance and multimedia installation artists known as Los Cybrids: La Raza Techno-Crítica, and of Latino film director and digital media artist Alex Rivera's *Cybracero Systems* spoof labour outsourcing website. The chapter concludes that while the representation of raced bodies permanently runs the risk of falling into the traps of essentialism and fetishisation and while the representation of *mestiza/o* cyborgs arguably makes this more rather than less likely, a concerted attempt to perform what we term 'a *mestiza/o* cyborg principle' as seen in the latter two examples helps to keep the negotiation of *mestizaje* critical in all senses.

The final chapter of our volume explores the discourse of Latin American-ness that has arguably been the most obvious subject of reinvigoration and/ or resemanticisation in online cultural production, both because of the proven ability of networked digital media to bring about social change and because of the tendency to refer to both social and technological change with the same terminology. In '*Revolución.com?* The Latin American Revolutionary Tradition in the Age of New Media (Revolutions)' we briefly explore the association of Latin America, and by extension Latin American-ness, with the concept of revolution, before going on to examine how two online cultural products/projects position themselves with respect to the Latin American revolutionary tradition, as well as how they use new media to either attempt to reinvigorate or more directly challenge that tradition. The cultural producers studied are the infamous Cuban blogger Yoani Sánchez whose *Generación Y* blog has catapulted her to international celebrity status for its critique of the Castro regime, and itinerant Mexican media artist and activist Fran Ilich whose work to create a utopian online community via his own *possibleworlds.org* server is directly related to the ethos and practice of (Digital) Zapatismo. Although difficulties abound in the creation of contestatory projects online, the chapter argues that both Sánchez and Ilich, despite their very different political positions, produce work that manages to retain a contestatory edge through their ongoing interrogation of the terms of the discourse of revolution, both with respect to traditional conceptualisations of revolution in Latin America and beyond, and with respect to the ways in which their interventions online negotiate the prevailing currents of circulation in new media.

As we have charted in this introduction, Latin American online cultural production is, we argue, a prime form through which we can explore the postregional configuration of Latin America today. In the chapters that follow, we explore the complex ways in which Latin American identity is renegotiated online, and analyse how these founding discourses are at times challenged and at times revitalised in their contemporary configurations. We now proceed to the first of our discourses—the cartographical imaginary that has mapped out the contours of the region—which we explore in depth in the following chapter.

1   Cartographic Imaginaries

Mapping Latin(o) America's Place in a World of Networked Digital Technologies

This chapter analyses the work of three Latin(o) American digital media artists who engage, albeit in very different ways, with the topographical, geopolitical and/or conceptual mapping of Latin America, both in relation to the history of cartographic representations of the region, and/or in relation to Latin America's place in the industrial practices and cultural imaginaries of (networked) digital technologies. It engages with recent research on the (neo-)colonialist impulses of mapping, both within cartography as a discipline (Harley 1989, Crampton 2001) and specifically in the mapping of the Americas/Latin America (Mignolo 2000 and 2005, Offen and Dym 2011). It also engages with debates in internet studies that have critiqued the early, neo-imperialist, 'frontiersman' discourse of the internet (Sardar 1995, Loader 1997, Dodge and Kitchin 2001b, Paasonen 2009), as well as with continuing debates on mapping out online space, specifically with respect to the politics of top-level domain names (Steinberg and McDowell 2003) and graphical representations of the internet and its traffic flows (Harpold 1999).

The chapter focuses particular attention on the Uruguayan net.artist, Brian Mackern whose *netart latino database* (2000–2005) both attempts to map out a place for Latin America in the global net.art community, and makes meta-critical comments on mapping and net.art as practices. It then goes on to examine more briefly the work of two Latina/o digital media artists: US-Salvadoran Eduardo Navas's animation *Plástico_2002_upDate* (2002) and US-Colombian Praba Pilar's *Cyberlabia* project (2005). Both Navas and Pilar further problematise the representation of Latin America through their deliberate inclusion of the Latino communities of North America and/or through their representation of this expanded Latin(o) America as part of a wider phenomenon in global relations in an era of informational capitalism supported by (and represented in) digital technologies. The chapter argues that these works evidence a desire to continue to revise hegemonic cartographies that seek to circumscribe, or even ignore entirely, Latin(o) America, and that they also engage in a sustained critique of its marginal place and role in cyberspace itself. Instead, they propose alternative cartographies and epistemologies of Latin(o) America and its place in a globalised world.

Starting first with the discipline of cartography, developments in the discipline from the 1980s onwards started to question the purported 'transparency' of the map and 'objectivity' of map-making as a process, and instead have encouraged us to understand cartography as a geopolitical enterprise. Harley's groundbreaking work in the 1980s on 'deconstructing the map' was one of the first to explore cartography as 'historically specific' (Harley 1989:3), and flagged up the need to 'search for the social forces that have structured cartography and to locate the presence of power—and its effects—in all map knowledge' (Harley 1989:2). More specifically, Harley urged that:

> we have to read between the lines of technical procedures or of the map's topographic content. They are related to values, such as those of ethnicity, politics, religion, or social class, and they are also embedded in the map-producing society at large. [. . .] In the map itself, social structures are often disguised beneath an abstract, instrumental space, or incarcerated in the coordinates.
>
> (Harley 1989:5)

This understanding of maps as naturalising representations necessitates our 'read[ing] between the lines of the map—"in the margins of the text"—and through its tropes to discover the silences and contradictions that challenge the apparent honesty of the image' (Harley 1989:3). Subsequent generations of scholars have built upon Harley's work, such as Crampton, who, summarising the understanding of cartography post-Harley, notes that this involves challenging the prevailing notion of cartography as 'the communication of information from the cartographer to the map user', and instead investigating how 'maps are part of a general discourse of power, which both enables and abridges possibilities for people to act' (Crampton 2001:236). This notion of maps as simultaneously enabling *and* abridging is central to the works under consideration in this chapter; that is, an understanding of maps as *abridging* entails exploring who is excluded from the map; while an understanding of maps as *enabling* entails exploring the possibilities of creating (temporary, tactical) alternative cartographies.

If such are the critiques of cartography as a global enterprise, in a (Latin) American context, notions of mapping as a geopolitical enterprise have been elaborated on in recent studies, in particular in the works of Walter Mignolo. Mignolo argues that the practice of mapping is integral to the very existence of the Americas as a whole:

> Before 1492 the Americas were not on anybody's map, not even on the map of the people inhabiting Anáhuac and Tawantinsuyu [. . .] the mass of land and the people were there, but they named their own places. [. . .] 'America', then, was never a continent waiting to be discovered. Rather, 'America' as we know it was an *invention* forged in the process

of European colonial history and the consolidation and expansion of the Western world view and institutions.

(Mignolo 2005:2)

If the process of mapping is thus central to the conceptualisation and very exis-tence of the Americas as an entity, Mignolo also stresses that this is an imperial project; in other words, the process of mapping the Americas was integral to (European) projects of empire in which 'modernity/coloniality' are conceptual-ised as 'two sides of the same coin', and thus 'the very idea of America cannot be separated from coloniality: the entire continent emerged as such in the Euro-pean consciousness' (Mignolo 2005:6–7). Extending Mignolo's argument, the very act of mapping the Americas carries with it its baggage of imperialism; the shape and contours of the continent were drawn in the interests of European imperialism. Hence, mapping is both central to the very concept of the Ameri-cas, and at the same time is imbued with its imperialist heritage.

While many critics have argued that the concept of a specifically 'Latin' America stems from an attempt to articulate French geopolitical interests in the mid-nineteenth century, in concordance with the imperialist history outlined above, within Latin America itself scholars such as Arturo Ardao have convinc-ingly attributed the creation and adoption of the term to Spanish-American intellectuals of a slightly earlier era who were seeking to draw out common-alities between the Spanish-speaking republics of the region (Ardao 1980).[1] In *Mapping Latin America: A Cartographic Reader* (2011), Karl Offen and Jordana Dym endorse this view of the early coalescence of a sense of regional identity and its conceptual mapping from within, and they go on to highlight the importance of the mapping of 'Nuestra América' ['Our America'] that was in evidence in José Martí's famous 1892 formulation that described the region as extending 'from the Río Bravo to the Straits of Magellan' (Martí, quoted in Offen and Dym 2011:3–4). What is significant in Martí's formulation—and the essay in which it appears—is that Latin America as geopolitical entity is constructed in explicit opposition to Anglo-America in the North. Furthermore, the fact that Martí felt the need to reclaim the region by discursively mapping out its contours in contradistinction to Anglo-America suggests that a sense of the power lying behind the hegemony of maps and mappings of the region had shifted by that point from Europe to the USA.

Over the course of the twentieth century and particularly in the Cold War era the concept of Latin America—now including Brazil with the Spanish-American states (Bethell 2010:478–79)—has been reworked to serve the United States' strategic interests, and the outline 'map-as-logo' of the region that encompasses Meso- and South America, together with the Caribbean, particularly in its shrunken Mercatorial projection which leaves it look-ing diminutive in comparison with North America, is most emblematic of that drive to divide up the non-anglophone world into manageable chunks. Nevertheless, although, as Benedict Anderson notes, the origins of the 'map-as-logo' derive from imperialist map-making where states coloured 'their colonies on maps with an imperial dye', the outline forms of states—

and arguably of geopolitical regions—'penetrated deep into the popular imagination' and, perhaps ironically, then began to serve as 'a powerful emblem' for anticolonial nationalisms (Anderson 1991:175) or, in the case of Latin America as a whole, for anti-imperialist resistance.

It can thus be argued that Latin Americans' cartographic projections of the region as a whole specifically seek to reclaim this logo-map—this regional outline—for themselves. This is already apparent in Uruguayan artist Joaquín Torres-García's early inversion of the map of Latin America (of this, more later). It is even clearer in the depictions of Latin America that circulated in revolutionary Cuban posters and cover designs for the journal *Tricontinental*, with, for example, the messianic figure of Che Guevara intimately fused with multiple outlines of the logo-map of the region (north at top).[2] Contemporary artists who engage with the cartographic representation of Latin America must deal not only with the European colonialist and more recent US imperialist history that underpins the mapping of the region, but also, in many cases, with the legacy of Latin American revisions of its relationship to the outside world and to the USA in particular as expressed in the regional map-as-logo. The cartographic representation of a bounded entity known as Latin America, whether intended to be abridging or enabling in its function, is furthermore highly problematic for Latinas/os who do not fit within or identify with the traditional regional boundaries.

The need to interrogate the norms of cartography and the discursive features of the map as raised by scholars such as Harley and Crampton becomes of even greater importance when analysing works designed for and published on the internet. Scholarship over the past two decades has brought to our attention the problematic mapping out of cyberspace, both in terms of the early predominantly metaphorical or conceptual approaches to the internet, as well as the structural features of html coding itself, both of which come under scrutiny for their role in endorsing implicitly neo-imperialist mappings of the internet. As Dodge and Kitchin note, the very term 'cyberspace' means 'navigatable space', the first part of the neologism being derived from the Greek *kyber* meaning 'to navigate' (Dodge and Kitchin 2001b:1), and the conceptual forms in which the internet is approached often tended, particularly in the work of earlier proponents, to reproduce (uncritically) a neo-imperialist, 'frontiersman' discourse. The notion of the 'electronic frontier', a term encapsulated in John Perry Barlow's influential 'Declaration of the Independence of Cyberspace' (Barlow 1996), is particularly representative of this early, *Wired*-influenced conceptualisation of the internet,[3] and has been much critiqued. Susana Paasonen questions the 'deeply American metaphor' underpinning this notion (Paasonen 2009:21), while Brian D. Loader pointedly notes that Barlow's advocation of free speech 'seemingly require[s] the world to speak English on the electronic frontier' (Loader 1997:6). The most sustained critique comes in a seminal article by Ziauddin Sardar who describes the electronic frontier as a 'mythic formulation' which has direct parallels with the 'colonization of non-Western cultures' (Sardar 1995:777), arguing that 'White man's burden, then, shifts from its moral obligation to civilize, democratize, urbanize and colonize non-Western cultures, to the colonization of cyberspace' (Sardar 1995:280). Such a conceptualisation has, as Kathleen K. Olson notes, now been largely superseded: the 'Western frontier metaphor' represented an early way of thinking about the internet which 'lost its power as the web became increasingly commercialised and privatised. Fences went up, legal rules were enforced, and the digital "wild West" was enclosed and divided into private parcels complete with "keep out" signs' (Olson 2005:15). Nevertheless, the influence of these earlier conceptualisations of cyberspace still lingers, particularly with regard to the politics of how the internet maps out space and reproduces geopolitical relations online.

More concretely, recent scholarship has focused on the assumptions encoded within the very protocols which structure or 'map out' internet content along neo-imperialist and/or nation-state lines. Here, the use of generic top-level domain extensions (gTLD) and country code top-level domain extensions (ccTLD) in URLs has been highlighted by scholars as both mapping out an implicit US neo-imperialism online, and at the same time attempting to draw boundaries around internet content in the interest of the nation-state. Steinberg and McDowell note how purportedly 'generic' top-level domains are in many cases available solely to refer to the US, with the .edu and .gov domains being particular cases in point. They go on to argue that the domain name structure reproduces the territorial divisions of the world, and that 'the internet naming system has all the signs of reproducing United States hegemony', since 'the hegemon defines its own naming system as the generic', while other states are given terms that are 'are suboptimal for would-be global actors' (Steinberg and McDowell 2003:55).

At the same time, the country code top-level domains have been critiqued for their assumption of English, or at least the twenty-six letters of Roman alphabetic and nonaccented script used in English, as lingua franca, as well as for their attempt to map out internet content according to nation-state boundaries. In the first case, it has been recognised that 'the design of the DNS [Domain Name System] presents formidable technical challenges for the accommodation of languages that use non-Roman characters', and even for those that simply use accents with Roman characters (Committee on Internet Navigation and the Domain Name System, National Research Council 2005:164). Nevertheless, speakers of key world languages such as Russian, have moved, in recent years, from an acceptance of their country code top-level domain as .su (later .ru in the wake of the break-up of the USSR), to the Cyrillic .рф [the Russian Federation] to indicate their scriptural nonconformity with English, as well as 'to signify the transnational, deterritorialised environment of the Russophone World Wide Web: that is the online activity of Russian-speaking communities in Russia proper, the near-abroad, Israel, the USA and other countries' (Strukov 2012:1585).

This latter consideration leads on to the second critique made of the DNS— its attempt to fit all internet domains within the boundaries of traditional nation-states which is a particular concern of those linguistic, religious or ethnic groups whose identity transcends the boundaries of the state. Indeed, the central concept embedded within the two-character country-level domain names is that of the nation-state; in the case of the many nations that do not have states—or, to use the suggestive term employed by Keating and others, 'stateless nations' (Keating 2001)—no *official* national representation is available online. Within a Hispanic context, the campaigns by Catalan nationalists for a domain name, under the auspices of the *Associació punt-CAT* group, founded by Amadeu Abril i Abril, and which eventually led to ICANN (Internet Corporation for Assigned Names and Numbers) approving the domain '.cat' in September 2005, are particularly illuminating in revealing how issues of visibility and national identity are negotiated online via domain names, as well as how nonnation-states can make strategic use of existing domain name regulations to forge their own sense of nonnation-state identity.[4] URLs, then 'map out' the geopolitical concerns of the offline world, and have come under critique by both scholars and campaigners for their reproduction of existing offline inequalities online.

In a similar vein, debates have also taken place regarding the attempts made by those now known as 'internet geographers' to produce graphical representations of the internet's structure or its traffic flows. As will be discussed in more detail later on, all too often these maps of internet geography are based on the same kinds of assumptions and elisions as hegemonic cartographies of the offline world have been over history. These assumptions and elisions encompass both the choice of data used to generate the maps and the graphical conventions, including form of projection and the use of logo-maps, employed to render them meaningful to viewers. Furthermore, such maps may also be seen as functioning to reify the spatial configuration of informational capitalism such that subtleties are erased and real alternatives abridged. While research on this topic is not as voluminous as that concerning the problems of the domain name system, critics such as Harpold (1999) have been quick to point out the 'pernicious metageographical' discourse evident in such representations.

Within this context, in which graphic and/or conceptual mapping both in offline and online domains, as well as the constant spaces of interconnection between the online and the offline, speaks to geopolitical concerns, the case studies in this chapter are seen as examples of resistant mappings; that is, mappings which tentatively speak back to some of the neo-imperialist or statist assumptions underpinning mapping practices. The mappings that we analyse cover a range of graphical and textual formats, given the impossibility of separating entirely the cartographic from the textual. This is true of mapping in general where the distinction between map and text, as we have already seen, is often blurred in academic analysis (Harley 1989:5), and of Latin America's self-representation in particular where key historical moments of resistant cartographic *self*-representation in/of the region as a whole, such as Martí's description of 'Nuestra América', have been couched in textual form. Furthermore, it is even more true of the representation of the internet itself which, while it relies on spatial concepts for its user-friendly 'navigation', uses cartographic terms in a more metaphorical than literal manner. While the domain name system, for example, suggests a 'mapping out' of cyberspace, it functions primarily as a taxonomy of cyberspace that might subsequently and not unproblematically be visualised cartographically. Therefore, in what follows, we have focused as much as possible on graphic representations of Latin America, but we have used the terms 'cartography' and 'mapping' to encompass taxonomic or more broadly conceptual forms of *textual* mapping where necessary.

REMAPPING LATIN AMERICA ONLINE:
MACKERN'S *NET.ART LATINO DATABASE*

Uruguayan net.artist and creator Brian Mackern is arguably one of the pioneers of net.art in the region, being one of the earliest in Latin America to explore the potential of the new medium for artistic expression. Mackern's many works, ranging from the early 1990s to the present, explore the formal aspects of the net and programming languages, as well as making meta-critical comments on the medium, and on net.art and experimental fiction as genres. His series of 'artef@ctos virtuales', for instance, include his *JODI/ web_o_matic [n]coder* (Mackern 2000) which pays a tongue-in-cheek homage to the pioneers of net.art, whereby the user types in a 'source code' which is then converted into 'lenguaje JODI'. The reference here is to the net.art duo, JODI (Joan Heemskerk and Dirk Paesmans), who were some of the first practitioners of net.art, particularly their 'browser art' which involved 'undermining the prescribed use value of everyday web authoring systems' (van Mourik Broekman 2003:222), and in which the conventions of the world wide web, such as pop-ups, error messages, and so forth, were the 'raw material of a body of structuralist, conceptual art works' (FACT 2004). The conceit of much of JODI's works was that the art lay in the code itself rather than the rendered page of the browser, whereby the 'meaning' of a work is 'hidden in a certain html code' (van Tomme 2011:34). Mackern's *JODI/ web_o_matic [n]coder*, therefore, enacts a form of ironic homage to JODI's practice, playing with the order of phenotext and genotext.[5] In Mackern's version, the 'source' is in fact conventional written language and the rendered 'result' is an increasingly complex set of ASCII commands in green phosphor screen-display font, a font typical of the iconic IBM 5151 monochrome monitors of the 1980s, and which has now become a visual metaphor for computer-generated code.[6] Another of Mackern's works, *Cort_azar*, involves a series of vowel sounds, as pronounced by Argentine boom writer, Julio Cortázar, which are remixed randomly on a series of loops, an allusion to the person who 'exploró las posibilidades de narrativas alternativas que ahora son posibles en internet' ['explored the possibilities for alternative narratives that are now possible on the internet'] (Mackern c.2002). Given that Cortázar, and particularly his 1963 novel, *Rayuela*, is frequently hailed as one of the precursors of hypertext fictions—or, in the words of Landow, a 'print proto-hypertext' (Landow 1992:38)—Mackern's homage to Cortázar both plays with the recombinant possibilities offered by new media technologies, and makes a meta-critical commentary on those same technologies.[7]

These pieces, along with many other of Mackern's works, both play with codes as generative of works of art and at the same time comment on the medium itself, by flagging up the very structures of the internet itself. Indeed, this dual impetus—the use of coding to generate the art, coupled with a meta-discourse on the medium itself—has been conceived by practitioners and scholars of net.art as central to the genre. Dieter Daniels's comprehensive 'modernist typology' underpinning net-based art cites 'reflection on the medium' and the 'revision of formalist approaches, referring to the network medium' as two of the principal tenets underpinning net.art (Daniels 2009:44–46), while Tilman Baumgärtel has similarly asserted that:

> Net art addresses its own medium. [. . .] It explores the possibilities that arise from its taking place within this electronic network and is therefore 'net specific'. Net art plays with the protocols of the Internet, with its technical peculiarities. It puts known or undiscovered errors within the system to its own use.
>
> (Baumgärtel 2001:24)

Echoing the assertions of Daniels and Baumgärtel, Julian Stallabrass sets out two central claims about internet art as being its use of the computer not 'as a tool but as its subject matter', and its exploitation of 'the particular qualities of hardware and software to the extent that it is "unthinkable without its medium, the Internet"' (Stallabrass 2003:139).[8]

Mackern's works are thus indicative of these two fundamental features—the use of codes to generate the art, and a meta-commentary on the medium itself—that underpin net.art, particularly earlier versions of the genre in the 1990s. Or rather, more properly, Mackern's works may be read as ironic reworkings of these underpinnings whereby, as this chapter reveals, his works engage with these early net.art aesthetics, but reencode them within a critical geopolitical perspective from the South.

The particular work of Mackern's under consideration in this chapter, his *netart latino database* (2000–2005), plays (along) with these two prominent conventions of early net.art, and yet reencodes them in a Latin(o) American–specific cultural context. The *netart latino database* draws together the work of leading net.artists in the region, and has played a leading role in sculpting a Latin(o) American sense of net.art community.[9] Yet, in much the same way as net.art conceives of coding as part and parcel of the art itself, so Mackern's conceptualisation here is not of a database as a purely transparent tool which should simply give access to its contents, but rather, the database itself is an art work in its own right. This is immediately evident from the structural features of the work, which invite metaphorical readings as much as offering ease of accessibility. Indeed, as will be discussed below, many of the structural features of the database are deliberately frustrating or nonintuitive, forcing the viewer/user into an active and critical position, and functioning for artistic effect rather than efficiency. Mackern's work here resonates with the practice of other net.artists and curators in Latin America, where it is the curatorial interface that it is also a net.art work in its own right; see, for instance, the *Women: Memory of Repression in Argentina* net.art exhibition of 2003, curated by Raquel Partnoy, where the curatorial environment, with its use of photographs, sound files, video files and linkings, has artistic as much as organisational functions; the 2005 ArteUna interface for the *30 Años de Golpe Militar Argentina* exhibition, whose jigsaw-format interface functions as a work of art and invites interpretation in its own right; or Eduardo Navas's many curatorial works, such as the *P2P[iece]* online exhibition of 2003–2004, where the structural features are as much a work of art as the contents themselves.

Again, as with JODI and many other net.artists of the early stages of the genre, Mackern's work of art exists not only in the main body of the work but also in the peripheral or paratextual features, such as the scroll bars, the title bar, or pop-up windows, among many others. In Mackern's case, the title bar at the top of the screen is particularly revealing in its function in not simply displaying the title, but in forming part of the work itself. It displays the following text: '['netart latino database—- > you connect the dots > > you pick up the pieces!]'. It is worth noting that the content of the title bar, after the title itself, is in the imperative form, issuing commands to the viewer/ user, invoking of course the commands of computer codes. The first of these commands, exhorting the viewer/user to 'connect the dots' refers to the deliberate organisational strategies of this work, as analysed below, which force the viewer into a more active position. That is, the command reflects the fact that the viewer/user must activate the work of art him/herself; the work of art in net.art does not exist *per se*, but must be activated by the viewer/user. Yet at the same time, of course, this command also refers to the content of this specific work of art in which, as will be analysed below, the central image is rendered not as a continuous line mapping out exact contours, but through the conjunction of three symbols repeated many times across the screen, with spaces between them. The viewer/user, therefore, must join the dots visually to 'see' the image represented by the database—a map of Latin America. In this command to join the dots there are, thus, also ludic connotations, following the classic predigital game format of joining the dots to reveal a (partially) hidden image; again, Mackern is here tapping into a common feature of net.art, whereby predigital genres are invoked and reworked in the context of new media technologies.[10] Here, Mackern's vision is one of tactical and resistant uses of joining-the-dots; joining the dots against the grain as the work both evokes the ludic features of the original game and yet encourages the viewer/user to construct a resistant mapping, as will be discussed in more depth below.[11]

The second of the commands again refers to the role of the viewer/user in activating the work, where the sense of 'picking up the pieces' invokes the act of connecting up the pieces, following the hyperlinks, picking and reassembling lexia, and so forth, which are common strategies in net.art, and are exemplified by this work. Yet the specific phrase used also conveys the utopian, explosive potential of net.art, since it implies picking up the pieces after an explosion, and here resonates with debates about the avant-gardist, radical impulses underlying net.art, as well as making a nod to explosive images within net.art itself. Regarding the former, while scholars and practitioners of net.art have not always agreed on the exact contours nor chronology of this emergent art form, where they have concurred is on the genre's historicity, identifying it as having radical impulses stretching back to the avant garde (Stallabrass 2003:48; Corby 2006:6; Bookchin 2006:69; Daniels 2009:29). Regarding the latter, it is worth remembering that one of the most iconic images of net.art is of course JODI's experimental webpage *wwwwwwwww.jodi.org*, in which viewing the source code reveals a diagram of a hydrogen bomb;[12] similarly, Mackern's own works, in indirect homage to JODI, have also played with this formula.[13] The notion of 'pick[ing] up the pieces' thus resonates with the view of net.art as a potentially radical, explosive practice; that is, how net.art, drawing on its shared roots with hacker ethics, tactical media and FOSS (Free Open-Source Software) movements, is envisaged as an (explosive) counter to dominant, corporate or state-sanctioned conceptualisations of the internet. Hence a conceptualisation of net.art as a genre involving the 'linking of technological progress, social change, and artistic innovation' (Daniels, D. 2009:29) is arguably invoked by this title bar, as it encourages the viewer/user to engage with the database, and the works within in it, as examples of potentially oppositional practice.

In addition to these two commands, the title bar also houses symbols which separate the three main elements (the title and the two commands), comprising the symbols -, >, ! and]. These symbols are common conventions in html tags, but again, as with much of Mackern's work, they are here used against the grain. The '>' symbol, conventionally used to close an html tag, is here combined with the '-' symbol not as a form of code, but to create the visual effect of an arrow, pointing the viewer forwards towards the next command. The exclamation mark, meanwhile, is an html tag indicating a comment—in other words, a portion of the text that can only be viewed in the source code, not in the rendered page in the browser. Of course, Mackern is using this tag tongue-in-cheek here, since this is precisely what we *do* see: the exclamation mark thus draws our attention to, rather than hides a comment, as in conventional html coding. The way in which these fragments of code appear, interspersed with the title and the commands framing the work, encourages us to read them as postdigital fragments; that is, fragments of code that appear on the margins of and yet are an integral part of the work of art itself. Here, the fragments or detritus of the postdigital age are reused constructively, a feature which also speaks to the notion of the tactical reuse of low-tech, as will be discussed further below. There is thus an equivalence drawn between the linguistic codes (the use of the imperative) and computer codes (the use of tags), as Mackern invites us to rethink some of the conventions of new media technologies.

Moving on from the paratextual information supplied in the title bar, the main browser window itself also provides the viewer/user with similarly meta-critical commentaries on new media technologies, net.art as a genre, and on the specifics of Latin America within the net.art community and within online space more broadly. In the main browser window itself, at the top of the screen, we do not see the title of the work, but instead an interrogative that poses for us a central question to consider as we access this work: '> ¿netart or notart? <'. Here, the work raises one of the central debates troubling net.artists (or perhaps, more strictly speaking, troubling art historians of conventional art as they grapple with art using new media): namely, the extent to which such works, making use of new media, can be termed 'art'. Given both the revisions to existing understandings of art that the genre of net.art has brought about, as well as the lack of agreement among net.artists themselves over exactly what net.art consists of,[14] Mackern's question to us encourages us to think through the contours of the genre as we explore his database.[15] Moreover, the question, of course, is posed not just about the medium but about this work more particularly; in other words, Mackern is inviting us to consider whether the work we are accessing is net.art, or not art. Thus once more, Mackern's question here functions as a meta-critical commentary on the genre and on this work in itself, encouraging us to question the role of this piece as art/not art, and not as purely a database. Again, the fact that this question is framed within the symbols '>' and '<' recalls conventional html tags, although these are here presented in reverse order (since in conventional html, '<' would open, and '>' would close the tag). This is thus another hint at the way in which code and new media technologies more broadly are used against the grain, a fact which is given further emphasis by the framing question marks around the statement, with the inverted question mark at the start indicating the socio-cultural context in which this question is posed. The Hispanicised format of the interrogative indicates that the (predominantly Anglo-European) conceptualisations of net.art will be interrogated from a Latin(o) American perspective, as well as implying more broadly the way in which new media technologies are redeployed in a particularly Latin(o) American (resistant) way in the contents of the database.

In terms of navigation, the work is deliberately challenging, and frustrates the user's expectations of ease of access, logical materialisation of data, and functionality implied by the term 'database'. As regards the home page, there are, for instance, no menus bars providing us with links to key features, no contents list providing us with an overview of the database, no search facility, nor any instructions informing us how to navigate the 'database'. The scroll-bar on the right-hand side, meanwhile—again, one of the peripheral features of a standard webpage, but here, once again, integral to the work of art—has been adapted, and is rendered as a solid grey column. The conventional 'up' and 'down' arrows, which function to aid the viewer in knowing where s/he is within a webpage, do not appear, thus again frustrating the viewer/user's navigation.

In terms of its visual presentation, the work consists of a white background, with only two other colours used: black font for the three characters, and blue for the hyperlinks. This deliberate sparseness of colour is a further instance of how Mackern's work refuses functionality and user-friendliness as its main goal, but instead functions as a work of art; here, the limited palette functions as a homage to an earlier generation of net.art, and to early generations of text-based browsers prior to the advent of graphical interfaces. Indeed, this effect is further reinforced by the visuals on the page, whereby the 'visual' interface is not, in fact, visual—there are no jpg, gif or other image files inserted into the page—instead, the only 'image' is that created by the repetition of a series of limited characters across the screen in courier font. Here, three characters — '+', '–' and '|' – are employed to map out the contours of Latin America across the screen [Fig. 1.1]. Again, this deliberate refusal to use a high-tech visual interface—particularly in the context of its creation, with the popularisation of graphical browsers in 1993 leading to the explosion of the world wide web as a visual interface in the mid-1990s[16]—signals Mackern's return to previous, pregraphical formats as a tactically resistant gesture. Moreover, the selection of courier font for this work—a font deliberately designed to replicate the output from a typewriter—again harks back to earlier, low-tech communication protocols, as well as paying homage to early ASCII-art.[17] When viewed at normal (100%) resolution, only part of the map is visible at any one time, again rendering a complete access to the database, or omniscient view of the map, impossible. In this sense, Mackern's map aims to provide a viewpoint which is resistant to the 'monarch of all I survey' trope which, as Mary Louise Pratt has persuasively argued, underpins the imperial gaze which mapped out the region for European interests (Pratt 1992:201–06). Mackern's map cannot be grasped in its entirety from an omniscient viewpoint, but instead must be negotiated, and then activated, for the viewer/user to gain access.

Cutting across the centre of this 'map' appears the title of the work, rendered thus:

|n|e|t|a|r|t|_|l|a|t|i|n|o| |d|a|t|a|b|a|s|e|

The way in which the title is broken up by the insertion of the '|' character is again reminiscent of early text-based browsers, where the different menus offered, usually at the foot of the page, were separated by this character—a feature which is nowadays, of course, obsolete and replaced by a more sophisticated use of graphics and buttons. Here, Mackern's knowing reuse of this character again makes a nod to low-tech precursors, and, in its breaking up of the reading flow, encourages us to read between the lines/characters of the title, posing yet again a meta-discursive statement on the work of art itself.

Outside the map, on the margins of the contours of the continent, the countries are indicated alongside their respective coastline, but not by their full country name; instead, they are represented by the country code top-level domains (ccTLDs) as used in html to indicate the URL of a site, where Argentina is represented by '.AR', Chile represented by '.CL' and so forth. The *netart latino database* thus produces a visual metaphor of the mapping out of cyberspace that is enacted within country code top-level domain extensions, and encourages us to think through some of the tensions and conjunctions between on- and offline space. Firstly, the use of the country code top-level domains raises recent debates on the carving out of cyberspace as indicated by the domain extensions, as discussed in the introduction to this chapter, engaging with what Enteen has called the 'spatial conceptions of URLs' (Enteen 2006). As Steinberg and McDowell have persuasively argued, the naming system within the URL 'simultaneously reproduces claims to globalism, state sovereignty, and the presumption of United States hegemony' (Steinberg and McDowell 2003:47). Similarly, Enteen has argued that 'current procedures for identifying the location of electronic data, Uniform Resource Locators (URLs) in particular, situate the internet and the world wide web as geographically-based systems with corresponding geopolitical reference points in the physical world' (Enteen 2006:230), and thus the practice of country code top-level domains in URL extensions encodes websites within geopolitical contexts. Indeed, empirical research on this phenomena has offered significant insights into this process: Enteen's research on Tamil Eelam websites that refuse to recognise the primacy of country code suffixes to denote national presence (Enteen 2006); Shklovski and Struthers's research into how in Kazakhstan country code top-level domain names are not mere markers but 'have real meaning and their importance increases in locations where notions of statehood are in flux' (Shklovski and Struthers 2010); and Steinberg and McDowell's research on how Pacific Island microstates use their internet domain names to 'construct new "virtual" identities outside the idealized nexus of nation, government, and territory' (Steinberg and McDowell 2003), all serve as important examples of how geospatial and related cultural and linguistic concerns are being negotiated in the contemporary world. Moreover, according to Enteen, the practice of country domain extensions is intricately linked with the practices of mapping, as she argues that 'conceptualizing webpages as locatable under the logic of domain names and URLs enforces the perspective of mapping, accompanied by its ideological implications' (Enteen 2006:235). It is thus particularly fitting that Mackern has chosen to use country codes rather than country names to mark out his map; if the

URL is a space in which geospatial concerns are played out, then Mackern's work interrogates these concerns.

At the same time, Mackern's use of the country domain code comments on the problem of establishing national domains in transnational space, one of the most hotly debated issues in digital culture. This concern—the extent to which particular content on the internet can be marked out as 'belonging' to a particular national space or imaginary—is precisely the crux of much online cultural production, and speaks to one of the central concerns of the present volume; namely, the extent to which national or regional cultures can be expressed in online space. Mackern's use of country domain names thus also brings up tensions over national/regional versus global flows of identity online, and explicitly organises our access to the works within the database according to national or regional paradigms, plotting out the contours of a regional, pan-Latin American identity. At the same time, Mackern's practice does not amount to the fixing of his map, and the contents within it, within the confines of the nation-state. Rather, Mackern's reuse of the country code top-level domains to mark out his map must be understood in the wider context of his resistant, ironic reuse of standard coding elsewhere within this work; in other words, given Mackern's ironic reworkings of html commands in the title bar, his deliberate frustrating of the standard conventions of database formats, and his use of characters not for conventional coding but in the service of ASCII-art, his use of the country top-level domains similarly cannot be taken purely at face value. Instead, we are encouraged to view his use of these country top-level domains against the grain, and question their role, just as the standard features of other new media codes and technologies are questioned throughout this work.

In addition to this, one of the crucial features of this layout, in much the same way in which Mackern's other works dialogue with existing net. art precursors and yet perform ironic reversals, lies in the presentation of the 'map/database' across the screen. The database is structured in the form of a map, representing Latin America, yet with Argentina at its topmost point, rather than at the bottom, as in conventional cartographic representations of the continent. This layout is an obvious homage to Uruguayan artist Joaquín Torres García's iconic drawing, *América invertida* [*Inverted America*] (1936), a work which has often been cited as encapsulating a sense of Latin American resistance to hegemonic powers. Torres García's drawing reversed the conventional representation of the American continent, excluding the USA from the map and locating Chile and Argentina at the top, thus implicitly reversing hierarchies and rejecting (neo-)colonial powers. Referring to motivations behind his drawing, in a paper first published in 1943, Torres García stated 'ahora ponemos el mapa al revés, y entonces ya tenemos justa idea de nuestra posición, y no como quieren en el resto del mundo. La punta de América, desde ahora, prolongándose, señala insistentemente el Sur, nuestro norte' ['now we turn the map upside down, and we've got a precise idea of our position, and not as the rest of the world would have it. The tip of the Americas, from now on, stretching out, points towards the South, to our North'] (Torres García 1943). For Carmen Alcaide, Torres García's Dadaist-inspired drawing served to 'expresar la rei-vindicación de otra mirada sobre la propia experiencia cultural' ['express the claim for another viewpoint on our own cultural experience'] (Alcaide 1997:229), carving out an alternative space for artistic expression. For Juan Pablo Dabove and Carlos Jáuregui, meanwhile, Torres García's image func-tioned to question 'la violencia epistemológica-metafórica del mapa "origi-nal"' ['the epistemological-metaphorical violence of the "original" map'] (Dabove and Jáuregui 2003:10). In other words, two central impulses can be traced back to Torres García's original drawing: the necessity of speak-ing back to (cultural) imperialism; and the necessity of speaking back to the violence intrinsic to cartography itself.

These two impulses, then, are inherent within Mackern's own, twenty-first-century reworking of Torres García, and indeed, Mackern has made specific reference to Torres García's image as one with which the *netart latino database* specifically dialogues. Commenting on the structure of his own work in a recent article, Mackern notes that it makes:

> humorous and cynical allusions to the situation in which we Latin Amer-icans found ourselves. Its interface, an inverted map of South America drawn in ASCII, is an obvious tribute to the work of Joaquín Torres García and uses 'poor' (low-tech) design resources (ASCII sketches had always been a useful tool for designs in net contexts that operated very slowly).
>
> (Mackern 2010:434–35)

In this way, if Torres García's work of an earlier era served to propose another viewpoint on Latin American cultural experience, and at the same time to question the violence of the map, then Mackern's new version revit-alises this proclamation of cultural identity in the face of hegemonic powers for the late capitalist era of the late twentieth and early twenty-first century. The structural features of Mackern's database/map visualise the 'inversion' of global conceptualisations, point to the creation of alternative cartog-raphies, and integrate the resistant use of low-tech resources; all of these notions which, as we argue throughout this volume, are integral to Latin(o) American cultural production online, and resonate with the tactics of many artists of the region. There are similarities, for instance, with Guillermo Gómez Peña's notion of the 'low-rider Mac', an image of the ironic and tac-tical reappropriation of dated technologies, following a *rasquache* aesthetic (Gómez-Peña 1996).[18] So, too, are there resonances with the Electronic Disturbance Theater's tactical combination of 'hi-fi, low-fi, and no-fi ele-ments' (Domínguez, in interview with Fusco 2003:155), as well as of course with Domínguez's recent and highly controversial tactical media project, the *Transborder Immigrant Tool* (2009), specifically designed for use on inexpensive low-tech mobile telephones.[19] The recourse to deliberately dated ASCII-art as a means of contestation in Mackern's work is thus, a potentially resistant one; while it shares impulses to a certain extent with the 'reprise of early computer graphics' to be found in much net.art in an Anglo-European context (Stallabrass 2003:48), in Mackern's work it also carries with it a Latin(o) American-specific sense of the creative and tactical reuse of dated or low-tech resources.

Indeed, the format of the companion volume to the database continues with this playing with deliberately dated computer aesthetics and the resistant reuse of low tech. Refusing any high-tech graphics, the cover of the volume consists of two pieces of rough-hewn, thick grey cardboard, on which the image of the database-map is imprinted. Such a strategy immediately recalls the aesthetic of Eloísa Cartonera and the other Latin American *cartonera* publishing projects of the mid-2000s, in which the recycling of detritus, the challenge to existing publishing norms and a creative response to the inequalities of neoliberalism are brought together; as Bilbija puts it, *Eloisa Cartonera* is 'literally a "waste manager" that converts societal excess and detritus created by a neo-liberal economy into new cultural and social tissue' (Bilbija 2008:88).[20] The choice of this form of book binding for the *netart latino* companion volume is, thus deliberate, and embeds this volume within wider resistant recycling projects in Latin America. Similarly, other features of the volume continue this overt play with low-tech: for instance, instead of an accompanying CD showcasing the database, there is a pull-out section at the back of the volume, printed on a continuous ream of perforated fanfold paper, of the type used in dot matrix printers in the 1970s. The pull-out thus references the early days of computing, while also, of course, purposely rendering the hotlinks of the original database functionless; their printing here on paper, rather than inclusion in a CD ROM, means that the reader cannot click on the links to access the work. These features combined, as with the database itself, call attention to the resistant use of low-tech, to the deliberate frustration of high-tech potential, and embed the work within a tradition of resistant recycling.

At the same time as overtly flagging up the use of low-tech in the work itself, and in the companion volume, Mackern also expressly frames his project as an attempt to carve out a specifically Latin(o) American space for net.art. Mackern notes that he conceived the work as a 'response to various European and North American (and even Latin American) theoretical works on net.art in which the same artists and artworks were mentioned over and over again' (Mackern 2010:435). In contrast, the *netart latino database* was created for the purpose of 'asserting, with touches of irony [. . .] that we have our own "heroes" and that many of the works touted as pioneering endeavours in other latitudes were also being developed simultaneously by us' (Mackern 2010:435). Indeed, it is worth noting the relative lack of any Latin(o) American examples in any of the main scholarly works on the genre; the vast majority of the works analysed in volumes such as Corby's *Network Art*, Stallabrass's *Internet Art*, Saper's *Networked Art* and Daniels and Reisinger's *Net Pioneers* are by US or European artists, and there is a tendency to ignore Latin America as the site of production of net.art.[21] In this sense, Mackern's database attempts to inscribe Latin America's place; literally putting Latin America on the net.art map, his net.art database aims to assert the originality and importance of Latin American net.artists.[22]

Indeed, this notion of a 'netart latino' community is created by the interactive features of the database; clicking on the domain names then makes the page scroll downwards, leading the viewer/user to the links associated with the domain name in question. These links are to prominent net.art works by artists of that particular country, provided both by Mackern himself, and by suggestions from users, enabled via the 'Registro de sitios' function on the site. These are, as with the 'map' itself, provided via text-based links only, with no graphical interface employed, and their organisation haphazard, with no obvious ordering via chronology, artist surname or title of the work. Significantly, the presence of these links means this 'map' has depth rather than being pure surface; in other words, what would be flattened geographical features of a standard map are in fact links to external works, which themselves have multiple layers and multiple linkings. In this sense, Mackern's map once again maps out a potentially resistant stance to the monarch-of-all-I-survey trope, since his map must be entered and approached through its depth, rather than immediately grasped in its entirety.

That said, this notion of the geocultural specificity of the *netart latino database*, as of the works collected within it, has come under scrutiny by those writing in the exhibition catalogue produced to accompany the work. Laura Baigorri's piece argues that the notion of locality, and of Latin American specificity, is meaningless on the internet, since,

> In the online universe, the discourses and production of *Latin art* cannot be focused through the lens of specificity, because net.art is created and disseminated using a medium of communication that makes it possible to construct a global meta-culture where the concepts of 'nation' or 'homeland' are foreign.
>
> (Baigorri 2009:72)

Pace Baigorri, however, we argue that, while Mackern's classification of net.art by country and by region might at first seem problematic, in fact, as has been analysed in this chapter, the *netart latino database* is far from proposing a hegemonic mapping out by region and nation-state. There is, granted, a certain sleight of hand in Mackern's classification, particularly regarding the origin of many Latina/o or Chicana/o artists, who frequently appear in his database classed under the country of their parentage, rather than classed under the US, or under an alternative term resistant to the boundaries of the nation-state.[23] Indeed, what Mackern does not provide for is a potential non-nation-state or cultural classification (there is no attempt to invent a domain name for the expression of Chicano or more broadly Latin(o)

American belonging—.azt, .xic or .lat, for example). That said, as has been noted, his work problematises rather than reaffirms the relationship between the nation-state and online cultural production. Indeed, as we argue throughout this volume, the relationship between cultural specificity and online presence is not a straightforward oppositional one, but is in fact complex and multiply inflected; in other words, it is important not to conceive of the internet as always and irrevocably global, and in Manichean opposition to the local, national or regional, but instead to explore the productive possibilities that new media technologies offer for local, national and regional forms of cultural expression. In this particular instance, Mackern's use not of country names but of URL domain names indicates that his work maps out not geographical place, but online conceptualisations of locality; the presentation of his map indicates that we are witnessing a *reverse mapping* out of the continent, rather than its conventional portrayal; the depth rather than surface of his map, as noted above, refuses the monarch-of-all-I-survey trope, and thus points to rich levels of data. In these and other ways, we argue that Mackern's classification of the works in his database, both on the level of country and region, is paradigmatic of the critical regionalism with which we ended our introduction; that is, it involves a meta-critical, self-reflexive understanding of what it means to be Latin(o) American, and, as such a similar meta-critical, self-reflexive understanding of the mapping out onto nation-states.

In summary, then, Mackern's *netart latino database* talks back to a series of dominant trends within mapping, within the net.art sphere more specifically, and more broadly within predominantly anglophone conceptualisations of online space. Firstly, Mackern's work talks back to cartographies of the Americas—originally mapped out as part of a European imperialist gaze, and subsequently reframed in a set of neo-imperialist relations with its wealthier neighbour to the North, Latin(o) American cartography is embued with geopolitical concerns. As such, Mackern's ironic ASCII-map charts, in a tactical and partial form, potentially resistant mappings of the contours of the continent. Secondly, the *netart latino database* talks back to existing mappings of net.art by scholars and practitioners who conceive of net.art as a predominantly Anglo-European phenomenon or as non-context-specific. Here, Mackern's visualisation of the subcontinent through ASCII-art reveals that even the most purportedly 'formalist' of net.art experimentation has geopolitical grounding. Thirdly, Mackern's work speaks back to the cartographic tropes of the internet *per se*, as encapsulated in domain names and more broadly in spatial conceptualisations of the internet. In this regard, Mackern's knowing reuse of html coding and other features of the standard browser format forms a way of talking back to and engaging with current debates on the locality and embeddedness of content on the internet. In summary, then, Mackern's work, much more than a mere database, provides illuminating commentaries on the mapping of Latin America through existing domain name protocols, and on the broad shape within which discourses of Latin American-ness can be understood online.

The two artists whose work is the subject of the remainder of this chapter can be seen as following in Mackern's footsteps in terms of their desire to problematise hegemonic forms of mapping, either on or offline, but they do this in ways that seek to find alternatives to the sleight of hand evident in Mackern's work for mapping Latina/o net.artists. In so doing they suggest a more unmistakably postregional approach that both comfortably embraces Latina/o subject positions as well as explores the interface between Latin(o) American regionalism and other ways of interpreting the dynamics of the contemporary world. Eduardo Navas is of Salvadoran origin, though he rarely presents himself as anything other than a net.artist (without a national, regional or ethnic epithet), having lived in the United States since early childhood.[24] In his art work in general Navas is critical of the existence of a concept of a discrete, regionally specific Latin American-ness in the world today, and, in the piece studied here, he represents this critique through a dialogic, textual form of mapping of what one might call 'delocalised *latinidad*'. Chameleonic multimedia artist Praba Pilar is of Colombian origin, although she spent much of her childhood in Mexico before moving to the US.[25] The art work examined here comprises a series of digital prints based on popular images of internet geography. Her objective in this work is to use such images critically to represent the complexity of relationships between different regions of the world in the age of informational capitalism. In this context Latin(o) America can be seen as offering a telling example of such complexities.

The Textual Mapping of Delocalised *Latinidad*: Eduardo Navas's *Plástico_2002_Update*

Eduardo Navas is an increasingly prominent media/net.artist, academic curator and editor (founder of the journal *netartreview*) and his work on 'Remix Theory' has been influential in the world of digital media art (Taylor 2012:194). Navas's theory essentially takes the concept of the remix from disc-jockeying practice and explores the substantial consonance but also subtle differences that the practice of copy and paste, of making 'mashups', has in the dynamics of internet culture. Informed by this theoretical work in sampling and recycling material, Navas's work frequently offers a self-reflexive critique of the medium with which he is working, as well as a critique of the dynamics of globalisation, with a particular awareness of the place of Latin(o) America in that. Some of his most significant works include *The Quixote* (2000)—a reworking of Jorge Luis Borges's reworking of Cervantes's 'original' text—and *Goobalization*, versions I to III (2005–07), a series of visually complex animated mash-ups of images downloaded from the internet that encourage the viewer to consider the dynamic between hegemonic and homogenising processes of globalisation and projects of resistance and cultural diversity within and even enabled by globalisation itself.[26]

Plástico_2002_upDate (2002) is a Flash animation that, after a brief definition of the noun 'plastic' in both Spanish and English, juxtaposes, against a black screen, the lyrics of the Willie Colón and Ruben Blades salsa smash-hit 'Plástico' (from the album *Siembra* [*Sowing Time*, 1978]), translated into English and positioned at the top left of the screen, with statistics about the nation-states of the Americas as a whole, as extracted from the *Info Please* website in 2002, occupying the bulk of the screen. The animation lasts for the duration of the playing of an audio file of the Colón and Blades track, unchanged in its musical form from its original 1978 release. While the track plays in Spanish, the lyrics in English change from grey to white as each line is sung. When each chunk of the lyrics displayed has been sung, the next chunk appears alongside data for the next nation-state, progressing in alphabetical order. In Navas's terms this is a fairly simple 'reflexive mashup' of the lyrics of a musical track with web-based data, with the original track functioning as something of a framing device. Although Navas argues that 'reflexive mashups' are often predominantly functional in their web-based applications, he also concedes that 'the reflexive mashup's foundation in functionality does not make it free from the allegorical tendency that other forms of Remix are dependent upon' (Navas 2010:171). Particularly in this case where the 'reflexive mashup' is presented as a discrete piece of net.art, the viewer is thus encouraged to read the materials presented critically, in order to capture that allegorical impulse.

Visually the animation is deliberately low-key. In comparison with Mackern's *netart latino database* which managed to evoke Latin America and its place in the world/net.art in graphic form so economically and so pertinently through its calligramme-like use of html textual symbols, in the night sky of the screen of *Plástico_2002_upDate* no constellations emerge; there is no graphic representation of the Latin America of the song or of the statistics to be found. Given his preference for exclusively textual representation in a medium such as digital animation that so clearly suggests the need for and potential of graphical representation, and given the subject matter—almost exhaustive coverage of the nation-states of the Americas as well as the provision of statistical and even topographical data that so often forms the basis of maps—Navas might seem to be making a statement about the function of (carto)graphic representation in itself. Nevertheless, although it is certainly the case that Navas, as a conceptual artist, often prefers text-based or text-heavy forms of artistic expression, rather than deliberately avoiding (carto)graphical forms of representation in this work, it might be argued that Navas has instead actively pursued a form of conceptual mapping in a dialogue between affective and statistical forms of textual material. *Plástico_2002_upDate* offers, then, a critical textual mapping of what we might term 'the idea of Latin(o) America'. In his presentation of the work on his website, Navas says that the animation aims to 'reevaluate emancipatory narratives that have affected Latin Americans since 1978', producing 'a metaphoric commentary on how hopeful gestures can quickly become absorbed by our current state of globalization'

(Navas, 'Plástico'). This critique is achieved through the 'reflexive mashup' of idealistic song lyrics and contemporary statistical data.

The Colón and Blades song 'Plástico' critiques the influence of US values ('modelos importados' ['imported models']) in Latin America where social climbing, white-supremacist attitudes, and an obsession with money, possessions and appearances are symbolised by the artificial nature of plastic and contrasted with the big-hearted naturalness of Latin America where the strong sun will melt plastic if given half a chance. The song then goes on to exhort 'Latinos' to be proud of who they are and to form 'una Latino-américa unida' ['a united Latin America'] and 'una raza unida' ['a united people'] like the one of which Simón Bolívar dreamed. It then lists an 'affective cartography' of the region in a roll-call coda that embraces Panama (Blades's birthplace), Puerto Rico, Mexico, Venezuela, Peru, the Dominican Republic, Cuba, Costa Rica, Colombia, Honduras, Ecuador, Bolivia, Argentina, 'Nicaragua sin Somoza', and finally 'el barrio' ['the neighbourhood'] and 'la esquina' ['the street corner'].[27] A selection of Spanish American countries such as Chile, Guatemala, El Salvador and Paraguay are missing, probably more for reasons of artistic economy than for their political leadership in 1978. More significantly, however, Brazil, Suriname and all anglophone and francophone nation-states in Meso- and South America and the Caribbean are also missing. Colón and Blades's Latin America is thus specifically Hispanic. It also does not really seem to countenance the mushrooming Latina/o presence in the United States as part of what being 'Latino' might include.[28] It is really quite essentialist, then, in its conceptualisation of Latin America as a discrete, and neatly bounded, set of Spanish-speaking nation-states, and diametrically opposed to the culture of Anglo-America.

The statistical data provided in the animation is no less problematic, though in a different way. It comes from the *Info Please* website which is the online version of one of the oldest and most popular almanacs in the United States, part of the Family Education Network and owned by Pearson Education Inc., 'the world's largest integrated education company' including the *Financial Times* and Penguin groups (*Info Please*, 1998–).[29] It is hence data of an authoritative and hegemonic nature, presented in a naturalised, matter-of-fact manner for school children. The almanac's primary achievement is to articulate the data provided in such a way that the user 'naturally' appreciates the economic and industrial might of the United States as 'leading industrial power in the world, highly diversified and technologically advanced' and major exporter of 'consumer goods' (*Info Please*, quoted in Navas's animation), in comparison with the considerably lesser development but sizeable and highly exploitable natural resources of Latin America. The data also omits information concerning the potentially denaturalising political 'colours' of the nation-states listed, though it does name current presidents and vice-presidents.

This data, though clearly biased, does not simply validate the message of the Colón and Blades song—its call for Latin American resistance and a sense of regional cultural identity—by providing proof that the US functions as the 'plastic' consumerist parasite encroaching upon edenic Latin American resources and corrupting its people. Instead it can be read as revealing the idealism of the 1978 song by evidencing 'our current state of globalization', in Navas's terms. The data provided covers almost all the nation-states of the Americas, including Canada, the USA, Brazil, Belize and Suriname,[30] rather than the Colón-Blades affective sketch of Latin, or more properly, Spanish America. The data on languages spoken and ethnicity/race, but also on trade relations and international disputes, given for each nation-state also give ample evidence of the imbrications of Anglo-America in Latin America and, even more importantly, the massive encroachment of Latin America on the USA in recent years.[31] The communications data for internet service providers and users might at first sight provide evidence of a digital divide where the US holds all the trumps in an age of informational capitalism, but it also demonstrates the fact that Latin America is connected, and over time, the same data would demonstrate the rapid growth in this respect that was experienced in Latin America in the 2000s. Indeed, as Navas elsewhere notes appreciatively, 'aun países que no tengan accesos a la última tecnología han hallado forma de incorporar la tecnología que pueden obtener para empujarse como cultura global' ['even countries which don't have access to the newest technology have found ways to incorporate the technologies that they can get their hands on in order to promote themselves as part of global culture'] (Navas, quoted by Yto.cl 2007). The statistical data, then, might be presented as facts about discrete nation-states, but in fact it demonstrates interdependence and connectedness, albeit not on entirely equal terms.

What Navas's *Plástico_2002_upDate* suggests through this use of statistical data, which might be hegemonic in origin but which also reveals the complexity of contemporary geopolitical relations, is that Latin America is not so easily locatable as Colón and Blades might have assumed. Indeed, in Navas's view it is perhaps more fruitful to conceive of oneself not as Latin American, or even Latino, but as part of a 'global culture' that has multiple, complementary centres. In this networked set-up Navas argues that the (local) artist needs to strive to make his/her work 'visible a nivel internacional y de esta manera deslocalizar las narrativas en práctica de momento' ['visible at an international level and in so doing make sure that the narratives of the moment are delocalised'] (Navas, quoted by Yto.cl 2007).[32] Navas's animation might be thus said to 'delocalise' traditional, discretely bounded, discourses of Latin American identity and to instead mobilise a complementary *latinidad* throughout global culture. This delocalised conceptualisation of *latinidad* is further underscored in Navas's curatorial essay 'The Influence of Non-Places in the Concept of Latin America' (Navas 2009). Here Navas elaborates various definitions of Latin America 'as a concept that moves across borders' (Navas 2009:3), as 'a non-place (a place in constant transition and redefinition)—an idea that can be re-enacted in different places according to the tendency of the locality' (Navas 2009:21) in the spirit of Marc Augé, and as a place/concept 'that can be *cited*, anywhere around the world' (Navas 2009:22; original italics). Furthermore, he consistently considers the predominantly Latin American media artists selected for the exhibition as glocal cultural producers, with the emphasis falling on their elucidation of local stories that can circulate globally and find parallels with other local stories. The idea of Latin America as bounded entity is thus put under considerable strain in Navas's work, even if he does not seek to move beyond the regional paradigm altogether. This is, in essence, a post-regionalist approach at work.

Exploring the Spatial Dynamics of Informational Capitalism: Praba Pilar's *Cyberlabia* Project

Where Navas's 2002 animation initiated a discourse of 'delocalisation' of Latin American-ness in an era of informational capitalism and chose to map the complexities of this out in textual form, Praba Pilar's work situates itself as already beyond the desire to represent Latin America or Latin American-ness, preferring instead to explore contemporary *global* relations. Arguably, however, the place of Latin(o) America in her work offers a telling example of the global issues she seeks to raise. In comparison with Navas and his textual mapping, Pilar's work focuses much more clearly on informational capitalism's spatial dynamics and on its forms of cartographic self-representation.

Over the last fifteen years, internet geographers have wrestled with the need to represent a particularly contemporary phenomenon—the interconnectedness of the 'wired' world and of the informational economy more generally—that defies two-dimensional representation even more resolutely than the globe itself and still presents challenges for meaningful representation through three-dimensional digital and interactive forms of representation. The result has been the development of a huge variety of different models of exponential complexity—arc maps, hyperbolic models, models that only function through interactive digital technologies and cannot in themselves be transferred to a two-dimensional, offline medium. These forms of cartographic representation have come to constitute an art form in itself where commentators frequently note the unintentional organic beauty of the forms created.[33] Nevertheless, some of the most commonly circulated images of internet geography such as the work of researchers at Bell Laboratories or the Cooperative Association for Internet Data Analysis (CAIDA) demonstrate that, while mapping complex global communications systems might be said to be achieved, their visualisation still suffers from the traditional hegemonic assumptions of mapmakers since time immemorial. The projection chosen may artificially shrink the global South in an extreme version of the Mercator projection (as seen in Stephen Eick and colleagues' arc map of internet traffic between countries in 1993 [Dodge and Kitchin 2001a: 59]).[34] Furthermore, the outline map-as-logo form still functions as the skeletal base for some of the most infamous representations, typically a white outline against a black 'night sky' screen or etched onto a globe represented as 'floating' in dark space.[35] In these visualisations the nation-states evidencing the most significant connectivity are often filled in with a primary colour (with connectivity being calculated almost inevitably according to personal connectivity rather than community connectivity), and large parts of Africa, Asia and Latin America are consequently left uncoloured, as 'framed voids' or 'dark continents', just as they were in the maps of the colonial era. As Harpold argues in his article 'Dark Continents: A Critique of Internet Metageographies',

> these depictions of network activity are embedded in unacknowledged and pernicious metageographies—sign systems that organize geographical knowledge into visual schemes that seem straightforward (how else to illustrate global Internet traffic if not on images of . . . the globe?), but which depend on historically—and politically—inflected misrepresentation of underlying material conditions.
>
> (Harpold 1999)

Of course, it is not just a case of individual internet geographers' naïve misrepresentation or more deliberate abridging of the real experiences of the peoples of the developing world. As documented at length by Manuel Castells, informational capitalism itself (including capital restructuring, as well as the 'new technological and organizational conditions of the Information Age') 'is intertwined with rising inequality and social exclusion throughout the world' (Castells 2000:68), and this has a spatial configuration which results in the development of 'dual cities', and in the opposition of 'glocal nodes' (Graham and Marvin, quoted in Castells 2001b: 238–39) with '*the black holes of informational capitalism*' (Castells 2000:165; original emphasis). It is the latter that Castells terms 'the Fourth World', arguing that, with the collapse of the USSR and hence the end of the 'three worlds theory', 'the First World has not become the all-embracing universe of neo-liberal mythology. Because a new world, the Fourth World, has emerged, made up of multiple black holes of social exclusion throughout the planet' (Castells 2000:168). It is this reality that internet geographers represent more or less subtly.

Castells's Fourth World comprises those totally excluded from information society and he is a firm believer in the existence of a form of 'global digital divide' (Castells 2001b: 241). What he pays less attention to are to the inequalities within social inclusion (which way the data packages are flowing and what messages they are carrying), and to forms of creative contestation.[36] Although Pilar expresses herself firmly in terms of a First World/Third World binary, in the series of seven digital prints known as *Cyberlabia* (or *Cyber.Labia*),[37] included in her *Cyberlabia: Gendered Thoughts and Conversations on Cyberspace* (2005) chapbook,[38] her reworkings of the iconic maps of internet geography described above actually suggest a rather more nuanced approach to the spatial logic of informational capitalism that focuses both on the place of the inhabitants of the Fourth World and of those included on unequal terms within informational capitalism.

Pilar currently describes herself on her website as a (San Francisco) 'Bay Area/Colombian [. . .] performance artist, technologist and cultural theorist' whose work explores 'aspects of emerging technologies which generate new forms of economic, environmental and sexual exploitation and erasure' through 'site works, performances, street theatre, writing and websites' ('Praba Pilar bio'). Her early work included installation art work in conjunction with the United Farm Workers Union in 1995 and with the art activist group The Hexterminators: SuperHeroes of the Biozoid Era in the late 1990s/ early 2000s, as well as sundry acts of protest in support of the antiglobalisation movement, all of which has earned her a mention in *The Civil Disobedience Handbook* (Tracy 2002:41–43). She was also a member of the infamous group Los Cybrids: La Raza Techno-Crítica, along with John Jota Leaños and René Garcia, during its lifespan from 1999–2003.[39]

While Los Cybrids aimed to critique new technologies, and the internet in particular, through a culturalist/racialised lens, in her subsequent solo work Pilar has focused less specifically on issues of Latin(o) American cultural or ethnoracial identity—though she still describes herself on her website as 'deeply rooted in Latino communities'—and instead focuses more on issues of cyberimperialism more broadly speaking, together with a nuanced, critical approach to cyberfeminist concerns. As such Pilar's perspective is in consonance with a growing body of what might be identified as *critical* cyberfeminism; a feminism that refuses the utopianist dreams of freedom and empowerment through disembodiment in virtual space typical of Euro-American cyberfeminism,[40] and is instead much more attentive to issues of race and class as they affect different groups of women, both on- and offline (cf. Fernández 2002; Daniels, J. 2009).[41] Pilar's *Cyberlabia* project is emblematic of this focus, and it has garnered her several mentions in the increasing numbers of volumes dedicated to (critical) cyberfeminism (cf. Hobson 2007:119–20; Ray 2007:33–37).

The *Cyberlabia* project is, in its book/pdf form, a compilation of interviews with prominent feminist and environmentalist critics of digital culture in both its on- and offline practices (Anne Balsamo, Sheila Davis and Paulina Borsook), as well as Art McGee, a key voice in the debates over how race, particularly African American-ness, intersects with networked digital culture. The title itself, as circumscribed by the definitions that Pilar offers from the *Larousse* dictionary, refers simply to 'chat' on the subject of networked culture—the Spanish word 'labia' means 'fluency' and the expression 'tener mucha labia' translates as 'to have the gift of the gab'. Nevertheless, it clearly also plays with the immediate gyno-anatomical connotations that the term will have in the minds of an anglophone reader (and the text, is, after all, written in English), as well as reasserts the importance of writing the body for (particularly French) feminist thought.[42] It is thus that the title suggests the critical cyberfeminist focus of its 'chat' on the subject of networked digital culture.

The book also includes the lyrics to Pilar's performance piece 'Computers Are a Girl's Best Friend' as well as a CD-ROM of the performance itself. This performance is thematically related to the interviews in its professed aim to 'get beyond superficial cries of the cyborgian revolution and examine the real impacts computers are having on women' (Pilar 2005:4). All this is interspersed by the element that is most relevant for analysis here—the series of homonymous digital prints which illustrate the themes of the interviews and performance. The prints are based on some of the most iconic images of internet geography discussed above—Eick and colleagues' arc map and globe visualisations, CAIDA's Walrus hyperbolic model, as well as others by John Risch and researchers at the Pacific Northwest National Laboratory, Ben Fry and Silicon Graphics. These images of internet geography are turned into digital collages by Pilar and combined with images of women taken from pornographic websites or of children sitting on top of piles of toxic high-tech waste.

It is clear from Pilar's statements on the *Cyberlabia* prints that she is predominantly concerned with the place of the Third World/global South in the flows of both digital material and obsolescent hardware. In the introductory description of the prints on her website, she states that the series is designed to promote 'the reflection that the pornography is made in the Third World, with the Internet traffic coming to the First World—while the hazardous waste is flowing in the opposite direction' ('Cyber.Labia 2005', in 'Projects'). In the interview with Anne Balsamo, Pilar also cites the Indian physicist Vandana Shiva's critique of the supposed neutrality of technology which argues that digital technologies respond to the 'particular culture, class and gender' preferences of the global North that are then 'foisted on the Global South', and that because these ICTs 'emerge from a dominating and colonizing culture, they are themselves colonizing' (Pilar 2005:14). This endorsement of Shiva's arguments thus emphasises the fact that Pilar's work is also intended to constitute a broadly postcolonialist critique structured around the binary spatial logic of First World/Third World and global North/global South.

Prints 2 and 8 in the series offer clear examples of the collection's critique of this contraflow system in information technology (online pornography in the case of Print 2 and the dumping of digital waste materials in the case of Print 8). Print 2 [Fig. 1.2] is based on a map of internet geography that Pilar credits to John Risch and other researchers at the Pacific Northwest National Laboratory and which comprises a traditional two-dimensional wall-chart style map of the United States in the top left-hand corner of the image, against a black background marked out by white gridlines and dotted with snippets of data.[43] White lines are depicted emerging from points on the wall-chart and converging in an abstract cube that occupies the bottom left-hand corner of the image. Entwined with this map and its abstractions,[44] yet dominating the screen, is the image of a dark-skinned, female cyber-sexworker who is outlined in neon hues and depicted drawing a largely disembodied erect penis (bottom left) towards her smiling mouth, while her elbow rests on a computer keyboard (bottom right). The composite image depicts the white lines that emerge from the wall-chart leading to the cyber-sexworker whose body occupies the same space as the cuboid structure of the original map. This suggests connections being made from the United States (the client) with the cyber-sexworker and thus that there is a (solicited) flow of pornographic data that originates somewhere outside the map and terminates in the heart of the First World.

Print 8 [Fig. 1.3] indicates the flow of high-tech waste in the opposite direction through its depiction of a dark-skinned young boy sitting on top of an almost abstract heap of garbage that indicates its high-tech nature through the visual cue of its neon-hued outline. This garbage heap obliterates almost the entirety of Eick and colleagues' arc map of internet traffic between countries in 1993. What the boy and the garbage heap do not obscure from view, however, is significant. Even though the garbage heap appears to disrupt the rhizomatic flows and the utopianist smooth space of the cartographic imaginaries of First World internet geographers suggested by the map, this is a simple superposition of images and the arcs continue to be visible at the top of the print, thus suggesting that the linking of the nation-states of the First World through networked digital technology goes on undisturbed 'behind' the garbage heap. The implication, then, is that the garbage heap is really located in the unconnected, outline-only parts of the map, which necessarily correspond to the Third World/global South. Thus, while the viewer might be encouraged towards a postcolonialist critical awareness of the power relations that underpin digital technologies, in both these images Pilar's representation of this relationship does not immediately appear to disrupt a sense of discrete 'worlds' that Castells's analysis of the spatial logic of informational capitalism suggests is really the case.

It is arguable, however, that Pilar's digital prints can be seen to do rather more justice to the complexity of representing contemporary networked culture—its multiple exclusions and partial inclusions. In the first place, the figures described above represent the Fourth World of total social exclusion (the women and children working in the high-tech waste disposal industry) and a more nuanced version of that Fourth World (the connected but exploited cyber-sexworker, for example). Secondly, in terms of mapping this more or less nuanced version of the Fourth World that is Pilar's subject (regardless of the terminology she uses), in line with Castells's description, these worlds constitute neither the homogeneous reality of the global South nor are they absent entirely from the global North. This complexity is neatly captured through a consideration of the presence of Latin America in these images.

Latin America is implicitly embraced as part of the Fourth World in the representation of the figures in Pilar's images as broadly 'women and children of colour', who may well be Asian or African, but who could just as easily be Latina or Brazilian. Nevertheless, while these figures might immediately seem to locate Latin America among the 'dark continents' of internet geography, the map of the region as it appears in some of these prints is also evidently part of the networked world. In Print 8, for example, the Latin American map-as-logo is not obliterated by the garbage heap and can be seen clearly, coloured predominantly in green and blue with only a few outline-only states. It may thus be a place where high-tech toxic waste is dumped in preference to leaving it on United States soil and where many people are indeed left in a position of social exclusion, but it is also a (fast-growing) part of the informational economy and certainly not uniformly part of Castells's Fourth World, even if there are also many inequalities of inclusion, referenced here in Pilar's images of cyber-sexworkers.[45]

Furthermore, in terms of demographics, Latin America is, of course, increasingly also Latino America—Pilar herself is part of this reality—and social exclusion and/or inequalities within inclusion are not quite so clearly locatable as uniquely 'south of the border'. As Harpold has argued, 'In the networked era, the heart of darkness is an interstitial formation—which is to say, its borders are drawn around and between us' (Harpold 1999). Indeed, in Print 2 the lines that seemingly link points on the wall-chart of the USA with the cyber-sexworker whose body emanates from the Latin America of the map. If, in the iconography of internet geography, what this might suggest is the refraction of a signal by a satellite, the conclusion that the viewer might draw from this is that the lines connect a client located in, say, Denver with a sexworker located in the San Francisco bay area. The 'heart of darkness' or the 'black holes of informational capitalism' are thus to be found in the United States of America, as much as they are in Latin America or elsewhere in the global South.

To return to the mainframe of this chapter—the questions of mapping and of Latin America in an era of informational capitalism enabled by digital technologies—like Mackern, Pilar problematises the conventions of cartographic representation by making the viewer reflect on what is left out (the map's abridging function in Crampton's terms) and what might be read in different ways (its enabling function). Like her fellow Latino, Navas, she also problematises the concept of Latin America as easily locatable, either in the South or even in a contestatory 'South as North', or even as a useful framework for a discussion of contemporary global relations. Pilar's South is more of a portable South—a more nuanced, intuitive version of Castells's Fourth World and an ongoing process of critical positioning rather than an identification with any particular region. As such it perhaps suggests an even more radical conceptualisation of a postregional approach than those put forward thus far.

The Shape of Latin(o) America Online

As our argument in this chapter has shown, given that mapping was arguably one of the founding practices by which the shape and form of Latin America was inscribed—particularly by imperial, and subsequently neo-imperial eyes—recent digital cultural practice in Latin America has continued in the vein of Torres García's gesture to interrogate and revise hegemonic cartographies. The three case studies we have investigated provide different takes on this process, and engage in a sustained critique of the place assigned to Latin America, both in official cartographies and in the conventions for mapping out internet content. In their different ways, they propose alternative cartographies of Latin(o) America and its place in a globalised world, and question the notion of Latin(o) America as a necessarily bounded entity. While the three case studies analysed in this chapter map out what might be termed the broader contours Latin American-ness, as we see in subsequent chapters, other cultural producers make use of the internet to focus on or interrogate specific discourses which have attempted to capture or represent Latin America over time.

2 Reworking the 'Lettered City'
The Resistant Reterritorialisation of Urban Place

This chapter follows on from the thread of the mapping out of identity along spatial lines that we analysed in the previous chapter, to now focus on one particular geographical-conceptual space: that of the city. Here, we explore one of the most influential discourses to emerge from Latin American studies in the second half of the twentieth century—that of the 'lettered city'—and analyse how this discourse is transmuted and challenged by contemporary online works. The original model of the 'lettered city' was developed by Ángel Rama in his hugely influential homonymous book, *La ciudad letrada* (1984), in which he argued that writing was fundamental to the formation of Latin American societies, and that cities were central in the control and diffusion of the power associated with it. Power structures within the city thus allied the elites with written discourse, meaning that the discourses that emanate from cities were the preserve of the colonial (and, later, creole) elite; these discourses must, perforce, function to the exclusion of nonelites (women, indigenous populations, lower classes and so forth).

Rama himself noted the transformations that this 'lettered city' underwent in the mid-twentieth century, mainly due to modernisation and education for the masses (see in particular Chapter Six of Rama's study). Recent works by Latin Americanist scholars have taken up this notion set forth by Rama, and continued with the thrust of his argument to explore further ways in which the 'lettered city' has undergone mutations in recent years. Jean Franco's *Decline and Fall of the Lettered City* (2002), for instance, explores a variety of ways in which the model of the 'lettered city' has been transformed in the latter half of the twentieth century, including via the recuperation of marginalised voices through the *testimonio* genre. In a different vein, Elena Ortega has posited that women writers function in a zone beyond the 'lettered city' (Ortega 2001:11), due to the complex and conflicted relations between women writers and the seat of literary power. Edmundo Paz-Soldán and Debra Castillo, in their introduction to their edited volume of 2001, invoke the trope of the 'lettered city', and explore how its status is profoundly altered by the rise of radio, cinema, and other mass media forms (Paz-Soldán and Castillo 2001:1–18). Ramón de la Campa, meanwhile, has argued that the questions raised by Rama lend themselves to 'an appraisal of the conflictive impact of global capitalism and market forces on cultural formation' (de la Campa 1999:143), thus updating Rama for our late capitalist context. In particular, de la Campa's comments are useful in the context of the present volume, since, as set out in our Introduction, the issues of globalisation and cultural formation/specificity come to the fore when analysing online cultural practice. Finally, a recent, although brief, reference to the notion of the 'lettered city' comes in Carlos Jáuregui's speculations that internet technologies allow for a critical practice 'outside an academic or specialized center' and thus 'the ruinous rings of Angel Rama's "lettered city" become permeable and flexible' (Jáuregui 2001:292). In all of these cases, scholars have indicated the continuing relevance of Rama's central concept, as well as suggesting ways in which Rama's model needs to be rethought in the light of contemporary debates around globalisation, (new) media, and communicative forms.

Drawing from and building upon these debates, this chapter argues that the transformations of the 'lettered city', as noted by Rama, and as developed by Franco, Ortega, de la Campa and others, are even more manifest in twenty-first century Latin American online culture. As is explored in this chapter, functioning within what Jesús Martín-Barbero has termed the 'desubicaciones y reubicaciones de la letra' ['de-locations and re-locations of lettered culture'] (Martín-Barbero 2003:383), brought about by new media technologies, Latin American online works force a rethinking of the model of the 'lettered city' in their portrayal of contestatory voices and perspectives. Via a two-pronged approach, in which the 'lettered city' is challenged both in terms of the primacy of lettered culture (that is, by giving voice to those previously excluded from lettered culture), and in terms of the centricity of the city (that is, by providing alternative perspectives of the city from new loci), Latin American online works attempt to remap the cityscape. This chapter therefore proposes a rereading of Rama by way of an analysis of Argentine Marina Zerbarini's net.art work *Tejido de memoria* [*Fabric of Memory*] (2003), and the literary-cultural works to be found on the Colombian website, *Hiperbarrio* (2007–), where the focus of expression shifts from the elites to the marginalised. While not claiming to be exhaustive, these two works are taken as illustrative of a broader trend in Latin American online culture which has seen a variety of works that attempt to produce resistant representations of offline place.[1] The chapter analyses firstly the resignification of the urban political centre as manifested in *Tejido de memoria*, highlighting how this work, in its reworking of images of Buenos Aires and its engagement with the Madres de Plaza de Mayo [Mothers of the Plaza de Mayo] undertakes a resignification of the city and urban space.[2] The chapter then focuses on the reformulations of the margins as exemplified in the *Hiperbarrio* website, exploring how the works it showcases attempt to convey urban experience from the marginalised, disenfranchised *barrios*, and posit the *barrio* as locus of cultural resistance. Functioning from ambivalent spaces which cross the boundaries of the 'lettered city', these two works make use of alternative modes of expression and dissemination enabled by the new media technologies to circumvent traditional channels of communication and power structures.

One particular way in which this model of the 'lettered city' is at once invoked and yet revised is through the constant referencing of both works to offline place. As the analysis in this chapter will reveal, the geographical tropes upon which these websites rely are both reinforced and transformed by their use online; if, as we discussed in our introduction, online practices entail not the loss of locatedness, but a reworking of the concept of locatedness, then these websites make use of the potential of the internet to force a rethinking of place and territory. This chapter argues that, just as the Madres' original conception of the Plaza de Mayo is predicated on the resignification of this space, following this logic, the internet may be seen to provide a further—and in some cases, more radical—opportunity for reterritorialisation and the recuperation of place. The processes of de- and reterritorialisation enabled by the advent of new media technologies thus do not function merely to further the interests of global informational capitalism but offer a potential space for tactical resistance. In this way, the analysis in this chapter engages with, but also contests, Deleuze and Guattari's theories of deterritorialisation and reterritorialisation. Deleuze and Guattari argued that capitalism, being based on social abstraction, involves deterritorialisation, and at the same time establishes 'factitious and artificial reterritorializations' which function 'in its own service' (Deleuze and Guattari 1977:303). Pace Deleuze and Guatarri, this chapter argues that the sites under analysis here are examples of what we could term *resistant* reterritorialisation, enabled by new media technologies, meaning that reterritorialisation online does not of necessity function in the service of capitalism, but instead, that tactical reterritorialisations via on- and offline practice may offer contestatory approaches which attempt to critique capitalism's logic. These potentially resistant reterritorialisations are undertaken through the tactical and resistant way in which Latin American online works engage with the productive tensions between online representations and offline places. As this chapter argues, rather than online cultural practice entailing the erasure of place-based concerns, instead, the way is open for new associations of place and for new formulations of territorial identity. In this regard, the works in this chapter are examined as examples of the creation of urban representations which function at the interface between the real and the virtual, and make tactical use of the tensions and interstices between these two realms.

RECONFIGURING THE CENTRIC: MARINA ZERBARINI'S *TEJIDO DE MEMORIA*

The Argentine digital artist and scholar Marina Zerbarini has been involved in research in art and technology since the mid-1990s, as well as developing her own multimedia and net.art works, many of which are hosted on her

website. Her online works to date include the hypertext narrative *Eveline,
fragmentos de una respuesta* [*Eveline, Fragments of a Reply*] (2004), which
is created from an aleatory and interactive combination of fragments from
the James Joyce short story, 'Eveline' (1914), remixed with photographic
images, videos, animations and sound files. Her net.art work, *Gemelos*
[*Twins*] (2005) takes the form of an interactive game, involving a mix of
sound files, texts and images taken from the web which are then incorporated by the user to create the effect of a 'Torre de Babel' ['Tower of Babel']
(Zerbarini 2005:76). More recently, her 'narrativa no lineal para internet'
['non-linear internet narrative'] *La borra* [*Sediment*] (2009) involves the creation of a narrative based on photographs of coffee grounds taken daily,
combined with a text extracted from horoscope predictions on the internet,
and a map image drawn from Google Earth, along with short comments by
the author. In all of these cases, as with Zerbarini's other pieces, her works
are characterised by the remixing of existing sources, the constant movement across multiple media (text, sound, still image and moving image),
the refusal to abide by conventional teleological narrative structure, and the
access to the work via a nonintuitive interface.[3]

This chapter focuses on her 2003 work, *Tejido de memoria*, an interactive online work which dialogues explicitly with the Madres de Plaza de
Mayo, and engages in an active reworking of the Buenos Aires cityscape.
Presented as part of the *Women: Memory of Repression in Argentina* exhibition of 2003 and curated by the artist and activist Raquel Partnoy, *Tejido de
memoria* is Zerbarini's most explicitly political work to date. In Partnoy's
vision, as explained in her curatorial statement, if the military 'wanted us to
forget', art has the potential to preserve what happened in the past (Partnoy
2004:2), and the works selected for this exhibition, including Zerbarini's, all
speak to this underlying impulse of recovering (memories of) the past. That
said, *Tejido de memoria*, as will be analysed below, undertakes a critique of
Argentina's recent past but also directs its critique at its present inequalities,
and, at the same time, problematises any easy access to the straightforward
recovery of memory. As with the other works included in this exhibition,
along with the curatorial interface itself, *Tejido de memoria*'s engagement
with this 'memory of repression' is closely tied to the representation of the
cityscape itself.[4]

An introductory gloss before we enter the work proper defines *Tejido* as
a 'work in progress', since, due to the incorporation of user comments, the
content of the site is constantly in flux, and identifies the themes of 'human
rights, poverty and social-memory inequality' (Zerbarini 2003) as central to
the work. Zerbarini then goes on to define the notion of 'tejido de memoria',
stating that a memory can be read as a 'weave that constructs and recon-
structs' the present in relation to the past (Zerbarini 2003). This notion of
'tejido', which is reflected in the title of the work itself, creates the image of
memory as text(ile), as weaving, and as an active construction of resistance.
The associations between weaving and memory are long-standing both in a

wider Western tradition, and in the Southern Cone of Latin America more specifically. Regarding the first of these, James Olney, in his seminal volume on the construction of memory, has noted that weaving has long been a 'characteristic metaphor for the operation of memory' at least as far back as the writings of Augustine. Olney argues that such a conception of memory as weaving means that:

> unlike the archaeological dig, the weaver's shuttle and loom constantly produce new and different patterns, designs and forms, and if the operation of memory is, like weaving, not archaeological but processual, then it will bring forth ever different memorial configurations.
>
> (Olney 1998:20)

Zerbarini's work engages with these processes identified by Olney, since her *Tejido de memoria* is involved in the construction of (contestatory) memorial configurations, and thus concurs with this conception of memory as processual. In this sense, Zerbarini's work indicates, as will be analysed below, that there is no straightforward, transparent access to the recovery of a simple, singular memory, and instead produces a complex process by which the viewer/user must engage in the active production of memory.

In a more culturally specific context, the image of weaving as (resistant) memory evokes, of course, the *arpillera* [tapestry weaving] movement of neighbouring Chile, which grew as a response to that country's experience of military dictatorship under the Pinochet regime of 1973–1990. From the movement's early inception in 1974, the act of weaving *arpilleras*, as well as the images they depict—scenes depicting the struggles of human rights activists, or images of the disappeared—represented resistance to a (patriarchal) dictatorship. In the words of Marjorie Agosín, whose volume *Tapestries of Hope*, now in its second edition, still remains the most authoritative on the genre, the *arpillera* is an 'amalgam of voices and histories' and functions as a 'story of memory' (Agosín 2008:15–16) commemorating the lives of the disappeared. In this image of the *arpillera*, then, close connections between textuality, fabric, commemoration, and gendered resistance are combined, connections which are undoubtedly evoked by Zerbarini's use of the term 'tejido'.

Moreover, Zerbarini's emphasis on memory, and on its construal as an active, constructive, textual-weaving process, is central to many Argentine cultural works of the postdictatorship era, from literature and cinema to performance art. Early films such as Luis Puenzo's *La historia oficial* [*The Official Story*] (1985) pitted a personalised quest for memory against an official historical rhetoric, while more recent projects have problematised existing models of memory recuperation, such as the *escraches* of the H.I.J.O.S.[5] in which protest, ceremony, street theatre and music combine to bring into public memory the human rights abusers of the Guerra Sucia [Dirty War] (1976–1983).[6] In these and many other similar works, the question of social memory, its recuperation, and its relevance to the present has been a constant in contemporary Argentine culture. Moreover, if, in recent cultural production such as Albertina Carri's *Los rubios* [*The Blonds*] (2003) and Luis César D'Angiolillo's *Potestad* (2002), a problematisation of existing models of memory recuperation is undertaken, Zerbarini's work, in which the recuperation of memory is never straightforward, linear, nor transparent, speaks to this recent trend.[7]

After Zerbarini's introduction to *Tejido*, we then enter the work proper. The main page has the same black-and-white image repeated several times in a mosaic format: a photograph of the interior of a building, with bare walls, concrete columns and high windows [Fig. 2.1]. The architecture, and the grey-scale, grainy quality of the image, recall images of the clandestine detention centres that were established during the Argentine dictatorship and which were responsible for the disappearance, torture and murder of an estimated 30,000 people.[8] While not overtly identified, the image bears striking resemblances to photographs of the ESMA (Escuela Superior de Mecánica de la Armada [Naval Mechanical School]) in Buenos Aires, the most notorious of the regime's torture centres where an estimated 5,000 people were detained, tortured and killed.[9] Given its notoriety and the frequency with which it is cited in survivors' testimonies, the ESMA has become a particularly emotive symbol in the Argentine national imaginary; as Di Paolantonio has argued, 'ESMA is vested with a particular memorial charge, which is fraught with complex and often contesting attempts to give representational content to the past victimization' (Di Paolantonio 2008:26). This image is therefore a politically and emotionally laden one, which, given its repetition in mosaic pattern across the screen, pervades this work. Significantly, clicking anywhere in the bottom third of the screen causes this background to scroll over to another screen, but it transpires that, whether we scroll left or right, we still end up with the same background image: all screens have in effect the same background, only with slightly different tones, ranging across grey, blue, beige and red. This repeated background suggests the omnipresence of the detention centres, and the lingering memory of them in the Argentine national imaginary and in the Buenos Aires cityscape.

The top left-hand corner of the site carries a date, which rapidly and constantly scrolls forward, from 1977 to the present day (2003, at the time the work was produced), and then restarts at 1977. Again, this scrolling date hints at an obsessive return to the past: 1977 is of course one year after the installation of the dictatorship, but also, more important in the context of this net.art work, the year of the establishment of the Madres de Plaza de Mayo. Meanwhile, 2003, as well as being the date of production of *Tejido*, is also the year in which then president Néstor Kirchner made the first steps towards the repealing of the Ley de obediencia debida [Due obedience law] and the Ley de punto final [Full stop law], and thus is a significant date as regards bringing the perpetrators of the crimes of the dictatorship to justice.[10] The scrolling date thus is doubly encoded; firstly, it serves as a reminder of past traumas which are constantly reemerging in the present, and how the logic of the dictatorship still impinges upon the present day—a feature we see explored throughout this work. Secondly, it functions as a commemoration of the setting up of the Madres association, and indicates how this association still has relevance in present day, postdictatorship Argentina, a fact which, again, is constantly enacted throughout *Tejido de memoria*.

In addition to the date, there are several named links, and other unnamed links, all of which are hidden in the visuals and link to the main content of the work. This content takes the form of video files, still photographs, texts, graphs, and user input, making this a fully multimedia work, in which the various materials are interwoven to produce an oppositional commentary on past and present Buenos Aires. In terms of how this content is navigated, the use of unnamed links, of icons which are constantly fluctuating, and the fact that the mouse cursor disappears at periodic intervals, making the user's navigation of the site frustrating and faltering, are all examples of the way in which this work recreates the sensation of disappearance, and of the need to search out the hidden meanings.

In the links themselves, there is a frequency of references—textual, visual, aural, statistical—to the city of Buenos Aires, as well as a repeated use of materials pertaining to the Madres de Plaza de Mayo in particular. Moreover, in addition to the use of historical sources (including, although not limited to, information from and about the Madres), there are also numerous statistics about contemporary poverty and inequality in Buenos Aires. The sources used in this work thus function to refocus the city and to contest the established meanings of the Buenos Aires cityscape from a dual perspective: from an engagement with historical sources which draw out the traumas of the dictatorship which still inhabit the modern city; and from an engagement with contemporary sources which underscore the inequalities still plaguing twenty-first-century Buenos Aires, as will be analysed below.

Regarding firstly the use of still images in this work, these are set on a rolling cycle, and appear in the bottom third of the screen, thus drawing our attention to this conventionally subordinate zone of screen space. The images are organised into three groups, and combine iconic views and monuments of Buenos Aires with oppositional images which contest the accepted meaning of the cityscape. In the first group of images, the rolling cycle starts with an archetypal image of modern Buenos Aires: a panoramic shot of the Buenos Aires waterfront with the skyscrapers of the Puerto Madero district reflected in the Río de la Plata [Fig. 2.2]. The image of the port has long functioned as a shorthand for Buenos Aires itself, with the term for the city's inhabitants—*porteños*—reflecting this elision, and the notion of the 'port city' representing Buenos Aires's much-vaunted cosmopolitan outlook and history of mass immigration.[11] The particular image here—the modern Puerto Madero district—reflects that district's regeneration following huge injections of foreign investment in the 1990s, in which finance and communications companies, among others, were relocated there. Yet the image we see is not the conventional tourist image, and indeed is one we would be unable to see in real life, for it is a mirror image, composed of a single shot of one part of the Puerto Madero district which is then doubled upon itself. After this image of the city, we then get brief glimpses of the following images which flash over it quickly before disappearing: an extreme close-up shot of a humanoid face with red eyes; a black-and-white photograph of a fountain; an image of several bald, alien-like figures supporting large spheres; and a black-and-white photograph of a person pedaling a bicycle cart.

These various images, set in the context of the main Puerto Madero image which frames them, function to contest the accepted meanings of the cityscape. The fountain, for instance, is the fountain located in the Plaza de Mayo, seen in this image with the Banco de la Nación Argentina and other government buildings visible in the background. The image is seen only fleetingly, as it moves swiftly up the screen before fading out, but even from this brief glance it is clear that the image has been altered, since the water in the fountain appears to run pink. Establishing a metonymical link to the preceding image of the face with red eyes, and to the subsequent image of alien bodies, this image functions as a commentary on both the dictatorship and on the contemporary neoliberal era in Argentina. The location of the fountain—the Plaza de Mayo—is clearly a highly charged setting in terms of the Guerra Sucia, and the pink water suggests the blood of those who were tortured and disappeared by the regime. At the same time, the perspective of the photograph, with the banking corporation in the background (rather than, for instance, the more expected tourist shot with the *Casa Rosada* presidential palace in the background) functions as a critique of finance capitalism as well as, or in place of, a critique of the earlier dictatorship. In this way, this image provides an implicit critique of the panoramic shot of the Puerto Madero district which serves as its backdrop: if Puerto Madero, as Pedro Pírez has argued, is one instance of the increasing fragmentation of Buenos Aires due to privatisation (Pírez 2002), then the image of the bleeding fountain with the major financial corporation in the background serves as an image of finance capitalism bleeding the country dry. The conjunction of these images thus establishes a link between the two regimes: between the human rights abuses of the dictatorship, and between the social stratification enacted by the neoliberal reforms of the Menem era and which continues up to the present day.[12]

The figure with the bicycle cart, meanwhile, while ostensibly providing a traditional image of the street vendors of Buenos Aires, is, in postcrash Argentina,[13] a much more highly charged image. The image of the street vendor/recycler with bicycle cart has become synonymous with the *cartoneros*,[14] the many thousands of people who, as a result of the crash in 2001 (and the preceding years of *menemista* privatisation and neoliberal policy which paved the way for the crash), were forced to make a living sorting through the rubbish of the wealthier areas of the city.[15] The image is thus emblematic of the harshness of life for many in modern Buenos Aires, and comments upon the neoliberal and privatisation policies of the Menem and post-Menem years which forced many to make their living in the grey economy and which saw an increase in inequality in Argentina. Again, the significance of this image as set against the backdrop of the Puerto Madero waterfront is paramount: if the official meaning of the Puerto Madero is of the triumph of privatisation and the insertion of Buenos Aires into global circuits of finance capital, then the image of the *cartonero* which fleetingly moves across it represents the rising inequalities and social stratification which these same policies of privatisation would disavow. In this way if, as Themis Chronopoulos has put it, 'the presence of *cartoneros* is one of the most visible and lasting effects of the 2001–2002 economic crisis of Argentina' (Chronopoulos 2006:167), then *Tejido de memoria* works to make tactical use of this visibility, resignifying the streets, and making visible the *cartoneros* over the official images of the cityscape.

These various images, and the way in which they are remixed, thus function to contest the accepted meanings of the Buenos Aires cityscape, and to resignify monumental space. If monumental spaces such as the Plaza de Mayo intend to signify a particular national discourse—in this case, celebrating the May Revolution of 1810 which ultimately led to Argentina's independence from Spain in 1816—then Zerbarini's net.art work aims to reappropriate this space, as the Plaza de Mayo is made to signify differently. In this tactic, *Tejido de memoria* continues the impetus behind much of the offline movements based in and around the Plaza de Mayo. The Madres de Plaza de Mayo were involved in the creation of alternative 'emotional geographies' (Bosco 2006:343); the *Siluetazo* movement of 1983 attempted the 'appropriation of the centric' (Longoni 2007:181) and the 'aesthetic capture' of the Plaza de Mayo (Amigo, cited in Longoni);[16] the Grupo Arte Callejero involved the creation of an 'alternative map of Argentina's sociohistorical space' (Taylor, D. 2006:71); the *escraches* and other protests of the H.I.J.O.S were an attempt at a 'metaphorical repossession of the streets' (Kaiser 2002:504) and the 'politiciz[ation] of the neighbourhood' (Benegas 2011:27). In all of these cases, attempts at the resignification of the cityscape underpin the protest and the production of memory, a tactic which is continued by *Tejido de memoria*. *Tejido de memoria*, thus, with its focus on the resignification of social space, fits into a trajectory of other, recent social and cultural movements in Argentina which have insisted on linking this recuperation of memory closely to issues of location and space.

Yet, where *Tejido de memoria* differs, of course, is in the fact that this work is hosted online; whereas the other movements mentioned above all involved the physical presence of protestors, actors, signposts or images in the Plaza de Mayo or in the streets of Buenos Aires, *Tejido de memoria* attempts to negotiate the cityspace and resignify it from an alternative locus: that of the internet. That is not to say, however, that *Tejido de memoria* is not located or embedded; rather, that it offers new sites of resistance which traverse real and virtual space. Indeed, we may argue, following Bosco's argument about the Madres' relationship to city space, that online space may prove a particularly fruitful and challenging site from which to contest the established meanings of the city. Bosco, in his 2006 article on the Madres' place-based practice, has argued that:

> When the emotional is incorporated into an understanding of embeddedness, the spatiality of social cohesion becomes more dynamic. Embeddedness does not necessarily remain dependent on relations of physical geographic proximity or on a locality, as it is typically assumed but, rather, evolves into a geographically flexible process that embraces a relational understanding of place. However, place still matters in a relational understanding of embededdness.
>
> (Bosco 2006:343)

Drawing on what Bosco argues here, we would argue that *Tejido de memoria*, as a web-based work, engages in precisely this 'relational understanding of embeddedness': relational, because it is not physically located in Euclidean space, yet embedded because *Tejido*'s commentary is embedded in the specificities of the Buenos Aires cityscape.

Similarly, a second group of rolling images provides contestations to the conventional meanings of the Buenos Aires cityscape. Here, we see a sepia photograph depicting the docks with a sailboat in the foreground, representing Buenos Aires's heritage and its heyday in the nineteenth century as a city built on immigration. This is followed by a modern photograph of the city, showing a building site with a crane, representing the boom in construction in the Puerto Madero zone under Menem, and then a romanticised photograph of Buenos Aires steeped in mist. These three initial photographs function as establishing shots of the traditional images of Buenos Aires, only to have three further images fade in, fleetingly, over them: a photograph of two men, with their hands on their heads; a photograph of a large line of people being rounded up, again with their hands on their heads; and a third photograph, in black and white, showing a large multitude of people grouped in front of a docking ship. These latter three images zoom in and then fade out so quickly we can hardly discern the exact figures they represent before they disappear again, and thus function as representatives of the shadowy figures haunting Buenos Aires. The first two of these, clearly referencing oppression and detention of civilians by the stances of the figures, finds its counterpart in the third, where the lack of specificity means the image could reference voluntary immigration rather than exile, although the location at the dockside is clear. The specific confluence of these images is significant, since the conjunction of the riverside with the brief superimposition of the images of *detenidos* ['detainees'] recalls the fact that during the dictatorship many of the *desaparecidos* ['disappeared'] were thrown to their deaths from the infamous 'death flights'. In this barbaric practice, victims of torture were drugged and, still alive, pushed out of planes into the Río de la Plata, their bodies to be found some hours or days later washed up on its shores.[17] This rolling cycle of images thus enacts a dynamics of trauma, where the shadowy, fleeting bodies of these barely glimpsed images come to haunt the images of the city and of the Río de la Plata in particular. This, one could argue, is an example of the 'hauntology' of Argentina, of which Diana Taylor has spoken (Taylor 1997:31), in which 'the *desaparecidos*, the ghosts of the forever missing, haunt the Argentine political scene' (Taylor 1997:142). The sequence of images presented in *Tejido* provides one such instance of 'performative hauntings' (Taylor 1997:31), in its cyclical, constantly repeated, imagescape of the shadowy, barely visible bodies which move across the cityscape.

The still photographs thus establish this work as one which will question the accepted meanings of the Buenos Aires cityscape, and attempt to give voice to the experiences which are disavowed in official discourse (whether this discourse be of the military regime, or of the neoliberal policies of the 1990s and 2000s). The other sources and links within the work also engage in this process: the video files, for example, provide the most explicit links within *Tejido* to the work of the Madres, as well as providing for alternative perspectives on the cityscape. Here, there are various links at the right-hand side of the screens which open up short films, some of which are artistic or fictional works, and others which are extracts of interviews with María del Carmen de Berrocal, one of the founding members of the Madres, and subsequently a member of the committee of the Asociación Madres de Plaza de Mayo.[18] These videos are organised into four groups, corresponding to each of the four different screens to which we can scroll. Of these groups, the one set on the blue-tone background is particularly revealing. Here, we are given three videos, the first two of which are excerpts of interviews with Berrocal, and the last a short fictional montage.

The first video, subtitled 'Inicios de la asociación' ['Beginnings of the association'] gives a brief introduction to the Madres, with Berrocal reaffirming the term 'locas' ['madwomen'] as a term of resistance. This appellation, given to the mothers by the military regime, was, in the words of Marguerite Guzmán Bouvard, intended to 'undermine their credibility in the public's eyes, and to keep them in their places—that is, marginal and invisible' (Guzmán Bouvard 1994:244). Here, Berrocal states that the Madres were, indeed, 'locas' in their decision to protest in the Plaza de Mayo, but reframes this as a positive stance of resistance, since they were 'locas de amor' ['mad with love'] for their disappeared children. Her affirmations here reveal the affective geographies drawn by the Madres in the Plaza, and set their protests against the discourse of violence perpetrated by the regime. The second video, subtitled 'Objetivos' ['Aims'], has Berrocal giving both the initial aims of the Madres—to find the disappeared children, and to have them recognised not as terrorists but as revolutionaries—and also the subsequent aims—of carrying on the fight for human rights that was started by their children. This is representative of the *Asociación*'s aims, postdictatorship, of standing up for human rights more broadly, as well as providing a fitting description of the way in which *Tejido* itself works, in its dual focus on the horrors of the past, and the inequalities of the present.

Finally the third video, a short artistic film rather than documentary footage, is composed of a montage sequence which cuts from a woman knitting, to a close-up of her hands, then to a still photograph of a face, over which a target is then superimposed, and finally cuts back to the close-up of the hands knitting again. The photograph of the face, in a passport-style format like those used by the Madres in their protests, represents the disappeared, while the imposition of the target over it, leaving the photograph itself mostly obscured, represents the military dictatorship obliterating identity and disappearing the person. The sequence of the woman knitting which frames this photographic still is a gendered image, recalling the mythical figure of Penelope, whose weavings of a shroud by day, and undoings of it by night enabled her to weave her own destiny. The implication in this montage is that women, through weaving (that is, through the resistant, processual construction of memory), bring to light the fate of the *desaparecidos*. Moreover, the notion of recuperating a socially sanctioned, gendered role (knitting/weaving) for oppositional purposes reflects the tactics of the Madres themselves, with their recuperation of the role of motherhood in order to oppose the regime and to demand justice. As scholars have noted, the Madres' tactic of assuming the appellation 'madres'—one of the conventional gendered roles for women within nationalistic discourse—in order to contest power involved a tactical use of that sanctioned role for oppositional ends. In this regard, Guzmán Bouvard has commented that the Madres 'while retaining the traditional expectations of femininity, such as motherhood, [. . .] have also transformed them by refusing to support a destructive nationalism' (Guzmán Bouvard 1994:188). In this way, the image of the female weaver in this video functions as a figure of agency and of the construction of resistant memory.

Furthermore, it is significant to note that the figure of Penelope, and the image of weaving more broadly, has also been championed recently as a metaphor for a gendered, resistant online practice. On weaving, theorists such as Sadie Plant have posited links between weaving and cyberfeminist practice (Plant 1999). On Penelope specifically, Plate has argued that she stands as a 'trope for digital textuality', representing women's negotiation of 'the current global medial ecology, with orality, print, and digital texts all concurrently present yet moving at different paces and in different spheres'. The loom thus functions as a metaphor for her subjectivity which is 'nomadic and shifting' (Plate 2007:52). If such are the connotations of weaving and new media technologies, then the image of knitting/weaving here can be understood as an image of the creation of resistant memory through digital media. Seen in conjunction with the Berrocal videos, and understood in the context of the work as a whole, this short montage thus functions to visualise the notion of 'tejido de memoria' which informs this work: essentially, the knitting represents the *tejido*, while the face represents the *memoria* of the disappeared. The imagery functions as a synecdoche for *Tejido de memoria* as a whole: to weave together images, videos, texts and user input to create a *tejido de memoria* in a gendered and resistant way. Thus in this sequence, as in the four other video sequences, through the interspersion of interview footage with art work, of documentary with fiction, there is an attempt to weave an alternative narrative of the Plaza de Mayo, and to bring forth the memory of those who were disappeared.

The sequences of still photographs and video files as discussed so far are supported by a further, unnamed section of the work in which eighteen individual documents—some text, some graphic and some photographic—provide supplementary information about the dictatorship, the Madres and contemporary inequality in Argentina. These are accessed via a series of icons at the left-hand side of the screen, icons which include a cassette tape, a CD, a clipboard, a document and recycling bin, and which reference both predigital, analogue formats (the cassette, the clipboard), as well as digital ones, again suggesting equivalences between earlier forms of government (the dictatorship) and present ones (the informational capitalism of the Menem and post-Menem era). These icons constantly fluctuate, flickering on and off, and, regardless of whichever is clicked, bring up the same image: a chess board with icons of people rather than chess pieces. Clicking on each individual person brings up a different document: these range from graphs and tables covering statistics on infant mortality, maternal mortality rates, poverty and unemployment in Buenos Aires; texts about the dictatorship and contemporary issues such as poverty and malnutrition in Argentina; and two photographic images.

Again, as with the rest of *Tejido de memoria*, the constituent documents in this section function collaboratively, such that the information included in one link resonates with statements or images given in another. For instance, one of the photographic images depicts a young woman holding a baby, with numbers and prices in white font superimposed over the black-and-white image. The significance of the image—perhaps somewhat opaque when seen in isolation—is drawn out as the user peruses the other files making up this section. For example, reading this image alongside the communiqué of the Madres which sets out their fight for the rights of political prisoners encourages us to view this picture as representing a *desaparecida* with her young child. Conversely, if we access this image directly after reading the graph entitled 'distribución de la mortalidad infantil argentina 1999' ['distribution of infant mortality in Argentina, 1999'], we may interpret this image as representing infant mortality, with the superimposed figures and prices representing the numbers of children who have died as a result of the inequalities caused by contemporary neoliberal policies in Argentina. The way in which these files are structured, and the fact that we jump from one to the other like figures across a chess board, rather than accessing them in sequential fashion, encourage us to make these and other connections as we read.

Similarly, another of the text files, entitled 'Un día después del Día de la Madre' ['The Day after Mother's Day'], is a short text by the Asociación Madres de Plaza de Mayo, originally published in 1996, and combines the memory of the dictatorship with a critique of contemporary capitalism, stating that 'el Día de la Madre la inventaron los comerciantes, pero nosotras, la Asociación Madres de la Plaza de Mayo, le dimos a la palabra "madre" un sentido especial' ['Mother's Day was invented by shopkeepers, but we, the Asociación Madres de Plaza de Mayo, have given the word "mother" a special meaning']. This text, when seen in the context of the graph showing the 'indice de la pobreza e indigencia' ['rates of poverty and destitution'] in Buenos Aires, reads as a critique of consumerism, and encourages the reader to establish links between such consumerism and the social inequalities it brings with it. Or, for instance, the text file entitled 'El trebol de cuatro hojas de las madres' ['The Madres' four-leafed clover'], a short journalistic piece about the Madres painting images of flowers on cards in November as a protest, resonates with *Tejido de memoria* itself as a work of protest art. In summary, this section provides many of the hard facts which will inform our understanding of the rest of the site, but is not without its own artistic merit since it is in its mixing of factual data with photographic images, and of historical sources with contemporary statistics in the form of a resistant and quasi-aleatory mash-up, that the section encourages us the users to make connections between the various sources, and to develop a critical understanding of the inequalities that they highlight.

Three further, unnamed sections of *Tejido* lie towards the top right-hand corner of three of the four screens, where four coloured bars each link to a different source. One set of these four bars links to files including two photographs, a text, and a scrolling series of quotations with images. Again, the lack of explicit guidance through these four sources encourages the user to establish links between them, and to develop a critical understanding of Buenos Aires's cityscape. For instance, one of the scrolling quotations—'la memoria es redundante: repite los símbolos para que la ciudad pueda existir' ['memory is repetitive: it repeats symbols so that the city can exist']—is an unacknowledged citation from Italo Calvino's novel *Le città invisibile* [*The Invisible Cities*] of 1972 (Calvino 1974:19). Calvino's novel, with its envisioning of new ways to approach the city, has frequently been the subject of attention by scholars and theorists researching the urban landscape, including Ángel Rama himself, who saw *Invisible Cities* as a work that encourages us to rethink social relations and the cityscape (cited in Franco 2002:191). With regard to the specific quotation used by Zerbarini, David Clarke and Marcus Doel, in their work on the cityscape in film, have illustrated how this statement, acknowledging the role of memory in sculpting the city, involves 'bringing questions of memory to bear on contemporary urban experience' (Clarke and Doel 2007:599). If this is the implication of the Calvino quote, the other sources which can be accessed alongside it shed light upon it, and enact the notion of 'bringing memory to bear' on the specifics of the Buenos

Aires cityscape. The short text, for example, explains why the Plaza de Mayo was a significant location for the Madres, and provides a particularly illuminating take on the Calvino quote: it is precisely due to the Madres' insistence on 'bringing memory to bear' on the Plaza de Mayo that a new, contestatory meaning of the city is produced. Similarly, another of the links brings up a black-and-white photograph of a protest march by the Madres, depicting protesters carrying a banner demanding '¿dónde están los centenares de bebés nacidos en cautiverio?' ['where are the hundreds of babies born in captivity?'], a reference to those children born to women held in torture and detention centres, and who were subsequently taken away from their mothers.[19] Fleetingly, below this image, the phrase 'el 2 de agosto de 2003 se anulan las leyes de punto final y obediencia debida' ['on 2 August 2003 the full stop law and due obedience law were repealed'] appears. Again, this image of the Madres occupying and resignifying the cityspace, in conjunction with a reminder that the two laws giving military personnel exemption from prosecution have now been repealed, visualises Calvino's statement about memory and the city: the repealing of the laws will allow the recuperation of memory, a memory which, through the actions of the Madres, is closely linked to the fabric of the Buenos Aires cityscape itself.

If the still images, video files, graphs and texts interweave a variety of sources in order to contest established meanings of the cityscape, another section of the work, entitled 'Comunicación' opens up a further space for the integration of new sources through the opportunity for interactivity. In this section, users are invited to add their comments to the site, which can then be accessed under the section 'Escritos' ['Writings'] (see below). User input is enabled through the completion of three screens where users have to input their data according to a preestablished format: firstly, by entering the name they want to use; secondly, by defining themselves in one word; then thirdly by setting down what they want to denounce, with the preprogrammed format starting, 'denuncia . . . ' ['denounces']. The instructions on each screen are given in the informal *vos* format, the interface has a human name ('Valentina'), and the use of a keyword is explained as a way in which Valentina/the interface can 'conocerte mejor' ['get to know you better'], all of which create a sense of intimacy, and again engage in the creation of affective geographies. Moreover, the experience being recreated here, with the highly charged wording beginning 'denuncia . . . ' has immediate resonances with the work of the Madres, whose first steps in the initial stages of the movement were to 'denunciar la desaparición' ['denounce the disappearance'] of their children and to petition for *habeas corpus*, the legal writ which allows a person to seek relief from unlawful detention.[20] The site thus recreates the actions of the Madres in their denouncement of the disappearances, while also allowing users to denounce contemporary injustices, since users are free to insert their own demands in the space provided. The emphasis on user interaction here is, thus, not to generate ludic pleasure as we will see in the works to be analysed in Chapter Three of this volume, but for the purpose of denouncing injustice.

The user input thus generated can then be viewed in the 'Escritos' section of *Tejido de memoria*, which is accessed via a link in the left-hand top corner of the screen. Each following the same format ('name, definition, denounces: [. . .]'), user input here ranges from reflections on the past, to criticisms of the present world order, including poverty, inequality, George W. Bush's presidency and the IMF. Statements here commenting on the 'memoria silenciosa' and the 'imágenes borrosas, opacadas pero nunca olvidadas . . .' ['silent memory'; 'images that are blurred, opaque, but never forgotten'] speak to the dynamics of *Tejido de memoria* in its retrieval of the shadowy memory of the *desaparecidos*. Similarly, the affirmation of another user that it is necessary to link memories of the past to 'el presente' ['the present'] brings together the discussion of past crimes and contemporary injustices. These various entries, conceived of not as user comments on *Tejido*, but as integral parts of the work itself, provide illuminating insights into the issues that *Tejido* raises, although, given the low-tech interface by which the entries can be uploaded (restricted to text-only), the overall effect is less visually stimulating than other sections of the work.

As this analysis has shown, *Tejido de memoria* is a complex work whose principal aim is to contest urban space from the very centre itself. By means of giving prominence to the subterranean, shadowy figures hidden under the city centre, and by providing new interpretations of the centric, *Tejido de memoria* resignifies urban space. The cityscape is renegotiated and contested via the multiple audio, visual, textual and statistical sources which compete and clash together to form this work, placing the user in an active role of rethinking the conventional representations of the city. In this way, Zerbarini's work provides us with a resistant, complex work which invites us to renegotiate the traditional 'lettered city' from an explicitly gendered, resistant perspective.

BLOGGING FROM THE MARGINS: *HIPERBARRIO* AND REPRESENTATIONS OF THE *COMUNAS*

Whereas the focus of *Tejido de memoria* was on subterranean, gendered forms of contestation hidden within the very centre of the city and of political power itself, the focus of the next case study in this chapter, the *Hiperbarrio* website, is on the mobilisation of subaltern voices from the margins of the city (both literally and figuratively).[21] *Hiperbarrio* is a project which brings together digital communities in working-class *barrios* of Medellín, Colombia's second-largest city, centred in particular around the *barrio* San Javier de la Loma, in the San Cristóbal *corregimiento* [district], some 11 kilometres to the north-west of the city centre. Given that Medellín has been described as 'a study in socio-economic contrasts' (Roldán 2003:163) due to the stark division between the wealth of its business district and the poor, precarious settlements on the slopes of the hillsides surrounding the city,

Hiperbarrio's attempt to recuperate voices from La Loma via blogs, videos and other activities is an attempt to resignify the city space from the margins.

The *Hiperbarrio* website hosts a variety of different literary, photographic and collaborative works developed by the participants in the various projects it runs. More open-ended than Zerbarini's net.art work (which did allow user input, but in a tightly structured way), *Hiperbarrio* aims to create online spaces for expression for the marginalised. Where, for Zerbarini's *Tejido de memoria*, user input was one element of the site, in *Hiperbarrio* user input is all, since the site is dedicated to digital inclusion, aiming to promote 'interacción participativa digital' ['interactive digital participation'] and the 'construcción colectiva de conocimiento desde la Cibercultura' ['the collective construction of knowledge via cyberculture'] ('Misión y visión de *Hiperbarrio*'). *Hiperbarrio* is, therefore, a site which is based on digital empowerment and internet activism, and as such is a project that owes its very existence to new media technologies.

Again, as with *Tejido de memoria*, *Hiperbarrio* places great emphasis on the recording of social memory; according to its stated aims, the site promotes 'la memoria histórica y cultural de nuestras localidades, las Bellas Artes la libre expresión y la Cultura Libre y abierta para todos' ['the historical and cultural memory of our localities, the Arts, free expression and free and open culture for all'] (*Hiperbarrio*). Here, *Hiperbarrio*'s rhetoric, with its emphasis on '*libre* expresión' and 'cultura *libre y abierta*' (added emphasis) implicitly links the issues of historic and cultural memory to debates over the digital commons.[22] The digital commons movements, and associated notions such as copyleft and Free (Libre) and Open Source Software (FOSS/FLOSS), arose as a reaction to the increasing commercialisation of digital space: basing their arguments on the notions of commons or common land of preindustrial agricultural societies, the digital commons movements envisaged their struggle as one of taking back digital space. As Sarah Coleman and Nick Dyer-Witheford explain it, 'as terrestrial enclosures had met with resistance, so some saw the cyber-spatial land grab facing a scattered but persistent "hydra-headed" insurrection' (Coleman and Dyer-Witheford 2007:395). Indeed, the frequency of terms which frame this struggle in topographical imagery—from the 'cyber-spatial land grab' of Coleman and Dyer-Witheford, to Kate Milberry and Steve Anderson's notions of 'cyber-enclosure' and a 'turf war in cyberspace' (Milberry and Anderson 2009: 394)—is evidence of how notions of the digital commons are conceived of in terms of geographical space. If *Hiperbarrio* thus frames its struggle for social memory in terms which recall the creative commons, then the close link between social memory and space (whether real Euclidean space, or virtual cyberspace), is again reinforced. This notion is, moreover, encapsulated by the very title of the site itself—*Hiperbarrio*—whose neologism implies the taking back of both virtual (*hiper*) and real (*barrio*) space. In *Hiperbarrio* the specifics of this taking back of space lie in giving over the 'lettered city' to those who are normally excluded from constructing its discourse: to the disenfranchised inhabitants of Medellín's poor *barrios*. If, thus, inequalities in Medellín are organised along 'social, spatial and economic' lines (Departamento de Planeación Nacional, cited in Roldán 2003:136), then the spatial praxis that *Hiperbarrio* undertakes is an attempt to make visible and remap these inequalities.

This notion of intertwinings of virtual and real space is further elaborated upon by the tagline of the site—'Historias locales, audiencia global' ['Local stories, global audience']—which indicates how *Hiperbarrio* attempts to combine place and virtual politics. Here, the 'historias locales' are those of the inhabitants of La Loma, while the 'audiencia global' are the readers and viewers of the site on the internet. This 'local/global' interplay dialogues with the famous antiglobalisation slogan 'think globally, act locally' (which itself drew on the environmentalist maxim of the 1980s), a slogan which, as Alexander Hicks, Thomas Janoski and Mildred Schwartz have noted, functions as way of bridging the 'conceptual gap' between local and global politics (Hicks, Janosky and Schwartz 2005:2). Indeed, as scholars have noted, internet activism is proving one of the most fruitful ways of enacting this slogan (see, for instance, Rupert 2005:46), and *Hiperbarrio*, in both its slogan and its tactics, thus taps into these dynamics.

At the same time, just as *Tejido de memoria* made reference to, and was informed by, several offline struggles, *Hiperbarrio* is, too, part of a wide network of resources, both on- and offline, a feature which is common to many activist groups and projects. *Hiperbarrio* is inextricably linked to the project of the then mayor of Medellín, Sergio Fajardo, who held office from 2003–2007, and which involved, among others, the building of modern libraries in the poorest neighbourhoods of the city. This link is not just ideo-logical—in that Fajardo's 'network of libraries' and *Hiperbarrio*'s projects have a shared aim of empowerment—but also in a very real, physical sense, since it is frequently the libraries in the *barrios* which provide the internet access through which users can go on the *Hiperbarrio* site, and in which the various workshops related to the project take place. Moreover, as will be seen in the examples given in this chapter, the activities undertaken in the various *Hiperbarrio* projects involve constant negotiations between real and virtual space, recalling Arturo Escobar's notion of the 'ongoing tacking back and forth between cyberpolitics [. . .] and place politics' (Escobar 1999:32). The dynamics of the *Hiperbarrio* project thus reveal the inter-linking of *Hiper* both place and virtual politics, and of online 'content' and offline issues of hardware, resources and access, in this mixture of virtual and place-based activities.

Of the various projects run by *Hiperbarrio*, one strand is the inclusion of blogs written by participants in the project, which are accessible via the link 'los blogs de hiperbarrio'. There are some 30 blogs listed, including both individual and group blogs, with their content ranging from commentaries on music, art, local events, social problems, and on *Hiperbarrio* itself. Some of these, such as *Esas voces que nos llegan* [*These Voices that Come to Us*], written by Jaime Gabriel Vanegas Montoya, deputy director of *Hiperbarrio* and head of the Biblioteca Pública Piloto, La Loma, in San Cristóbal, have many, quite dense entries, and give self-conscious reflections on the *Hiperbarrio* projects, including discussions of new media technologies and how these can be harnessed for social projects, and comments on recent events in Medellín. Interestingly, however, it is perhaps in the less self-consciously oppositional blogs where we see more of a use of alternative forms of self-expression. In the blog *El Parche* [*The Gang*], for instance, there is much less commentary on social issues (indeed, the focus of the blog is on music, night clubs and motorbikes), but the use of language is more vibrant and reflective of the language of the streets. In an entry of 5 September 2007, for example, we read:

> Parceros!!!, La tomba nos cojiô este domingo, asi fue:
>
> Estàbamos llegando al alto de las palmas pa darnos la guerra de ahì pa bajo, cuando pasò lo que tenía que pasar!
>
> [Hey guys!!! The police caught us this Sunday, like this:
>
> We had got as far as las palmas to start fighting down there, when what was going to happen, happened!]

The use of vernacular expressions, including contractions (such as 'pa bajo' for 'para abajo' ['down there']), and the use of *parlache* ('parceros' for 'amigos' ['friends'] and 'tomba' for 'policía' ['police']), give this posting, and others in the same blog, a strong flavour of life on the streets of Medellín. *Parlache*, the popular street slang of Medellín, spoken primarily by the young, started out in the marginalised, working-class sectors of the city. Luz Stella Castañeda, in her detailed study of the phenomenon, classifies *parlache* as 'la expresión simbólica de la exclusión urbana' ['the symbolic expression of urban exclusion'] (Castañeda 2005:81), and argues that it arose 'como una de las respuestas que los grupos sociales excluidos dan a los otros sectores de la sociedad que los margina' ['as the response that the excluded social groups give to those sectors of society that have marginalised them'] (Castañeda 2005:78). If *parlache* thus conventionally stands in opposition to standard lettered speech, then its use in this blog, as in others included in *Hiperbarrio*, attempts to affirm the place of *parlache* in the urban order and gives prominence to this 'nonlettered' use of language from the margins.[23]

In addition to the blogs, some striking examples of oppositional tactics and reencoding of the cityscape can be found in the short films made as a result of video workshops run through *Hiperbarrio*, under the title *Videobarrio*. Here, videos made by participants in the workshops are accessible on YouTube. One of these in particular, *Historia de Suso* [*Suso's Story*], has generated a strong response, with over 24,000 views of the video to date,[24] dozens of blog posts, press coverage, and an associated campaign, 'Campaña Pro Suso' ['The Support Suso Campaign']. The subtitle of the video—*'Personaje típico* de La Loma, Corregimiento de San Cristóbal, Medellín' ['*Typical character from La Loma, San Cristóbal District, Medellín*'] (added emphasis)—implies that, as with the narrative genre of *testimonio* on which the video draws, we are to read Suso's story as the 'story of his *barrio*'[25] as much as simply a personal tale, and, indeed, the video shares many features with *testimonio*. These shared features are evident not only in this paratextual framing of the story, but also in the tensions that *Historia de Suso* shares with *testimonio*, since many of the central concerns regarding *testimonio*, such as issues of mediation, editorship and filtering, are also present in this new media work. Just as the genre of *testimonio* has been the subject of debate due to its mediation and filtering of subaltern voices through an elite, educated editor/compiler, so too this video, given that it is made by several participants in the *Hiperbarrio* workshops, and that it does not include Suso in the credits as an active co-producer, filters the experience of Suso through an editing process. There is, thus, from the outset a tension between the desire to tell a story representing the collective of the *barrio*, and the filtering processes of the means of production of the video itself. Such a filtering is made explicit throughout the video itself, where the use of photo montage as technique, the intrusive use of on-screen titles, and the lack of diegetic sound all point to the constructed status of the video.

The video tells the story of Suso, a marginalised figure from La Loma, using images to convey his cityscape which are vastly different from the standard images used to depict Medellín as one of Colombia's success stories of commerce and urban renewal, such as that of the new metro (inaugurated 1995), symbolic of Medellín's technological achievements, or those of the *barrio* El Poblado, Medellín's wealthy business district which represents its status as a 'major industrial hub' and 'financial nexus' (Roldán 2003:129). The video starts with a child's drawing of a man standing next to an outdoor water pipe (presumably meant to represent Suso), and is then followed by several on-screen titles, much in the vein of silent movies, which narrate the story from the perspective of a child who has just encountered Suso in the Biblioteca de La Loma. After this framing story, we then enter the story proper of Suso, as we learn from the titles that his parents donated the land where La Loma's parish church, library and school are all built. Montage sequences of images of Suso's house then illustrate the conditions in which he currently lives: interior shots show crumbling walls, green mould, bare earth floors, and strips of corrugated iron slipping from the roof. The images themselves, particularly in their framing and camera angles, encourage us to read Suso's story as representative of the collective experience of the *barrio*: the depth of field in many of the shots means that we are constantly aware of the city as backdrop, while the fact that Suso only ever appears in mid-shot rather than close-up, and is always framed against the fabric of the house or the wider *barrio*, establishes a strong link between his lived experience and the collective experience of the *barrio*. At mid-way through the video, the on-screen titles call for Suso's rights for a house in a decent condition with amenities, with these titles followed by images showing parts of his house open to the elements, and facilities such as the toilet and washing area in a state of disrepair. The video concludes with the request that we should recognise his parents' gesture—'reconozcamos el gesto de sus padres'—a reference to the 'Pro Suso' campaign which collected donations towards rebuilding Suso's home. The various images which make up Suso's story clearly aim to resignify urban space: as such, *Historia de Suso* is an attempt both to tell the story of the marginalised in Medellín (and in the *barrio* La Loma in particular), and to fight for the improvement in their living conditions. Again, this illustrates the constant negotiations between on- and offline activism which characterise *Hiperbarrio*, and the way in which an online work (the video) is inextricably linked to the creation of offline, real space (the rebuilding of Suso's house).

Another video, entitled *Rayones [Tags]*, although not having had the phenomenal success of *Historia de Suso,* has had over 600 views to date, and provides, through its showcasing of graffiti in La Loma, a record of alternative inscriptions of the cityscape. As with *Historia de Suso, Rayones* makes use of on-screen titles which are interspersed with the main images of the video, some 31 still photographs of graffiti in La Loma. Using the informal second-person form of address, the titles interpellate the viewer and locate him/her in La Loma from the outset: 'caminas por tu barrio y algo se te cruza a la vista' ['you walk through your *barrio* and something jumps out at you']. Following the introductory titles, there then follow a series of still images of graffiti, interspersed at intervals with further titles. The graffiti shown cover topics ranging from declarations of love ('Cristian te amo putamente nunca lo olvides' ['Cristian, I bloody love you, never forget that']), sporting affiliations ('América', referring to the football club América de Cali); musical preferences ('solo punk'; 'Rap, 100% rap'); and political statements (such as the graffito which simply states 'AUC', in reference to the Autodefensas Unidas de Colombia, a paramilitary organisation), among others. The language of the inscriptions shows again the presence of *parlache* slang inscribing the cityscape, with the use of words such as 'chapolos' (for 'borrachos' ['drunks']), 'piroba' (an insulting term for a woman), 'gonorrea' (a *parlache* insult) and 'pichonas' (slang for woman).[26] The prevalence of *parlache* slang in the images reveals the city to be inscribed with competing discourses, with a particular focus here, through the images captured and their framing, on the popular discursive forms of the marginalised and of urban youth.

The majority of the photographs show graffiti on the fabric of the city itself: inscribed across bricks, planks and cement walls, the graffiti in these images link self-expression to the cityscape in a very literal way. These images, seen together in a sequence, reveal how the inhabitants of La Loma themselves have marked out and inscribed their *barrio*, and, in their remixing via this montage, suggest graffiti as a partially oppositional urban practice. If, as Faye Docuyanan has put it, 'graffiti writers actively engage in *place-making* activities' (Docuyanan 2000:105), then this video shows how graffiti in La Loma work to inscribe and make place for contestatory voices. This can be seen, for instance, in some of the photographs which show graffiti in clearly identifiable locations. The first of these is an image of the exterior of a school cafeteria, with its sign—'Secretaría de bienestar social: Restaurante escolar' ['Ministry of social welfare—school canteen']—hanging off its hinges. Crossways over the sign can be seen a short graffito in which obscenities and insults prevail: although some words are illegible, those which can be clearly made out include 'Duber gay tonto maricón' ['Duber stupid gay queer']. Here the graffiti, which reclaim an official sign for the purpose of making personalised statements, function as an alternative signage to replace the official one whose use is deteriorating (since the sideways sign can no longer be easily read), and exemplifies the way in which graffiti function as (partial) 'signs of resistance' (Kane 2009:11) to a dominant urban order. That said, there is no sense here of an outright opposition between the official ruling order and graffiti as resistant practice; the content of the graffiti itself, with its implied homophobia, does not function solely as a 'sign of resistance' (Kane 2009:11) to a dominant urban order, but reproduces that implicitly patriarchal order. In this sense, as with much popular cultural expression, the graffiti selected in this frame are not (purely) oppositional, but instead function both within and without official discourse/signage. Here, the markings undertaken by members of the *barrio* to change the original meaning of the officially sanctioned sign serve both as an example of how graffiti work to 'lead the viewers' gaze onward (or inward) in diverse directions, some performative, some informative' (Kane 2009:11), as the image here shows how graffiti force us to read the cityscape other-wise, *and* as an example of how graffiti may also mimic the dominant libidinal economy.

A similar example can be seen in the image of the exterior of the Biblioteca San Javier de la Loma, site of the *Hiperbarrio* project itself, with the graffito 'Checho' inscribed on the wall. Here, the use of the personal name on the exterior of the public building functions to personalise the public space, and inscribe individual experience into the cityscape. In many ways, this encapsulates what *Hiperbarrio* aims to do: to enable the inscription of the individual experiences of inhabitants of the *barrio* into the city and into lettered culture. The wall of the library in this image thus functions as the interface between personalised expression (the exterior, voice of the *barrio*) and mediated, public space (the interior space of the library). At the same time, given that the library is the seat of the *Hiperbarrio* project, the image captured here is ambivalent; while potentially representing resistance to the official urban order, it also implicitly represents resistance to *Hiperbarrio* itself. This image is thus, as with the example mentioned above, ambiguously encoded, revealing graffiti to be not purely oppositional but existing in a space of tension between resistance and affirmation of a dominant urban order.

This notion of the close relationship between cityscape and personal/collective expression is taken up throughout the on-screen titles that periodically intersperse the images. The titles encourage us to draw connections between the images with which we are presented and the urban space in which they are inscribed, as the graffiti are personified as 'aquellos inconfundibles veci-nos nuestros' ['those unmistakable neighbours of ours'], linking them to notions of the *vecindario* ['neighbourhood'] and of local belonging. Later, the graffiti are described as simultaneously being 'parte del paisaje' ['part of the scenery'] and 'parte de la historia' ['part of history'], thus linking social memory to spatial praxis, and insisting on the very physical presence of the graffiti in urban space. Similarly, the affirmation 'cualquier lugar es un lienzo útil para que les den vida' ['any place is a useful canvass where they can be given life'] takes up an artistic metaphor for the graffiti artists, thus valorising their work, and suggesting that the *lienzo* for the twenty-first-century city is no longer the space of the elite artist of the 'lettered city', but the open space of the streets for the street artists. Finally, the titles, and the video as a whole, end on a series of interrogatives posed to the viewer, including the questions 'Es esto cultura o no? . . . Es producto de lo vivido en La Loma?' ['Is this culture or not? . . . Is it the product of lived experience in La Loma?'], again stressing the link between the *barrio*, urban space and cultural expression. In these ways, it is the video's (re-)framing of graffiti, and its working of graffiti into a narrative of grassroots expression and cul-tural identity of the *barrio*, which aims to create a sense of resistant practice.

The framing of graffiti as a (partially) resistant urban practice is further emphasised in the video by the use of sound, since there is no spoken dia-logue in the video, the only sound being the song 'Antaño' ['Long Ago'] from the 2002 album *Dolor* [*Pain*] by Colombian hip-hop singer Chonta (aka Mauricio Rodríguez). Hip-hop is a particularly apt choice of musical genre as soundtrack for this video, since it engages with both the graffiti aesthetic and the notion of urban youth culture. Regarding the first of these issues, Ruth Adkins Robinson, in her article on the history of the genre, identifies graffiti as one of the four core elements of hip-hop culture (the other three being rap, breakdancing and DJing; Robinson 1999:38), and, indeed, the album cover for *Dolor* reflects this, with its use of fonts that resemble spray-can graffiti. Regarding the second issue, as has been noted by scholars, hip-hop lyrics represent the experiences of marginalised urban youth; in the words of Arlene Tickner, hip-hop serves as a tool 'for poor, marginalized youth to reflect on their lived experiences' (Tickner 2008:121). In Colombia in particular, hip-hop has become an important genre since the 1980s, with the narratives told by Colombian hip-hop covering 'lyrical rep-resentations of suffering in marginal populations, street life in the country's urban ghettos, and domestic and international facets of the internal war' (Tickner 2008:137). The use of hip-hop in this video thus provides an addi-tional commentary on the encoding of urban space and the disenfranchised voices that speak from the city's margins.

Moreover, in addition to the generic relevance of hip-hop to the aesthet-ics and content of the video, the individual song chosen proves particularly revealing when heard alongside the images. The lyrics of 'Antaño' combine frequent references to local space and the *barrio* (the word 'barrio' is used at least twice, as well as a variety of other topographical markers), with references to the recuperation of the past. The notion expressed in the song that the music we are hearing is 'el legado de [. . .] este barrio, producto de lo vivido en el pasado' ['the legacy of [. . .] this barrio, the product of what we've lived in the past'] provides a fitting description of the images we see: the legacy of the *barrio* as inscribed on its very fabric through graffiti, and the product of lived experience. The lyrics of 'Antaño' thus reflect the notion underlying *Hiperbarrio*—that of recuperating and valorising the 'memoria histórica y social' of the *barrio*.

Yet perhaps the most innovative and contestatory activity engaged in by *Hiperbarrio* is one which makes tactical use of the interplay between virtual and real space: the creation of a 'collective cartography' through the 'Cartografía colectiva' project. This project involves members of the *barrio* La Loma using a mix of high- and low-tech equipment (GPS systems accessed via mobile telephones, OpenStreetMap software,[27] paper and pencils) to map out La Loma, and thus record their own cityscape. The end product—the collective map—is accessible through the *ConVerGentes* blog, where users can click on the 'Cartografía colectiva' link to access the map and see, for the first time, their streets and buildings mapped out. Users can zoom in and out, see their *barrio* in detail, and add their own input as the project progresses. In this way, the members of the community themselves are involved in mapping their own *barrio* in a nonofficial, collective project, and thus serve as an example of what scholars have termed 'participatory mapping' or 'counter mapping' which aims to counter existing tendencies and omissions in official cartographies. If, as noted in Chapter One of this volume, official cartographies are as much representations of power relations as mere transcriptions of topographical features—as Jeremy Crampton puts it, cartography exists 'in a field of power relations' through which 'knowledge is constructed' (Crampton 2001:235–36)—then participatory mapping can prove a way for those on the margins of power to map out their own space. Indeed, Crampton has recently argued that participatory mapping is a way of 'trying to redress the silences and erasures of mapping representations' (Crampton 2009:842), a notion which proves illuminating when considering *Hiperbarrio*'s 'Cartografía colectiva' project. An entry in the *ConVerGentes* blog which explains the motivations behind the 'Cartografía colectiva' states that 'como muchas comunidades en la ciudad o el país, la información geográfica de La Loma es prácticamente escasa, no se visibiliza en los mapas' ['as in many communities in the city and in our country, geographical information about La Loma is scarce, it isn't visibilised on maps'] (19/12/09). Here, reflecting Crampton's comments on redressing silences, the 'Cartografía colectiva' project aims, quite literally, to put the *barrio* La Loma onto the map, to make the experience of La Loma visible in the cartographies of the city and of the nation.

Moreover, the existing lack of visibility is due precisely to the marginalised status of La Loma, to the lack of infrastructure, and to the lack of official recognition by the state of the precarious settlements—again issues which relate to the notion of cartographies and power relations. The same blog entry reflects on this:

> Es necesario para un territorio como La Loma comenzar a visibilizarse geográficamente, ya que como grupo nuestra finalidad es la recuperación de la memoria histórica y cultural de un sector que ha sufrido (como muchos otros), por mucho tiempo el abandono por parte del estado [. . .] estos ejercicios con nuevas tecnologías nos están ayudando a poder alcanzar dicha visibilización.

> [For a territory such as La Loma, it is necessary to start to become visible geographically, since as a group our aim is the recuperation of the historical and cultural memory of a sector that has suffered (just as many others have) from being abandoned by the state [. . .] these exercises with new technologies are helping us to achieve said visibility.]
>
> (*ConVerGentes* 19/12/09)

Here, it is no longer a question of the 'lettered city' dictating to the margins; instead, where the state ('lettered city') has failed to record *barrios* such as La Loma in official cartographies, the community action by the members of the *barrio* themselves provides their own, contestatory, cartography. If, as Kenneth Bauer has argued in relation to Tibetan participatory mapping projects, such 'cartographic interventions can identify and delineate political boundaries in ways that may allow local or indigenous groups some measure of autonomy' (Bauer 2009:230), then here the creation of citizen cartographies in the 'Cartografía colectiva' project aims to grant autonomy to those on the margins to map their own experiences. Moreover, the references in these two quotations to visibility ('visibilizar' and 'visibilización') resonates with the theory of mapping as a visualisation of power relations; the alternative mapping proposed by *Hiperbarrio* will, thus, provide a visualisation of those normally excluded from official cartographies. That said, this impulse towards autonomy, and the associated rhetoric over cultural memory in the blog entry above, is qualified by equally emotive rhetoric over the abandonment of the *barrio* by the state. There is, thus, a split impulse between a desire for autonomy and an implicit rejection of the role of the state, and, at the same time, a desire for representation and visibilisation.

This split impulse is, fittingly, encapsulated by the ambivalences in the means of production of the project itself. Located in an ambivalent space between official state cartographies such as those undertaken by the Instituto Geográfico Agustín Codazzi on the one hand,[28] and the globalising enterprises of multimedia giants such as Google with their Google Maps and Google Earth technologies on the other, the 'Cartografía colectiva' project involves inevitable tensions in the use of globalising new media technologies to represent grassroots cultural memory. Regarding the latter, controversies over data privacy arising from Google Earth, as well as ethical questions over ownership of data, have dogged discussions of Google's mapping technologies in recent years. As Roopali Phadke sums it up, concerns raised about 'Google Earth's reshaping of geospatiality' range from its '"digital peep box" effect, its use as a weapon for panoptic geopolitical surveillance, its implication in racial digital divides, and its use in promoting disaster voyeurism' (Phadke 2010:268). Moreover, for many, the recent battles between various nation-states and Google Earth are read as 'an engagement between an older form of sovereignty and a newer one' in which new media giants such as Google represent a 'new modality of power' (Kumar 2010:154). It is, of course, significant that the *Hiperbarrio* project has chosen to employ OpenStreetMap, a project supported by the not-for-profit entity, OpenStreetMap Foundation, rather than the Google Earth product of the multibillion-dollar company, Google. As such, it is a potentially resistant gesture both to official state cartographies and multinationals such as Google, although it exists nevertheless in a site of tension, or a squeezed space, between competing forces.

The 'Cartografía colectiva' project thus attempts to situate itself between the (fading) powers of the nation-state in mapping its terrain, and the (increasing) powers of neoliberal transnational capitalism in mapping out global territories for its own gain. Here, the project aims to carve out a space for grassroots expression in the face of both these powers, striving to map out the *barrio* from below by making tactical use of new media technologies against the grain. Again, as with other strands of the project, it is worthy of note that the importance of these new cartographies is voiced in this blog entry in relation to the project of social memory ('la memoria histórica y cultural'), again reinforcing how spatial praxis is inextricable from social experience. In many ways we can thus see the 'Cartografía colectiva' project as attempting to visualise what the *Hiperbarrio* umbrella project as a whole aims to do: create new cartographies through which to express the hitherto unmapped urban margins.

As this analysis has shown, the *Hiperbarrio* website, and the various textual, visual and practice-based activities it showcases, provide a variety of oppositional images of the cityscape, and attempt to reinscribe the city not from the point of view of the lettered centre, but from the marginalised peripheries. The projects, and the associated activities, involve constant negotiation between on- and offline space, and propose the reinscription of the Medellín cityscape in order to give voice to the margins.

CITYSCAPE, MEMORY AND CONTESTATION: ONLINE SPACE AND THE RETHINKING OF OFFLINE PLACE

Both the sites under discussion in this chapter are actively involved in forcing the user to rethink notions of the cityscape and its encoding in official discourse. For *Tejido de memoria*, the resignification of the city lay in the gendering of urban space and the reencoding of monumental space in order to voice those experiences which would be silenced by the official, elite, discourse of the 'lettered city'. For *Hiperbarrio*, the resignification of the cityscape is undertaken from the margins, and involves inscription often on the very fabric of the city itself. *Tejido de memoria* exemplified how a social movement which preexisted the internet can subsequently be mobilised by cultural production on the web; *Hiperbarrio*, by contrast, is a social movement whose very existence has come about due to the new technologies. Both make equally successful use of online space to contest the accepted meanings of offline place and, in so doing, revalorise voices and experiences that are conventionally excluded from the 'lettered city'. Yet at the same time, both projects problematise any easy assumption of a purely oppositional use of new media technologies: *Tejido de memoria* engages with myriad images and texts of Argentina's recent past, and yet problematises the construction of memory as a transparent, linear narrative; *Hiperbarrio* overtly states its aim of preserving social memory of the *barrio*, but then locates its practice in a squeezed space between the waning powers of the nation-state, and the rising powers of multinationals. In both cases, the city is depicted as a contested space, and the reworking of sources and struggles for inscription onto the city are figured as continuing battles for the control of meaning of the cityscape.

3 From Macondo to Macon.doc
Contemporary Latin American Hypertext Fiction

In the present chapter, we now move from the representation of physical locales that characterised the previous chapter to the consideration of a central mythical locale in the Latin American literary landscape—that of Macondo—although we then expand from this locale to models of literary creation more widely. Our chapter here thus takes as its starting point the persistence of 'Macondo' as one of the defining keywords of twentieth-century Latin American fiction. 'Macondo', often used as shorthand for the boom generation, for the literary questions thrown up by García Márquez's iconic *Cien años de soledad* [*One Hundred Years of Solitude*] (1967), and more broadly, for a magical-realist style of writing that extended beyond the boom to more properly postboom writers such as Allende or Esquivel, has been an overdetermined and ubiquitous term in Latin American literary studies of the twentieth century. Even where generations have explicitly set out to counteract Macondo—the most prominent of which being the McOndo movement of the 1990s, and their rejection of the exoticism of magical realism in favour of a more urban and technologically influenced narrative style[1]—reference is still made to the overriding presence of this paradigm, albeit within the argument about its necessary destruction.

This chapter, therefore, starts from the premise that the notion of Macondo is one which is still being worked through in contemporary Latin American narrative. This is not to argue that magical realism, nor García Márquez's novel, is the paradigm *par excellence* of contemporary Latin American narrative; rather that the spectre of Macondo, and some of the central literary questions raised in the novel in which it figures, is one which is still haunting contemporary literature, and is being compulsively played out and negotiated online. The aim of this chapter, therefore, is to chart how contemporary Latin American hypertext fictions both speak back to a Latin American–specific heritage of literary experimentation, and at the same time dialogue with prevailing discourses of new media and hypertext. Taking as two case studies Colombian author Jaime Alejandro Rodríguez's *Gabriella infinita* [*Infinite Gabriella*] (1999–) and Argentine author Belén Gache's *WordToys* (2006a), the chapter focuses on three key issues that, as scholars have argued, came to the fore in García Márquez's paradigmatic work: the representation of a (mythical) Latin American locale; the potential for reconfigurations or 'second chances'; and the role of the author-god. The pun on the term 'Macondo' given in the title to this chapter, therefore, is intended to indicate how new hypertext fictions both speak back to these previous literary paradigms, and at the same time dialogue with the discourses and potentialities of new media.[2]

Firstly, the chapter explores how the sense of (a paradigmatic, Latin American) location inherent to the notion of Macondo is played out in twenty-first-century hypertext fiction. Macondo, García Márquez's fictional town, reenacted the founding myths of Latin America—the period of discovery, the conquest of the jungle, settlement, independence, civil war—playing out anxieties with origins and location. As Roberto González Echevarría has argued, *Cien años de soledad* is concerned with the rewriting of 'the fictions Latin American culture has created to understand itself', and the story of Macondo is, thus, the telling of the myths of Latin America (González Echevarría 1998:18).[3] Moreover, as Mario Vargas Llosa has noted, Macondo as a location represents the entirety of the Latin American landscape: 'in the landscapes around Macondo, this village tucked between steep sierras and steamy marshes, the whole spectrum of American nature, its eternal snow, its mountain ranges, its yellow deserts, its rains and earthquakes, is paraded before us' (Vargas Llosa 1995:60). If the original Macondo, thus, was a mythical location where the founding narratives of Latin America were played out and where Latin American geography in its entirety was inscribed, this chapter explores how in twenty-first-century hypertext fictions we find dystopian (although no less mythical) reenactments of Latin American space. Here, the chapter details how practitioners of hypertext fictions engage in the playing out of the predominant myths or concerns of the contemporary, twenty-first-century Latin American situation.

Secondly, a consideration of the reconfiguratory potential of Latin American hypertext fictions speaks both to a Latin American–specific literary heritage, and also to global trends in hypertext theory. Regarding the former, if the original inhabitants of García Márquez's Macondo famously had no second chance—'porque las estirpes condenadas a cien años de soledad no tenían una segunda oportunidad sobre la tierra' ['because the bloodline condemned to one hundred years of solitude did not have a second opportunity on this earth'] (García Márquez 1978:325)—now, in the new formats enabled by hypertext fiction, the potentials for characters, plot lines and events to have second (and third, and fourth . . .) chances in their constant reworkings in the hands of the user are explored by authors of this new genre. Such an understanding also speaks to Jesús Martín-Barbero's recent speculations on the potentialities of new media for Latin American letters, where he hypothesised that the 'second opportunity' of which García Márquez spoke may, indeed, be found in the 'convergence between cultural oralities and new visualities and cybernetic writings' (Martín-Barbero 2009:156). In this regard, the notion of 'second opportunities' or the reconfiguratory potential of literature speaks also to features which have been the subject of much debate among hypertext theorists. From early conceptualisations of the genre, such as the works of Landow (1992) and Bolter (1991) which stressed the consequences that hypertext had for traditional understandings of literary textuality, to later theorisations which provided a more nuanced understanding of these features, issues of nonsequentiality, multilinearity and 'multiform stories' (Murray 1998:30–38) offered by digital technologies have been a constant.[4] Our chapter here aims not to endorse these issues as utopian answers to questions of the restrictiveness of conventional literary form, linearity or the printed page, but instead to explore their possibilities and limitations. Thus the focus in this chapter on the transformatory potentials of hypertext with regard to existing notions of literary practice is not intended to reinforce technological determinism, of the kind that Aarseth has so eloquently warned against (Aarseth 1997:18), but rather, to indicate the productive ways in which these features are explored in contemporary Latin American hypertext fiction. In other words, our analysis here is not so much of the technology itself as inevitably offering a rupture with conventional understandings of literary form, as of the moments of self-reflexivity enacted in the two works under consideration. That is, this chapter focuses on how these works explore the possibilities offered by digital technologies, all the while making self-referential comments about both the enabling possibilities *and* the limitations of these technologies.

Thirdly, the chapter reflects on the function of the author/reader in hypertext narrative, again a feature which both engages with one of the most hotly debated issues in recent global hypertext theory, and speaks to the specificities of a Latin American literary heritage. Regarding the latter, in García Márquez's novel the figure of Melquíades functioned as an image of the author-god and his creative power: In the words of Emily Hicks, Melquíades is the 'omnipotent god' (Hicks 1991:5), and each of the characters in the novel is 'controlled by the text of Melquíades' (Hicks 1991:9). García Márquez's literary play with the author-god figure itself of course spoke to a long tradition in Hispanic letters of the questioning of the author-god role, ranging from, although by no means restricted to, Jorge Luis Borges's multiple playing with authors in his *Ficciones* [*Fictions*] (1944), Miguel de Unamuno's play with the author-god and character in *Niebla* [*Mist*] (1914), right back to Miguel de Cervantes's multiple author figures in *Don Quijote* [*Don Quixote*] (1605). New hypertext fictions in Latin America, with their focus on author-reader figures, thus continue this rich tradition of the exploration of the (limits of) the author-god.

At the same time, the at-times-outright questioning of the author-god in Latin American hypertext fictions, and the concomitant exploration of the potential for the reader him/herself to take up the active status as creator of meaning and controller of the structuring order of the narrative, dialogues with theorisations of hypertext in a broader context. Here, these fictions speak to debates such as those raised by Aarseth who analyses the increasing attention on the 'consumer, or user, of the text, as a more integrated figure than even reader-response theorists would claim' since 'nontrivial effort is required to allow the reader to traverse the text' (Aarseth 1997:1), and where texts, in the words of Murray 'invit[e] readers/viewers to imagine themselves in the role of author' (Murray 1997). These explorations have given rise to new and hybrid terms to describe the 'active intrusive reader' (Landow 1992:90), such as Montfort's 'interactor' (Montfort 2003:vii) or Murray's 'cyberbard' (Murray 1997:208–13), which envisage a more active, creative role for the reader. Yet, at the same time, as Hayles cautions, it is a fallacy to associate 'the hyperlink with the empowerment of the reader/user' since the 'reader/user can only follow the links that have been scripted' (Hayles 2008:31). Hayles neatly sums up here one of the central debates within hypertext theory, namely, that while new media technologies may appear to pave the way for active *wreaders*, this should not be interpreted as hypertext radically undoing author-reader conventions, nor, indeed, that all hypertext of necessity involves a postmodern, liberatory, emancipated reader.[5] In the case of the hypertext fictions analysed here, the chapter argues that the author-reader dynamic is that captured succinctly within Murray's description of the reader *imagining* him/herself in the role of author: In other words, these fictional works do not propose this as ever fully achievable, but are more concerned with the processes towards, and self-reflection on, the potential of a revised role for the reader, rather than its actualisation. It is thus the *imaginary*—and hence potentially *illusory*—role of the *wreader* that comes under scrutiny in these new hypertext fictions, dialoguing with a rich Hispanic tradition of the refiguring and questionings of the author-reader relationship, as well as with discourses of new media technologies.

GABRIELLA INFINITA: SCOPIC POWER, PERSPECTIVE AND THE (LIMITATIONS OF) THE IDEALISED *WREADER*

Gabriella infinita (1999–) is a hypertext narrative by Colombian author and scholar Jaime Alejandro Rodríguez. Lecturer at the Universidad Javeriana in Bogotá, Rodríguez is by now well-known for his theorisations on narratology, with a particular focus on digital narrative and hypertext, as well as his publications on technoculture and new technologies more broadly (see, for instance, Rodríguez 2004, 2005, 2006, 2011). He has also risen to prominence in recent years for his fictional output, which, in terms of his print texts includes his collections of short stories such as *Album de cuentos* [*Short Story Album*] (1995) and *Ficción y olvido* [*Fiction and Forgetting*] (2007a), and his novels *Debido proceso* [*Due process*] (2000) and *El infierno de Amaury* [*Amaury's Hell*] (2006). Yet it is perhaps his new media works for which he is most famous: Rodríguez is arguably the leading hypertext author in Colombia and his *Gabriella infinita*, as well as his later *Golpe de gracia* [*Fatal Blow*] (2006), have won him a series of awards and nominations, and put him at the forefront of literary experimentation in that country.

Gabriella infinita, the work under consideration in this chapter is, like *Golpe de gracia*, a complex hypertext narrative, involving a combination of text, images and audio files which the reader must negotiate in order to assemble the narrative. There are, tellingly, no contents pages, no user guides, and no page numbers on the initial page: in short, none of the established markers which would guide the reader through the conventional print novel.[6] The initial page of the work is characterised by sparse images: although the interface is predominantly visual, the images that do appear are monochrome, and tend to use the same spectrum, with dull greens and greys predominating. Links to the various lexia and sound files are hidden in the visuals, and it is only through exploring the interface and testing out possible entry routes that the reader/user enters into the narrative, meaning that the reader has to participate actively in the construction of meaning. The bonds between these lexia are looser than in the conventional print novel, and the text is dispersed, while chronological order is also unclear.

In addition to the images, lexia and sound files constructed by Rodríguez and his creative team,[7] the work also contains interactive elements, allowing user input via a link to 'escriba su historia' ['write your/their story'] at the end of each lexia. This links to a blog, which to date has hundreds of user comments responding to various aspects of the narrative, including character, location and time period (Rodríguez 2007b). In this way, while the narrative is not fully open to user modification—the users cannot overwrite the existing lexia, for instance—what users can do is contribute additional information to supplement the existing narrative. Notably, one character—Federico—is essentially vacant, and the user is invited to fill in the gaps by participating in the blog; in this way, user input helps to construct characters, as will be discussed in more depth below.

Indeed, the title of the narrative—*Gabriella infinita*—suggests infinite possible combinations, and signals an attempt at challenging conventional reading modes. Rather than linear, the story presents itself as rhizomatic, recalling Deleuze and Guattari's definition of the rhizome as having 'neither beginning nor end', and as pertaining to 'a map that must be produced, constructed, a map that is always detachable, connectable, reversible, modifiable, and has multiple entryways and exits' (Deleuze and Guattari 2004:23). Deleuze and Guattari's notion of the rhizome has been seen as paradigmatic of hypertext narrative *per se*, most notably by Stuart Moulthrop, who uses their concepts to define hypertext as a work in which 'the reader's implicit task [. . .] is to build a network of virtual connections' (Moulthrop 1994:301). The 'multiple entryways and exits' and the map that is 'connectable' of which Deleuze and Guattari speak, then, provide an accurate reflection of the way in which *Gabriella infinita* presents itself although, as will be analysed below, the possibilities of a fully liberated, rhizomatic text are questioned in the lexia as we follow the story of the protagonist.

If one of the defining features of the earlier Macondine fictions was the representation of locale, and the ways in which the locale reflected current concerns in Latin American identity, then *Gabriella infinita* provides, from the outset, a fascinating commentary on the possibilities and limitations of locatedness in hypertext fictions. One of the most striking features of this work is its almost obsessive reworking of the coordinates of space: space, both real and abstract, is painstakingly evoked throughout the lexia and audio files making up the narrative.

The narrative is clearly set in Colombia's capital, Bogota, and a series of references to immediately identifiable landmarks of the city are made in several of the early lexia as well as in the opening image which the reader sees before entering the narrative. This initial image portrays a cityscape with high-rise tower blocks dominated in the background by jagged hills, one of which is marked by a large cross, and the other by a statue of the Virgin with open arms. These landmarks are immediately identifiable, the hill with the cross being Monserrate, and the hill with the statue being the Cerro de Guadalupe with its famous statue of La Virgen de Guadalupe. The opening image, therefore, is an iconic one of Bogota, in which the old and the new are co-existent: the skyscrapers of the Centro Internacional represent Colombia's insertion into global circuits of finance capital, while the religious monuments are reminders of Colombia's Catholic heritage and past [Fig. 3.1]. Indeed, as will be discussed below, this dynamic between past and present—between the spectres of past national traumas on the one hand, and the visualisation of contemporary regimes of control[8]—is one constantly played out within the narrative.

Similarly, the lexia also make reference to several immediately recognisable locations in Bogota, including the Plaza de Lourdes (the main square in the Chapinero *barrio*), the Avenida Central, the Calle Diecinueve (one of the main thoroughfares which cuts through the city), and the Barrio Viejo (La Candelaria). *Gabriella infinita* is, thus, clearly set in Bogota—although the word 'Bogota' itself is never used—but, as soon as the narrative unfolds, and whichever lexia we may choose to access first, the images presented are of an apocalyptic Bogota. If García Márquez's original Macondo was an idealised locale which represented the mythical unfolding of Latin America's history—albeit one which subsequently declined and met its own apocalyptic end[9]—here, right from the outset, the locale is an apocalyptic one. As the reader discovers and pieces together the various lexia, it becomes apparent that the depiction of urban space is one of devastation and destruction:

El paisaje de una ciudad, ahora desolada, no podía ser más aterrador: contra el reloj de la avenida, un autobús ardía todavía, mientras algunos buitres intentaban violar sus ventanas en busca de carroña. Un viento mortecino levantaba papeles y basura en cortinas que obligaban a los transeúntes a doblar los brazos a la altura de sus cabezas para protegerse. Desde las ventanas altas de los edificios, descendía un hollín pegajoso que, poco a poco, cubría los árboles y las calles. Al fondo, el Cerro Tutelar lucía calvo y envejecido.

[The cityscape, now desolate, could not be more terrifying: a bus that had crashed into the clock in the avenue was still burning, while some vultures tried to break through its windows in search of decaying meat. A deathly wind lifted up entire curtains of paper and rubbish which forced passers-by to cover their heads with their arms to protect themselves. From the high windows of the buildings, a sticky soot came down which, bit by bit, covered the trees and streets. In the background, the Guardian Hill stood bald and aged.]

('Gabriella ve con dolor la destrucción de la ciudad' ['Gabriella, pained, sees the destruction of the city'])

Here, the depiction of urban space is clearly one of failure and chaos, rather than the triumph of the capital city as representative of modernity and progress. The topos of the vulture—a literary shorthand for destruction—is allied with the image of violation to create a portrait of a city destroyed and vulnerable. Moreover, the hill in the description is Monserrat, whose normal moniker as the 'Cerro Tutelar' conveys celestial protection, as the notion of the 'ángel tutelar' ['guardian angel'] is embodied in the hill. Here, in a deliberate oxymoron, Monserrat is personified as 'bald and aged', and thus the image of the mountain which conventionally represents hope and sanctity is now one which represents desolation.

Clearly, these images relate on a superficial level to the plot: set in the not-too-distant future, the narrative tells of the destruction of the city after attacks by unidentified forces. Yet the images also demand to be analysed in relation to Bogota's recent past and present: As has frequently been noted by scholars, science fiction as a genre is as much a reflection on past and present anxieties as a projection of a radically different future.[10] As David Seed has put it, science fiction works by 'defamiliaris[ing] metaphors of the times by rendering them as concrete metonyms' (Seed 1999:2), meaning that futuristic projections frequently encode contemporary anxieties and concerns. *Gabriella infinita* is no exception to this rule, and the images of this futuristic city recall both past and present moments in Colombia's history.

Regarding the first of these—the imprints of the past—it is striking how the depictions of the cityscape in this extract, and in others like it, recall a defining moment of Colombia's history, one whose very name includes the city itself: the Bogotazo of 1948, also known as the '9 de abril'. On 9 April, 1948, the leader of the liberal party and candidate for the presidency, Jorge Eliécer Gaitán, was assassinated in central Bogota. His assassination led to riots in the capital, with mobs burning down many of the buildings in the historic city centre, looting shops and attacking public buildings. While death tolls remain unconfirmed, scholars have estimated that the dead in Bogota alone numbered above 2,000, and the wave of violence (which later came to be known as *La Violencia*) spread to Colombia's other major cities and to the countryside.[11]

Scholars have noted that the Bogotazo has profoundly marked the Colombian psyche: Jorge Orlando Melo has commented on 'la permanencia de representaciones colectivas del 9 de abril y de Gaitán [. . .] en la conciencia de los colombianos' ['the permanence of collective representations of the 9 of April and of Gaitán [. . .] in Colombians' consciousness' (Melo 1997), while Daniel Pécaut argues that 'the 9th of April remains among Colombians like an unburied corpse', because 'there is still no comprehensive historical synthesis of the period' (Pécaut 2000:142). More recently, Rory O'Bryen, talking more broadly about the period of *La Violencia* unleashed by the Bogotazo, discusses how 'spectres of *la violencia*' haunt subsequent Colombian literature and culture. For O'Byren, these spectres 'belong exclusively neither to past, present or futures' but instead 'bring about the experience of a more profound "anachronicity"' (O'Bryen 2008:21). Our contention here is that this notion of 'profound anachronicity' is precisely what lies at the heart of science fiction narrative, and that the futuristic narration of *Gabriella infinita* is a way of both rescuscitating these spectres of the past, and of actualising the anachronicity of which O'Bryen speaks. This futuristic Bogota is, thus, haunted by the spectre of Gaitán and the Bogotazo, which still permeate the fabric of the cityscape.

This haunting appears most noticeably in the description of the effects of the conflict on the cityscape and its architecture, which hold parallels with images, both written and photographic, of the Bogotazo. As Gabriella makes her way through the streets, the images she encounters parallel those recorded in eye-witness accounts of the Bogotazo:

> Como si aún no hubiera despertado de su última pesadilla, Gabriella Ángel se encontró de pronto en medio del caos de unas calles repletas de automóviles abandonados y de gente que, intentando esquivar los latigazos que descargaban las ondas explosivas de las bombas, corría de un lado a otro enloquecida.

> [As if she had still not awoken from her last nightmare, Gabriella Ángel found herself suddenly in the midst of the chaos, in streets filled with abandoned cars and with people who, trying to avoid the lashes caused by the explosive waves of the bombs, madly ran from one place to the next.]

> ('Gabriella sale a la calle en busca de Federico' ['Gabriella goes out into the street to look for Federico'])

While the images of abandoned cars, bombs and frenzied crowds may be common to many accounts of civil disturbances worldwide, they recall eye-witness accounts of the Bogotazo, in particular due to their framing. The conveying of Gabriella's experiences of the disturbances via the simile of the nightmare implies this sense of haunting of which Pécaut, O'Bryen and others have spoken. The images are thus implied as oneiric remnants of past traumas imprinted upon the contemporary cityscape.

Yet there is also, arguably, a third layer of interpretation that the reader can bring to the depictions of this futuristic urban space, one which has resonances with García Márquez's original location of Macondo, in which locality was seen to encapsulate a prevailing sense of Latin American identity. Whereas García Márquez's original Macondo, encapsulating the history of the Americas, spoke to Latin America's past but also hinted at a potentially revolutionary future, here Rodríguez's twenty-first-century locale speaks to the image of Colombia (and, by extension, Latin America) in the era of late capitalism. That is, critics have argued in relation to García Márquez's original Macondo that its dissolution at the end of the novel posited a potentially positive, revolutionary impulse in which the vestiges of (neo-)colonial rule were overthrown. In the words of James Higgins, 'the ending of the novel reflects, at least on the socio-political level, the optimism generated throughout Latin America in the 1960s by the triumph of the Cuban Revolution' (Higgins 1990:154), and the destruction of Macondo and of the Buendías at the novel's close is a necessary step towards 'a new socialist ethos which will do away with the old oligarchic and neo-colonial order' (Higgins 1990:155). Thus, in the context of the 1960s, a period of radicalism in Latin America, with the Cuban Revolution seemingly paving the way for the installation of left-leaning movements across the region, Macondo's destruction at the end of the novel is read as a moment of revolutionary hope. Now, however, the destruction of the locale in the twenty-first century takes place in the era of late capitalism in which, to borrow Lyotard's term, the 'grand narratives' of emancipation that fuelled the sense of revolutionary optimism in Latin America have collapsed.[12] There is, thus, no truly oppositional space in the regime of control constituting late capitalism, and indeed, this is evidenced in Rodríguez's depiction of the locale in his work. The locale is in a state of partial destruction *throughout* the narrative; there is, thus, no sense of a regime being overthrown, and indeed, power is dispersed throughout the society as depicted by this nightmarish cityscape.

In this sense, this futuristic city and the images of devastation it contains function as allegories for the devastation wreaked by neoliberal policies on its inhabitants, and, more broadly, on the opportunity for oppositional practice. Edward Soja, paraphrasing Henri Lefebvre, has argued that 'urbanization was a summative metaphor for the *spatialization* of modernity and the strategic "planning" of everyday life that has allowed capitalism to survive' (Soja 1989:50). If, therefore, we take urbanisation and the representation of space as a metaphor for modernity, the devastation of the cityscape in this narrative can be read as an allegory for the destruction of civic society and of oppositional movements in late capitalist, neoliberal Colombia. Our reading here chimes with work by Geoffrey Kantaris on recent Colombian cinema, in which he analyses how the cityscape in these films 'provides an allegorical backdrop for a visible politics of space, from the dissolution and recombination of (local) place under the speculative flows of economic (and cultural) capital, to the decorporealization of space within the aggressive (global) realm of visualization and the simulacrum' (Kantaris 1998). This notion of the cityscape allegorising the politics of space applies to *Gabriella infinita*, in which the cityscape arguably represents the Colombian social fabric under late capitalism. The destruction of the city, therefore, represents the dissolution of social space under extreme neoliberal policies and privatisation, and the concomitant dispersal of control throughout the social fabric of this society. The use of the phrase 'había estallido' which appears in various lexia to refer to the outbreak of hostilities refers not only backwards to the Bogotazo, but also signifies contemporaneously: Social cohesion has been burst apart by finance capital, and the new regime of control has dispersed its power throughout the social body.

Inevitably, such a reading of the cityscape in *Gabriella infinita* as representing late (informational) capitalism must take into account the procedural enactment of the work through new media technologies. For this era—that of late capitalism—has also been seen by many theorists as being underpinned by new media technologies; what Manuel Castells has termed 'informational capitalism' (Castells 2001a) or Christian Fuchs has called 'global network capitalism' (Fuchs 2008), in which the regimes of accumulation are based on new media technologies. There is thus, following the arguments of these theorists, a direct implication of new media technologies with late capitalism, although this is not to say that all use of such technologies must, of necessity, function in the service of these regimes. Indeed, to dismiss all hypertext fiction as necessarily complicit with late (informational, network) capitalism would be both to fall into technological determinism, and to ignore the rich and continuing history of tactical media which has proved so central to Latin(o) American uses and understandings of new media technologies. Rather, the uses of new media technologies in this work are ambiguously encoded, both through the imagery employed to depict the regime itself, and through the self-reflexive comments on the limitations of such technologies. Regarding the former, the abundance of images in the lexia and in the visuals of abandoned technologies, of broken machines, of failed or partial capture of data by analogue and digital media—the accumulated detruitus of late capitalist society—imply a critique of late capitalism's logic. The images here function to question, as much as to support, the trope of the regime of control. Regarding the latter, as will be analysed in more depth in the following paragraphs, critiques of the regime of control are also enacted through the self-reflexive commentaries on the potentials and limits of new media technologies that are undertaken throughout the lexia.

Central to the representation of Bogota and its urban space as discussed above is the figure of the protagonist and the ways in which she negotiates this space. The story that we navigate is at once the story of Gabriella's quest to find Federico, and a commentary on the processes of hypertext narrative itself. The reader is allied with Gabriella from the outset of the narrative, as a variety of strategies provide a suturing of the reader's subjectivity with that of Gabriella's: Features such as the title, the focalisation of the narrative, the insights into Gabriella's thought processes, the *style indirect libre*, the images of her body, and the reader's discovery of the story at the same point as Gabriella does, all function to position the reader as Gabriella.[13]

Gabriella is thus both the entry point for the reader into the text, and also proxy for the experiences of the reader. In this way, as the reader progresses through the narrative, Gabriella's experiences come to stand as a guide for approaching hypertext narratives. For example, we witness her, as she goes into Federico's apartment, trying to analyse the objects that are strewn there:

> Pero ahora, Gabriella tenía la necesidad de saber algo más, de comprender el motivo de los movimientos de Federico en estos últimos seis meses; y ahí estaban sus cosas, invitándola a construir la historia, la verdadera historia.

> [But now, Gabriella needed to know something more, to understand the reasons for Federico's movements in the last six months; and here were his things, inviting her to piece together the story, the real story.]

> ('Tal vez la ausencia de Federico tenía algún sentido' ['Maybe there was a meaning behind Federico's absence'])

This sensation is, on a purely plot-driven level, that which Gabriella feels due to Federico's absence, and the understanding of the motives would be the understanding of the reasons for his leaving her. But at the same time, Gabriella's thoughts here serve as instructions for understanding hypertext fictions: The desire to 'construir la historia, la verdadera historia' is a representation of the reader who has to actively contstruct the story as s/he navigates between the different elements making up the narrative. The objects in Federico's room therefore represent the lexia of a hypertext narrative, awaiting decoding by Gabriella who represents the hypertext reader.

Indeed, this literary device—whereby Gabriella's sensations and experience stand for the experience of the reader of hypertext narratives—is woven throughout the narrative. We witness, for instance, Gabriella perusing Federico's bookshelves and attempting to make an order out of the apparent disorder in which the books are arranged—a clear metaphor for the work of the reader of the hypertext narrative, constructing an order from the dispersed lexia. We see her examining loose sheets of newspaper strewn on the floor of Federico's apartment, and finding that 'al ordenarlas, le han revelado relaciones insospechadas' ['when she put them together, they revealed unexpected connections to her']—again, an image of the reader of hypertext fiction creating his/her own order from the dispersed links, with the primacy on the reader, not the writer, to establish the 'relaciones insospechadas'. We also read Gabriella's quest frequently framed within interrogatives, mirroring the experiences of the reader of hypertext:

> ¿Qué era todo eso realmente: una broma, una equivocación, una locura? ¿Cómo entender esa extravagancia de un "principio de ilusión"? [. . .] ¿Qué tipo de realidad? ¿Qué tipo de ficción? . . .

> [What, really, was all this: a joke, a mistake, a moment of madness? How could she understand this extravagant 'principle of illusion'? What type of reality? What type of fiction?]

> ('Siempre quiso hacer cine' ['He always wanted to make a film'])

Here, the questions Gabriella asks about Federico's absence stand for those of the reader as s/he negotiates the new form of narrative that hypertext provides.

All of these examples go to show how Gabriella functions as a cipher for the reader of the hypertext narrative in her positioning as reader and decipherer of the clues Federico has left. This suturing of Gabriella and the (ideal) hypertext reader is brought to its apex in one particularly revealing lexia, which comes in the section entitled 'Mudanza' ['Moving']. The section opens on a video file which provides a panning shot of images in the form of cutouts or collages: Deliberately not pixelated, these images are immediately paradoxical, refusing to make full use of technologically enhanced images or computer-generated graphics. Instead, the images are overtly presented as cutouts, as if undermining the normal use of depth cues in planes of vision, by rendering them in a jagged, awkward and deliberately obtrusive fashion. Bordwell and Thompson's definition of 'depth cues' as 'the factors in the image that help create [. . .] a sense of space' (Bordwell and Thompson 2004:212), explicitly highlight that in order to create this sense of a three-dimensional space, depth cues are used to create volume. In their words: 'we do not think of the actors' faces as flat cutouts, like paper dolls' (Bordwell and Thompson 2004:212). Yet the video in *Gabriella infinita* does precisely the opposite: The images *are* flat cutouts, and the planes which would normally be indicated subtly to create a sense of real, three-dimensional space are instead presented as simple layers. The video thus engages in a purposeful playing with perspective, and self-consciously highlights its own construction. This feature—the playing with perspective and the deliberate manipulation of depth—gains significance as the reader continues accessing and reading the lexia, since, as will be discussed below, perspective proves crucial to the location of Gabriella as active *wreader* of the narrative. [Fig. 3.2]

The lexia accompanying these images take up and develop this preoccupation with perspective and deliberate construction of optical illusions, with the most revealing of these being the one entitled 'Federico la mira desde la puerta' ['Federico watches her from the door'], which in many ways reads as a comment on the narrative as a whole and on the functioning of hypertext narrative as a genre. In this extract, Gabriella's musings on the scene before her and its possible links with Picasso's work *Las Meninas* [*The Maids of Honour*] provide an extended explanation of the workings of hypertext fiction:

> Gabriella se quedó observando desde la puerta el interior del cuarto. Recordó entonces la fascinante explicación de Federico acerca de la función de la sombra que aparece en el último plano del cuadro 'Las Meninas' que Picasso adaptó del original de Velázquez.

> [Gabriella stood looking into the room from the doorway. She remembered the fascinating explanation that Federico had given about the function of the shadow that appears in the background of the painting 'Las Meninas' that Picasso adapted from Velázquez's original.]

The intertextual references in this passage immediately alert the reader to the self-reflexive status of this lexia, since Picasso's *Las Meninas* series of paintings are famous both for their playing with perspective and their intertextuality, being reworkings of Velázquez's 1656 original.[14] Hence Gabriella's questionings here become questionings regarding the narrative that we are reading: *Las meninas*, in its playing with reality and reflection, between original and copy, is emblematic of the constant tensions between the real and the virtual that typify hypertext narrative.

As Gabriella continues reminiscing about her conversations with Federico, her comments highlight the particularly self-reflexive nature of Picasso's art. Here, she recalls how Federico described the work as a 'juego, engañoso y complejo' ['deceptive, complex play'] which functions as an 'auto-reflexión pictórica' ['painterly self-reflection'], and highlighted how the painter himself appeared in the painting as he 'observa la escena desde la puerta del fondo' ['observes the scene from the door in the background']. As scholars have shown, the central conundrum in Velázquez's playing with perspective in *Las Meninas* is the issue of where the painter stands in relation to the work, a subject which has generated substantial debate among critics.[15] Similarly, with regard to Picasso's studies on Velázquez, as Enriqueta Harris has put it, these works play with 'the enigmatic relationship between artist, subject and spectator' (Harris 1982:177). If the location of the artist-creator to his work is, thus, one of the central enigmas of Velázquez's original, and of Picasso's homage to it, so too the issue of the writer-creator and his location in the work becomes central to the narrative of *Gabriella infinita*. The reference in this excerpt to 'auto-reflexión' can, thus, be read as self-reflexive on the narrative we are reading, and on the role that the author plays in the work.

This notion of 'auto-reflexión' thus proves central to the understanding of the dynamics of the author-reader relationship in hypertext fiction. If initially we might assume the author/writer to be Federico—and indeed the title of the lexia, 'Federico la miraba desde la puerta' ['Federico looks at her from the doorway'] encourages us to make this connection—on closer inspection Gabriella is given greater agency in this scenario. For the lexia begins by informing us that it is *she* who is looking through the door: '*Gabriella* se quedó observando desde la puerta el interior del cuarto' ['*Gabriella* stood looking into the room from the doorway'] (added emphasis). If Gabriella is given scopic primacy in this scene, and if Federico's apartment metaphorically represents the lexia of hypertext fiction awaiting decoding, then Gabriella stands in for the mysterious figure in the doorway in *Las Meninas*, for the figure of power who decides upon the meaning of the scene before him/her.

This is confirmed towards the close of this lexia, where issues of reflection, mirror imagery and perspective come together with the figures of the author and interpreter. Initially, the narrative takes up the notion of artifice implied by Velázquez's highly constructed work of art to suggest the notion of 'setting up', and develops it in relation to Gabriella's situation:

> Quizás, pensó Gabriella antes de entrar, esta presencia suya en el cuarto, todo su loco deambular por las calles de la ciudad, [. . .] no eran más que los elementos de una escena en la complicada fábula de Federico; tal vez, ella estaba ahora-aquí sólo para cumplir la función de la sombra de Picasso: el reconocimiento del 'montaje' que el autor había preparado de antemano. ¿Acaso, durante su relación con Federico, ella había tenido alguna vez el control de las 'escenas?'

> [Perhaps, thought Gabriella before she went in, her presence in his room, all her mad wanderings through the city streets, [. . .] were no more than elements in one of the scenes of Federico's complicated plot; perhaps she was only here now to play the role of Picasso's shadow: the recognition of the 'set-up' that the author had prepared beforehand. At any point during her relationship with Federico, had she ever really been in control of the 'scenes'?]

This episode hints at the 'revelations' we discover elsewhere in the lexia, when Gabriella becomes aware of the 'new dimension'. Initially, the preponderance here of terminology related to representation—*escena, fábula, montaje*—hints at the fact that Gabriella may have been set up in more ways than one: she is an element in Federico's set-up, just as she is an element in the set-up of the hypertext fiction we are reading. Yet on close inspection, the lexia reveals Gabriella to be much more than the pawn in Federico's game: If she functions as 'Picasso's shadow'—the shadowy figure in the doorway who holds scopic power over the scene—then she stands for the active, constructive, participatory reader of hypertext fiction.

This is particularly evident in the section of the narrative entitled 'Revelaciones' ['Revelations'], in which the reader is presented with a series of discoveries on the part of Gabriella. One episode in this section, entitled 'Gabriella tiene voz' ['Gabriella speaks'], is accessed by clicking on the image of a door, with both image and title hinting at the growing access of Gabriella to previously hidden knowledge and self-expression. Within the lexia, Gabriella comes to the realisation that her role in the affair is less to find Federico (a task she never achieves), and more to enter an alternative reality to which her searching has led her:

> Y esa esperanza la hará sentir irreal, pero feliz; como si estuviese a punto de nacer a una dimensión verdadera, aunque no pueda explicarlo, aunque no quiera explicarlo.
>
> [And that hope would make her feel unreal, but happy; as if she were about to be born into a true dimension, even if she couldn't explain it, even if she didn't want to explain it.]

This is the moment of anagnorisis when Gabriella grasps the nature of hypertext fiction. The apparent paradox encapsulated in Gabriella's musings—the sensation of being '*irreal*' ['unreal'] while witnessing the birth of a 'dimensión *verdadera*' ['true dimension']—represents her rebirth into the virtual reality of the realm of hypertext. This *irreal/verdadera* paradox resonates with the oxymoron 'virtual reality': this new dimension is where the real and the virtual are combined, and where new experiences are possible.

Thus Gabriella enters a new realm, that of virtual reality and hypertext in which, potentially, the reader/co-creator gains supremacy over the author-god. The author-god figure, as embodied in Melquíades in an earlier era, is now displaced in favour of the *wreader* figure, as embodied in Gabriella and her negotiations of the lexia of hypertext. Yet, given that Gabriella, thus, stands for the empowered reader of hypertext narrative, it is significant that her portrayal throughout the story has been polarised in gendered terms. Gabriella is overwhelmingly corporeal: Images abound of her material, heavy, bodily status, with frequent references to corporeality, as the reader is given descriptions of her tears, sweat, pregnancy, heavy belly and so forth. Federico, by contrast, is weightless, vacant, incorporeal; quite literally absent from the narrative, Federico inhabits the world of the ethereal. The reader only has access to him through Gabriella's memories, her dreams and the traces (of texts, sound files, diskettes, videos) that he has left behind. Where we do get a brief glimpse of Federico as he appears in one of Gabriella's dreams, he appears only as lack: Firstly 'tapado con una gran manta que le cubría hasta el rostro' ['covered with a large blanket that hid even his face'], Federico is then revealed as a 'calavera, horrenda y sonriente' ['horrifying, grinning skull']. Federico's image, then, is of lack.

On the one hand, therefore, we could read this narrative as one which reinforces standard gendered binaries: the masculine/feminine roles are, at first sight, troublingly conventional, encoding femininity as corporeal and masculinity as cerebral. Yet, reading through these gendered roles in the light of the revisionary potential of hypertext fiction may provide for an alternative reading: If the male author of modernist fiction was the author-god, with the text releasing a single, 'theological meaning' (Barthes 1977:146),[16] in hypertext fiction the male author-god figure is defunct, and it is the female reader-creator who gains power. This female reader-creator is not the *lector hembra* ['female reader'] of Cortázar's infamous theory,[17] but the active reader-creator who makes meaning and who forms the shape of the narrative. At the same time, and as with the other features of this work, Rodríguez's conceptualisation of Gabriella as the idealised *wreader* speaks also to debates within global hypertext theory, and in particular refuses to engage with the by-now much-critiqued cyberpunk ideal of 'leaving the meat behind', instead positioning the ideal *wreader* as resolutely corporeal.[18] Hence Gabriella represents the idealised user/co-creator of the hypertext narrative: Both firmly corporeal *and* idealised, Gabriella stands in for the hypertext reader.

That said, as mentioned in the introduction to this chapter, the active role for the reader in this hypertext narrative is actualised within the mechanics of this work only up to a point; the 'escribe su historia' link at the end of each lexia allows the reader to post to a blog, but the reader cannot rewrite the existing lexia, add new links, insert new visuals, nor delete any of the available material. Similarly, the reader can follow the links in random order, and can access the work through multiple entry and exit points, but can only access the links established by the author; the reader cannot add his/her own links to the central narrative itself. *Gabriella infinita* is thus not fully open to user input, as is perhaps more in evidence in works such as Doménico Chiappe's collective multimedia novel, *La huella de Cosmos* [*The Trace of Cosmos*] (2005).

What is potentially illuminating in this regard is the response of readers to the opportunities for participation. For instance, of the blog posts grouped under the 'Federico: un enigma' ['Federico: an enigma'] category, it is interesting to note that the vast majority of the users here talk *about* Federico, pondering what might motivate this character, discussing the character in context, and relating his experiences to their own. Only one is a fictional addition to the narrative, in the form of a fictionalised interview with Federico; in other words, only one respondent so far has taken up the opportunity to add to the fictional corpus itself.

In this way, *Gabriella infinita*'s explorations of the author-reader relationship point to the liberatory potentials for the reader to become active co-creator/author, while at the same time point to their limitations. The idealised *wreader* is explored through the narrative lexia and images, yet Gabriella's exploration of her growing scriptural and scopic power is always couched in terms of potential rather than actuality. Similarly, in the interactive features of the text, the reader becomes active but with certain caveats: the reader navigates at will, but within the existing lexia; the reader fills in the gaps of characterisation, but does not create entire new characters; the reader can play around with chronological order, but cannot add new time frames to the narrative itself. Negotiating between Latin American literary heritage and global hypertext trends, and negotiating between the potentials of new media technologies and their limitations, *Gabriella infinita* offers up to the reader a metafictional story of the genre, and a reflection on his/her own practice as s/he navigates the text.

WORDTOYS: VAMPIRIC REMIXES, BUTTERFLY CITATIONS AND THE QUESTIONING OF THE POWER OF THE *WREADER*

The Argentine writer Belén Gache is by now well known for her experimental fiction—both online and offline—including net poetry, literary blogs, *video-poesía* and hypertext fictions. Gache's works of net poetry include *Manifies-tos Robot* [*Robot Manifestos*] (2009), in which audio poems are generated by a system that searches for keywords on the internet and then verbalises them using prerecorded phonemes, and *Radikal Karaoke* (2010), in which randomised multimedia poems are generated via web-based searches. Her literary blogs include *Diario del niño burbuja* [*Diary of the Bubble Boy*] (2004), which comprises 100 blog posts based on images selected at random using an image search engine, and *El blog de los sueños* [*Dream Blog*], a blog in which Gache has recorded her dreams between 2007 and 2008. Her *videopoesía* consists of a series of performances of the work of major poets, under the collective title 'Lecturas' ['Readings'], while her hyptertext works include *El libro del fin del mundo* [*The Book of the End of the World*] (2002), and *WordToys*, the object of study of this chapter. She is also founder member of the *Fin del mundo* net.art group, along with Jorge Haro, Gustavo Romano and Carlos Triknick, and has been involved in curatorial projects as part of this group, as well as contributing significantly to theoretical writings on experimental literature and hypertext.[19]

Her 2006 work, *WordToys*, contains fourteen individual short fictions which combine images, text and sound. The work constantly plays with the tensions between print and digital formats; right from the start, we are presented with what initially looks like simply an online version of a print novel, with a front cover, dated black-and-white front image, contents page, and even dog-eared pages we can 'turn' by clicking the mouse. Yet once we click and enter each short fiction, what we 'read' turns out to be far from a linear print text presented in electronic form, but a myriad of sound, image and text files interlinked in experimental ways. As this section will argue, Gache's work, like Rodríguez's, involves the creation of alternative locales, but ones which, in the case of Gache, speak more to preexisting images of a (mythical) Latin American locale and to images of cyberspace than to the specificities of the late capitalist era. Following on from this, the section also focuses on the highly self-referential nature of Gache's work, highlighting how her short fictions reflect on the possibilities and limitations of textual multiplicity, nonlinearity and multisequentiality as afforded by digital technologies. Finally, the section moves on to consider the figures of the author/reader in her work, exploring her questioning of the possibilities of giving real agency to the reader.

Gache's work is much less immediately rooted in a strong sense of physical location than Rodríguez's was: Her *WordToys*, heavily influenced by Surrealism, is more involved in depicting dreamscapes than in real-life geographical locations. That said, it would be a mistake to dismiss this work as having no relevance to issues of locatedness and of the associated notions of Latin American (mythical) identity which García Márquez's Macondo, and Rodríguez's subsequent dystopian version, recalled. Indeed the very notion of space and location is central to Gache's project, and, moreover, her overtly Surrealist approach to the depiction of other-worldly locales arguably speaks to the mythical, magically real locales of García Márquez's original. Moreover, locale and mythical identity often resurface in Gache in the form of already-existing texts which are reused in the context of her fiction; frequently, the texts upon which Gache draws are some of the most iconic ones defining Latin American identity and its mythical locale. Thus it is in the coordinates of cyberspace, of hypertext, and of experimental (re-)writing that Gache explores this mythical locale, an exploration which then provides inroads into an investigation of the writing process and of the author/reader relationship.

The chapter 'Southern Heavens' is one such example of the ways in which Gache's work simultaneously draws on existing conceptualisations of Euclidean space and yet actualises (in a tongue-in-cheek way), new understandings of surreal, other-worldly locales. The introductory paragraph framing this piece makes explicit reference to cartography, mentioning the 'cartas náuticas pre-cartográficas' ['precartographic nautical maps'] in which 'el diseño del espacio permanecía aun centrado en las propias experiencias del viajante' ['the representation of space was still centred on the experiences of the traveller himself']. The paragraph then goes on to describe the birth of modern cartography, in which 'los itinerarios se volvieron abstractos y no vividos' ['the itineraries became abstract, not lived'], and then poses a question for the reader:

> ¿Será que la frecuencia y longitud de nuestros trayectos determinan el espacio?
>
> [Can it be that the frequency and length of our journeys determine space?]

The question here, while ostensibly relating to a past moment of the creation of modern cartographies, can also clearly be read as the need for the creation of new understandings of cyberspace: a space which is no longer the Euclidean space of classic cartography, but one where, indeed, the frequency and length of our journeys determine space. That is, Gache's questions resonate with debates in cybercultural studies that have demonstrated that cyberspace does not exist as an *exterior*, Euclidean space visited by human subjects who are external to it: Cyberspace is, as theorists have strenuously argued, rather the *interface* between human subjectivity and technology, and it is only in this moment of interface (the moment at which we experience it) that cyberspace can ever exist at all.[20] Given that cyberspace, if it exists at all as a spatial phenomenon—and Gache's narrative, as will be seen below, problematises some of the spatial commonplaces in the conception of cyberspace—comes into being at the moment that human beings navigate it, in this sense, the 'locale' is not exterior, but is indeed determined by the 'frecuencia y longitud de nuestros trayectos'.

The sound and image files which accompany this lexia provide an ironic actualisation of this experience of navigating (cyber)space, and function to problematise some of the easy assumptions associated with this concept. The image file consists of an interactive astronomical map over which the user can move the plane, in the shape of a cartoon image of a Douglas N70C. Both of these images—the astronomical map and the cartoon of the aeroplane—are deliberately dated; the aeroplane is a two-tone, brown-and-beige, one-dimensional cutout of a 1950s model, while the map is a Zodiacal map of the celestial heavens, mapping out the astrological figures across the months of the year, rather than a contemporary, accurate map of space [Fig. 3.3]. A deliberate disjuncture is thus created between these anachronistic images and the accompanying sound file, which establishes that our voyage is a futuristic, intergalactic one lasting 100 million light years. Moreover, the contents of this sound file provide a further ironic take on the intergalactic journey, since the voice-over is a parody of the instructions given by the cabin crew to passengers on modern-day flights, combining the commonplaces of airline travel—oxygen masks, the location of the emergency exits—with more esoteric comments on the intergalactic journey being undertaken, as we are alerted to the fact that 'afuera [. . .] todo estará inmóvil y callado' ['outside [. . .] everything will be immobile and silent'], that we are passing through 'un espacio sin tiempo' ['a space without time'], that by looking out of the window we can glimpse 'el fondo de un lugar sin fondo' ['the end of a place without end'] and that we are flying on 'el vuelo que nunca termina' ['the flight that never ends']. As well as ostensibly guiding us through outerspace, the depiction of the journey clearly functions as an allegory for the (idealised) journey that the contemporary websurfer takes when navigating cyberspace, although this journey and the notion of the websurfer itself are parodied and undercut throughout. The 'space without time' recalls contemporary discourses on the rapid pace of technological change and the speeding-up of communications around the globe under contemporary conditions of late capitalism. The phrase resonates with David Harvey's suggestive term of 'time-space compression' in which space 'appears to shrink to a "global village" of technological communications' and 'time horizons shorten to the point where the present is all there is' (Harvey 1990:240). Similarly, the oxymoron 'el fondo de un lugar sin fondo' recalls early utopian conceptualisations of cyberspace, which conceived of it as never-ending, non-Euclidean, infinitely traversable, and having no edge; in the words of John Perry Barlow in his oft-cited manifesto, 'A Declaration of the Independence of Cyberspace', cyberspace was conceived of as a 'world that is both everywhere and nowhere' (Barlow 1996).

It is therefore striking how, in Gache's short narrative, these assumptions underpinning the notion of cyberspace, the websurfer and communications technologies more broadly are undercut. In addition to the constant ironising via the anachronistic images and the voice-over, the interactive elements themselves provide a further way in which the conventional understandings of cyberspace are troubled. Here, while listening to the accompanying voice-over narrative, as the user manipulates the plane, s/he is able to move the plane entirely off the map, and into the blank spaces beyond. That is, if we move the mouse sufficiently to the left or to the right, the plane (our avatar) gets beyond the limits of this purportedly limitless space. In other words, Gache's ironic narrative implies that this space does indeed have a 'fondo' or limits after all, and, so too, there are limits to the idealised image of the websurfer. Here, Gache's aesthetic production of space, in which certain commonplaces are manipulated and yet thwarted, points towards some of the contradictions within these easy metaphors of cyberspace, and encourages our deconstruction, rather than blind acceptance, of them.

Thus, while Gache's short narrative here differs from Rodríguez's sustained representation of urban geographies under late capitalism, certain parallels are nevertheless discernible. Gache's narrative may not function in the same, immediately politicised sense as Rodríguez's did in *Gabriella infinita*; the images, sound files and interactive features within this short narration do not propose a dystopian representation of the ravages of late capitalism on contemporary society. Gache's approach here is undoubtedly more ludic than overtly political, yet, while her short narrative does not provide an immediately obvious retort to the systemic violence of informational capitalism, the contestatory impulse arguably lies in its mocking of the neo-imperialist or corporate impulses behind contemporary conceptualisations of cyberspace and its navigators.

If the chapter 'Southern Heavens' problematised some of the easy metaphors of cyberspace, other chapters within *WordToys* provide alternative readings of real, Euclidean space which are at the same time refigured as new and other-worldly. The short narrative 'Mujeres vampiro invaden Colonia del Sacramento' ['Vampire Women Invade Colonia del Sacramento'] makes immediate reference in its title to the city of Colonia del Sacramento in Uruguay, located on the shores of the Río de la Plata, facing Buenos Aires. Colonia del Sacramento has suffered a series of invasions and conquests throughout its history, being disputed between Spanish and Portuguese rule. This city, therefore, refers to real-life geographical space, but also, in its status as disputed territory, represents a border zone or a frontier, conjuring up one of the central, and highly contested, metaphors of cyberspace: that of the 'electronic frontier'.[21] The 'invaden' of the title, therefore, refers not just to the multiple invasions to which Colonia del Sacramento was subjected, but also to new space-invaders (*mujeres vampiro*) and their negotiation of cyberspace.

The narrative opens with a deliberately sparse initial interface, comprising a black background and the three names given to the *mujeres vampiro* displayed across the centre of the screen in blue font: Celeste, Jezabel and Camila. Clicking on each name brings up a short lexia making up that woman's story, as the name disappears and a half-moon image appears at the top of the screen. At the same time, a sound file is activated—a monotonous, repetitive sound, resembling a ticking clock or a dripping tap—which continually resonates once the link has been activated. As each new link is opened, a new sound file is activated, resulting eventually in three competing sounds running alongside each other but perpetually out of synch with each other.

Of the three protagonists in this story, the first of these, Celeste, is both a woman's name, and the term used to describe the main colour in the Argentine national flag. Metaphorically, therefore, we are encouraged to read her story as figuring Argentine national identity as feminine, as an experimental fiction imagining what would happen if, rather than patria, the national symbol was a woman. The second, Jezabel, is a name resonant of women who dare to defy the norm: A Phoenician princess of the Old Testament, Jezabel married King Ahab and converted him to the worship of the Phoenician God, Baal. While the name 'Jezabel' has popularly come to stand for women who are sexually provocative and dangerous, the figure has been recuperated in recent feminist rereadings of the Bible, which read her as a character who usurped male authority.[22] Finally, the third of these vampiric women is named Camila, an obvious reference to a major figure in the Argentine national psyche. Symbolic of opposition to Rosas's bloody regime of the nineteenth century, and allegorised as resistance to the twentieth-century dictatorship in María Luisa Bemberg's 1984 film,[23] Camila represents resistant femininity, standing up against totalitarian state power, and yet mobilises stereotypical codes—those of romance and illicit love—in a partial, complicitous critique.

These three figures thus represent, in their different ways, resistance to dominant patriarcal conceptions of the nation and women's roles within it. At the same time, all are vampiric, with each of the female figures using existing codes and vampirising them. In this way, the *mujeres vampiro* and the vampirism they undertake are representative of the options open to women: the taking up and reuse of existing codes of gendered behaviour. This notion has frequently been expressed in recent feminist and queer theory, and is perhaps most aptly summed up by Chela Sandoval's notion of 'survival skills under subordination' which conceives of consciousness as a 'masquerade' in which loyalties 'can be withdrawn and relocated depending on survival, moral, and/or political imperatives' (Sandoval 2000:31). In this sense, the options for women in the expression of their subjectivity lie in the selection and reuse (or, to use Gache's metaphor, the vampirisation) of existing codes.

At the same time, these *mujeres vampiro* also stand in for the active reader of hypertext narratives; each of their short narratives represents a moment of (partial) scopic capture, mapping out (tentatively) omniscient viewpoints. The lexia comprising the narratives of these three *mujeres vampiro* consists of very short, one-paragraph accounts narrated in the first person, each recounting an oneiric, nocturnal episode. The narrative relating to Celeste, entitled 'El viejo faro' ['The old lighthouse'], provides an image which encapsulates the activities of these vampiric, other-worldly women/ *wreaders*:

> Desde la cima del viejo faro observo los techos coloniales. Desde aquí, la ciudad parece un mapa nocturno sobre el que las débiles luces de los faroles señalan un itinerario de sueños.

> [From the top of the old lighthouse, I look down on the colonial rooftops. From here, the city looks like a night map on which the faint lights of the streetlamps sketch out a dream itinerary.]

Here, Celeste is given scopic primacy, much in the same way as Gabriella was in *Gabriella infinita*, and her position of power enables her to grasp and gain entry to the 'mapa nocturno' spread out beneath her. Literally a map created from a composite of images taken by orbiting satellites at night, in which the light sources indicate population density, the *mapa nocturno* represents a textual/representational form composed of multiple sources, and as such stands for hypertext narrative, in its drawing on multiple sources and linkings in its constitution. Such a reading of the *mapa nocturno* is of course strengthened by its use in a Latin American context, where the term has been recently theorised by Jesús Martín-Barbero in his work on mediations to mean 'a map which enables us to study domination, production and labour from the other side of the picture' (Martín-Barbero 1993:212). The notion of the *mapa nocturno*, therefore, carries within it notions of interrogating media and mediations, and thus stands as an image of the hypertext narrative, with the *mujeres vampiro* as the *wreaders*.

In this way, the *mapa nocturno* is, in its turn, interrogated by the *mujeres vampiro*, and the images of vampirism represent the author/reader of hypertext narratives, in his/her use and reworking of existing texts, images, and sound files. The *mujeres vampiro* thus represent the options open to the *wreaders* of hypertext narrative: the reconfiguration of lexia to form their own connections and narratives. Yet, of course, this role, as with the roles represented by the women's names, is only partially liberatory; just as Celeste, Jezabel and Camila each negotiated partially oppositional stances by reusing the codes available to them, so too the *wreader* of hypertext narrative finds his/her role not in a stance of complete liberty, but in the navigation and reworking of the available lexia. Vampire women, then, stand as the ideal image of the *wreader* in Gache's work, just as the pregnant Gabriella did in Jaime Alejandro Rodríguez's. Not figured as omniscient author with all its connotations of originality and genius, but as vampiric, the *wreader* of hypertext fictions makes use of the available material, and any originality lies in its productive reworking.

This notion of the reuse of existing sources as exemplary of the workings of hypertext fiction is explored throughout Gache's narratives in this collection, and leads to sustained reflections on the possibilities (and limitations) for textual multiplicity, nonlinearity and multisequentiality. As with Rodríguez's *Gabriella infinita*, Gache's work explores these potential 'second chances' through the structural features of the fictions which allow for random sequences, multiple choices and new linkages. Some of the narratives deliberately use new media technologies to attempt to reconfigure the conventional, linear reading pattern although also bring the reader face to face with the limitations of these same technologies. An example here is the short story '¿Por qué se suicidó la señorita Chao?' ['Why Did Miss Chao Commit Suicide?'] in which the story—the response to the question posed in the title—is generated at random by an algorithm. After a short introductory preamble setting out the genesis of the story—the images in Blue Willow porcelain, and an article written by Mao Zedong in his youth—the user then clicks upon the 'ingresar' ['enter'] link, which generates the response to the question. The response takes the form of a sequence of lexia in different coloured fonts in which a series of principal actors in the story—'la sociedad china', 'la señorita Li' and 'sus padres' ['Chinese society', 'Miss Li' and 'her parents']—are recombined along with a series of set phrases and outcomes. Below this, a link named 'otra respuesta' ['another response'] enables the reader to click again, which generates a new response, with different protagonists taking up different roles in the narrative. Here, the possibilities for narrative multisequentiality as enabled by new media technologies are brought to the fore, as new versions of the narrative are generated, producing a different set of motivations for, and outcomes of, the suicide. Similarly, the role of character within this new narratology—one of the most hotly debated elements in recent hypertext scholarship—is foregrounded, since roles and outcomes are swapped by characters seemingly at random. Gache's practice here thus speaks to global debates in hypertext theory which have explored the extent to which existing understandings of characterisation remain valid when considering procedural fictions.

That said, Gache's practice at the same time brings the reader up against the limits of these potentially liberatory new media technologies. Even though we are in the realm of a computer-generated narrative in this short story, authorship nevertheless still adheres, albeit in the guise of what Murray has termed 'procedural authorship' (Murray 1997:153). Given that the codes are written by the author, not the reader, and that the reader is merely navigating the available possibilities set down by those codes, the procedural author, in the words of Murray, has 'created the world of narrative possibilities' (Murray 1997:153). Indeed, this sense of the limitations of procedural narrative is made clear at each short story's conclusion since, at the end of each randomised version, the conclusion to the story is always the same. However many times we try the 'otra respuesta' link, we will end up with the same concluding sentence to the story:

> Dado que la sociedad se ha tornado en extremo peligrosa, debemos estar alertas para evitar que nos infrinja a nosotros mismos su golpe fatal.

> [Given that society has become extremely dangerous, we must remain alert in order to ensure that it does not deal us a fatal blow.]

Here, the reader is alerted to the fact that, however many apparently randomised versions are available, the narrative conclusion is always the same, conveying a sense of the limitations of literary experimentation. Moreover, given that this conclusion is in itself a Bowdlerised version of the conclusion to Mao Tse Tung's original article (accessible via a link in the preamble to this narrative), the reader constantly comes up against the uncomfortable feeling that the conclusion to the story is already prewritten, and, however it may be reconfigured, is forced to fit into a predetermined agenda by its close. The multiple stories in this short narrative thus function as an exploration of the possibilities, and yet also the limitations, of narrative multilinearity as enabled (or as controlled) by new media technologies.

Indeed, just as with *Gabriella infinita*, this notion of potentially infinite chances and infinite rewritings is explored in the many self-reflexive commentaries on the nature of hypertext fiction within these short narratives: Again, it is less the case of the radical actualisation of *wreaderly* freedom in these works, and more a case of the reflection on its possibilities and limits. One particular case in point is the chapter 'Mariposas-Libro' ['Butterflies-Books'], which contains several self-reflexive comments that guide the reader through the process of negotiating a hypertext narrative. The introductory lexia for this chapter informs us that:

> La escritura detiene, cristaliza, de alguna manera mata a la palabra conservando su cadáver. Un cadáver etéreo como el de una mariposa disecada. Parto aquí de la idea de colección. Al igual que Linneo clasificaba sus insectos en diferentes clases, colores, tamaños; al igual que un entomólogo caza mariposas y las ordena luego clavando sus cuerpos con alfileres, aquí coleccionaré citas-mariposa. (Teniendo en cuenta, además, que las mariposas se parecen topológicamente a los libros). La idea es formar una colección infinita de citas (si el concepto de infinito no atentara contra el de colección).

> [Writing fixes, crystallises, to an extent kills the word, preserving its corpse. An ethereal corpse like that of a mounted butterfly. From this I develop the idea of a collection. Just as Linnaeus classified his insects in different classes, colours, sizes; just as an entomologist hunts butterflies and puts them in order, sticking their bodies down with pins, so here I

will collect butterfly-quotations. (Taking into account, as well, that but-terflies, topologically, look like books).

The idea is to create an infinite collection of citations (if the concept of infinity doesn't contradict that of collection).]

'Mariposas-Libro' thus represents new possibilities offered by hypertext, firstly, in the opportunity offered for infinite citations and connections to be drawn in the production of this 'infinite collection', a notion which, as Gache points out, goes against conventional classificatory systems. Secondly, the new possibilities offered by hypertext are present in the importance of user input, since in this chapter users are invited to contribute further quota-tions, and so continue expanding this 'infinite' collection.

From this initial page, the reader then enters the chapter proper. The chapter opens with a set of six colour images of butterflies set against a green background, with a literary quotation appearing in the centre of the screen; the images are not of butterflies caught in flight, but rather displayed as if pinned down in a collection. Clicking on any one of these butterflies activates a link which brings up at random a quotation about butterflies from a literary or scientific text, which is then displayed in the centre of the screen, while the original image of the butterfly is replaced by another. These quotations come from a variety of literary and scientific sources, including the works of Aristotle, Sigmund Freud, Jean Baudrillard, and many leading Latin American authors. From the outset, therefore, this work is an intertex-tual and self-referential one, in which quotations from eminent authors are brought together in new and revealing ways as the reader clicks at random on the images on the page. Several of the quotations, as well as dealing with butterflies, also deal with the nature of fiction itself, an analogy hinted at by the fact that Gache identifies butterflies with literary quotations as noted above. Given that Gache parallels quotations with butterflies, they stand as an image of the text, and hence quotations such as the following draw our attention to textuality as much as to butterflies as a species:

'Chuang-Tzú soñó que era una mariposa. Al despertar, ignoraba si era Tzú que había soñado que era una mariposa o si era una mariposa y estaba soñando que era Chuang-Tzú.'

['Chuang-Tzu dreamt that he was a butterfly. On waking up, he wasn't sure if he were Tzu who had dreamt he was a butterfly, or a butterfly who was dreaming he was Chuang-Tzu.']

Gache's choice of quotation here, drawn from Jorge Luis Borges, is revealing both in terms of its content and in terms of the selected author. Regarding the latter, Borges is frequently cited by scholars as writing proto-hypertext fiction, and of envisioning the internet and electronic literature *avant la lettre*.[24] Regarding the former, the specific quotation in this case—from the Taoist philosopher Chuang-Tzu—has been the subject of an extended enquiry by Borges in his 'A New Refutation of Time' of 1944 in which he interprets Chuang-Tzu's dilemma via Berkeley and Hulme, in order to conclude that 'there is no other reality for idealism than mental processes' (Borges 1999:329). The central concern here—the difficulty of distinguishing reality from dream—stands as an image of hypertext, poised as it is between the real and the virtual, and where the text only exists in the moment of its enactment. Moreover, if Eleni Kefala has shown that 'for Borges the terms *soñador* and *autor* [dreamer and author] are inexorably interchangeable' (Kefala 2007:371), then the image of Chuang-Tzu represents once again the image of the (idealised) *wreader* of hypertext narratives, constantly navigating across the various links and files to create meaning.

Similarly, the quotation included from Cortázar's *Rayuela* [*Hopscotch*] (1963) is significant more for what it tells us about hypertext fiction than about butterflies themselves. The quotation is taken from Chapter 146 of *Rayuela*, one of the 'capitulos prescindibles' ['expendable chapters'] of Cortázar's novel, and takes the form of a fictional letter to *The Observer* newspaper.[25] The particular extract thus provides us with a series of recursive images of the writer/reader: We start with Gache, the author of *WordToys*, and progress back through the author Cortázar, to the fictive author of this letter (M. Washbourn), and thence to the fictive readers of *The Observer*.[26] This Chinese box of quotations alerts the reader to the intertextuality of Gache's work, and also of the functioning of hypertext fictions: That is, this quotation stands as an image of the intricate, multiple linkings between lexia which create traces from one text/author to the next. Moreover, *Rayuela*, like Borges's labyrinthine fictions, has been seen as a precursor of hypertext, with Landow describing it as an 'analogue print hypertext', and 'fully hypertextual because it suggests specific multiple paths of reading' (Landow 2009:447). Gache's choice of quotation thus again functions meta-critically, calling our attention to the formal aspects of *Rayuela*, in which the reader was offered a choice in the reading pattern and thus a potentially more an active involvement in the construction of the narrative.[27] On the one hand, thus, Gache sets herself within a long line of literary precedents, embedding her work within a strong tradition of literary experimentation in Latin American letters. On the other hand, the fact that the lexia within this chapter are all preexisting quotations highlights an essential lack of originality to this piece, and so tempers some of the more utopian proclamations about the radical originality of new media fictions: Originality, Gache implies, lies more in the recombination of existing texts.

Nestled among the highly self-referential quotations from Borges and Cortázar come several quotations of authors writing about the Latin American landscape, including Pablo Neruda and Abel Posse, among others. This is where Gache's citational strategy comes full circle, in that her quotations combine commentaries on experimental fiction and authorship with commentaries on mythical locales and Euclidean space. Their juxtaposition—a

juxtaposition enacted at random, and in different order as each reader negotiates the work—leads to their being reread in new, telling ways. We are thus
encouraged to read these depictions of Latin America as, similarly, metafictional and discursive: That is, Latin America is highlighted as a *discourse*,
to return to the notions set out in the introduction to this volume. Gache's
citational practice thus highlights how Latin America is constructed through
the discourses written about it.

One example of this can be seen in the citation of Abel Posse's 1987
novel *Los perros del paraíso* [*The Dogs of Paradise*] which reenacts the
foundational discourses in the construction of Latin America, and in which
the butterflies in the jungle are described as 'nacidos de la corrupción de
la paleta del Tintoretto' ['born from a corruption of Tintoretto's palette'].
Posse's novel, a fictionalised version of historical events in Latin America's
conquest, critiqued and debunked the central myths of the discovery and
founding of Latin America. In this particular extract, the images of the butterflies, and of the other features of the natural landscape, are images of
illusion: The butterflies appear as if they are painted, and, by association,
Latin America is formed by the myths that construct it. The extract from
Posse's text thus speaks both to the mythical, constructed status of the Latin
American locale, and also, via Gache's *citas-mariposa* analogy, to the inherent citationality of Posse's original novel.

Throughout this chapter, then, Gache's technique is one of the recombination of existing literary excerpts which address both the Latin American
locale and an infinite chain of author/reader citations. The originality of
Gache's work lies in the way in which these quotations are constantly (and
randomly) reconfigured; access to the quotations is generated through the
random clicking on an image of a butterfly, producing new sequences as the
quotations are displayed in a different order each time. The citations are, thus,
in addition to their original meaning, put together in new and productively
clashing ways. Here, Gache's technique has strong resonances with the Surrealist shock image, on which much of her work draws. The Surrealist shock
image functions, in the words of its most famous proponent, André Breton in
his 1924 manifesto, not through comparison but via the 'rapprochement de
deux réalités plus ou moins eloignées' ['bringing together of two more or less
distant realities'] (Breton 1962:43).[28] Yet at the same time, and as with much
of Gache's practice, her work in this chapter also speaks to new developments
in the theorisation of digital media, particularly the notion of mash-up cultures, whereby works of art are composed of the remixings of existing sources,
lexia and sounds.[29] This chapter as a whole, thus, engages with the discursive
production of the Latin American locale, while also exploring the productive
capacities of new media technologies, in which it is not the case that the reader
is given free reign to become an author, but in which the creative recombina-
tions of available lexia provide space for partial agency for the reader.

Similarly, the chapter 'El idioma de los pájaros' ['The Language of Birds']
can be read as much as a treatise on hypertext fiction as an investigation

into birdsong. Here, we encounter an introductory page followed by five images of birds which, when clicked, recite lines of poetry from famous poets (Rubén Darío, Guillaume Apollinaire, Edgar Allen Poe, Gustavo Aldolfo Bécquer and Charles Baudelaire). The introductory lexia informs us that 'Los pájaros de "El idioma de los pájaros" son máquinas-poetas. [Están] programados para re-citar palabras.' ['The birds of "The Language of Birds" are poet-machines. They are programmed to re-cite words']. The *pájaros* here stand as a metaphor for hypertext fiction: As 'poet-machines' they are preprogrammed and represent the linking of lexia in innovative ways that is offered by both poetry and hypertext. Poetry and hypertext are, therefore, analogous: Both working by using words in new contexts and reconfiguring conventional meanings, poetry and hypertext play with the codes of language.

This notion of playing with codes is reinforced by Gache's citation of Italo Calvino, which explores the notion of language as a code:

> Italo Calvino decía que, en última instancia, todo escritor es una máquina: trabaja colocando una palabra tras otra siguiendo reglas pre-definidas, códigos, instrucciones adecuadas. [. . .] O, en el mejor de los casos, movilizada a partir del llamado de lo indecible, continúa su trágica lucha por salirse de los límites de las mismas sin lograrlo.

> [Italo Calvino said that, in the end, every writer is a machine: s/he works by placing one word after another, following predefined rules, codes, and appropriate instructions. [. . .]. Or, at best, moved by the call of the unsayable, the writer continues her tragic struggle to get beyond the limits of these rules, without success.]

Through this intertextual reference to Calvino, Gache develops the notion of writing as always being rewriting, since writing and poetry can only function by reworking the existing codes of language. In this sense, language play, and language itself, is already ripe for hypertexualisation: Language as a code, analogous to machine codes and hypertext codes which generate electronic literature, is inescapable, but it is the task of each poet/*wreader* to reconfigure and recreate on the basis of these available codes. The *máquinas-poetas*, therefore, encapsulate both the machine codes of computer-generated fictions, and poetry's playing with language codes, and represent the actualisation of poetry in electronic form.

As is evidenced by the self-reflexive nature of Gache's fiction, the vast majority of the chapters in *WordToys* have writers or readers as their subject matter, from monks reading a sermon in 'El jardín de la emperatriz Suiko' ['Empress Suiko's Garden'] to dreamers searching for a lost scrap of paper in 'Los sueños' ['Dreams'] and to the surreal 'Rimbaudian word processor' in 'Procesador de textos rimbaudiano', to name but a few. There are, thus, a variety of figures who stand in for the author-god—or, more properly, the reader-god—of hypertext narrative. One of the most striking in this regard is the chapter entitled 'Escribe tu propio Quijote' ['Write Your Own Quixote'], which, after an opening lexia, provides the reader with a word-processing package in which s/he may write his/her own version of the *Quixote*. The opening lexia provides us with instructions both on the purpose of this particular work and on negotiating hypertext *per se*. Under the subheading 'Todos somos Rembrandt, todos somos Cervantes' ['We Are All Rembrandt, We Are All Cervantes'], we are told that:

> Cuando en 1962 Andy Warhol realizó sus *Do it yourself flowers*, remitía a un producto propio de la cultura de masas: las pinturas *Do it yourself* [. . .] El lema publicitario de estas pinturas era, precisamente, *Every man a Rembrandt* [. . .].
>
> *Escribe tu propio Quijote* está realizado con este mismo espíritu.
>
> [When Andy Warhol made his *Do It Yourself flowers* in 1962, he was referring to a product of mass culture: the *Do it yourself* paintings [. . .] The marketing slogan of these paintings was *Every man a Rembrandt* [. . .].
>
> *Write Your Own Quixote* was conceived in the same spirit.]

Again, Gache's technique of creating a recursive chain of authors/artists—whereby we back-track from Gache through Warhol to Rembrandt, and thereby to Cervantes—highlights this chapter, as with many of her others, as a self-reflexive work. Here, the notion of the kit—in which instead of there existing a finished work of art, the artist/user can create a work from the available pieces set in front of him/her—functions as a metaphor for the hypertext narrative in which the *wreader* is given partial agency in the creation of the work in his/her recombination of lexia, sound and image files. Again, Gache's practice here both speaks to a Hispanic literary heritage, and to contemporary debates in hypertext theory. Regarding the former, Gache's words here evoke note only the *Quixote*, but also more recent precedents such as Cortázar's *62:modelo para armar* [*62:A Model Kit*] (1968). Regarding the latter, following the hype of early theorisations in hypertext which envisioned users as co-artists and co-creators of the work, every *wreader* is a Rembrandt, we might say.

Following on from this, Gache makes specific reference to the image of the author in the *Quixote*, listing the chain of authorial figures—from Cervantes, Cide Hamete Benengeli, Alfonso Avellaneda, Borges and Pierre Menard—associated with this iconic text. Gache's choice of intertext here is striking for its multiple *mises-en-abîme*: *Don Quijote*, of course, tells us the tale of a man who fashioned himself as a knight in imitation of chivalric literature, whose telling is relayed through the fictional author figure of Cide Hamete Benengeli, which is then rendered by a potentially unreliable translator, and which is framed via a metafictional prologue which, as Friedman has shown, is 'about the writing of prologues' (Friedman 1994:113). The original *Don Quijote*, then, is highly metafictional. The *mises-en-abîme* are continued by Borges's famous, ironic retelling of the *Quixote* via another fictional author, Pierre Menard, meaning that all the protagonists of this recursive tale—Don Quijote, Cide Hamete, Borges, Pierre Menard—are readers/writers.

We, the *wreaders* of this work, are then inserted into a long line of apocryphal Cervantes, as we are invited to write our own version of the *Quixote*, by clicking a link which opens up a blank word processor page. However, as we start typing, irrespective of which keys we press—including the 'delete' and 'backspace' keys—the same sentences appear: the opening paragraph of *Don Quijote* ('En un lugar de La Mancha, de cuyo nombre no quiero acordarme . . .') ['Somewhere in La Mancha, in a place whose name I don't want to recall . . .']. Here, the rewriting of the *Quixote* offers, pointedly, no deviation from the original, leading to a central tension: Gache here is deliberately denying the *wreader* the reconfiguratory potential of hypertext fictions.[30] On the one hand, this work thus actualises, in stark terms, the importance of *Don Quijote* for all subsequent generations of writers: Namely, that *Don Quijote* is the great intertext with which all Hispanic authors inevitably find themselves dialoguing. On the other hand, Gache's strategy here is again one which calls into question the purported liberatory effects of new media technologies on the reader; here, as we witness, agency is at once tantalisingly promised to the reader, and then denied, as s/he is physically unable to writer his/her own *Quixote* with the tools provided. Once again, then, Gache's work initially draws us into a compelling narrative of *wreaderly* freedom, and then brings us up against the failings of such a utopian notion. It is, thus, particularly fitting that this chapter is the last in the book, bar the interactive bibliography ('La biblioteca') at the end. 'Escribe tu propio Quijote' closes the collection with a resounding reminder to us to explore the limitations of new media technologies, and to not take proclamations of the utopian potential of hypertext at face value.

SITUATING HYPERTEXTUAL PRACTICE IN A LATIN AMERICAN LITERARY TRADITION

Drawing on the notion of extension—the file extension implied in the term '.doc' as given in the neologism of this chapter's title—this chapter has argued that Latin American hypertext fictions are neither the radically other/new, nor simply repetitions of the same. Rather, they nod to the new possibilities enabled by digital media, but at the same time maintain close dialogues with predigital, extant literary discourses. As has been shown, the issues of mythical locale, literary self-consciousness, and the shifting relationship between the author and the reader are central to discussions within these works. Regarding the first of these, the issue of (mythical) locale is worked through both as representative of our contemporary, late-capitalist era, and as speaking back to previous discursive constructions of Latin American-ness. Regarding the second point, as has been shown, the hypertext fictions analysed present fictional worlds and characters that are resoundingly self-conscious and comment on the medium itself. Here, the emphasis is less on digital media as offering a proliferation of new, antilinear, revolution-ary reading patterns *per se*, and more on the potentials and limitations of these technologies. Finally, these fictions present new conceptualisations of the author-reader relationship, and, again, explore to what extent greater *wreaderly* agency is ever truly possible. Speaking here to a long literary heritage of authors attempting to give greater agency to their readers, these fictions dramatise a new relationship between author and reader, but at the same time indicate its impossibility in the actual procedural enactment of the work.

4 Civilisation and Barbarism
New Frontiers and Barbarous Borders Online

Following on from our previous chapter which focused on models of literary creativity as encapsulated in Macondo, here in Chapter Four we move onto another founding discourse which maintains some elements of spatiality via the image of the frontier, but which more properly sets up conceptual rather than geographical borders: the well-established and much-debated dichotomy between civilisation and barbarism. As early as the first chronicles of the *conquistadores* whose depiction of barbarous cannibals 'marked Amerindians as savages' (Restrepo 2003:53), and Jan van der Straet's emblematic painting *America* (c.1575) which functioned as a 'visualization of discovery as the advance of civilization' (Montrose 1991:5), the Americas has been figured as a zone in which the competing forces of civilisation and barbarism are played out. The civilisation/barbarism dichotomy is thus, in the words of Mabel Moraña, one of 'the enduring dichotomies established by imperial authority' (Moraña 2004:643), a legacy which in itself was an import of prior theories from Europe which stretch back as far as Greek and Roman times.[1] In this way, dating from classical antiquity, the barbarian has been figured as foreign/ alien, and the civilisation/barbarism dichotomy has functioned as the theoretical framework through which colonial actors conceived of the Americas.

While the roots of the civilisation/barbarism dichotomy can thus be found in colonial attitudes towards the indigenous populations of the Americas, themselves based on concepts borrowed from classical antiquity, the most infamous and high-profile exposition of this binary comes, of course, in Domingo Faustino Sarmiento's notion of *civilización y barbarie* as expounded in his *Facundo* of 1848. Sarmiento's notorious pronouncements, which presented his native Argentina—and, by extension, Latin America as a whole—as being caught in 'la lucha entre la civilización europea y la barbarie indígena' ['the battle between European civilisation and indigenous barbarism'] (Sarmiento 1848:49), have profoundly marked Latin American culture. That Sarmiento was both statesman and writer, and that his *Facundo* was published during the period in which the emergent Latin American countries were defining themselves as nation-states, is of profound importance, for Sarmiento's binary was embroiled in the debates about the very nature and substance of Latin America itself, and in the definitions of Latin American-ness as the concept developed. Indeed, the impact of Sarmiento's theories can be seen in the fact that subsequent generations of Latin American writers have returned almost obsessively to his binary. This is evidenced in texts ranging from José Enrique Rodó's *Ariel* (1900), which rehearsed Sarmiento's battle between civilisation and barbarism, although in this case pitting the civilised Latin Americans against the 'barbarous', utilitarian North Americans, to the *novela de la tierra* ['regionalist novels'] of the 1920s and 1930s which enacted the binary through fictional means,[2] through to Fernández Retamar's *Calibán* (1971) which reversed the terms of Rodó's rereading of Sarmiento, among others. As Alicia Ríos has noted, 'the need to overcome "the barbarous" will be a theme repeated or inverted throughout Latin American history, as will the values of civilization and of "culture"' (Ríos 2004:18–19).

Civilisation and barbarism is thus perhaps *the* founding binary of Latin America as a concept, given that it is a notion which has informed conceptualisations of the Americas from the conquest onwards, and one which was widely mobilised in nineteenth-century independence movements, proving central to the very formation of the independent Latin American nation-states. Thus it is no surprise to find that the key terms of Sarmiento's debate are taken up with frequency even today: for example, many Latin American online practitioners invoke these terms in creative and challenging ways, and either dispute the dichotomy, or reread it in the light of globalisation and contemporary conflicts. This chapter focuses on the work of two such artists: Mexican/Chicano performance artist Guillermo Gómez-Peña, and Colombian net.artist Marta Patricia Niño, in order to illuminate the extent to which their works interrogate this founding dichotomy.

There are three important features to draw out of the civilisation/barbarism debates as they have to date been analysed by Latin Americanist scholars which prove particularly relevant when analysing online cultural production: first, the centrality of the (metaphor of) the border to the dichotomy; second, the battle between autochthonous and foreign forces as represented by this dichotomy; and third, the concept of 'barbarian theorizing'. Regarding the first of these, the civilisation/barbarism debate, as articulated by Sarmiento in the nineteenth century, was drawn along the frontier—both literal and figurative—between 'civilised' urban society and the barbarous pampas.[3] The civilisation/barbarism dichotomy was thus mapped out along a conceptual borderland or frontier that was fundamental to conceptions of the state (and, we may extrapolate, conceptions of Latin American-ness).[4] As Walter Mignolo has observed, the notion of the 'frontier' was a vital component of nineteenth-century conceptualisations of the state in Argentina, with the frontier representing 'the movable (westward) landmark of the civilizing mission, the line dividing civilization from barbarism' (Mignolo 2000:298). Mignolo goes on to note that this notion of the 'the frontier of civilization' subsequently becomes the 'borderland' of the end of the twentieth century, where a new consciousness or 'border gnosis' emerges (Mignolo 2000:299).

The borderland or frontier, is, thus the topographical representation of the civilisation/barbarism dichotomy and, as this chapter will show, this topographical fixation is constantly reenacted online. If Mignolo traced a development in the mapping of the civilisation/barbarism dichotomy from frontiers in the nineteenth century to borderlands in the twentieth, this chapter argues that in contemporary online practice borders are both material and electronic. The mobilisation of metaphors of borders and frontiers in Latin American net.art is ubiquitous, both as images and as structuring features of the works. These borders refer, arguably, both to the frontiers and borders of online space, thus engaging with, and in some cases problematising, the highly contentious notion of the internet as the 'electronic frontier' of which we spoke in Chapter One of this volume. At the same time, these borders also speak to the contemporary flows of data in a purportedly borderless world of multinational finance capitalism; in this way, by their deliberate highlighting of the disavowed borders subtending this system, the works studied in this chapter highlight the cracks in the system. In this way, the frontier—a founding term of the internet, yet one which has been severely critiqued in recent years—is bound up closely with notions of civilisation and barbarism, and Latin American online cultural works, in their conscious playing with border-crossers, boundaries and barbarous bodies, engage with and critique this metaphor. Allied with this, and integral to the conceptualisation of the civilisation/barbarism dichotomy as being represented through borders, is the notion of the necessary policing and surveillance of these borders, a feature which often comes to the fore in Latin American cultural works online, due to the frequent positioning of Latin Americans as 'illegal' immigrants in the US popular mindset and US foreign and domestic policy.

Regarding the second point, that of the tensions between autochthonous and foreign influences, Philip Swanson, writing in 2003, argued that civilisation versus barbarism remains 'an unresolved dilemma' for much Latin American thought and culture up to the present since 'this tension is a defining features of the various culture wars or debates that rage in the academy over Latin American cultural studies, with regard to diverse but related areas such as transculturation, modernity, globalistion' (Swanson 2003:79). Swanson raises a key point here, in his contention that the civilisation/barbarism dichotomy, grounded as it was in the dispute between autochthonous and external influences in its foundational, nineteenth-century formulation, is still being played out today in the constant tensions between autochthonous versus foreign/globalising forces in Latin American identity. In this regard, Latin American online cultural production can be seen as an ideal space within which to interrogate these tensions. That is, such works, located precisely at the interface between globalising technologies and localised stories, in which identity is negotiated at the boundaries of the local and the global, is, thus, perhaps the ideal medium through which to explore the civilisation/barbarism dichotomy. In this way, reading through Walter Mignolo's call for the elaboration of local histories within and against global designs as noted in the introduction to this volume, new media arts can provide fruitful ways of tactically, temporarily, carving a space for these local histories, all the while piggy-backing on global designs.

Regarding the third principal point, that of 'barbarian theorizing', as scholars charting its history have shown, the notion of the barbarous implies at its most basic level the impossibility of, or negation of, thinking and theorising. Taking its origins from the Greek term βάρβαρος the term evokes babbling (that is, speaking a non-Greek language), and thus represents those who do not speak in a 'civilised' tongue.[5] Since, for the Greeks, language was one of the primary indicators of man's rational mind, those who were barbarous were, by definition, lacking in reason: As Anthony Pagden has neatly summed it up, 'the inability to speak Greek was regarded not merely as a linguistic shortcoming, for a close association in the Greek mind between intelligible speech and reason made it possible to take the view that those who were devoid of *logos* in one sense might also be devoid of it in another' (Pagden 1986:16). The origins of the term 'barbarous' thus lie in the incomprehensibility of alien languages and imply a lack of capacity for thought and reason. As Mexican philosopher Leopoldo Zea notes, in his seminal work on the origins of barbarism, the very term itself is thus based on lack of access to the *logos*, since the barbarous in its original sense means:

> balbuceo de la verdad, del *logos* que no se posee. Bárbaro será entonces el que no posee la verdad y con ella la palabra que la expresa. (Zea 1988:23)
>
> [babbling of truth, the lack of access to the logos. The barbarous person, therefore, is he who does not possess the truth, and, at the same time, the words with which to express it.]

If the notion of the barbarous in its conventional form is the very negation of thinking and theorising, Latin American(ist) scholars have recently developed the concept of 'barbarian thinking/theorizing' as an oppositional practice. Traces of this concept can be found in many of the works of oppositional thought in recent Latin American letters, such as José David Saldívar's notion of the 'School of Caliban' which involves rethinking 'our American culture and identity from the perspective of the Other—Caliban— a protagonist excluded, ruled, and exploited' (Saldívar 1991:135). It also resurfaces, perhaps most famously, in Fernández Retamar's works; in this regard, Hugo Achugar, in his rereading of Fernández Retamar's *Calibán: apuntes sobre la cultura en nuestra América* (1971) and *Para una teoría de la literatura hispanoamericana y otras aproximaciones* (1975), notes how Fernández Retamar problematises the notions of universal reasoning and universal theorising, and puts forward the possibility of local knowledge production. For Achugar, this raises the following questions:

> Can barbaric Latin Americans theorize? Should they 'Prospereanly' speak or can they 'barbarically' babble? Speaking differently used to mark one

off as barbarian; it was, literally, 'to babble'. Is there only one way of theorizing? Can I as a barbarian have the right to my own discourse?

(Achugar 2003:134)

Achugar's argument here links the civilisation/barbarism dichotomy to theorising and epistemologies: Thinking, and what constitutes knowledge, is marked out along the dividing line between civilisation and barbarism. In essence, Achugar argues, the 'civilised' have always represented themselves as the owners of thought and theory, while the 'barbarous'—those who refuse to abide by the rules of 'civilised' discourse—are reduced to babbling. 'Barbarian theorizing' as proposed by Achugar here would therefore be 'non-hegemonic theoretical thought', a discourse 'produced outside the rules of the theoretical discourse of the "centre"' (Achugar 2003:134).

Walter Mignolo, meanwhile, has also discussed at length the notion of 'border thinking' or 'barbarian theorizing' in his *Local Histories/Global Designs*, and links this phenomenon to globalisation, arguing that 'the economic conditions created by globalization contributed to the rise of "barbarian theorizing" (e.g. border gnosis, double consciousness)' (Mignolo 2000:308). Crucially, Mignolo argues that these conditions of production (that is, globalisation) do not mean an imposition of a singular global design, but instead that 'barbarian theorizing' can provide for a contestatory positioning. Here, Mignolo contends, once we accept 'barbarian theorizing' as 'border gnosis' and as 'epistemology emerging from the conditions created by the last and perhaps more radical stage of globalization', this then provides us with the possibility of 'theorizing from the border', or, in other words, of combining:

> both the formation in 'civilized theorizing' and the experience of someone who lives and experiences [. . .] in communities that have been precisely subalternized and placed in the margins by the very concept and expansion of European civilization.

(Mignolo 2000:309)

Both Achugar and Mignolo thus shed important light on the barbarous in its formulation as 'barbarian theorizing': firstly, that this is a theorising which is characterised by speaking differently and by refusing to obey hegemonic thought (Achugar); and secondly, that it is simultaneously produced by conditions of globalisation and can provide a contestatory discourse to them (Mignolo).

Such potential for 'barbarian theorizing'—a theorising which is barbarous, a theorising which refuses to abide by conventional, Western, teleological thinking, a theorising which 'oppos[es] the clean and rational concept of knowledge and theory' (Mignolo 2000:109)—is precisely what the online art works studied in this chapter offer. The works studied offer the possibility of a thinking which is not bound by linear presentation or rationality but which is instead multisequential, rhizomatic and fluctuating. We argue that 'barbarian theorizing', as exemplified by Latin American net.art and online performance art, is thus the negotiation of the dilemma that Swanson had identified with regard to the constant tensions between autochthonous expression and foreign influences in the configurations of Latin American identity: That is, these artists, in their practice of barbarian theorising, provide for a form of thinking and of identity formation which transgresses the boundaries of the local and the global, and which formulates a partially resistant form of thinking and theorising.

BARBAROUS BODIES: GUILLERMO GÓMEZ-PEÑA

This chapter first considers the work of the Mexican/Chicano performance artist, Guillermo Gómez-Peña. Gómez-Peña is well known for his challenging, satirical performances using multiple media, including installation, video, radio, the internet and theatre. His works, whether artistic, performative or theoretical, frequently engage with the metaphor of the border, and both invoke it and problematise it as representative of Chicano identity. From his 1993 manifesto, 'The Border Is . . . (A Manifesto)' (Gómez-Peña 1993), in which he sets out definitions of border culture, through his 1996 collection of performance texts, poems and essays, *The New World Border* (Gómez-Peña 1996), to his 2000 collection of performance documents, interviews and 'chronicles', *Dangerous Border Crossers* (2000), the border for Gómez-Peña has remained the location of his theorising, and site for interrogation of identity. Many of the key terms and figures in Gómez-Peña's work, such as *borderismos* or the Border Brujo,[6] engage explicitly or implicitly with the metaphor of the border, and his use of, and deconstruction of, the border-as-metaphor and border-as-Chicano-identity has been frequently analysed by critics. For Jill S. Kuhnheim, in her discussion of Gómez-Peña's 1996 work *The New World Border*, the importance of Gómez-Peña's tactics is that he

> deterritorializes his production in several categories simultaneously, expanding the concept of the border to interrogate academic disciplines as well as linguistic, social, and epistemological domains.
>
> (Kuhnheim 1998:24)

Here, Kuhnheim's comments are particularly illuminating as regards the way in which Gómez-Peña's use of the border moves beyond the purely territorial, and involves at the same time an epistemological endeavour, suggesting a questioning of conventional thinking and theorising. For Stacy Alaimo, meanwhile, the importance of Gómez-Peña's playing with borders lies in its contestation of identity, particularly in relation to the way in which they 'they offer up spectacles of difference even as they contest the borders of identity and fracture the gaze of mastery' (Alaimo 2000:173). Here,

Alaimo's emphasis on spectacles of difference and on the fracturing of the gaze in Gómez-Peña's work proves particularly revealing in the case of the works under investigation in this chapter which, as the analysis below will show, involve the interpellation of the viewer/user, and the subsequent problematisation of the viewer's (anthropological) gaze.

The border is, thus, a fundamental trope in Gómez-Peña's works. Where his earlier works, and the critical response they have generated, have tended to situate his use of the border in relation to the question of *mestizaje* and to the problematisation of Chicano identity,[7] this chapter focuses instead on his later works in which border-crosser figures become symptomatic of the omnipresence of the *civilización/barbarie* debate both within the Latin American imaginary, and in US projections of Latinos and ethnic others. Two recent online works by Gómez-Peña and La Pocha Nostra, in collaboration with other artists, specifically foreground the barbarous in their border crossings: *The Chica-Iranian Project* (Gómez-Peña 2005b) and *The New Barbarians* (Gómez-Peña 2008b).[8] These works will be examined with a view to how they provide for playful yet disturbing revisions of the *civilización/barbarie* debate, and identify the creation of new 'barbarians' in the post–9/11 era.

Regarding the first of these, *The Chica-Iranian Project: Orientalism Gone Wrong in Aztlán* (2005b) is an online work which makes use of images taken from Gómez-Peña and La Pocha Nostra's performances, and inserts them into an ironic and disturbing online 'game' for the viewer.[9] The opening page presents the viewer with a black background, over which fade in from top left the credits in blue font, followed by the title in red font, and subsequently twelve thumbnail images across the horizontal axis of the screen, showing different performance personae. These images are constantly flickering, while behind them lies a barely discernible, shifting red line, bearing a resemblance to a jagged rope or barbed wire. Directly below these images, instructions inform us that we are about to enter 'a performance photo essay on the dangers of ethnic profiling in the post 9/11 era'. Here, it is worth noting Gómez-Peña's use of the term 'essay', since what we in fact enter, as will be analysed below, is not presented in traditional essayistic format; in this respect, the structuring of this work, with its explicit framing as an essay yet its rejection of the structural norms prescribed by this genre, represents a movement towards 'barbarian theorizing', and an attempt to produce (essayistic, theoretical) thought by nondiscursive means.

Clicking on a red arrow to the right of these instructions then loads the work itself. The initial page disappears and instead, on the same black background, instructions appear in green font across the top portion of the screen, inviting the user to 'test [his/her] ethnic profiling skills' by matching the name of the artist with the persona portrayed. Below these instructions, a larger version of one of the thumbnail images glimpsed in the initial page reappears in the left half of the screen, while the right half of the screen contains a list of the names of the performance artists with radio buttons.

Below the image lies the title of the image in yellow font, which reflects on the ethnic stereotypes presented in the image, with names such as 'La Kurdish Llorona', 'Typical Arab Chola', and 'Palestinian Vato Loco'. The user then has to select the name to match the personae portrayed by clicking on the appropriate radio button.

The subtitle to this online performative work—'Orientalism gone wrong in Aztlán'—is clearly a reference to Edward Said's groundbreaking work of the late 1970s, *Orientalism* (first published in 1978). Said's eloquent and highly influential volume—seen by many as laying down the foundations for what would later become postcolonial studies[10]—explored how the West constructs the 'Orient' as its negative mirror image, or, in the words of Said himself, how the 'Orient' is one of Europe's 'deepest and most recurring images of the other' (Said 2003:1). Said's work demonstrated how clichéd notions of an Oriental other in the Western imagination were closely linked with colonial politics, and thus how such romanticised images of the 'Orient' served European and North American imperial ambitions.[11] Importantly, for Said, 'Orientalism' refers not just to infrastructure—to the 'corporate institution for dealing with the Orient'—but more profoundly to a 'western style for dominating, restructuring, and having authority over the Orient' (Said 2003:3). Orientalism, thus, more than simply institutions, is a question of ontology and epistemology; as Sara R. Farris has argued,

> By disclosing the profound prejudices against the East, and especially the Arab world, that had been spread for centuries by European writers, presenting them as if they were the 'true' Orient, Said also engaged in an epistemological and political struggle. He demonstrated how knowledge is deeply entangled with power [. . .] and how, thus, representation itself in these uneven power relations—of the West over the East and of the West over its own intellectuals—can easily become a tool and outcome of this control.
>
> (Farris 2010:268)

In this sense, Said's quest in *Orientalism* was to unmask commonplace assumptions regarding the 'Oriental other', to question power relations, and to engage in an epistemological struggle, all notions which relate to and illuminate Gómez-Peña's practice in the works under consideration in this chapter.

Indeed, Gómez-Peña's *Chica-Iranian Project* engages directly with the postcolonial impulses of Said's work, in particular as regards (un)masking and epistemological struggles. On the one hand, the *Chica-Iranian Project* borrows from *Orientalism* the framework that constructs the other as barbarous and exotic, and, to an extent, plays (along) with some of the clichéd commonplaces about the Oriental/Chicano other. At the same time, however, as the insistence in the title that this is 'orientalism *gone wrong*' (our italics) indicates, this project deliberately questions the assumptions underlying Orientalism, and troubles its coordinates. Thus the stereotypes presented in this work, all the while engaging with the tropes of Orientalism—for the images frequently make use of erotic, romanticised types, as will be analysed below—resist classification and ultimately attempt to undo the stereotypes they proffer. Indeed, the predominance of masks and masking in the images within this work highlights these images as compelled performance and points to the struggle for epistemological power within the work. That is, as will be examined below, the overt putting on of multiple masks and costumes in this work, in which the multiple layers often clash among themselves, questions any essentialism underlying the images portrayed, and reveals such images to be constructed.

Examples of this troubling of ethnic stereotypes, and of the play between masking/unmasking can be seen, for instance, in the image entitled 'La Kurdish Llorona' [Fig. 4.1]. The title makes reference to the iconic image of Mexican/Chicana womanhood, La Llorona, the weeping woman of popular folklore who, after drowning her own children in order to pursue a sexual relationship, is doomed to weep for her dead children for all time. This conventional Mexican image of womanhood as exclusively defined by childbearing and in which female sexuality is punished—in Norma Alarcón's words, La Llorona as a figure for 'controlling, interpreting, or visualizing women' (Alarcón 1982:182)—is then othered by the insertion of the term 'Kurdish', an insertion which immediately problematises the cultural specificity of this iconic figure. Indeed, this othering or troubling is also enacted by the image depicted, since the veil—the conventional item of clothing representing La Llorona—is here made to signify in two ethnic contexts, namely Kurdish and Mexican, making the cultural specificity of the veil unclear. Moreover, where La Llorona is conventionally portrayed as shrouded either in a diaphanous, grey-white veil or a black cloak, here the veil is turned into the visual excess of the multiple layers of deep pink and pastel blue fabric.[12] The stereotypes of Mexican/Chicana feminine identity are thus othered, entailing an undoing of the stereotype by excess. In effect, these multiple layers of material present a double shrouding or masking, suggesting the multiple layers of identity performance, and indicating the attempt to deconstruct a stereotyped image of womanhood, demonstrating gender identity to be performative.

Moreover, this image, and the legend of La Llorona which it interrogates and demystifies, has important resonances as regards postcolonial power relations. Domino Renee Perez's recent volume on La Llorona has revealed the disavowed Aztec origins of the tale, arguing that 'European motifs were assimilated into or grafted onto Native stories about the Gritona' (Perez 2008:18). For Perez, thus, La Llorona as a figure is used to 'comment on the changing worldview of the Mexicas both pre- and post-conquest' (Perez 2008:18), and as such 'La Llorona's story narrates the origins of an ongoing colonial project' (Perez 2008:19). Gómez-Peña's mobilisation of the figure of La Llorona here, thus, speaks to the colonial past of this figure, as well as to similar ongoing (neo)colonial projects of the present, including US neo-colonial relations with Mexico, and those of the Turkish state's interest in Kurdish lands.

Finally, the playing with and (un)masking of identities in this image takes a further twist in the procedural enactment of the game itself since, on playing the game, the personae turns out to be performed by Emiko R. Lewis, identified on the website as Hapa/half Japanese. There are, thus, no Mexicans, Chicanas or Kurds in sight—nor any women, for that matter. The image clearly plays on our stereotyped notions of Chicana and Arab womanhood, and confounds those stereotypes by revealing how such identities are constructed, rather than essences.

The other images which make up this online game provide similarly ironic and challenging images which constantly play with ethnic stereotypes. The persona entitled 'Afgani Immigrant in Texas', for instance, portrays a woman wearing a hijab which on closer inspection is composed of a repeated pattern of the stars and stripes. Here, the iconic national symbols—the flag and the hijab—are troubled in their uneasy combination, and the image makes the viewer contemplate the multiple identifications of immigrants in the US. Moreover, given the make-up of the costume—in effect, the stars and stripes are superimposed upon the hijab, quite literally imprinted upon the fabric—the image also invites the viewer to reflect upon US neo-imperialism and the imposition of cultural values. This sense of unease is furthered by the stance of the actor, who holds her hands, palm outward, across what must be the lower half of her face, but which is obscured by the hijab. The implication here is that the woman does not speak for herself, but is being spoken for by the two national symbols. This visual metaphor for the muffling or silencing of the woman's voice functions here, however, less in the conventional sense in which the hijab is often interpreted as a symbol of the oppression of women, but more in the sense of how we, as spectators and players of this game, rush to classify the woman. Again, as with La Kurdish Llorona, on playing the game the persona turns out to be played by Liz Lerman, a Chicana performance artist. Once more, the two key terms of the persona—Afgani and Texan—are revealed as absences, reinforcing once again the performativity of national and ethnic identity.

The persona named 'Generic Terrorist', meanwhile, is played by Gómez-Peña himself, and depicts him wielding a scimitar, wearing a *lucha-libre* wrestling-style mask, and with the words 'pleez do not liberate me!' emblazoned across his bare chest. Again, cultural and ethnic markers—the scimitar as a (contested) visual shorthand for Arab culture, from the first crusades to the present day,[13] and *lucha-libre* as an emblematic Mexican national sport—are juxtaposed, indicating how these two distinct cultures are often lumped together as alien others in the US imaginary. The slogan across the performer's chest, meanwhile, implies that 'liberation' may not be the preferred outcome. In the context of the making of this piece, with the US 'liberation' of Iraq (March–May 2003) fresh in viewer's minds, the connotations are unmistakable; the Iraq War, also known as Operation Iraqi

Freedom, involved the invasion of a sovereign country by US troops, and as such, we are inclined to read the slogan as protesting against such invasions made in the name of 'liberation'. Coupled with this, the title itself of this persona, 'Generic Terrorist', again highlights the arbitrary classification of entire ethnicities as barbarous terrorists by the Bush administration, providing a textual counterpart to the mixing of Arab and Mexican cultural artifacts in the visuals. Here, the notion of 'orientalism gone wrong' as noted in the subtitle to this work, is given a biting, politicised meaning through its linking to contemporary global politics.

At the same time, the slogan painted across the performer's chest is also an intertextual reference to one of Gómez-Peña's own earlier performance works, 'El Warrior for Gringostroika' (1992) which featured the artist in a similar *lucha-libre*–style mask although this time coupled with a *mariachi* costume, with the words 'please don't discover me!' on his chest. The slogan painted in 'El Warrior for Gringostroika' formed a critique of the discourse of the 'discovery' of the Americas—a 'discovery' which in fact meant conquest, genocide and forced conversion of the indigenous populations to an imposed religion, Catholicism—and now transposed onto a post–cold war mentality, with the implicit critique of US cultural imperialism. As Thomas Foster notes with regard to this earlier piece, 'El Warrior for Gringostroika', 'tied border cultures worldwide to the breakup of the Soviet Union and the collapse of the three-worlds model' (Foster 2002:49). In the updated version provided by 'Generic Terrorist', this intertextual reference is now focused on drawing out the implications of 'liberation'; in other words, the reality of the Bush regime's strategies for the 'liberation' of Iraq is undercut by the urge not to liberate, encouraging the viewer to consider Bush's strategies not as liberation, but as neo-imperialism.

These various personae, and the others which make up this game, are thus characterised by a predominance of maskings and veilings, pointing towards ethnic performativity, and also towards the vying for interpretative and epistemological power. This epistemological struggle, read through Said as implied in the subtitle to the game, has undeniably postcolonial undertones, and is intended to force the reader to question the easy, at-first-glance values by which the images can be interpreted. Instead, as we play the game, we become increasingly aware of the complexity of the images, and the interpretative power of the viewer/user is questioned. As such, these personae can be seen as examples of what Gómez-Peña has called 'ethnocyborgs', composite entities that are 'one-quarter stereotype, one-quarter audience projection, one-quarter esthetic artifact, and one-quarter unpredictable personal/social monster' (Gómez-Peña 2005a:81). This tongue-in-cheek statement, if applied to *The Chica-Iranian Project*, indicates how the images constructed within it are intended to play on the audience's preconceptions, and force us to question our own assumptions and worldview. For Gómez-Peña, such ethnocyborgs are '"artificial savages"' or in other words 'cultural projections of First World desire/fear of its surrounding subcultures and the so-called "Third World Other"' (Gómez-Peña 2005a:89). Gómez-Peña's comments here bring the personae of *The Chica-Iranian Project* back round to the founding question of civilisation and barbarism; namely, these ethnocyborgs are involved in laying bare the construction of savages as a threatening/exotic other in the Western mindset. In this way, the personae in this performance and its accompanying online game represent precisely these 'artificial savages'; artificial both in that they are composed of cultural projections rather than essences, and, more profoundly, in that they lay bare the projections of the West as regards ethnic/cultural others. The work itself aims to demystify such projections and, as we play the game, it is our own preconceptions and prejudices we are forced to confront.[14]

At the end of this ironic game, when the user has successfully matched all the personae with their respective actors, and has thus returned these troubling bodies to their 'correct' boxes, the user is presented with a black screen, as words in green font appear across the centre of the screen, congratulating him/her: 'Thanks for participating in our (non)objective risk classification exercise. You've added greatly to our store of targeted intelligence. We feel much safer now.' These valedictory words, which ape the overhyped terminology of the then Bush administration's 'war on terror', are clearly ironic, and leave the user feeling uncomfortable at the ease with which they have been interpellated into the game and have participated in this ethnic classification. The *Chica-Iranian Project*, therefore, performs— and forces the user to perform—anxieties over ethnicity. In its aggressive positioning of the user as policer of the personae s/he is presented with, it forces us to confront our own stereotyping tendencies, as the user plays the role of border control. Moreover, given that we can only progress through the game when we have selected the 'right' answer (and so pinned down these potentially troubling bodies), it highlights the desire to classify border-crossing bodies, rather than maintain them in a hybrid contestatory state. That is, it is only on clicking upon the 'correct' answer that we can progress to the next screen and view the subsequent image. If we select the incorrect answer, we hear a low buzzing sound and remain on the same screen; if we select the correct one, a gong sounds, ironically rewarding us in our efforts, and, via a sound bridge, resonates over onto the next screen. There is, thus, a clear parallel drawn between playing the game and playing (along with) the system; our compulsion to play and to select the 'right' answer correlates to the systemic desire to assign 'correct' classification to these troubling bodies.

Playful yet serious, the *Chica-Iranian Project* thus speaks to contemporary socio-political concerns regarding the quest to identify the threatening ethnic other in contemporary US foreign and domestic policy. Speaking to what Gómez-Peña himself has flagged up in recent interviews and essayistic works (see, for instance, Gómez-Peña 2005a:275; Gómez-Peña 2008a:197), the *Chica-Iranian Project* engages with the troubling redeployment of the age-old civilisation/barbarism dichotomy by hegemonic groups, and forces the viewer/ user to confront how his/her interpellation into the game is, at the same time, his/her interpellation into US foreign and domestic policy. This chimes with the assertions of Idelber Avelar who, in a contribution to the recent edited volume, *Ideologies of Hispanism* (2005), has suggested that the treatment of Mexicans and Chicanos in the US post–9/11 is due to fears of the alien/barbarous other:

> The various stories of Mexicans recently being objects of hostile attacks in the U.S.—by being or not confused with Middle Easterners—are emblematic: not white enough, the Latin American *mestizo* is subject to the xenophobic attack by evoking the image of the feared other, the dark, the impenetrable, the Eastern.
>
> (Avelar 2005:270)

Avelar's argument here that Latin Americans and Middle Easterners alike are figured as the threatening other in the US imaginary provides a useful summary of the impulse underlying *The Chica-Iranian Project*, in the attempt to explore the ways in which the US worldview constructs its barbarous others. Moreover, it is worth noting how Avelar's argument, and Gómez-Peña's performances, resonate with Sarmiento's original formulation of the *civilización/barbarie* dichotomy; throughout *Facundo*, Sarmiento famously drew parallels between the barbarous inhabitants of the pampas and Arabs, Bedouins and Berbers. As Christina Civantos aptly sums up, 'Sarmiento uses a deeply rooted European figure of the other, the Arab, as an analogy or metaphor for the Argentine other' (Civantos 2006:41). In this way, if the original *civilización/barbarie* debates mobilised European fears of an Arab/Middle Eastern other in order identify the potentially troubling gaucho other, here, in the twenty-first-century context, Gómez-Peña is revealing how the elision of the two terms—the Latin American and the Arab—is remobilised in the service of contemporary anxieties about ethnic identity and the war on terror.

Indeed, the *Chica-Iranian Project* can thus be seen not just in terms of the contemporary experience of Chicanos in the US, but, more broadly, as engaging with the very conceptualisation of Latin(o) America itself. Walter Mignolo, in his seminal work on the origins of the term 'Latin America', has demonstrated that, in the 'global designs' of the European imaginary, Latin America is conceived of not as the Orient but the 'extreme Occident'. Basing his observations on the historical configuration of the Americas, Mignolo argues that:

> The Occident, however, was never Europe's Other but the difference within sameness: Indias Occidentales (as you can see in the very name) and later America (in Buffon, Hegel, etc), was the extreme West, not its alterity. America, contrary to Asia and Africa, was included as part of Europe's extension and not as its difference [. . .]. Occidentalism was a transatlantic construction precisely in the sense that the Americas became conceptualized as the expansion of Europe.
>
> (Mignolo 2000:58)[15]

Hence it makes perfect sense for Gómez-Peña to subtitle his *Chica-Iranian Project* 'orientalism *gone wrong* in Aztlán' (added emphasis); in effect, what we see enacted in this work is a form of slippage from one to the other, in which the extreme Occident becomes mistaken for the threatening Orient. The *Chica-Iranian Project* thus reveals an elision of the two discourses—the extreme Occident and the Orient—in the eyes of the West, as well as calling into question the definition itself of Latin(o) American identity. Moreover, these questions are inextricably linked with the founding discourses of Sarmiento and his civilisation/barbarism binary: As Mignolo argues, for intellectuals such as Sarmiento, '"Latin America" was not the Orient but the "extreme Occident"', and Sarmiento and his contemporaries 'appointed themselves as the leaders of the civilizing mission in their own country, thus opening the gates for a long history of intellectual internal colonialism' (Mignolo 2000:55). In this way, the terms of 'Orient/Occident' are inextricably linked with both the defining of Latin America itself, and with the specific dichotomy of civilisation and barbarism according to which the region's identity has oft been plotted; Gómez-Peña's resistant, ironic reworking of these terms thus brings into play the geopolitical significance of these terms for defining Latin(o) Americans today.

Regarding the second of Gómez-Peña's recent works, the three photo-performance portfolios 'Ethno-Techno: Evil Others and Identity Thieves', 'Post-Mexico in X-Paña' and 'The Chi-Canarian Expo' form part of the larger body of work entitled *The New Barbarians* that, in the words of the artist himself, 'explores the cultural fears of the West after 9/11' (Gómez-Peña 2008b). The title makes ironic reference to Sarmiento's founding binary, while the images within the portfolios present beings who cross boundaries, and who refuse to be locatable on either side of the civilisation/barbarism divide.

Gómez-Peña's strategy in this work, as in *The Chica-Iranian Project*, is to position the viewer in relation to the images in a way which is deliberately challenging and uncomfortable, and which questions the viewer's own gaze. Examples of this strategy include 'En el hall del genocidio' [Fig. 4.2], which provides an example of the 'reverse anthropology' of the type that Thomas Foster noted in Gómez-Peña's earlier work (Foster 2002:50–51).[16] In this image, Gómez-Peña is standing, wearing an indigenous headdress, upper-body armour, a *poblana*-style skirt and high heels, and carrying a machine gun. Behind him, rows of skulls in display cases take on the appearance of museum exhibits, and are reflected in a glass door to the left of the image. This image deconstructs the anthropological gaze, firstly, by refusing to offer us a museum exhibit of the traditional ethnic figure which is the conventional subject of anthropology: Here, the transnational array of props, which combine hypermodern tools of warfare with tribal headgear, refuses any easy classification according to ethnic and cultural types, and provides instead a hybrid image.[17] Secondly, the rows of display cabinets behind him which clearly reference museums of anthropology (bringing to mind, perhaps, the monumental Museo Nacional de Antropología in Mexico City) are deconstructed by the skulls they display and the title of the piece; that this museum exhibit celebrates genocide reveals the (neo-)imperialist underpinnings of anthropology as a discipline.[18] Thus the machine gun that Gómez-Peña carries stands for resistance: indigenous resistance to the anthropological gaze and, more important, resistance to our gaze as viewers and implied visitors to the museum. In this sense, this image attempts to resist the anthropological gaze that classifies ethnic others, and deliberately implicates the viewer in this process.

Similarly, the image entitled 'Abu Ghraib Reanactment' engages with and problematises the classification of others, and complicates the viewer's gaze. The image shows two male actors, one of whom holds a machine gun, is wearing a camouflage jacket, and has his face bound by barbed wire. The other wears a vest, shorts and fishnet tights, with his entire body bound by barbed wire, and wearing a bandana on his head. The title of the piece is a reference to the Abu Ghraib jail in central Baghdad, the site of the torture, rape and homicide of Iraqi prisoners by US military personnel in 2004. Gómez-Peña's reenactment engages with this context, and yet infuses it with new meanings; the addition of the fishnet tights, for example, suggests a transposition of the conflict onto the policing of sexuality, with the implication that nonnormative sexuality is subject to control and surveillance. Moreover, given that the prisoner has an implied Mexican identity through the use of the bandana, this is a further example of how the barbarous other in the US mindset is interchangeably Mexican/Arab. Finally, the use of barbed wire is doubly encoded, since it functions in two cultural contexts. Firstly, the barbed wire is a recognised feature of the Abu Ghraib prison and as such stands for the containment of Iraqi prisoners by US imperialism, yet it is also a synecdoche frequently used to represent the US/Mexican border, and as such speaks to US immigration politics of the border. Again, Gómez-Peña's image here invites the viewer to reflect upon the elision of these two distinct cultural and ethnic groups in the US mindset, as well as providing a visual metaphor for the construction and containment of Mexican and Arab identities as barbed/barbarous others. Here, the revision of the concept of barbarous others as *barbed* others is doubly encoded: on the one hand, it clearly inserts the notion of the barbarous into contemporary global politics, and yet, via the image of the barbs, suggests a potentially resistant stance of those who are so named.

Similarly, images in other sections of the work provide reflections on the creations of new barbarians. Those in the section 'Post-Mexico en X-Paña' play on the notion of othering, a fact which is implied by the deliberately resistant title, where the conventional orthography of the word 'Spain' (España) is othered by the use of the Aztec-influenced 'X' in place of 'Es'—a strategy recalling Chicano poetics/politics of linguistic resistance. The constituent images of this collection, such as 'Sagrada familia' or 'Re-enactment', produce new and challenging takes on conventional European discourses and images, as implied by this title. One particular instance of this can be seen in the piece 'Piedad Post-colonial' [Fig. 4.3], in which Gómez-Peña is seated, wearing an indigenous headdress, with bones hanging from his neck and carrying a machete. He cradles in his arms a female figure who is naked bar a pair of boots, whose face is painted red and who has three crosses painted on her torso. The image is clearly a play on Michelangelo's 1499 sculpture, *La Pietà*, a key art work of the Renaissance showing the Virgin holding the dead Christ. That this is specifically flagged as a 'post-colonial' version sheds new light on the work; what is being lamented here is the genocide of the indigenous population of the Americas during the Iberian conquest, with the inert body of the female actor representing the death of these peoples. Moreover, this reenactment provides a new encoding of Michelangelo's (European) original; if the original lamented the death of Christ—the central figure in Christian iconography—this reenactment laments the death of indigenous peoples who died as a result of an invading force which was fighting precisely in the name of that same Christianity.

These various images comprising *The New Barbarians* function to display and then challenge stereotypes of ethnic identity, and also to involve the viewer/user in this challenge. In this way, they undertake a similar strategy to that noted by Alaimo in relation to 'Border Brujo', namely that, 'what Gómez-Pena confronts, of course, is not the individual audience member *per se*, but, more crucially, the way in which the gaze of mastery is structured' and he thus makes 'the audience members realize their own inability to arrest, to circumscribe, and to master this text, forcing them to relinquish the delusion of omniscience' (Alaimo 2000:179). In *The New Barbarians*, the viewer's gaze is constantly challenged and implicated in the power structures that each piece reenacts and deconstructs.

However, one potential source of ambiguity in Gómez-Peña's work lies in the fact that the bodies he presents, for all their staged barbarity, are sensuous, eroticised bodies; we are not presented with troubling, shadowy bodies as in Argentina's *siluetazo* movement, nor with the harrowing dismembered plastic limbs used by the *mujeres de negro* to denounce the Ciudad Júarez/Chihuaha killings.[19] Instead, the bodies in Gómez-Peña's work are highly aestheticised; the female form, in particular, is highly sexualised, with his actors notable for their attractive, youthful bodies. The 'Supermodelo Zapatista', for example, with machine gun, bare breasts and high heels, may provide an ironic take on the classical image of Zapatista militancy, but ultimately ends up reinforcing the Mexican-Chicana body as sensual, erotic, and the object of an implied male gaze. Many of the other images employing female actors function in similar ways, and there is a marked lack of representation of the female body as a quotidian entity, much less as ageing or unattractive according to conventional patriarchal norms of feminine beauty.

This has resonances with Kuhnheim's observations about Gómez-Peña's earlier work, *The New World Border*; here, Kuhnheim argues that Gómez-Peña 'maintains a unified speaking position [. . .] that ultimately reinforces his authority as artist and as emblem of a particularly masculine bicultural identity' (Kuhnheim 1998:27). Critiquing in particular his use of gendered identities in this work, Kuhnheim argues that:

> The absolutes of gendered identities, for example, are reinforced rather than taken apart in this text. In several instances in *The New World Border*, he pokes fun at possible feminist critiques, closing off dialogue with these perspectives rather than opening it [...]. The book includes many traditional female images, both verbal and visual, and near the end of the text he allies woman with the land: 'on whose breasts will I be resting next century? / on whose land will I be resting for good?'
>
> (Kuhnheim 1998:234)

Kuhnheim's critique here could well be levelled at the images on display in *The New Barbarians*, since the images of the barbarous bodies as simultaneously pleasurable and erotic have a long history in European definitions of the indigenous American other, from early figurations of indigenous women as Amazons and onwards.[20] Regarding this long history, scholars such as Anne McClintock have argued that the colonial gaze was a type of 'porno-tropics' in which women functioned as 'imperial boundary markers' (McClintock 1995:25), while Fernanda Peñaloza has discussed how the portrayal of indigenous women as 'highly eroticised object[s] performing for the benefit of male pleasure' is part of 'larger tropes of territorial conquest' (Peñaloza 2010:470). In this light, the question therefore remains of whether Gómez-Peña's work ends up reexoticising the Chicana body. Undoubtedly the intent of Gómez-Peña's playing with these images is to question their validity, in the same way in which Alaimo, in her discussion of 'Border Brujo' has argued that the very hyperabundance of Mexican and Mexican American characters is a deconstructive strategy which 'allows it to resist reification, commodification, and epistemologies of control' (Alaimo 2000:178). That said, in *The New Barbarians*, it remains to be seen whether such hyperabundance is enough, or whether it ends up reinforcing stereotypes of barbarous/erotic female bodies.

BARBAROUS BORDERS AND 'BARBARIAN THEORIZING': MARTHA PATRICIA NIÑO

The second work under analysis in this chapter is Martha Patricia Niño's *Relational Border Map* of 2007. Martha Patricia Niño is a Colombian creative multimedia artist and scholar at the Departamento de Artes Visuales of the Universidad Javeriana in Bogotá, Colombia. Her artistic works include several digital installations such as *Peligro biológico* [*Biological Threat*] (1999), in which a robot roams art galleries, criticising works and harassing spectators; *Recorridos del cartucho* [*Travels around El Cartucho*] (2003), in which interactive systems provide *testimonios* of the *barrio* Santa Inés del

Cartucho in Bogotá; and *Hack-able Curator* (2007), which involves a curating programme that searches for photographs based on algorithms. *Relational Border Map*, one of Niño's recent online works, is a net.art work which imaginatively combines a series of terms that provide links to external sites.

The main page of *Relational Border Map* consists of a black background, with a series of key terms in neon-green letters in angular font [Fig. 4.4]. Again, this font apes the same iconic green phosphor screen-display font as employed in Mackern's works (see Chapter One in this volume), and, as such, is both deliberately anachronistic and self-referential, drawing attention to the formal qualities of computer code. The words rendered in this font are linked by lines, thus creating the relational map of which the title speaks. These words constantly move across the screen, and as they do, they create new relations with each other, new lines are drawn, and old ones erased. Clicking on each word turns the font colour to red and brings up a small pop-up box with a brief lexia; these lexia then link to external sites relating to each word. There is a finite number of lexia—27—used in the work, and the terms included are politicised terms, relating to the contemporary world of new technologies, terrorism, corporatism and state control.[21]

The top of the page carries the heading 'The map is not the territory', an unacknowledged citation of the famous phrase by the scientist and philosopher, Alfred Korzybski (Korzybski 1994:58). In his 1934 work *Science and Sanity*, Korzybski examined the human capacity for abstraction, using the map as an allegory for all human systems of classification. Robert P. Pula, in his preface to the 1994 edition, glosses Korzybski's reasoning thus: 'Korzybski realised the importance of *visualization* for human understanding. He knew, then, that to make some of the higher order, overarching relationships of his system accessible, *visible*, he must make a diagram, a model, a map' (Pula 1994:xvii). The quote from Korzybski, thus, with its reference to the need to create maps, while at the same time reminding us that the map is not the territory (that is, an abstraction is not the same as the actual entity it represents), provides an illuminating introduction to Niño's work, since the making visible of overarching relationships through mapping is central to the project of *Relational Border Map*.

Moreover, *Relational Border Map* engages with the notions of frontiers and borders as represented by the civilisation/barbarism dichotomy: Specifically foregrounding borders in the title itself, Niño's work engages with the frontier/border metaphor, and frames this metaphor in terms related to control, surveillance, mapping and policing. We therefore propose seeing this work as an example of 'barbarian/border thinking', in that, as the analysis will show, the mapping Niño proposes is a remapping, and a rethinking of relations. While the Latin(o) American aspect of *Relational Border Map* is less immediately obvious than in the work of Gómez-Peña, what Niño's work does show is, through the use of mostly anglophone writings, an oppositional perspective, creating a contestatory position (a key feature of 'barbarian theorizing' according to Mignolo and Achugar).

Examples of this 'barbarian thinking' can be found both in the links provided by the lexia, and in their juxtaposition with other key terms. Regarding the first of these—internal contradictions within any one key term—an example can be seen in the term 'World Trade', which brings up a pop-up window with two links: the first to a site entitled *World Trade Organization* (http://www.gatt.org/), and the second to *The Yes Men*. While the first of these sites may appear at first glance to be the official site of the World Trade Organization, carrying the official WTO logo and using the same menus and fonts as the real WTO website (http://www.wto.org/), on closer inspection this turns out to be a hactivist site. Items on its 'News' section provide ironic commentaries on the exploitative nature of world trade, such as the announcement of 'the creation of a new, much-improved form of slavery for the parts of Africa that have been hardest hit by the 500-year history of free trade there'. Here, the text apes the discourse of development common to many of the WTO's pronouncements and yet turns it on its head as it is employed to reveal how purportedly developmentalist and 'free trade' policies result in the perpetuation of North-South inequalities. Similarly, the section 'About the WTO' borrows from standard neoliberal rhetoric but uses this to announce the imminent disbandment of the WTO, claiming that 'numerous studies have shown that current trade liberalisation rules and policies have led to increased poverty and inequality, and have eroded democratic principles, with a disproportionately large effect on the poorest countries'. In both these cases free market rhetoric is used against the grain, and speaks to popular resistance to the WTO, a growing movement since the mid-1990s and whose most high-profile campaign came in the shape of the Seattle protests of 1999 against the WTO's Ministerial Conference held in that city. As Venter and Swart note, institutions such as the WTO are seen by antiglobalisation protest movements as 'promot[ing] and facilitat[ing] corporate power' and as imposing a 'monolithic system of universal rules imposed by highly centralised institutions to further the interests of U.S. corporations' (Venter and Swart 2002:61). For many, thus, the WTO represents, in the words of Stanley Aronowitz, the 'third leg of the international economic cooperation fashioned by the "advanced" industrial countries and international financial institutions to control the developing world' (Aronowitz 2009:204). As such, the WTO, despite advocating free trade and purportedly promoting development, functions in the eyes of many to maintain countries of the global South in neo-colonial conditions of exploitation. In this way, exploring the links associated with this lexia leads us to question the term itself, and encourages us to unpick the rhetoric and so read the term in a resistant fashion.

Similarly, the second of the sites linked to this same lexia also offers us an alternative perspective on the purportedly transparent and self-evident term 'free trade'. This second site is that of the *The Yes Men*, a media activist group started by Jacques Servin and Igor Vamos, under the pseudonyms Andy Bichlbaum and Mike Bonanno, respectively, which was initially inspired by the antiglobalisation movement, and which hijacks corporate events, opposes the WTO, and encourages readers to join civil disobedience networks. In fact, *The Yes Men* are authors of the fake WTO website accessed via the first link, although this fact is not made clear by Niño; instead, it is the linking of the two sites within the one lexia which encourages the connection to be made by the viewer.

Moreover, a further twist to the notion of 'free trade' is added by the varied activities of *The Yes Men*; in addition to their protests against the WTO, *The Yes Men* have often taken on corporate giants, including Exxon Mobil, Chevron and others. Famous for their near-perfect aping of corporate and neoliberal rhetoric, one of *The Yes Men*'s most prominent tactics is the creation of fake PR websites for multinational corporations, to the extent that these sites are frequently mistaken for the real thing, most famously in their 2004 response to Union Carbide's Bhopal disaster of 1984 which led to *The Yes Men* being interviewed on the BBC.[22] In this sense, therefore, the notion of 'world trade' takes on a further, oppositional/critical meaning: We are encouraged to read 'world trade' not through its official representation via the WTO, but instead to read each word more literally, and scrutinise the practices of those corporations who trade globally. In the light of the Union Carbide scandal, for example, we may ponder how environmental disasters in one part of the world are disavowed by multinational corporations, all the while profiting from cheaper production costs afforded by that location, and so, extrapolating from this, question the strategies by which such corporations trade across the world in unequal terms.[23] In this sense, after visiting *The Yes Men*'s site, we are inclined to consider the manipulation of the terms of world trade (and global corporate responsibility) by large multinationals, and so again read the term against the grain.

Moreover, within the context of Niño's work, it is significant that both of the sites linked within this term function via the manipulation of new media technologies, a fact which reflects back on Niño's own practice. That is, the first site makes use of the gatt.org domain name for oppositional purposes, capitalising on the possibility of purchasing domain names, while the second documents a range of protests undertaken frequently through the creation of fake websites, as well as promoting electronic civil disobedience more broadly. These two links, then, frame Niño's own work within a tradition of media hacktivism and electronic civil disobedience, and encourage us to view *Relational Border Map* as a potential example of tactical media. Here, tactical media can be understood through the definition proposed by its most vocal proponents, the Critical Art Ensemble, as the 'critical usage and theorization of media practices that draw on all forms of old and new, both lucid and sophisticated media, for achieving a variety of noncommercial goals and pushing all kinds of potentially subversive political issues' (Critical Art Ensemble 2001:5). With regard to Niño, the interlinking within her own work to some of the leading proponents of tactical media, as well as the overt structural features, such as the green phosphor display font, which immediately flag up her work as questioning the use to which the formal aspects of new media technologies may be put, ally *Relational Border Map* with these tendencies, and encourage us to view it as speaking tactically, within and yet against the system.

Brought together here in Niño's work, the *Yes Men* site and the fake WTO site thus highlight the inherent contradictions within, and offer new meanings of, the term 'World Trade'. If, in its officially sanctioned meaning, 'World Trade' means to 'open trade for the benefit of all', with the justification that 'the opening of national markets to international trade, with justifiable exceptions or with adequate flexibilities, will encourage and contribute to sustainable development, raise people's welfare, reduce poverty, and foster peace and stability' (WTO Mission Statement), here, we are encouraged to explore the internal contradictions in the WTO's own rhetoric. That is, Niño's work uses these terms resistantly, forcing them to function against their own logic, and, as we explore the links which spread out from the seemingly self-evident term, we are forced into a position of 'barbarian thinking'. In other words, as we explore these links we think these terms from the margins/borders rather than from their official representation.

Another example of the ways in which links within one single key term provide clashing and productive new meanings is the term '1984' which brings up a pop-up window with three links, all relating to George Orwell's influential novel, *1984*, but which bring up important and revealing contrasts. The first of these, entitled '1949–orwell 1984' brings up a link to a sound file of the 1949 radio adaptation of *1984*, starring David Niven, and posted on the Indymedia UK website (Indymedia 2005). Before the performance itself starts, the radio announcer highlights for the audience the issues of authoritarianism as brought to light by Orwell's work. The second link is to a video file of Apple's 1984 commercial, a short film directed by Ridley Scott which uses Orwell's *1984* as counterpart to its own product, the Apple Mac personal computer. Referencing Orwell's novel in both its rhetoric and imagery, the film shows a screen with a Big Brother figure who declares that 'Our Unification of Thoughts is more powerful a weapon than any fleet or army on earth', and ends with a voice-over from Apple reassuring us that 'you'll see why 1984 won't be like "1984"'. Meant to symbolise the fight for the control of computer technology as the few against the many (Cellini 2004)—and read by many as Apple pitting itself against the mighty corporate giant IBM—the commercial used Orwell's dystopic scenario as an allegory for contemporary battles over media content and control. Finally, the third link, entitled 'Orwell Rolls in his Grave' is a link to a video file which brings up Robert Kane Pappas's documentary film, *Orwell Rolls in his Grave* (2003). Pappas's film explores the relationship between the media, corporate interests and the US government, and reveals how large multinationals have monopoly interests in media outlets, and hence control information flow. The film argues that the media are 'not a healthy counterpart to government, but work with it' and that 'mainstream media is an impediment to democracy in United States'.

In her bringing together of these three sites, Niño forces the user to engage in multiple viewing/auditory strategies: The viewer/user must digest audio and visual material which is not presented sequentially, but linked rhizomatically. This bringing together provides for a reflection on the key term, '1984', that unites them: Firstly, the sites she has drawn together encourage us to perceive that 1984 might not be so far away, since corporate control of the media, Big Brother–style, is not simply a feature of a futuristic dystopian fantasy, but already exists in actuality in the US today. Orwell's *1984* famously predicted the development of new media technologies in the shape of his all-intrusive 'telescreen', and linked these to the repressive powers of a totalitarian superstate. Here, reading through Niño's multiple links, we are encouraged to view new media technologies as functioning in the interests not of the state but of transnational media corporations. Indeed, the location of the sound file of the radio play in the first link—the Indymedia UK website—encourages such a reading. The Indymedia network, having its origins in the 1999 Seattle protests against the World Trade Organization and the neoliberal model it promoted, has since spread worldwide, and has played a leading role in alternative media, open publishing and participatory journalism.[24] That the sound file is tagged on the accompanying Indymedia page with the terms 'anti-militarism' and 'repression' indicates how the dated radio play is meant to be understood in contemporary terms within Indymedia's aims of questioning corporate control of media content. In this sense, the links within this lexia make reference to this fundamental issue of the manipulation of the media so eloquently foreshadowed by Orwell, and yet update it for our late capitalist, twenty-first-century context in which the interests of multinational media giants transcend the boundaries of the nation-state.

Furthermore, more than simply just linking the three sites uncritically, Niño's work also encourages us to consider whether there may be internal contradictions between the three links: whether, for instance, media giants such as Apple disavow their actual relationship to Big Brother–style corporatism. The film's huge budget—some $900,000, which was an astronomical sum for a commercial at that time—seems to belie Apple's claim to represent the small, independent freedom fighter standing up to the media giants. As Ted Friedman has noted, Apple was already a $500 million company at the time, adding that 'Apple may present itself as a smaller, kinder, gentler corporation, but it operates by the same rules of the marketplace as everybody else' (Friedman 2005). In this way, the links contained within '1984' encourage the user/viewer to construct his/her own narrative linking the three sites, and, thereby, produce new and productive meanings.

Yet it is perhaps the second type of 'barbarian thinking' offered by *Relational Border Map* that is the most radical: namely, the one which lies in its internal structure. The multiple and constantly shifting relationships between the key terms as they constantly reconfigure on screen encourage the reader to investigate his/her own connections between these terms. Within these constantly fluctuating combinations, suggestive ones are constantly forming, disappearing, and then reforming, with links being drawn between terms such as War, Oil, Race; 9/11, War, Fear; Culture, Order, Time; World Trade, Fear, Control; or Police, Paranoia, Alien. In these fleeting moments, Niño is suggesting the intricate connections between the key terms informing our contemporary worldview, and, encouraging us to glimpse momentarily their mutual imbrications.

As an example of this, the combination of the terms 'Border Patrol', 'Alien' and 'Police' provides for some thought-provoking interconnections. The first of these terms, 'Border Patrol', links to the 1994 digital art work of the same name by digital media artist and activist Paul Garrin in conjunction with David Rokeby (Garrin 1994–1996). The work consists of an object tracking system in which stationary cameras function as sensors to an interface which controls the position of 'snipercams' which lock onto 'targets' (that is, the viewer's head), and then produces the audio sound of gun shots. Garrin's work frequently shows a particular concern for technology and freedom, such as his *Name.Space* project (1996), which aims to divest US-sanctioned monopolies of their control of the domain name system, or his media activist site *MediaFilter* (1995), explicitly flagged up on its homepage as a tactical media project.[25] Here, in *Border Patrol*, Garrin interrogates how technology may be put to use for surveillance and control, and interpolates the viewer into his project. As Laura Baigorri has succinctly summed up, in *Border Patrol* Garrin 'trata de la tecnología como instrumento de control y poder, y de los ciudadanos sometidos involuntariamente a ella' ['deals with technology as an instrument of control and power, and how citizens are involuntarily subject to it'] (Baigorri 2010:155), and as such this work immediately encourages us to think through not only the border, but new media technologies themselves.

The second term linked here, 'Alien', brings up a pop-up box with a short lexia providing a dictionary definition of the term which reads as follows: 'alien; ālyən; ālēən; adjective: belonging to a foreign country or nation; unfamiliar and disturbing or distasteful; relating to or denoting beings supposedly from other worlds—extraterrestrial'. Below this short text are two links: the first, to a short BBC news article, 'Maybe We Are the Martians', by journalist Helen Briggs (Briggs 2003), and the second to the Wikipedia entry for 'Goobacks', about an episode of the television cartoon *South Park* in which futuristic beings travel back in time to the present. In the first article, a representative of NASA is quoted as conjecturing whether, since the Earth and Mars exchanged material in the early days when life was forming on Earth, 'Was Mars part of our past? Maybe we are the Martians', while the second link, providing detailed plot summary of the *South Park* episode, comments that it functions as a 'satire of immigration' and the debates surrounding it in the US. Read in conjunction, these two links prompt the reader to question exactly who the aliens are, and to reflect on the way in which societies construct their own barbarous aliens.

Finally, the third term in this brief connection, 'Police', links to an article entitled 'The Police State Is Closer than You Think' by Paul Craig Roberts on the anti-interventionist website *Anti War* (Roberts 2005). The article discusses how, in the aftermath of 9/11, the then President Bush attempted to erode the right to *habeas corpus*, a central tenet of the US justice system and enshrined in the US Constitution.[26] Roberts concludes by arguing that 'everyone is disturbed about this barbaric and illegal practice except the Bush administration'. While Roberts's short article does not make the link explicit, it is clear that the implication here is that barbarism is exhibited not on the part of the purported terrorists, but on the part of the government who acts against the Constitution and human rights as enshrined in the Geneva Convention. Roberts's strategy here involves revealing how acts of the purported 'civilised' are in fact barbaric, a strategy which has often been theorised in a broadly postcolonial context, from as early as Aimé Césaire's *Discours sur le colonialisme* (1955), which condemned the colonisers as barbaric, through to Paulo Freire's arguments about the 'violence of the oppressors' made in 1972. Here, Freire argues that,

> For the oppressors [. . .] it is always the oppressed [. . .] who are disaffected, who are 'violent', 'barbaric', 'wicked' or 'ferocious', when they react to the violence of the oppressors. [. . .] Whereas the violence of the oppressors prevents the oppressed from being fully human, the response of the latter to this violence is grounded in the desire to pursue the right to be human.
>
> (Freire 1993:273)

Freire's comments here reveal the underlying power relations behind the wielding of the term 'barbaric', and point to the essential contradiction at its heart; namely, it is the very same violent oppressors (who, due to their violence, are barbaric) who then name their oppressed other as 'barbaric'. In this sense, we can read the encoding of the US government here as barbaric as a moment of uncovering this essential 'violence of the oppressors' or, to use Žižek's term, the 'systemic violence' that subtends late capitalism (Žižek 2006). Thus here, encoding the Bush regime as barbaric, more than a mere rhetorical strategy, means uncovering the disavowed barbarity of the oppressors, and of the neoliberal regime they represent.

These three key terms—'Border Patrol', 'Alien', 'Police'—brought together fleetingly in Niño's work, produce new meanings through their interconnections. Garrin's *Border Patrol*, for instance—a digital art installation work produced several years before 9/11—takes on a new meaning when read alongside Roberts's 'The Police State Is Closer than You Think', which explores how the police state in actuality is policing its citizens. Similarly, the conjunction of the link between 'Police' and 'Alien' encourages the reader to think through the links between the two, and to explore how US policy constructs the alien and the foreign as barbarous threats, all the while engaging itself in barbarous acts against basic judicial rights. The synopsis of the *South Park* episode, meanwhile, with its description of apparently futuristic aliens who turn out to be time-immigrants from the future, is infused with a new and more politicised meaning when considered alongside Garrin's *Border Patrol*: Here, the conjunction of anxieties over aliens/immigrants and the policing of borders makes for productive reflections on the US Border Patrol Agency, and its policies of defining and policing barbarous others.

Through its structural make-up, therefore, Niño's *Relational Border Map* encourages us to participate in what we might classify as 'barbarian/border thinking'. The thinking offered up to us by *Relational Border Map* is barbarous firstly because of its constant troubling of borders—the border being, we recall, the fundamental conceptual and spatial dividing line between civilisation and barbarism. Given that the thinking in *Relational Border Map* is produced along the continuously shifting borders and links between the key terms, it is precisely in the borders, in the contact zones in which two or more terms are momentarily brought together, in the liminal spaces where the barbarous and the nonbarbarous meet, that this theorising occurs.

Secondly, *Relational Border Map*'s proposed mode of thinking is barbarous in that it is a nonlinear, nonteleological, nonhierarchical thinking. In contradistinction to the established modes of civilised thinking which function according to established syntax and are unidirectional, here the onus is on us as viewers and readers to navigate the works, trace our own links, and construct our own meaning/theorising. Theorising is thus given over to the barbarous, in the nonlinear and oppositional thinking in which the reader engages.

And finally, *Relational Border Map* is barbarous in its stance of speaking back to power: The key terms it uses are critically resignified through the complex and shifting interlinkings to which they are subjected. In this way, the established meanings of terms such 'Border Patrol' or 'Police' are challenged, as the original sources are imbued with new meanings through their constant interconnections with other terms. In these ways, *Relational Border Map* enacts, and impels the reader/user to enact, an oppositional discourse of the barbarous.

REPRESENTING AND THEORISING THE BARBAROUS ONLINE

The two artists considered in this chapter provide different forms of 'barbarian theorizing' and barbarous border-crossings online. Gómez-Peña's work engages more explicitly than Niño's with images of barbarian cultural artefacts, in its playing with the stereotypes of ethnic others. Gómez-Peña's approach is essentially visual, focusing on bodies as the particular site of anxieties over the barbarian and border crossers. Where he approaches the issue of 'barbarian theorizing', this lies in his critique of linear thinking, implicit, for instance, in the ironic congratulation we get when we successfully classify the disconcerting bodies in *The Chica-Iranian Project*. Here,

Gómez-Peña offers a critique of linear (civilised) thinking, with the desire to classify and return the disquieting bodies to their rightful place, but does not allow the viewer/user the space to construct an alternative. That is, the viewer/user cannot progress through the game other-wise, constructing his/her own, barbarous tactics of resistant classification or, indeed, of nonclassification. In this sense, the *The Chica-Iranian Project* when considered in terms of 'barbarian theorizing' remains at the level of critique of civilised thinking, but does not offer the opportunity for a specific 'barbarian theorizing' in its place.

Niño's work, meanwhile, places less emphasis on the bodily and on visual images of the barbarian, and as such does not engage as explicitly as Gómez-Peña with the politics of barbarous bodies. That said, while her work has less to say about the policing of barbarous bodies, her resistant relinkings and constantly shifting structures arguably provide a more successful format for the production of 'barbarian theorizing' than Gómez-Peña's works. *Relational Border Map* offers more space for the user/viewer to construct a resistant and constantly shifting form of thinking/theorising, producing a form of barbarian resistance in the contestation of the accepted meaning of the original (civilised) terms. Both artists, in their different ways, attempt to produce works of resistant digital culture: works which necessarily exist at the borders of the world system, but which use the very tools provided by that system—online 'games', hyperlinking, (fake) websites—to contest it.

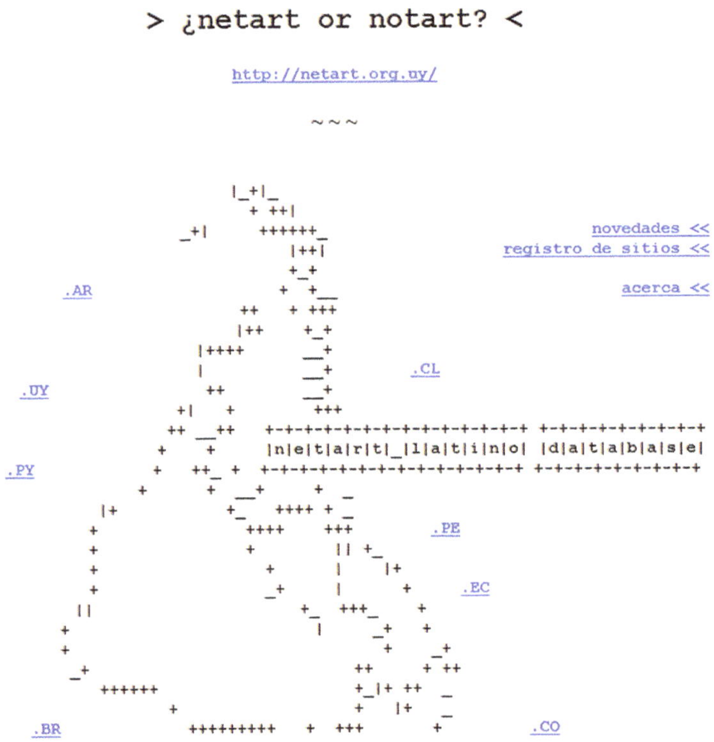

Fig. 1.1 Brian Mackern, *netart latino database*, opening screen.

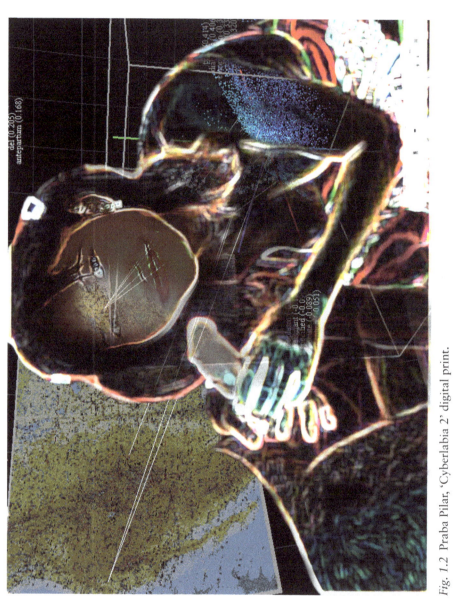

Fig. 1.2 Praba Pilar, 'Cyberlabia 2' digital print.

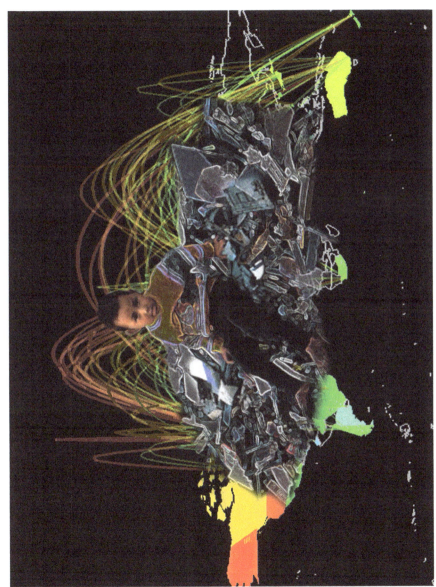

Fig. 1.3 Praba Pilar, 'Cyberlabia 8' digital print.

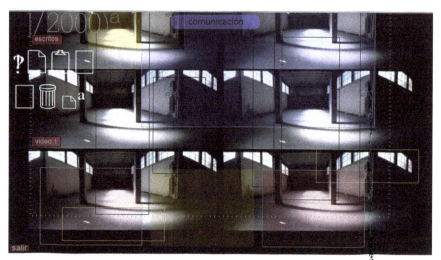

Fig. 2.1 Marina Zerbarini, *Tejido de memoria*, opening screen.

Fig. 2.2 Marina Zerbarini, *Tejido de memoria*, cycle of images.

Fig. 3.1 Jaime Alejandro Rodríguez, *Gabriella infinita*, opening screen.

Fig. 3.2 Jaime Alejandro Rodríguez, *Gabriella infinita*, 'Mudanza'.

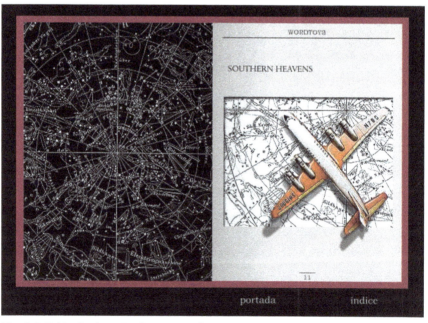

Fig. 3.3 Belén Gache, *WordToys*, 'Southern Heavens'.

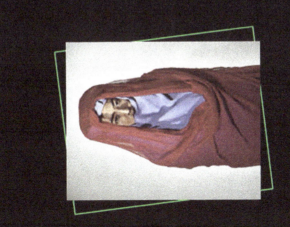

Fig. 4.1 Guillermo Gómez-Peña, *The Chica-Iranian Project: Orientalism Gone Wrong in Aztlán*, 'Kurdish Llorona'.

Fig. 4.2 Guillermo Gómez-Peña, *The New Barbarians*, 'En el hall del genocidio'.

Fig. 4.3 Guillermo Gómez-Peña, *The New Barbarians*, 'Piedad Post-colonial'.

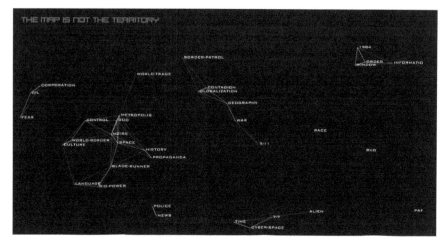

Fig. 4.4 Martha Patricia Niño, *Relational Border Map*, opening screen.

Fig. 5.1 Guillermo Gómez-Peña, 'Ethno-Techno: A Virtual Museum of Radical Latino Imagery and Fetishized Identities', photograph of El Ethnographic Loco.

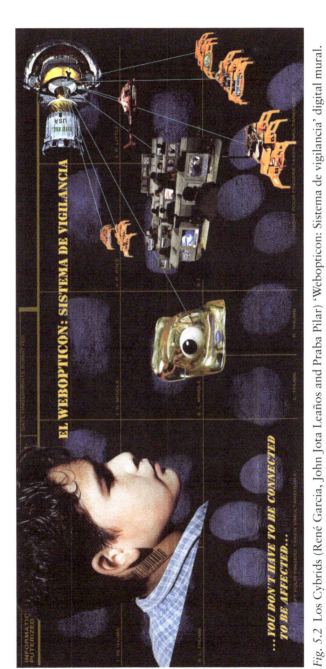

Fig. 5.2 Los Cybrids (René Garcia, John Jota Leaños and Praba Pilar) 'Webopticon: Sistema de vigilancia' digital mural.

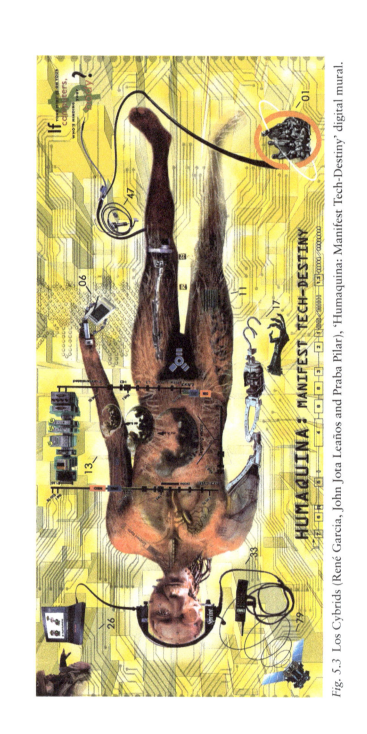

Fig. 5.3 Los Cybrids (René García, John Jota Leaños and Praba Pilar), 'Humaquina: Manifest Tech-Destiny' digital mural.

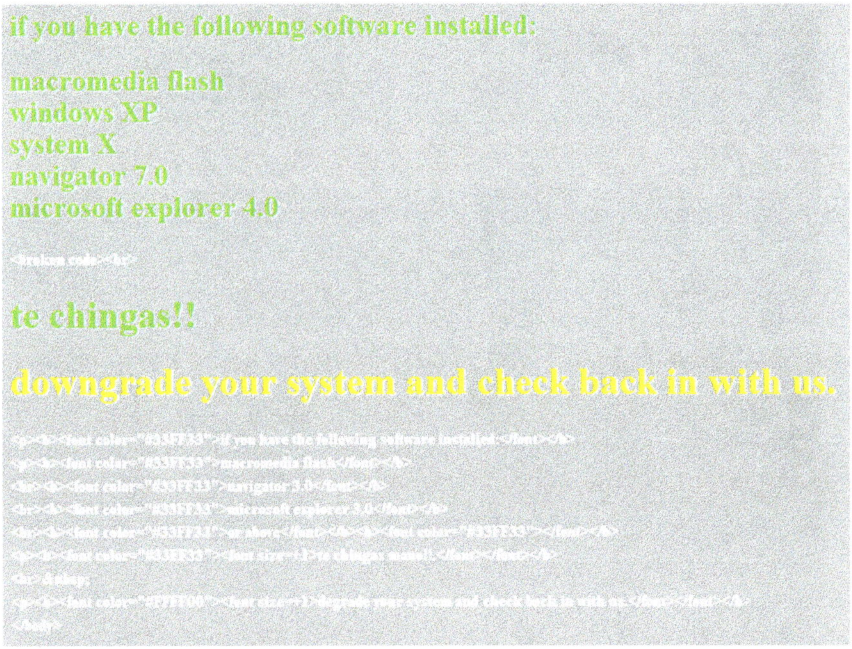

if you have the following software installed:

macromedia flash
windows XP
system X
navigator 7.0
microsoft explorer 4.0

te chingas!!

downgrade your system and check back in with us.

Fig. 5.4 Los Cybrids (René Garcia, John Jota Leaños and Praba Pilar), screen from opening sequence of website.

Fig. 5.5 Alex Rivera, *Cybracero Systems*, opening screen.

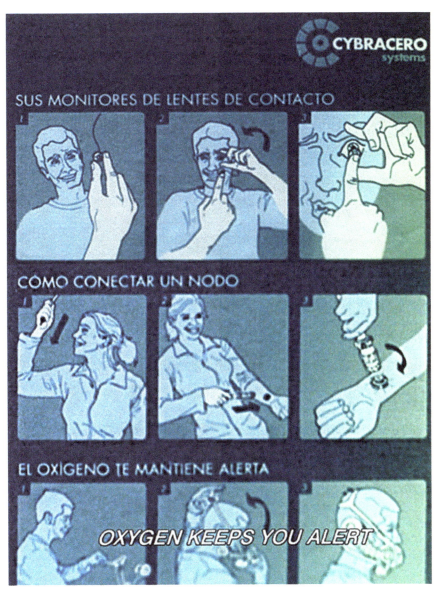

Fig. 5.6 Alex Rivera, *Cybracero Systems*, 'How to Node Up'.

Fig. 6.1 Fran Ilich, *possibleworlds.org* logo, from opening screen.

5   *Mestiz*@ Cyborgs

The Performance of Latin American-ness as (Critical) Racial Identity

FROM CIVILISATION AND BARBARISM TO *MESTIZAJE*

Where the previous chapter explored the continuing responses to the civilisation versus barbarism dichotomy that can be seen in online cultural products created by Latin Americans and Latinas/os,[1] this chapter focuses on a discourse of Latin American-ness that constructs its subject in an almost diametrically opposed manner: Instead of a discourse of dichotomy, the discourse of *mestizaje* is one of synthesis. Although the term *mestizaje* was used prominently to indicate the issue of racial mixture in the system of *castas* ['castes'] established at the inception of the colonial era,[2] a discourse of *mestizaje* designed to give a more positive appreciation of the mixed racial composition of the region started to emerge at the beginning of the Independence period in the speeches and writings of Simón Bolívar and then later in those of José Martí. It was given added impetus in the wake of the Mexican Revolution by José Vasconcelos's treatise *La raza cósmica* [*The Cosmic Race*] (1925), which had a notable impact across the region.

In the first instances of its positive resemanticisation *mestizaje* was conceptualised in primarily political terms and exalted as that which made the process of gaining independence from Spain necessary. In Bolívar's view, the fact that so many of the inhabitants of the colonies constituted 'a species midway between the legitimate proprietors [of the region] and the Spanish usurpers' meant that they needed to govern themselves to consolidate a sense of legitimacy (Bolívar, quoted in Miller 2004:8). *Mestizaje* was subsequently also identified as one of the key features that distinguished those in the Spanish-speaking parts of the Americas ('our *mestizo* America' in Martí's terms) from those in the English-speaking parts and in particular from the United States' obsession with (white) racial purity, both in terms of appearance and in terms of temperament and values. As a consequence of both of these uses, but of the latter in particular, it is truly fundamental to the emergence of a conceptualisation of specifically 'Latin American' identity both within the region and in the United States/Europe. Indeed, Marilyn Grace Miller also argues that the adoption of the term *Latin* America to define the region appealed to intellectuals such as Bolívar and Martí precisely because of the heterogeneity of the populations of classical antiquity and the discursive embrace of such heterogeneity in the writings of that era (Miller 2004:15).

Mestizaje as we know it today is a highly complex discourse. In its Bolivarian adaptation it was more about polity than race, and it has subsequently come to embrace all forms of cultural mixing. Nevertheless, the racial underpinnings that stem from the *casta* classification system can never be entirely theorised out of *mestizaje*. Despite acknowledging the overarching will in recent theorisations of terms such as *mestizaje* and hybridity to transcend racially determinist ways of thinking, Joshua Lund emphatically argues that '*to theorize hybridity is to operate within a discourse of race*' (Lund 2006:3; original emphasis). Furthermore, with respect to the discourse of *mestizaje* in particular, Miller also notes that it has tended to be reified by Latin American intellectuals, as well as by external commentators, who have paradoxically lost sight of the discourse's *a priori* focus on heterogeneity and process, and have instead attempted to fix it 'as the mark of Latin American *sameness*, as the most recognizable and pervasive condition of all peoples and cultural productions found south of the Rio Grande, as the mark of *la raza*' (Miller 2004:x; original emphasis). While Miller's discussion of *mestizaje* conceives of it as a discourse that goes well beyond issues of race, the racial underpinnings of the discourse are evident in the terms she chooses to use ('the mark of *la raza*'). Moreover, the prevalence of a racial discourse in the United States which focuses in particular on questions of hypodescent and phenotype, or even just skin colour—the 'marks' of race—has worked to further propagate an ever-more reified form of the discourse among and about today's Latino communities in which *mestizaje*, *raza*, *latinidad*, 'Latin looks', and even 'brownness' are all interchangeable and instead of an ongoing process where *mestizaje* is 'produced through a series of concrete *practices* that can never be reduced to a type of *body*' (González 2000a:47; original emphasis), 'real' *mestizaje* is lost to view and substituted by an *a priori* thing, an 'essential' brown body.[3] Furthermore, Miller argues that this reified conceptualisation of *mestizaje* as 'the mark of *la raza*' 'now becomes a synonym for all Latino expression *in* the United States' (Miller 2004:142, original italics).

Yet despite the threat of reification, cooption by the mainstream and sheer overuse, there are still cultural producers who work to create alternative expressions of *mestizaje* that are resistant to these dangers. Such approaches are the heirs to subaltern and subversive manifestations of *mestizaje* through history where the concept figures as a cipher for resistance to dominant ideologies, and, most importantly, they focus decisively on *mestizaje* as process rather than product. It is this kind of *mestizaje* that Rafael Pérez-Torres terms 'critical mestizaje'. As he warns, 'mestizaje, on either a cultural or a racial level, does not guarantee contestation. Only a constantly critical and questioning deployment of mestizaje—a mestizaje on the margins, so to speak—can move processes of identification beyond established and disabling social scripts' (Pérez-Torres 2006:66).

In order to start to identify the kinds of materials to be studied in this chapter and to grasp exactly how they might relate to Pérez-Torres's concept of 'critical mestizaje', it is useful to compare in more detail the discourses of civilisation/barbarism and *mestizaje*. Although the two discourses exist palimpsestically and in close dialogue with each other, there are fundamental differences in their application that need to be explored further. Unlike *mestizaje* and its racial underpinnings, the discourse concerning the civilisation versus barbarism dichotomy does not have to focus on the relationship between explicitly racialised groups—barbarians might be deemed to be different and hence inferior to civilised people, but they do not have to look different from civilised people at the level of the body itself. Questions of civilisation and barbarism are thus more of a matter of power, perspective and *performance*, and, in the analysis of the civilisation versus barbarism dichotomy as played out on the human body in the previous chapter, the focus was on denaturalising this performance of predominantly ethnic, cultural and/or national identities, achieved largely through the use of props (masks, veils and so on). It responded to the 'Where are you from?' question that defines ethnicity for Peter Wade (Wade 2010:17).

Although the conceptualisation of ethnicity is so close to that of race that the terms are often used interchangeably in common parlance, and although in academic discourse reference to 'ethnoracial' identities or groups is often the most accurate descriptor to be invoked, Wade's illuminating comparison of the conceptual reach of race in opposition to that of ethnicity is helpful in establishing the different ways in which these discourses work. Although both are social constructs rather than natural facts, 'racial identifications use aspects of phenotype as a cue for categorisation' and such categorisations have more often been used as the basis for discrimination than in the case of ethnicity (Wade 2010:19–20). Furthermore, Jennifer González emphasises that race is an 'importantly *visual* system of power' and that 'the visual truth effect of race has very real consequences even if the facts about race as a category or discourse reveal it to be primarily an ideological construction' (González 2006:341; original emphasis). As a result of the visual nature of race it tends to be interpreted as less of a matter of performance than as a natural fact revealed by the naked body (rather than through the use of selected props). Representations that seek to reveal race always run the risk of reifying it in an unhelpful way, whatever the intentions of their creators.[4] In comparison with the discourse of civilisation/barbarism and the performance of ethnicity, then, the racial discourse of *mestizaje* is much more of a tug-of-war between the tendency to reify the raced body through representation and the potential to keep manifestations of the raced body performative.

This chapter therefore seeks out not cultural products that offer examples of the performance of Latin American-ness through the deployment of culturally significant props above all else, but ones that foreground, problematise and question the integrity of the Latin(o) American racialised body, particularly in the context of new (networked) technologies. These are materials that more often than not impress upon the viewer their desire to explore issues of race through their exposure of significant expanses of *brown* flesh. Nevertheless, in order to avoid the dangers of reification and offer examples of Pérez-Torres's 'critical mestizaje', cultural products that seek to explore race and racial mixing in innovative, *critical* ways will still need to move beyond the display of phenotypical racial markers to a *performance* of race in order to underscore its constructed-ness and its historical specificity, in particular the never-complete process of *mestizaje*.

LATINO (AMERICAN) *MESTIZAJE* AND CYBORG CONSCIOUSNESS

There are very close parallels to be drawn between a discourse of racial mixing such as *mestizaje* and discourses concerning the threatened integrity of the human body in our present era of techno-scientific inventions and networked digital technologies. The exponentially increasing possibilities of hybridising human bodies and machines have been both celebrated and feared. While much popular *Wired*-inspired discourse championed the emancipatory potential of new technologies to enhance and extend human lives through implants and other interventions, or to free us from the limitations of our bodies altogether in the apparently raceless, genderless expanses of 'cyberspace', such utopianist dreams were quickly checked by more critical work that has focused on the rather less liberatory effects of the medical technologies now available and on the persistence of gender, and later race, as signifiers of inequality in virtual environments. The maximum cipher of these changes and challenges to human ontology is the figure of the cyborg, a (human) organism integrated with (networked) technologies. The cyborg has been interpreted by Steve Dixon (not unproblematically) as, in the first instance, 'a technological response to existential and spiritual uncertainties and crises within late industrial Western societies, symbolizing a human desire for wholeness within an alchemical, technological matrix' as well as 'a quest to leave the frail and fallible mortal body behind, and to enter an immortal (or at least, endlessly upgradable) machine one' (Dixon 2007:306). According to Dixon, the concept of the cyborg thus suggests both a positive embrace of disembodiment, freedom from the 'meat' of material existence and the liberation of consciousness, even if it also expresses in its monstrosity our qualms about what might be lost along the way.

Theoretical works elaborating on the nature of cyborgs developed rapidly from the mid-1980s with the publication of Donna Haraway's seminal work on 'cyborg consciousness', 'A Cyborg Manifesto: Science, Technology, and Socialist-Feminism in the Late Twentieth Century',[5] and they peaked in the mid- to late 1990s with the publication of Chris Hables Gray's anthology *The Cyborg Handbook* (1995), and a series of influential works on 'posthumanism', most notably Judith Halberstam and Ira Livingstone's *Posthuman Bodies* (1995) and N. Katherine Hayles's *How We Became Posthuman: Virtual Bodies in Cybernetics, Literature and Informatics* (1999).

Representations and performances of cyborgic personae emerged in dialogue with cyborg theory—both inspiring it and responding to it, and this in both on- and offline media. According to Dixon, cyborg figures in performance art in particular have sometimes sought to take cyborg theory to its logical conclusions—here the work of Australian performance artist Stelarc and Brazilian Eduardo Kac is paradigmatic, with both announcing through their cyborgic performances the obsolescence of the body (Stelarc) and of the skin (Kac) (Dixon 2007:306–21). Nevertheless cyborg figures in performance art more often seem to offer a critique of the theorisations of disembodiment through the manifest materiality of both flesh and frequently of metal, too. Given the general preference in much performance art for imposing, and often fairly low-tech, metallic prostheses to signal cyborgism—as opposed to the highly sophisticated prosthetics of Stelarc or unobtrusive computer chip implants *à la* Kac—they 'frequently [celebrate] an eroticized sexuality of metal' and 'exalt in the conjunction of the hard and the soft; the natural and the technological; the metal and the meat' (Dixon 2007:331). This Dixon identifies as a camp aesthetic in its reliance on excessive theatricality. Nevertheless, a question that this chapter will pose itself is whether, if cyborg bodies also reveal the raced body as the base organism with which prostheses are melded, they will still be read as camp. Can the critical function of the cyborg in performance art be sustained under such conditions or will the appearance of the raced body—particularly in conjunction with 'eroticized sexuality'—disturb this critical function and instead see the figures collapse into the mainstream reification of the racialised other?

Given that the figure of the cyborg has clear parallels with that of the *mestiza/o*, it would seem reasonable to expect that cyborgs would also appear in Latin(o) American cultural production with an interest in, or made for dissemination via, new (networked) technologies and that these figures would be used to reflect critically on racial mixing in the contemporary, technologically mediated world. Nevertheless, in Andrew Brown's *Cyborgs in Latin America* (2010), there is only one passing reference to the conjunction of cyborg and *mestiza/o* subjectivities via Jerry Hoeg's early and highly suggestive, but non-racially specific, formulation of 'cybermestizaje'.[6] In fact the real focus of Brown's chapter is on the issue of posthumanism and gender in a Latin American context, and the book as a whole concerns responses to posthumanism in the region and typically reads the cyborg in relation to neoliberalism or postdictatorship society rather than as a figure with any statement to make about race. Brown's monograph undoubtedly seeks to do justice to the nature of those cyborgs appearing in Latin American literature and film and the conclusion to be drawn is that there is a dearth of *mestiza/o* cyborgs that seek to reflect on the conjunction of *mestizaje* and cyborgism in the offline Latin American cultural production examined. A brief study of Latin American online cultural production also reveals few cyborgs—despite the projects of Kac mentioned above—and fewer still which set out to reflect on the relationship of cyborgs to the discourse of *mestizaje*.

Nevertheless, a startlingly different picture emerges if one considers the online cultural production of Latinas/os where there is a proliferation of cyborg figures, most of which evidence a clearly racialised (if also cyborgic) body. Given the prevalence of the racialisation of Latina/o identities in the United States, it is no real surprise to find that questions of racial identity and Latino (American)-ness are frequently of central importance in such online work. Where this is examined with a specific focus on the dialogue between new technology and racial identity, this is often focalised via the figure of the *mestiza/o* cyborg. Furthermore, the figure of the cyborg is arguably the most significant vehicle for a discussion of race in Latino (American) online cultural production—other more naturalistic representations of brown bodies online tend to be more closely aligned with discourses and performances of ethnic/cultural identity than specifically with issues of race.[7] However, it is not simply a case of such cultural producers focusing on the figure of the cyborg in order to challenge mainstream US society's assumptions that certain racial groups are 'primitive' and hence unsuited to dealing with high technology, let alone integrating it into their own bodies. Nor is it just a case of excessive revelling in all possible forms of hybridity to emphasise the hybrid nature of these Latina/o artists' *mestiza/o* identities. While all this is of relevance, the Latina/o interest in cyborgs is also very timely. It suggests a dialogue with, possibly even a challenge to, the mainstream Anglo-American academy and its move in the 1980s and 1990s to appropriate *mestizaje* via cooption into a more generic discourse of hybridity/cyborgism. It also suggests a way of trying to problematise the reification and fetishisation of the brown body seen in mainstream US society's commodification of the sexy Latina/o brown body and its demonisation of the pathological and dangerous (usually male) brown body during the same period.[8] Latina/o cyborgs may thus signify an attempt to redeploy the discourse of *mestizaje* in all its specificity and disturbing messiness, although again, this comes with multiple caveats about the achievability of such an enterprise.

With respect to the desire to challenge the Anglo-American academy's attempted appropriation of *mestizaje*, it should be noted that many of the Latino/a cultural producers in question were closely involved in the Southern Californian academic world that was the birthplace of cyborg theory in the late 1980s and early 1990s, and they would have undoubtedly been aware of the association of the figure of *la mestiza* and that of the cyborg that was at the heart of Donna Haraway's work on 'cyborg consciousness'. In 'A Cyborg Manifesto', an essay that began appearing in different versions from the mid-1980s onwards, Haraway used Chicana cultural theory as a key support for her own theorisations and the link has been made repeatedly, for better or for worse, by subsequent theorists who have drawn on her formulations. In the essay itself Haraway warns that 'by the late twentieth century, our time, a mythic time, we are all chimeras, theorized and fabricated hybrids of machine and organism; in short, we are cyborgs' (Haraway 1991:150). That is to say that modern science offers us all technological implants/interfaces that enhance and maintain us (pacemakers, crowns or simply access to computers and other gadgets). Furthermore, she warns that with the growth in nanotechnology, 'The ubiquity and invisibility of cyborgs is precisely why these sunshine-belt machines are so deadly. They are as hard to see politically as materially' (Haraway 1991:153). Much cyborg-related technology, then, is very reactionary in nature—it is simply an extension of capitalist/patriarchal/state control over us in order to ensure the maintenance of a smooth-running and compliant workforce. Nevertheless, what Haraway hopes for in her manifesto is that 'liberation rests on the construction of the consciousness, the imaginative apprehension, of oppression, and so of possibility' (Haraway 1991:149). What she wants to identify and promote is a 'cyborg consciousness' that, despite being the product of powerful interests, can critique and challenge that paradigm of control: 'The main trouble with cyborgs, of course, is that they are the illegitimate offspring of militarism and patriarchal capitalism, not to mention state socialism. But illegitimate offspring are often exceedingly unfaithful to their origins' (Haraway 1991:151). According to Haraway, it is those unfaithful ones that will be most resistant/conscious. Furthermore, given that Haraway argues that invisible cyborgs are the most reactionary, it follows that the most resistant ones will also be visible. Only where cyborgs are visible can they prompt reflection on what they mean.

Much of the remainder of Haraway's manifesto then goes on to compare the resistant 'cyborg' with the subject of Third World feminism, with prominent references to the figure of La Malinche,[9] and in so doing she draws heavily on the work of Chela Sandoval whose doctoral thesis focused on Chicana/Latina/Third World feminisms and made judicious, grounded use of Chicana feminist Gloria Anzaldúa's theorisations of '*mestiza* consciousness'. In particular Haraway identifies Sandoval's work on 'oppositional consciousness' and the resistant methodologies ('technologies') of 'women of color' as having strong parallels with her formulation of 'cyborg consciousness'.

In Sandoval's 1995 essay written in response to Haraway's, 'New Sciences: Cyborg Feminism and the Methodology of the Repressed', and published in *The Cyborg Handbook*, Sandoval critiques Haraway for parts of her early formulation of cyborg consciousness (although she does allow that Haraway has subsequently revised her position). Sandoval contends that '[Haraway's] work inadvertently contributed to [the] tendency to elide the specific theoretical contributions of U.S. third world feminist criticism by turning many of its approaches, methods, forms and skills into examples of cyborg feminism' (Sandoval 1999:255), whence the endless references to '*la mestiza*', with or without reference to Anzaldúa's work, in so much cyborg and cyberfeminist criticism regarding identity formation.[10] Sandoval also notes that Haraway's work posits 'oppositional "cyborg" politics' as something new, an argument that Sandoval's work has always sought to counter: 'My argument has been that colonized peoples of the Americas have already developed the cyborg skills required for survival under techno-human conditions as a requisite for survival under domination of the last three hundred years' (Sandoval 1999:248). To sum up her position, then, Sandoval concedes that she is writing in order to address the elisions described above and to specify simply that 'cyborg consciousness can be understood as the technological embodiment of a particular and specific form of oppositional consciousness that [she has] elsewhere described as "U.S. third world feminism"' (Sandoval 1999:248). She then goes on to flesh out more fully the commonalities that 'cyborg feminism' has with the 'techniques and terminologies' such as *mestizaje*, derived from Third World feminism.

Sandoval's response to Haraway attempts to ensure that the relationship of cyborg theory to *mestizaje* is more carefully acknowledged and it challenges the fuzzy multiculturalist political stance that slips too easily from the statement that 'we are [all] cyborgs' to the implicit claim that 'we are all *mestizas/os*'.[11] We might expect Latina/o cultural producers to effect a similar manoeuvre to Sandoval in their cyborgic performances, as they make apparent their Latina/o cyborgic specificity, yet without dismantling Haraway's optimistic arguments about the potential for resistance to the system altogether. After all, apart from eliding *mestizaje* with cyborg consciousness, Haraway's manifesto argues for precisely the kind of resistant stance that lies at the base of (critical) *mestizaje*. One might also assume that the performance of a visibly *mestiza/o* cyborg—doubly visible, through the brown skin tone and the prostheses that identify it as cyborg—would serve to emphasise the resistant nature of the '*mestiza/o* cyborg consciousness' that the creator of that figure wishes to deploy.[12] But again, these assumptions based on Haraway's manifesto may prove too optimistic and, instead, as suggested earlier, the visibility of race may simply combine with the alternately violent and sexually titillating signs of cyborgism as outlined by Dixon and reduce the performance to an example of the reification of race so prevalent in mainstream American media. *Mestizaje* and cyborgism may simply function to neutralise each other.

While the consideration of race and its representation online[13] did not emerge as strongly in the first instance as the exploration of issues of gender and online representation including cyborg consciousness,[14] there has been a line of criticism that stretches back as far as *The Cyborg Handbook* that is attentive to the conjunction of issues of race/subalternity/postcoloniality and cyborgism and that seriously questions whether a resistant cyborgic subject position of this nature can exist at all. In stark contradiction to Haraway's theories, Joseba Gabilondo asserted provocatively that 'there is no such thing/subject as a "postcolonial cyborg"' since 'postcolonial subject positions are always left outside cyberspace' (Gabilondo 1995:424), although, to be sure, by 'cyborg' Gabilondo means the particular subjectivity to be found in cyberspace, rather than any more literal fusion of human and machine. Jennifer González has interpreted Gabilondo's statement to mean that if we see something that *looks like* a 'postcolonial cyborg' it will have already been commodified and incorporated into mainstream popular culture and its ability to resist will have been thus neutralised (González 2000a:43–45). An identifiable raced cyborg figure in circulation online, therefore, will be simply (interpreted as) an unproblematic commodity rather than as a prompt for critical reflection because popular culture does not believe race or racism to have any place online. David J. Hess's article, 'On Low-Tech Cyborgs', also in *The Cyborg Handbook*, concedes that subaltern, raced, cyborgs do exist, but interprets them as playing an expendable, subordinate role in an ongoing grand narrative that Anglo-American popular culture tells itself to ensure its hegemony. He suggests that (more literal) cyborgs in US popular culture seem to recycle 'the same old tale of the Lone Ranger and Tonto, a story about American culture's fundamental problem with the acceptance of ethnic or racial difference' and that a film such as *Terminator II* (dir. James Cameron 1991) 'might be read as revealing white America's insecurity in a multicultural society: the cyborgetic Tontos emerge strong and powerful, but the movie also ends by throwing, quite literally, the cyborgs into the great melting pot' (Hess 1995:372).[15] Finally, in a brief overview of literal cyborgs that are 'racially "marked" as not "white"' in contemporary offline popular culture and which typically correspond to '(mostly male) cyborg fantasies' of 'a powerful, yet vulnerable, combination of sex toy and techno-sophisticate', Jennifer González concludes that 'Cyborg bodies [. . . do not]—as yet—function as radical alternatives. It may be that the cyborg is now in a new and progressive phase, but its "racial" body politics have a long way to go' (González 2000b:548–50).

A similar picture emerges when we move to examine the way that mixed-race identities have been represented online—a subject position that is frequently elided with that of the more literal cyborg either on- or offline on account of the overlap between discourses of racial hybridity and cyborgism and because the online dimension of the representation of human subjectivities already leads to cyborg subjectivities in Gabilondo's terms. Lisa Nakamura has argued that the architecture of mainstream user interfaces such as drop-down menus has tended to work to abridge options for the expression of mixed-race identities altogether (Nakamura 2002:101–35). By contrast Jennifer González's study of the representation of novel racial 'combinations' in two net.art projects finds that there is an overwhelming tendency to flaunt the endless possibilities of racial mixing via combinations of different body parts, but that this simply trades in racial stereotypes that ultimately offer nothing new, if not are downright reactionary. She finds that these net.art projects, despite their best intentions, offer 'a narrow or ahistorical conception of hybridity' and cause problems for themselves by equating 'cultural identity or self-representation [. . .] with a configuration of body parts' (González 2000a:46&47). This kind of uncritical hybridity works to erase the violence done to racially 'other' bodies during the history of colonial expansion. Furthermore, while combinations of body parts might seem to be a good way of signalling a nonessentialist conceptualisation of race and racial hybridity in visual terms by denaturalising the mixture, they are too easily subsumed by a confluence of eugenicist thought and online consumerism.

The vast majority of the reified examples of (mixed-)race cyborgs given above are produced by mainstream media conglomerates or at the very least not by artists of colour. For Latina/o cultural producers their representation of *mestiza/o* cyborg figures will not automatically be read as more resistant. While this chapter is necessarily cautious about the potential of any cyborg figure to avoid reification and resist 'the system', if there is a way to do this, it will be encapsulated in the production of noticeable, yet mutable, *mestiza/o* cyborg figures in performative online environments where they are less easily reified. Arguably a key part of what may signal the difference between reactionary (mixed-)race cyborgs produced by mainstream Anglo-America and (potentially resistant) Latina/o *mestiza/o* cyborgs will be simply the framing or staging of the work, the signature, the artist's homepage, the URL. While performance art often requires a disturbing of the frame in order to be effective, where the frame is lost altogether the resistant objectives of the cultural producer behind the performance may be lost too.

MESTIZA/O CYBORGS

With all this in mind, this chapter now proposes to examine in more detail the work of three (groups of) Latina/o cultural producers who have devoted significant attention to the representation of *mestiza/o* cyborgs, and, beyond the obvious stacking up of evidence of the proliferation of such figures, to try to tease out the different aims and achievements of each. In doing this the balance between the fetishisation of the brown body and the performance of a more critical (although still racially focused) form of *mestizaje* is key. The examples chosen for study in the remainder of the chapter unsurprisingly all have some relationship to performance art. The first artist to be studied is Guillermo Gómez-Peña (along with his performance troupe La Pocha Nostra) who has played a seminal conscience-raising role with respect to the issue of race and (networked) digital technology. As noted in the previous chapter, his work has tended to move from a focus on race and *mestizaje* in his early performance art to broader questions of globalisation and civilisation versus barbarism in his more recent, post–9/11 work. While his early work that is the subject of this chapter tended to be predominantly offline, where Gómez-Peña does use the internet to disseminate aspects of his offline performances, he tends to use it simply as an online gallery space rather than in the interactive—hence more fully performative—game format of some of his later work such as that examined in the previous chapter. While the frame of the online gallery space provides a context that ensures resistant readings based on the artist's reputation, Gómez-Peña's representation of *mestiza/o* cyborg figures itself does run a significant risk of reification through loss of performativity.

The second group of artists known as Los Cybrids: La Raza Techno-Crítica [The Cybrids: The Techno-Critical Race] also tended to perform and to create multimedia and installation art offline in the early 2000s, mainly with a view to dismissing new technology as having a nefarious impact on the Latino community (the group is 'techno-crítica'), and only using the internet to better disseminate its offline work. However, this chapter also deems significant its *performance* of a *mestiza/o* 'cybrid' identity, particularly in the disturbing opening sequence of its website. Finally, the chapter moves on to the work of film director and digital media artist Alex Rivera who, again, has generally used the internet as simply a means of disseminating his short films/mockumentaries. Nevertheless, his *Cybracero Systems* website is another example of how a website can function as a performance in itself. It is these rather more difficult to circumscribe examples of online performance art that provide the most sophisticated approaches to the representation/performance of race through their deployment of *mestiza/o* cyborg figures and principles, even if they simultaneously run the risk of losing the frame, and hence their critical context, altogether.

GUILLERMO GÓMEZ-PEÑA'S EVER-MUTATING ETHNO-CYBORGS AND HYPER-RACIALISED REPLICANTS

The work of Guillermo Gómez-Peña offers a highly suggestive starting point for the discussion of virtually any aspect of *latinidad* and networked digital culture. His statements about cyberspace and its implicit borders that exclude Latin Americans and other subaltern subjects might have justified inclusion in Chapter One with its focus on cartographic imaginaries; his conceptualisation of an alternative Latino 'virtual' or 'cyber barrio' might have seen him figure in the Chapter Two with respect to the discourse of the Lettered City; his invocation of revolution and resistance through reference to the Zapatistas might have justified his inclusion in Chapter Six; and indeed his work that revises the civilisation versus barbarism dichotomy is already the subject of detailed study in Chapter Four of the present study. Nevertheless, it is absolutely inevitable that his work should also be considered in some detail in the context of a chapter on *latinidad* as a (mixed-) racial identity. It is, arguably, this aspect of his work that has attracted most attention from critics, particularly those working on cyberculture/digital culture/new media within the anglophone academy.[16]

Given that so much of what Gómez-Peña has had to say on the subject of a clearly racialised concept of *latinidad*, particularly in conjunction with the subject of new technologies/the internet, has been so often repeated both by critics and by Gómez-Peña himself, no broad introduction will be provided here (although, tellingly, it is the nature of these repetitions and their ongoing mutations and contradictions that already suggest a key to interpreting Gómez-Peña's work). The argument that this section proposes to advance with regard to Gómez-Peña's representation and/or performance of *mestiza/o* cyborgs is as follows: Gómez-Peña's statements on race and *mestizaje* fluctuate between essentialism and a more critical approach. In particular, his approach to the relationship between Latin(o) Americans and new technologies/the internet, although suggesting a healthy challenge to mainstream (white) American assumptions on the subject based on this group's racialised and racist approach to *latinidad* (in Gómez-Peña estimation) and hence evidencing Gómez-Peña's desire to move beyond mainstream society's essentialist approach to race, also clearly relies on an amount of strategic essentialism (and downright exaggeration) to define both groups. Where he creates figures that he denominates 'ethno-cyborgs'[17] and puts them into circulation in online 'galleries' (as an extension of his offline performances), should we expect to find figures that challenge the prevalent reification of raced bodies online, in particular, perhaps, because of their articulation of a 'disturbing' and unstable combination of raced bodies and technology? Or will his (strategic) essentialism mean that these figures are too easily reincorporated into the fears and desires of the mainstream (racist) imaginary that he purports to challenge as proof that Gabilondo was right when he declared that there was no such thing as a 'postcolonial cyborg'? In short, is what Gómez-Peña thinks he is doing demonstrable by results?

In terms of Gómez-Peña's attitude to race and *mestizaje*, in Foster's estimation he 'has acknowledged his willingness to move between a strategic essentialism and a strategic antiessentialism, depending on audience' (Foster 2002:58). Nevertheless, the real, heart-felt rather than strategic, approach in Gómez-Peña's own view is clearly anti-essentialist. As he stated in an interview with Jennifer González with reference to traditional, reified conceptualisations of *mestizaje*,

> *Mestizaje* is a thing of the past. Binary models are no longer operative [. . .]. What do you do with Post-Mexicanos? We're the product of several racial mixtures and many overlapping subcultures. What are we then? Post-mestizos? Meta-mestizos? [. . .] Our identities are in permanent flux. [. . .] More than mestizos, our multiracial and multicultural kids are poly-cultural (and poly-gendered) cyborgs.
>
> (González and Gómez-Peña 2009:253).[18]

Despite his rejection of *mestizaje per se*, these comments are entirely consonant with Pérez-Torres's definition of 'critical mestizaje' as 'a constantly critical and questioning deployment' (Pérez-Torres 2006:66). And based on the above, cyborg figures, either literal or more metaphorical, are where this kind of approach to race should be in evidence.

However, in terms of Gómez-Peña's approach to new technologies, where he attempts to appropriate and infiltrate the world of high technology on behalf of Latin(o) Americans, there is almost always a rather more pola-rised racial dynamic to his thinking. Gómez-Peña's interest in challenging the mainstream (white) American assumption that Latin Americans are primitives and hence that their racial genealogy itself means that they are unsuited to dealing with technology predates his move to comment on the role of the internet or produce material for circulation online (Gómez-Peña 2000:251–52). With the advent of the internet in the early 1990s, he quickly began to articulate an updated set of concerns. In his much reedited mani-festo-like essay, 'The Virtual Barrio @ The Other Frontier; or, The Chicano Interneta' (1995–97),[19] he challenged the utopianist conceptualisation of a 'cyberspace' that was purportedly raceless but tacitly white and anglophone, arguing that, 'forced to assume the unpleasant but necessary roles of web-backs, cyber-aliens, techno-pirates, and virtual *coyotes*',[20] Chicana/o artists would attempt 'to "brownify" virtual space; to "spanglishize" the net, and "infect" the *linguas francas*' (Gómez-Peña 2000:258–59).

This racial, as well as linguistic, polarisation is also apparent—alongside other polarising discourses such as that of civilisation versus barbarism—in a slightly later performance piece, 'Tech-illa Sunrise (.txt dot con Sangrita)', co-authored with Rafael Lozano-Hemmer, which narrates 'excerpts from the cyber-testament'. In this account the explicitly white frontiersman (of so much of the early rhetoric of cyberspace) ironically recalls the 'good old days' of 'the Cambrian era of cyberspace': 'We were young, ambitious and white, / & there was no one else around to bother us.' He then goes on to narrate the loss of that cyber-eden: 'Then came the Others, / brown people, tar people, e-mongrels of sorts, / speaking bizarre linguas polutas. / The cybarbarians came from the South of nothingness, / & rapidly moved North into "the zone"' (Lozano-Hemmer and Gómez-Peña 2001).

What is evident in all of the above is Gómez-Peña's direct challenge to what he sees as the hegemonic conceptualisation of new technology as white and pure. Instead he attempts to reverse the dynamics of the new medium point for point. He hence challenges the dazzling whiteness and the frontiersman/colonialist rhetoric of early anglophone cyberspace with a determination to 'pollute' and 'brownify' those spaces via a process of 'unauthorised' colonisation (the creation of a 'virtual barrio' of 'web-backs' and 'e-mongrels'). It is this point-for-point approach that substitutes white for brown, pure for mongrel, and hegemonic colonisation for subaltern infiltration (yet a form of colonisation nonetheless), that has the potential to be the Achilles' heel of Gómez-Peña's approach. He might articulate opposition to hegemonic positions but, in the (strategic) essentialism of his approach, he still remains bound by hegemonic paradigms of thought themselves. He still works within the binaristic racialised discourse of mainstream US society.

Nevertheless, Gómez-Peña's stance on race in/and cyberspace is not quite so easily dismissed as just a simple politics of inversion which actually delivers more of the same. In 'Tech-illa Sunrise' Lozano-Hemmer and Gómez-Peña posit 'brown' not so much as the opposite of white as might elsewhere appear to be the case, but as a contrast to the US racial polarities of black and white: it is a third position. They propose that Lupita, a (voracious) Latina service provider,

> has long ago dropped the binary code in favour of a recombinant self-organizing system of neural nets interconnected via EMR fields that allow for complex emergent phenomena, lighter and deeper shades of brown.
>
> El ciberespacio es café, no blanco ni negro, remember [. . .]
>
> [Cyberspace is coffee-coloured, not black nor white][21]
>
> (Lozano-Hemmer and Gómez-Peña 2001)

While this kind of tactic might essentialise black and white bodies and subject positions, it provides a more radical conceptualisation of brown ones. The brown bodies that Gómez-Peña wants to see infiltrating cyberspace are also implicitly not (just) attractive, aspirational Latina/o bodies with smooth (milky) coffee-coloured skin as commodified by corporate America as the 'generic pan-Hispanic' (cf. Dávila 2002:272–73). The invented verb 'to brownify' and the reference to 'brown people, tar people, e-mongrels of sorts' suggest distaste and dirtiness. These terms are semantically unappealing, unassimilatable by mainstream culture, and hence suggest that Gómez-Peña is invoking a radical form of *mestizaje*, one that mutates and recombines to keep up its challenge to unsettle the binaries of hegemonic culture—if coffee-coloured mixtures are now acceptable, an invocation of more disturbing and complex mixtures follows.

The potential to mutate and propagate exponentially also chimes with Gómez-Peña's championing of virality as modus operandi. In 'The Virtual Barrio' Gómez-Peña argued that Latin(o) American 'Web-backs' should aim to constitute 'el nuevo virus virtual' (Gómez-Peña 2000:260), and in 'Tech-illa Sunrise' Lonzano-Hemmer and Gómez-Peña scripted a parodic virus alert for what they called 'QuetZalcoat-82L or simply "The Mexican Bug"' (Lonzano-Hemmer and Gómez-Peña 2001), made more realistic by the fact that so many known computer viruses have stemmed from Latin America.[22] These positive invocations of Latino virality seek to challenge the popular imaginary and its hasty association of race with infection and disease, contamination and dirtiness. As Nakamura has argued on the subject of attempts by chatroom users to identify themselves racially,

> race in cyberspace is conceptualized as a bug, something an efficient computer user would eradicate since it contaminates her work/play. The unexpected occurrence of race has the potential, by its very unexpectedness, to sabotage the ideology-machine's routines.
>
> (Nakamura 2002:48–49)[23]

They also seek to turn on its head the history of (self-)conceptualisations of Latin America as more passively, congenitally diseased, in large part on account of its racial make-up (cf. Trigo 2000). In Gómez-Peña's work the dynamics of racial mixing are thus articulated as a mutant, recombinant bug, and they are conceived as extremely efficient in their functioning as such. Furthermore, the association of *mestizaje* with virality helps Gómez-Peña keep *mestizaje* critical—virality is a dynamic that is much less easily reified into a resultant body than *mestizaje* because it is more a question of an unseen agent or principle than an identifiable body in itself.

Theories of *mestizaje* and virality might sound very promising; however, the visual representation and performance of such theories is another matter. In order to appreciate Gómez-Peña's approach to *mestizaje* online, this chapter will now focus on a more detailed analysis of the appearance on his websites of key performance personae. As proof of his determination to gatecrash white cyberspace, in 1994 Gómez-Peña started to create performances that incorporated an interactive online dimension, most notably *The Temple of Confessions*, later known as *The Ethno-Cyberpunk Trading Post and Curio Shop on the Electronic Frontier*. The interactive online element comprised a questionnaire concerning mainstream 'white' fears and desires regarding the racialised Latina/o other that was used to gather data which would directly inform the creation of performance personae in subsequent work such as the *Mexterminator* project (1995–). The questionnaire elicited such a significant volume of responses of an openly confessional nature that it was kept online and used as a source of material for a number of years (Gómez-Peña 2000:47). In 1998 Gómez-Peña and his performance troupe, La Pocha Nostra, launched their first website—entitled *La Pocha Nostra*—that gathered together extant materials from their various offline projects (Gómez-Peña and La Pocha Nostra 1998–2003). This was superseded in 2003 by a newer, more elaborate version entitled *Gómez-Peña's Pocha Nostra* and which contained some works intended exclusively for circulation online (Gómez-Peña 2003–).

There is a common thread that leads from the materials gathered from *The Ethno-Cyberpunk Trading Post* questionnaire through to the composite performance personae of the *Mexterminator* project (an ironic reworking of the iconography and message of the *Terminator* films [1991–] and their mainstream assimilation of the racial-other-as-cyborg referenced earlier). It then continues through the online dissemination of images from the *Mexterminator* project on the first *Pocha* website (see, for example, 'Ethno-Techno: A Virtual Museum of Radical Latino Imagery and Fetishized Identities' [1998–c.2000]),[24] and on to the more fully internet-based work on the current website (see, for example, *The Chica-Iranian Project* [2005b]).[25] That common thread is Gómez-Peña's predilection for what he chooses to call 'ethno-cyborgs'. Many of the early ethno-cyborgs from the *Mexterminator* project have appeared reworked in slightly different configurations in Gómez-Peña's other projects from the last fifteen years—films, 'video-graffitis', public radio interviews and so on—and personae such as El Mad Mex and Cyber-Vato have come to be some of the most instantly recognisable characters in his repertoire.

There is no doubt that in his work with ethno-cyborgs Gómez-Peña is responding to academic debates on cyborgism and the (prosthetic?) appropriation of *mestiza/o* subjectivity therein. Thomas Foster notes the similarities between Gómez-Peña's conceptualisation of La Chingada[26] as part of a Fifth (virtual) world—an ethno-cyborgic figure, therefore—in his *New World Border* (1996) and Haraway's 'Cyborg Manifesto' and its association of the cyborg figure with La Malinche (Foster 2002:47). Furthermore, in the introduction to his essay 'Ethno-cyborgs and Genetically Engineered Mexicans: Recent Experiments in "Ethno-Techno" Art', Gómez-Peña explicitly outlines the debates on the status of the human body in relation to new technologies in the mid-1990s in the US art world (Gómez-Peña 2000:45). He argues that the art world's response to new technologies is either all celebratory, all machine with a consequent erasure of race or it effects a retreat into 'neotribal paganism', and that 'none of these options were viable [. . .] for Chicano/Latino performance artists and other politicized artists of color interested in new technologies' (Gómez-Peña 2000:45). The remainder of the essay traces the development of his response to this, articulated specifically via the figure of the ethno-cyborg.

Gómez-Peña's conceptualisation of the ethno-cyborg is deliberately very loose such that it can refer metaphorically to the ethnic/cultural/national composite figures, identifiable above all else by their clashing costumes and props, that were analysed in Chapter Four of this volume, as well as to more literal cyborg figures which display visible signs of their part-raced-human, part-machine composition. In work from the *Mexterminator* period, metaphorical ethno-cyborgs included La Cultural Transvestite, performed by Sara Shelton-Mann and only identifiable as a cyborg in Gómez-Peña's description of his work with ethno-cyborg figures (Gómez-Peña 2000:54). Other ethno-cyborgs such as El Mad Mex (performed by Gómez-Peña himself, and also referred to as El Mexterminator or El Ethnographic Loco in other versions) and Cyber-Vato (performed by Roberto Cifuentes) were much more easily recognisable as figures that combined clearly raced human bodies (via the exposure of expanses of naked brown flesh, as well as significant amounts of luxuriant brown hair) and machines (typically via low-tech prosthetic arms made of plastic painted silver [Dixon 2007:328]).

It is of course the case that many ethno-cyborgs in Gómez-Peña and colleagues' repertoire blur such distinctions between the literal and the metaphoric. Visible prostheses, for example—particularly very low-tech, 'techno-rascuache' ones, in Gómez-Peña's terms, that are more postfracture supportive orthosis than permanent prosthesis—may be read as simply another form of ethnocultural prop and interpreted as part of the low-brow, kitsch-looking bricolage approach of Chicano *rasquache* aesthetics.[27] Nevertheless, in the conceptualisation of the more literal ethno-cyborg personae in

Gómez-Peña's 'new pantheon of mighty robo-Mexicans', although working in conjunction with the props, it is the display of the raced body itself that is set centre-stage. Gómez-Peña describes these 'robo-Mexicans' as being 'armed with mysterious shamanic artifacts and sci-fi automatic weapons, their bodies enhanced with prosthetic implants and their *brown skin* decorated with Aztec tattoos' (Gómez-Peña 2000:50; added emphasis), and as 'refracting fetishized constructs of identity through the spectacle of [their] *"primitive," eroticized bodies on display*' (Gómez-Peña 2000:49; added emphasis). These personae are also referred to interchangeably as 'hyper-racialised replicants',[28] borrowing the term 'replicant' from *Blade Runner* (dir. Ridley Scott 1982) where it was coined to designate a cyborg that is all machine on the inside with only the form/the skin of a human. While this use of the term might help embrace the more metaphorical ethno-cyborgs within the 'pantheon of mighty robo-Mexicans', in its highly ironic application to literal ethno-cyborgs that do display visible traces of cyborgism such as El Mad Mex and Cyber-Vato, it works to further underscore the centrality of race to Gómez-Peña's articulation of these personae. It is thus these more literal cyborg figures that are the subject of the current chapter because it is in these cases that Gómez-Peña may be seen to dialogue with the question of racial identity most decisively.

El Mad Mex, for example, is a character part shaman, part gangsta as evidenced by his props (a skull on a pole and a high-tech–looking weapon in one incarnation[29]). In a variation on the theme, he wears a basque suggesting a transvestite/transgender identity, and his crutch and US army jacket also suggest that he is a war veteran, and insist upon his closeness to mainstream, Anglo-American society. Nevertheless, these items of costume and props are arguably outweighed by the overt display of the raced body and cyborgic signifiers. Particularly in the enraptured/agonising pose captured by Eugenio Castro and displayed in 'Ethno-Techno: A Virtual Museum of Radical Latino Imagery and Fetishized Identities' as 'El Ethnographic Loco', Gómez-Peña shows off most prominently his brown skin and long, part loose, part braided brown hair [see Fig. 5.1]. This is enhanced by the low lighting of this black-and-white photograph where the only significant props picked out by the spotlight, bar the US army insignia on the jacket, are those that reveal the character's cyborgic nature: not only the orthotic armature attached to his left arm, but his more fully prosthetic right hand (although clearly this latter is a plastic toy and his real hand can be seen manipulating the controls).

What is the effect of the conjunction of mixed-race body and cyborgic signifiers in these images of ethno-cyborgic performance personae? In the first instance we may posit that race and resistance are closely entwined in Gómez-Peña's ethno-cyborgs. Gómez-Peña uses the discourse of *mestizaje* to provoke those who might have either thought new technology and/or the internet were racially pure safe havens or that mixing humans and machines was something entirely divorced from the ongoing mixing of humans that has characterised history. The logic of the discourse of *mestizaje* would even suggest that Latinas/os are 'congenitally' predisposed to mixing, including mixing human and machine or the real and the virtual and hence destined to reproduce rapidly and more suited to life in (dialogue with) cyberspace than those who would conceive of themselves as racially pure. In a tongue-in-cheek riff on Haraway's most contentious statement Lozano-Hemmer and Gómez-Peña claim, 'Nosotros, los otros . . . / We are all ethno-cyborgs, chiborgs, cyBorges, ciboricuas y demás [. . .] / We R slowly corrupting your default configuration. / [. . .] / We are reverse engineering your ass' (Lozano-Hemmer and Gómez-Peña 2001). *Mestiza/o* cyborgs are threatening to take over cyberspace. Furthermore, as Thomas Foster points out, the image of the ethno-cyborg's prosthesis might symbolise 'the transnational imbrications of the Mexican and United States economies as having a prosthetic relation to an imagined social body' where Mexicans and Mexican Americans are imagined 'as a mere supplement to or departure from American norms' (Foster 2002:53). It may, however, in the light of Allucquère Rosanne Stone's discussion of the role of the prosthesis as opposed to the instrument or tool, more positively signify 'a less easily dismissed process of incorporation without assimilation' that keeps *mestizaje* critical and messy by challenging 'primitivist ideologies [that] may imagine the spatial coexistence of temporally distinct and bounded populations, a nonsynchrony that serves as a defense against possibilities for cultural', and one might add racial, 'mixing necessarily implied by coexistence' (Foster 2002:53).

However, there are a number of caveats that accompany such a positive assessment of Gómez-Peña's interpretation of literal ethno-cyborg figures and the meaning of the confluence of their raced bodies and prosthetic limbs. In particular what remains of the performance of such figures in the images that circulate online is less convincingly resistant. El Ethnographic Loco is depicted with his toy prosthetic right hand clawing at his own mouth suggesting a conflicted, nonassimilated, unstable cyborgic identity, but one where the (fake) technology is rebelling against the (raced) human who would otherwise direct it. There is an ironic reference here to Stelarc's high-tech third arm and his exploration of how technology can enhance human capabilities—Gómez-Peña's low-tech prosthesis suggests that it will more likely cause disability in 'the wrong hands' than overcome any natural or accidental limitations to human ability. This reading thus evokes mainstream conceptions of Latinas/os as unsuited to handling technology. And while the technology is depicted as turning against Gómez-Peña in this image, the potential is also there (and released in other similar images) for the violence to be turned outwards. Gómez-Peña's literal ethno-cyborg figures thus also explore mainstream US society's fear and outright rejection of the (almost always male) racial other. They are dystopian, disturbing images of the unhinged Latino male made more threatening via prosthetic limbs and weapons.

Clearly, in Gómez-Peña's view, these images are meant to be read as a critique of the mainstream fears, fantasies and prejudices evoked—Gómez-Peña claims that the vast majority of his ethno-cyborgs are the result of collating ideas supplied by the general public rather than the result of his own preconceptions or imagination (Gómez-Peña 2000:49–50). Yet does just reflecting that material back to the same audience, even with a bit of exaggeration, actually guarantee that the images will be perceived as critiquing mainstream perceptions of Latinas/os? Arguably, without a willing assumption of criticality on behalf of the viewer, they run the risk of being seen as simply indulgent of both racist and sexist stereotypes of *latinidad*. Other critics have also expressed concern that 'the decision to put forward stereotypes can have the effect of immunizing the audience from careful reflection about what they are seeing' (McGahan 2008:79).[30] Furthermore, does the fact that these images circulate online alongside those on pornography websites, for example, where sadomasochism and racial fetishes are amply indulged, or those on gaming sites where the player can combine cross-racial desire and consumerism in the construction and collection of hybrid avatars, mean that they will inevitably be neutralised in their impact by the dominance of these other graphic regimes in cyberspace in particular?

Really, what distinguishes Gómez-Peña's ethno-cyborg images from these others is the question of their framing/context. The way Gómez-Peña has used the internet is of note here. While the material that produced the ethno-cyborg figures allegedly all stems from the online questionnaire and might thus qualify as a type of digital performance art in this respect, the ethno-cyborgs themselves circulate online in stills from the performances or poses for the camera of photographer Eugenio Castro. Many of the posed images appeared in a section of the first *Pocha Nostra* website as 'Ethno-Techno: A Virtual Museum of Radical Latino Imagery and Fetishized Identities'; the stills and some of the more formally posed images also appeared in the 'Pocha Nostra Photo Gallery' on the same website. While this use of the internet as a supplement to live performance through the display of still images is potentially unhelpful since the danger of reification of raced bodies is far greater with discreet, static images than it is with performance itself, and particularly so online, the mere fact of framing and of labelling them is what makes it clear that they are not intended to be consumed in the same way that those images on pornography or gaming websites are.[31] Furthermore, the fact that so many of the images are so elaborately posed can help promote critical viewing—as Gómez-Peña clarifies, his poses strive to offer 'the conscious staging of artificial authenticity, [. . .] the questioning of this staging process, as it happens in front of an audience or in front of the camera' (González and Gómez-Peña 2009:243), rather than simply the types of raced bodies that mainstream society expects. Thus, even in a still image there is still a performative dimension evoked.

Finally, while Gómez-Peña's interest in cyborgs has perhaps started to wane in recent years, a last feature that has helped him avoid some of the traps of essentialism in his display of the *mestizo/a* cyborg online is the endless reworking and revision of these cyborgic performance personae, where different actors perform similar but related personae, and where the same cyborgic character is captured in ever-evolving incarnations. An overview of the images in the 'Pocha Nostra Photo Gallery' (Gómez-Peña and La Pocha Nostra 1998–c.2003) provides ample evidence of the permutations of Gómez-Peña's ethno-cyborgs since the beginning of the century. There we find Gómez-Peña's 'Tijuana Stelarc', Juan Ybarra's 'Robowarrior', and others besides. Furthermore, given that these are images that are meant to be viewed as part of series of such images, as 'photo-performances' in Gómez-Peña's terms, they reference the 'process of production as much as [. . .] the final result' (Gónzalez and Gómez-Peña 2009:238). In sum, this more nuanced appreciation of the framing of Gómez-Peña's ethno-cyborgs online helps underscore the reason why his work on mixed-race subject positions still falls within the parameters of a discourse of 'critical mestizaje'.

CYBRIDS AND CYBRACEROS: COMPLIANCE OR DISTURBANCE?

Where Gómez-Peña and colleagues present their viewers with an ever-mutating array of images of hyper-racialised cyborgs which contrive to retain the power to unsettle the viewer and provoke a revision of racial paradigms, the two cultural products, or better projects, that are examined side by side in this section, although clearly influenced by Gómez-Peña's ground-breaking work from the late 1990s, offer a rather different, potentially more radical (because more fully performative) approach to the subject. In the first instance, they put into online circulation representations of *mestiza/o* cyborgs which suggest total disempowerment and/or subjection to the demands of US neoliberal economy and the constraints of racist ideology. Nevertheless, while such images, like Gómez-Peña's, can provoke critical awareness of the issues in themselves (through their framing), they work in conjunction with the performance of a *mestiza/o* cyborg 'principle', seeking ways to disrupt 'white', anglophone cyberspace in terms of their circulation online. It is this approach that arguably offers a more unsettling form of online performance of racial hybridity than Gómez-Peña's ethno-cyborg gallery images could do.

   This section thus focuses on materials contained on the two websites in question as well as on these websites' performative role online. The first website belongs to a group known as Los Cybrids: La Raza Techno-Crítica made up of three Latina/o artists: 'New York/Colombian' Praba Pilar,[32] John Jota Leaños ('born and raised in Los Angeles in a Mexican-Italian-American family') and René Garcia ('a Mexican born in California').[33] Active from 1999–2003, they defined themselves as 'a junta of three poly-ethnic cultural diggers of the Latino sort dedicated to the critique of cyber-cultural negotiation via techno-artístico activity', and their work included (predominantly offline) performance, installation and digital art designed to 'undermine the passive acceptance and unacknowledged overarching social, cultural and environmental consequences of Information Technologies'.[34] They were generally very negative about the potential for a productive relationship between Latinas/os and new technologies, especially the internet (Miesz-kowski 2000), arguing that the digital revolution was marginalising Latinas/os in low-paid service jobs or being used by those in power to conduct surveillance of ethnic others more effectively (Gonzalez, A. 2001). In all this they were very explicit about the racial basis of the digital divide: 'The new economy doesn't solve inequalities, but rather perpetuates them along the lines of racial divide' (Los Cybrids, glossed by Gonzalez 2001). Yes despite arguing that Latinas/os should 'Get the fuck off the Web!' (Mieszkowski 2000), they had their own website from mid-2001.[35]

Included on the group's website are links to its various offline projects, one of which is of particular significance with regard to the figure of the *mestiza/o* cyborg. The project involved the creation of three digital murals that were produced for display on a billboard outside the Galería de La Raza in San Francisco in 2001–02. In fact, Leaños was the instigator and curator for a series of nine specifically digital murals made for the site; a site which has been in constant use by Latina/o artists engaged in tactical media since it was reclaimed from the advertising company that owned it in 1975. The series of digital murals comprised work by different artists and collectives and was exhibited over the period 1999–2002; marrying form and content, its aim was to 'offer sharp critiques of issues such as racial profiling, the Digital Divide, surveillance, sexual equality, and posthumanism' (Leaños c.2005). In the work produced for the series by Los Cybrids to respond to these themes, the figure of the *mestiza/o* cyborg looms large. Although Los Cybrids' digital murals were quite clearly not created for online circulation, their focus on the effects on the Latino community of new technology, specifically the internet, illustrated with cyborg figures, makes it relevant for discussion here. Furthermore, these murals have arguably had more long-lasting impact online than they can have had during their short lifespan on the billboard itself[36] and they remain central to the identity of Los Cybrids as a group—the group's name, the *mestiza/o* cyborgs of the murals and the disruptive performance of the group's website itself must be considered as interrelated aspects of its *mestiza/o* cyborg tactical approach to issues of race and new media.

The second website is the work of Alex Rivera, a digital media artist and filmmaker, 'born in 1973 to a native of Peru and a native of New Jersey' and for whom 'Growing up in a bi-cultural channel surfing tract home led him to rethink some assumptions about race, immigration, identity, and the global economy'.[37] After gaining a degree in political science Rivera has dedicated himself to the creative exploration of these topics in a variety of different media. His proclivity for parodic remixing of publicly available materials in order to effect his critique of the dominant order is something that Rivera himself identifies as a specifically '*rasquache* aesthetic' (Decena and Gray 2006:131). In this the influence of Gómez-Peña and colleagues is clear to see.[38]

Rivera has been producing short films that he has distributed online since the late 1990s via his *Invisible Cinema* website. Many of these short fiction films, activist documentaries and 'mockumentaries' evidence an interest in exploring the relationship of information technology with issues of immigration and globalisation. One of the 'mockumentaries' entitled *Why Cybraceros?* (1997) remixes in parodic fashion a 1959 promotional short film, *Why Braceros?*, made by the US government to explain the Bracero Program to the general public.[39] According to Rivera *Why Cybraceros?* is a 'surrealist satire of anti-immigrant politics and internet utopianism' ('CNYPG' 2009) which sees migrant workers no longer needing to cross the border (and thus constitute a 'social problem' for Anglo-America) because, in this imaginative business model, they can control robots in the fields of southern California via networked computer terminals in their home countries.

As a spin-off from the short film—and as an alternative home for the short film itself in its different versions—Rivera went on to create a 'spoof migrant labour outsourcing website' (Castillo 2011).[40] The website, which has a URL of its own, entirely independent from Rivera's homepage and other artistic projects, was first launched in 2000, entitled *The Cybracero Program: An Initiative of Remote Labor Systems Inc.*, and has been redesigned at key points to respond to the changing political climate in the US as well as to supplement Rivera's other artistic projects. According to Debra A. Castillo, 'the original site focused on the incoherencies of the so-called immigration debate with its careful avoidance of the glaringly obvious fact of racial discrimination' (Castillo 2011) in its use of maps rather than figurative images to illustrate human traffic. In Castillo's analysis 'the update from 2003 specifically references post 9/11/01 anti-terrorist rhetoric' (Castillo 2011), and it incorporates an updated version of the short film where the robots in the fields are correspondingly depicted in more menacing, insectoid fashion than was previously the case. The site was renamed at that point *Remote Labor Systems: Market Driven Solutions for Today's World Order.*

Finally, after a period of dormancy, Rivera's website was relaunched in early 2009 in a slick, new format and entitled *Cybracero Systems*, to coincide with the launch of Rivera's related prize-winning feature-length science-fiction film, *Sleep Dealer* (USA/Mexico 2008). In this latest version, the site is 'framed by allusion to the global economic crisis' (Castillo 2011) in its references to cheap labour and squeezed budgets. The visual elements of the new site mimic the sanitising discourse prevalent in real labour outsourcing websites that makes it possible to render *virtual* brown-bodied and explicitly Latin American—rather than domestic Latina/o—workers as a cheap, efficient, pleasant and even attractive solution that is both cleansed and contained by its location online. Indeed, in Lisa Nakamura's terms, this is clearly suggestive of the workings of 'cosmetic multiculturalism' which is constituted by a 'disavowal of the recognition of race in local contexts in favour of comfortably distant global ones. In the new landscape of cyberspace, other countries (i.e., markets, and sources of cheap expert immigrant labour in information fields) exist, but not American minorities' (Nakamura 2002:22). It is this last version of Rivera's website that is of interest in the context of this chapter on account of the prominence given on the site, in counter-distinction to the previous versions of the site, to these images of clearly *mestiza/o* figures who, in the dispensation of their duties as members of the offshore labour force on offer, of necessity are also represented as (cosmetically multicultural) cyborgs.

In her earliest work on cyborgs, Jennifer González expressed concern at the frequency of representations in the mainstream media of specifically *subaltern* cyborg bodies (by race or gender) that evidenced subjugation and disempowerment. Running contrary to the common assumption that the figure of the cyborg referenced the posthumanist enhancement of human life, she argued that 'This is not a cyborg of possibilities, it is a cyborg of slavery' (González 2000b:545). Responding to this disempowering trend in mainstream representations of subaltern cyborg bodies as subservient, sexy or both simultaneously, Los Cybrids and Alex Rivera put into circulation exaggerated images of precisely such disempowered *mestiza/o* cyborgs.

The digital murals produced by Los Cybrids relate closely to the group's primary concerns: the simplistic rhetoric in mainstream media concerning the digital divide; the relationship between information technology and increased surveillance of targeted social groups; the potential enslavement of human beings and loss of human values as the counterside of posthumanist technological advances. In all of this, the focus is particularly on how new technologies impact negatively on 'people of color' and/or the poor.[41]

In the top left-hand corner of the second of the murals, 'Webopticon: Sistema de vigilancia' [see Fig. 5.2], the head-and-shoulders image of a young Latino boy, in profile as if posing for an ID photograph, reveals his cyborg status through the barcode seemingly tattooed on his neck. The background of the mural is composed of a blue-on-black 'digital' record of fingerprints, rendered in a grid format as per the information gathered by the US Immigration and Naturalization Service's biometric computer system IDENT to identify illegal immigrants.[42] In the top right-hand corner the links are drawn between a satellite, a helicopter, a bank of computer monitors with busy workers and various recording devices. Finally, the caption in the bottom left-hand corner, runs ' . . . you don't have to be connected to be affected . . . '. The message here clearly that new technologies are being used to better keep racially defined others such as young Latino men, typically profiled as criminals and/or illegal aliens by mainstream society, under surveillance. The fingerprints and other biometric information kept on file are thrown into relief by the rather more absurd appearance of the barcode on his neck.[43] What might so easily have been a self-empowering 'placa' '[insignia'] tattoo to identify his membership of a gang is swapped for a code that could be used to track and contain him. He is thus represented as an (unwittingly) disempowered cyborg figure.

The third mural in the series, 'Humaquina: Manifest Tech-Destiny' [see Fig. 5.3], represents a naked cyborg figure, full frontal but lying across the mural, head left, against a yellow-and-grey background of the circuitry of a motherboard, into which the figure blurs in places. The largely flayed body is depicted as enhanced by numerous implants and prostheses, seemingly to improve functionality/economic return. On the left-hand side of the image the headset worn by the cyborg links to a satellite (bottom left) and a laptop with a combat-clad figure pictured next to it (top left) for the purposes of command and control. The cyborg itself is depicted with a prosthetic right arm ending in a hook with an optional green 'glove' attachment, its left hand also ends fused with a kind of palm-top computer, a whole block of gadgetry is shown as suitable to be fitted into the stomach cavity once it is emptied of a foetus-like creature, and the genitals are replaced by an abstract, unisex 'logo'.

The image is reminiscent of an anatomical textbook, a user manual (with numbered parts) or a catalogue for cyborg workers/slaves (with a large green dollar sign in the top right-hand corner). The 'price' that is written over the dollar sign is expressed as 'If your mind is on your computers, who's minding your body?' and thus suggests anxieties over posthuman technological developments as something that should be everyone's concern. Nevertheless, many other features of the billboard point towards the extra anxieties that 'cyborg exploration' has for 'people of color' and the poor. The cyborg's unflayed body is clearly dark-skinned and its features are evocative of both Afro-Latina/o and *mestiza/o* heritage. On the right-hand side of the image, attaching to the cyborg's lower legs are cables that lead to the human-value price-tag (top right) and to a thumbnail group portrait, as per those of non-white groups in traditional ethnographic accounts (bottom right). The image's subtitle, 'Manifest Tech-Destiny', also suggests that the technological colonisation of the human body will be in the service of a hegemonic 'white' United States—the ability of new technologies to enhance human life, will, the group argues, 'accrue exclusively to first world beneficiaries', and not to 'poor nations and individuals'.[44] Furthermore, the mural suggests that where hegemonic society imposes cyborg technologies on subaltern groups it will be all the better to exploit them. Los Cybrids show viewers an extreme image of what these cyborgs of slavery and surveillance might look like.[45]

Clearly these digital murals were designed for offline display in the first instance. In their original installation on the billboard outside the Galería de la Raza, they constituted deliberate tactical media installations—they stole back a space from corporate culture and undermined its purpose. Leaños himself has argued that these works of 'Xican@ digital muralism' strove for 'decolonial consciousness and the promotion of a *política de fondo*' ['grass-roots politics'] (Leaños c.2005). Furthermore, Guisela Latorre argues that in 'Humaquina' in particular, the cyborg's 'centrality in the mural's composition as well as the figure's monumentality of scale disrupt and even overturn the colonizing process' (Latorre 2008:238). While monumentality of scale is most certainly lost in the murals' online circulation, these works do still retain a consciousness-raising purpose that is indicated by their titles and ironic captions, as well as the context provided by the websites on which they appear (that of Los Cybrids and that of the Galería de la Raza), as well as by their departure from verisimilitude to absurdity and exaggeration.

Nevertheless, the work of Los Cybrids, particularly its website, moves beyond figurative representation of the *mestiza/o* cyborg, whether aggressive or subjugated, to a performance of *mestiza/o* cyborg identity that more convincingly achieves the above aims. The website bore the group's name as its title and this, in itself, is significant in terms of how it 'positioned itself' in cyberspace. The use of the term 'cybrid', although a real word,[46] clearly indicates the group's identification with the concept of a mixed-race cyborg, combining as it does the 'cy-' prefix with the term 'hybrid'. Its use of the Spanish masculine plural definite article ('Los' Cybrids), as well as the group's subtitle (La Raza Techno-Crítica), also focuses attention on its laying claim to the term 'cybrid' on behalf of Latinas/os, and this comes articulated as a *critical*, self-aware statement of identity, thus challenging the depoliticising conflation of *mestizas/os* and cyborgs in Haraway *et al.*'s cyborg theory.[47]

The group's website also performed a *mestiza/o* cyborg principle by simulating viral infection. Before reaching the group's homepage, viewers would see a series of black screens with text in white, green and yellow which simulated the programming commands of pre-Windows computing. The first screen was headed by the statement: '<!-- ORALE, WE'RE GONNA LAY DOWN A DOWNGRADE', and other revealing terms embedded in the commands on this and the following two screens included 'cybrid', 'jotascript', and 'te chingas!!' [see Fig. 5.4].[48] These screens would seem to flash rapidly on and off[49] before a pop-up warning appeared saying: 'WARNING! Los Cybrids Ideological Bacteria version 3.1 has been released into the neural network! The Global Inequality Virus has infected all systems. Downgrade now!', with an 'OK' or 'Cancel' option.[50] Clicking 'Cancel' would take users on a loop back to the flashing screen, thus making them think they had really got a viral/bacterial infection and their computer had seized up. Clicking 'OK' would take users to Los Cybrids' website itself. Only those in the know and with a real interest in accessing Los Cybrids' website would have been likely to dare to click 'OK'. As Pilar has noted,

We were hoping to get web hits from people outside of activist/artist circles, who would not be in on the 'joke' of the ideological virus. It was interventionist in nature. We assumed there would be many many people scared of/by the site [. . .]. Additionally, when we received the Creative Work Fund, we spent some of the funds on creating an invitation for our year of events that was a CD. While the CD cover was printed with all of our upcoming events, the CD inside was printed with a warning that it contained a virus. Many many people received the invite and called us and Galeria to complain the CD had given them a virus, as it didn't 'work'. Well, actually, the CD was blank.

(Pilar 2012)

It is this performance of viral infection on behalf of a racialised minority group in its website's opening sequence that most succinctly expresses Los Cybrids' political agenda. Taking issue with the mindset of mainstream Anglo-American society that posits cyberspace as pure (and white) and in need of protection, and simultaneously associates the concept of race—and particularly racial hybridity—with impurity, pollution and disease, Los Cybrids was determined to act out these fears. It thus performed the viral infection of race and more generalised subalternity online.[51] Moreover, the principle of the *mestiza/o* cyborg—*el cybrid*—was what underpinned and authorised this endeavour. This was a *mestiza/o* cyborgic form of performance.

Alex Rivera's *Cybracero Systems* website perhaps relies more heavily than Los Cybrids does on the visual representation of corporate, commodified *mestiza/o* cyborgs to achieve its aims, but it also goes beyond representation to performance through the site's ostensible function as a business enterprise. At first sight the website appears reassuringly normal. Its slick appearance is 'visually within the norms for familiar, legitimate outsourcing companies' (Castillo 2011).[52] As Castillo notes, it uses a similar colour scheme and features tabbed drop-down menus 'for easy navigation', a sidebar with links to news items, and a footer with logos and endorsements to suggest its sanctioning by others in the industry. Even more notable is the scrolling banner at the top of every page that displays images of clearly brown-skinned, dark-haired, Latina/o 'cybraceros' who are well groomed and happily compliant in appearance. These are examples of Nakamura's 'cosmetically multicultural' workers discussed earlier. Castillo notes that this is a common feature in labour outsourcing websites where the banner serves to convey to would-be clients 'an image of reassuring modernity in the off-shore site (frequently in the form of a slide show interspersing gleaming offices with attractive young people of exotic hues)' (Castillo 2011). Where Rivera's site departs slightly from the norm in visual terms is in the depiction of the workers at their work stations, wired up with multiple neon-blue cables and wearing a headset and mouth piece, like so many high-tech marionettes [see Fig. 5.5]. Nevertheless, the sanitised work environments depicted, the happy faces of the workers and the convincingly proactive discourse of the website replete with quotes from satisfied workers and clients suggest that this kind of cyborg worker is entirely realistic and an unproblematic solution for both employer and employee.

At first sight, then, Rivera's *mestiza/o* cyborgs present the acceptable and totally convincing image of *latinidad* controlled through information technology that fits the expectations of hegemonic US society. Nevertheless, the website is a parody of a labour outsourcing website and the viewer's credulity must at some point be revealed to him/her. Castillo (2011) argues that this happens mainly through the text. While much of the site reads and functions in a smoothly corporate and bona fide manner with only modest exaggerations, a note under the banner on the homepage has read since the site's revamping: 'PLEASE NOTE: Cybracero warns people that the movie *Sleep Dealer* opening this weekend is an inaccurate and undeservedly critical portrait of our pioneering business model and is not representational of our business'. The disavowal of Rivera's other, more high-profile, artistic ventures that are so closely entwined with the website itself ought to alert the viewer to the duplicitous status of the *Cybracero Systems* site. However, it is even more likely at a visual level that the most credulous viewer will finally be made critically aware of the parodic nature of the site.

If the clever logo where a letter C wraps around a zero, and the colours of the letters pick out the 'cero' ['zero'] of *Cybracero* in light blue do not trigger awareness of the site's functional 'emptiness', the material that purports to explain the pragmatics of cyborgic work in the *Cybracero* model will do. The rough-and-ready graphics of the 'How to node up!' installation guide (with instructions provided in Spanish for the workers) [see Fig. 5.6] are reminiscent of airplane emergency egress instruction cards and cover how to fit the contact lenses dangling at the end of fibre optic cables into one's eyes, how to connect other cables to 'nodes' that have been installed in various parts of one's body, with a final (more reassuring because believable) warning to keep the breathing apparatus on because 'el oxígeno te mantiene alerta' ['oxygen keeps you alert']. Nevertheless, the absurdity of fitting cables into nodes on one's body in order to work is inescapable, and it is glossed with a text that does little to explain or reassure: 'Nodes are simple and easy to implant in a human body. A Cybracero's nervous system hooks up to a computer on the net. However, THEY MUST BE DONE BY A NODE INSTALLATION SPECIALIST. Beware of imitators and don't try this at home.'

It is through the figure of the *mestiza/o* cyborg—at first sight believable, at closer inspection quite clearly farcical—then, that Rivera's website proposes to encourage its viewers to confront their credulity and thus achieve its parodic function. Nevertheless, as with those members of the general public who wrote in to complain that materials distributed by Los Cybrids had given their computers a virus, there is evidence that some members of the general public that have discovered Rivera's earlier *Cybracero* sites did not spot the joke (cf. Thompson 2002; González, M. 2003). While performance art relies on its ability to disturb the frame to achieve its effect, it also still relies on some retention of the frame in order for it to be recognised as art and for its critical approach to be given due recognition. Where the frame is lost altogether the risk is that the critical function of the art will also be lost. The *Cybracero Systems* website is a piece of performance art in itself which nudges the viewer to consider the question of racism in an age of networked capitalism, but given that Rivera's site is less of an all-out assault on the viewer than that of Los Cybrids, it runs a greater risk that its more gentle, gradually revealed duplicity will be missed.

VIRAL *LATINIDAD*: *MESTIZA/O* CYBORG BODIES AS SYMPTOM OR PATHOGEN?

In 'Envisioning Cyborg Bodies', Jennifer González observes, 'I do not see the cyborg body as primarily a surface or a simulacrum which signifies only itself; rather the cyborg is like a symptom—it represents that which cannot otherwise be represented' (González 2000b:541). Yet while this may be true for the way in which cyborgs (and their earlier avatars) have worked in mainstream Western culture over the centuries, what we may conclude from this examination of *mestiza/o* cyborg figures, and the more performative ways in which they may be invoked online, is that for Latina/o artists, rather than a symptom, the *mestiza/o* cyborg is conceived as a pathogen, an active agent; not a rash or an inflammation signalling malaise about racial boundaries and their crossing but a cipher for the deployment of (a particularly hybrid form) of racial identity as a principle of bacterial or viral contamination. As such, with its threat that it can spread racial hybridity, literally through bodily contact or metaphorically through the corruption of files and hard drives, the *mestiza/o* cyborg and its discourse has much greater power to disturb those who would chance upon it and to challenge the reifying tendency of the visual power system that is race. Furthermore if, in its contemporary form, *latinidad* is found to be more 'contagious' than ever, 'circulating through the most diverse of networks' (Beasley-Murray 2003:223) and hence may be described, loosely, in today's computer-savvy terminology as 'viral', it is the more self-possessed and deliberately challenging virality of the *mestiza/o* cyborg, created explicitly to challenge US conceptions and 'pop cultural images of Latinos' and the contemporary global dissemination of such (Gómez-Peña 2000:51), that is arguably the best expression of this messy, unsettling and critical 'viral *latinidad*'.

6 'Revolución.com?

The Latin American Revolutionary Tradition in the Age of New Media (Revolutions)

The association of Latin America, and by extension Latin American-ness, with the concept of revolution is both long-standing and, this final chapter contends, a feature of Latin American cultural identity that has arguably seen the most substantial efforts at resemanticisation and reinvigoration in online cultural production, prompted both by contemporary political situations of differing sorts, as well as by the coincidence of the concept of 'revolution' in a sociopolitical sense with what is rather more loosely termed a 'revolution' in new media technologies—their invention *per se* as well as their practical deployment to promote social change.

This association of Latin America and revolutionary projects is well documented and, depending on the source, highlights from this trajectory may stretch from the Independence Wars of the nineteenth century, through the Mexican Revolution (1910–20), the Cuban Revolution (1959–) and the Nicaraguan Revolution (1979–90), to the uprising orchestrated by the Ejército Zapatista de Liberación Nacional in Chiapas in 1994, the Bolivarian Revolution in Venezuela (1998–) and other more recent social movements. While more sceptical critics warn that 'the stereotype that vindicates the natural right of these lands to revolution' is 'unproductive' (Herlinghaus 2004:563), other more ardent admirers of Latin American revolutionary projects still claim that Latin America 'was and is the world region which has generated the most original and vigorous popular and revolutionary movements' (Raby 2006:x).

Steering a less partisan course, in *Art and Revolution in Latin America, 1910–1990* David Craven seeks to identify exactly what Latin America has contributed to the meaning of the term 'revolution' in its traditional late twentieth-century (but pre-internet) usage. He argues that the Manichean Cold War capitalist-versus-communist schema for conceptualising revolutions since the 1950s as simply the changing of regimes between the two options proposed by the world's superpowers has been inadequate as a framework for understanding Latin American revolution (although it has been often used in the mainstream literature in the West concerning the region). Instead, Latin American revolutions should be understood as broad-based social movements rather than as battles of a specifically ideological or partisan nature; they may achieve their aims by militant or more peaceful means (and most frequently through a combination of the two); they affect all aspects of a society (education, health, welfare, even art), not just its form of government; and they result in the 'fundamental transformation of the institutions of power on behalf of social justice' (Craven 2002:8). This end result is best described as being constituted by a form of direct, popular or participatory democracy (as opposed to liberal or parliamentary concepts of democracy) and it almost goes without saying that, given their popular nature, 'real' Latin American revolutionary movements are clearly left-wing political projects.

However, Latin American revolutionary movements have not all fared well over time. Where the process has become institutionalised such that participatory democracy is seen to be a sham and the old order reigns unchanged except in name, or it has become mired in its adherence to ideology to the extent that numerous human rights violations are seen to occur in the name of the revolutionary cause, for many the discourse of revolution becomes associated with oppression rather than liberation. According to Jorge Castañeda, the crisis of the Latin American left since the end of the Cold War has been in part associated with the fear that 'the idea of revolution has withered and virtually died because its outcome has [. . .] become reversible' (Castañeda 1993:240–41). It is this potential of the term 'revolution' to mean radically different things to different people at different times—its 'revolving definitions' in Craven's terms—that must be borne in mind in any analysis of the way the discourse of revolution is deployed in Latin American cultural products.

This attention to the meaning of the term is even more important now given its new use as an epithet accompanying references to networked digital communications technologies to describe not only their newness, popular spread and more general ability to change the way we conduct our business, but also their potential for activist uses of proportions that are significant enough to bring down regimes that many might have thought eternal. The employment of the internet as part of a 'revolutionary'—new and different—strategy to help pursue a 'revolutionary'—although non-traditional—political agenda has been most notably pursued by the Mexican Zapatistas.[1] Their cause and various campaigns have offered the world a highly successful synergy of 'revolutions' and, in so doing, they have done much to reignite the old association of Latin America and revolutionary change. But is an embrace of the potential of new media technologies to change the offline world, or even to facilitate a space for imagining utopian possibilities online, enough in itself to really reinvigorate a concept that in Castañeda's terms has been in danger of 'withering and dying'? Will the sociopolitical concept of revolution not also need some serious attention irrespective of its new media platform? The answer, as we shall see, is that all elements in the equation need to be reexamined, realigned, and regularly so.

This chapter focuses on how the complexities of the discourse of revolution are employed in two online projects which are located at the crossroads of online activist practices and digital cultural production and which thus combine strategic and artistic concerns in varying measures. As intimated above by Craven's identification of art as intrinsically bound up in the work of Latin American revolutionary projects, it has quickly become apparent that, while the internet offered exciting new opportunities for activism that were exploited with alacrity by Latin American activists, the role of creativity, of art, in this enterprise was not insignificant. Hacktivism/tactical media can be considered politically motivated art forms as much as they are social practices with potentially revolutionary goals—they are the Dada movements of their day.[2] And, in the same way that Craven argues that Latin America has given a particular meaning to the word 'revolution', Zapatista-inspired hacktivism has been particularly influential across the world. While activism and art are indissociable in the objects of study selected for this chapter, given considerations of space and the specific remit of this volume, the analysis of the works does not focus to any great extent on the practices of digital activism and the success or failure of these works in this respect. Instead attention is devoted to the internal logic of these cultural products and the ways in which they negotiate their relationship to the 'traditional' discourse of (Latin American) revolution and how they nuance this with respect to the 'revolutionary' aspects of new media.

The chapter's first case study focuses on *Generación Y* (2007–), a blog written by the Cuban Yoani Sánchez and which tackles directly the official monopolisation of the discourse of revolution in Cuba. Nevertheless, the blog also goes on to suggest blogging and other forms of social networking as an alternative, but nonetheless revolutionary, discourse. The analysis of Sánchez's blog considers the extent to which she is successful in proposing this alternative discourse and whether she manages to escape the centripetal force of the official discourse of revolution. The second case study focuses on the Mexican media artist and activist Fran Ilich's conceptualisation of his own server, *possibleworlds.org* (2005–), and related projects, as a utopian online space created in the spirit of Zapatismo. In Ilich's case the focus will be on considering the extent to which his project positions itself as a descendant of the tradition of Latin American (and global) revolutionary discourse, but also on how a reading of his work that recognises it as employing a poetics of Digital Zapatista 'semantic disruption' offers a way of appreciating its more subtle and innovative aspects. While undoubtedly the development of Digital Zapatismo (as political praxis and as art) predates the practice of blogging in Cuba, and the networking of the Web 2.0 'generation' is a direct descendant of the early 'social netwar' that the original Zapatista Uprising orchestrated with Web 1.0 technologies (and a host of more traditional forms of communication to boot), the case studies are approached in this order because a more detailed appreciation of the resonance of the traditional discourse of revolution in contemporary Cuba is a useful prelude to considering the ways in which Ilich positions his project within a framework of Latin American and global revolutionary discourse.

INDEPENDENT JOURNALISM AND THE CUBAN BLOGOSPHERE

To understand the context in which Yoani Sánchez's blog has come about, it is important to consider the development of a practice of independent journalism on the island during the 1990s, and the importance of the internet in facilitating circulation in (and beyond) contemporary Cuba. Since the beginning of the Cuban Revolution the State has controlled all media outlets and any other form of journalistic practice has been a punishable offence (Voeux 2008:1; Pérez Valdés 2009). In the early decades of the Revolution there was strong support for its utopian aims and many journalists who would later identify as independent found roles for themselves within state-sanctioned media outlets. However, during the 1990s increasing numbers of Cubans felt the desire to publicly question their own system of governance and report on the hardships of daily life in the Período Especial en Tiempos de Paz [Special Period in Times of Peace] occasioned by the withdrawal of Soviet economic support and the evident unravelling of the Soviet Communist system (Pérez Valdés 2009). Furthermore, the catalyst for the development of an 'independent press movement' was the release from prison in 1995 of journalist Yndamiro Restano who had founded the country's 'first non-official journalism organization in 1987' (Bilello 1996).

It is worth noting here that the 'independent press movement' should not be considered entirely synonymous with the expression of dissidence from the Cuban regime, although the two are closely entwined (Voeux 2008:5). Their stated aims are, rather, to report on events without the restrictions of censorship, to contribute to debates on key topics affecting Cuba and Cubans, and to promote the construction of a sense of civil society on the island. While exact numbers of independent journalists working from Cuba are hard to calculate, most informed sources consider that the number has grown considerably since the mid-1990s and there has been increased evidence of organisation around agencies such as the Asociación de Periodistas Independientes de Cuba (Voeux 2008:2; Pérez Valdés 2009).[3] The increasing visibility of the practice on the island is evidenced by the attention it has received from the Cuban government in terms of its systematic attempts at repression. Twenty-seven journalists were imprisoned as a result of the round-ups of those identified as dissidents of the regime in the 'Primavera Negra' [Black Spring] of 2003, with further arrests of journalists having been made since then (Voeux 2008:5). Although all the detained journalists had been released by April 2011, the majority had gone/been forced into exile ('No More Journalists Left in Cuban Prisons', 2011).

The distribution of independent journalism via print media has typically been extremely limited on an island where the foreign newspapers in which the articles are ultimately printed are not available for purchase. As such the readership of such journalism has tended to be international rather than national. Nevertheless, despite severe restrictions on internet access for Cuban citizens detailed below, networked digital technologies have significantly increased the ability of independent journalism to function on the island, as well as its sense of potential to achieve its aims.

Connectivity in Cuba is famed for being the least extensive in the whole of the Americas, lagging behind Haiti even. According to Carlos Uxó, the most reliable estimates on direct connectivity for 2007 embraced a mere 3% of the population, yet arguably 100% of the population indirectly benefited from the internet as deployed by the government (Uxó 2010:12.9). The analysis of the reasons for the first figure is typically polarised with anti-Castro sources blaming the Cuban government for hampering development to fend off influence from the rest of the (capitalist) world, and with official Cuban sources blaming the US embargo for impeding access to the technology while nevertheless still identifying the internet as 'one of the "myths of contemporary development" used to "subvert our Revolution"'.[4]

The reality of the situation requires a more nuanced appreciation of the Cuban government's approach to information technology and how the 100% figure might be adduced. As Uxó argues, rather than promoting *personal* computing and *individual* access to the internet, the regime has preferred a collectivist and anti-capitalist approach, investing in those resources that will benefit its people the most (websites such as *Infomed* that provide medical personnel with up-to-date information relevant to scientific advances in their field), or in the development of websites for its own press organs such as the newspaper *Granma*. The government has also promoted the use of Linux systems, as well as developed other free software programmes and its own internet search engine, Dos por Tres, in line with its anti-imperialist politics (Uxó 2010:12.7). Many statistics regarding Cuban internet connectivity in comparison with other parts of the world are thus misleading since they are typically based on ownership of personal accounts and cannot account for collectivist models of access nor the way that different media intervene in the dissemination of online materials to offline groups and individuals. Nevertheless, despite the potentially much higher levels of community connectivity, the Cuban government has also largely worked to develop a Cuban 'intranet' available to a limited number of citizens via their workplaces and to impede access to an uncensored world wide web, both via content-management tools as well as policies making it illegal for Cubans to own personal computers, open internet accounts or to access these services in public places.[5] The US embargo has also significantly contributed to the digital isolation of Cuba with the blockage of shipments of hardware, service providers such as Google and Microsoft Internet Messenger unavailable to those on the island or of Cuban citizenship, and the undersea cabling that provides high-speed connectivity for the rest of the Caribbean also bypassing the island only a few kilometres off the coast.

While domestic and international political agendas have undoubtedly shaped access to the internet in Cuba, it is nevertheless the case that ordinary Cubans have demonstrated substantial resourcefulness in finding their own ways to access the technologies they desire. Both hardware and software have been traded on the black market and imported in the suitcases of foreign visitors; Cubans wanting internet access have bribed their way to accessing colleagues' workplace accounts or found their ways to the computer points in the lobbies of hotels reserved for foreign tourists, and they have learnt many skills in computer literacy as well as other, less high-tech, tactics in order to evade government censorship (Uxó 2010:12.9). Such determination does not, however, necessarily equate with outright dissidence or demonstrate in a nutshell the democratic nature of the medium. It has been argued that the surfing habits of Cubans are not as overtly politicised as such limited access and freedom of expression might suggest and, instead, downloading US music or identifying online the goods that they would like relatives living abroad to bring them on their next visit is the focus of at least some illegal personal access of the internet (Venegas 2010:177).

Despite such caveats about access and practice, the use of the internet in Cuba for the dissemination of independent journalism has developed significantly since the late 2000s and, alongside independent online journals, the practice of blogging has been the most popular form of self-expression.[6] Protagonised by the remaining exponents of independent journalism on the island after the Primavera Negra crackdown, together with a growing number of younger bloggers without a pre-digital, independent journalist past, and achieved through sheer persistence, creative subterfuge and downright illegality, the 'blogosfera cubana' ['Cuban blogosphere'] has snowballed since 2007.

Although in Beatriz Calvo Peña's anthology *Buena Vista Social Blog: Internet y libertad de expresión en Cuba* (2010a) the Cuban blogosphere is defined as encompassing all blogs concerning Cuba wherever they are written, and although a good case is made for the difficulty in producing reliable statistics concerning any of this blogging activity, it is clear that island-based bloggers account for about a quarter of those included in the survey on which some of the articles are based (or c.250 blogs in total) (Monett 2010:63&80). Salient characteristics of the island-based bloggers include the fact that, in comparison with the work of bloggers in the diaspora, their blogs are rather less clear-cut in their dissidence. Instead they tend to be more plural in terms of political positions adopted and more dialogic in their enactment of their politics, focused on sharing information and experiences (Monett 2010:70). Bloggers on the island are less aware of those blogging about Cuba elsewhere in the world (Monett 2010:76), instead tending to read each other's work, and this despite the Cuban government's attempts at censorship. However, the network created through blogging, and the way in which the outside world has come to look to island-based bloggers for information, has allowed those based in Cuba an important means of breaking out of their physical confinement on the island, and, like the Zapatistas before them, of shielding themselves from the worst excesses of governmental repression through the publicity afforded by their appeal to international support networks.

The most prominent group of island-based bloggers are those that have sprung up around the portal *Desde Cuba* (2008–) set up by independent journalist Reinaldo Escobar and a close group of friends and relatives including his wife, Yoani María Sánchez Cordero, or Yoani Sánchez as she is most often known. Despite their professed tolerance for differing political views, according to Calvo Peña the core members of this group have traced a trajectory in their blogs from personal 'desahogo' ['therapy'] to political commentary to dissidence proper and the organisation of offline activism (Calvo Peña 2010:164; see also Henken 2010). Increasingly they identify themselves as forming the 'blogosfera alternativa cubana' ['alternative Cuban blogosphere'] focused on producing 'periodismo ciudadano' ['citizen journalism']. The portal today comprises the work of over 40 different bloggers including the photo-blogs of Orlando Luis Pardo Lazo (*Lunes de post-revolución* [*Post-Revolutionary Mondays*], 2008–; *Boring Home Utopics*, 2009–), and the text-based blogs of Reinaldo Escobar (*Desde aquí* [*From Here*], 2007–) and Miriam Celaya (*Sin EVAsión* [*Without EVAsion*],[7] 2008–).[8] Nevertheless, the most renowned blog by far is Yoani Sánchez's *Generación Y* [*Generation Y*] (2007–). Although not necessarily the best or even the most representative blogger in Cuba, Yoani Sánchez was one of the first to take up this form of writing on the island and has become one of the most influential bloggers in the world since she launched her blog on 9 April 2007.[9] It is on account of her international reputation as well as her sustained engagement with the issues that this chapter seeks to discuss that Sánchez is selected for particular attention here.

YOANI SÁNCHEZ, BLIND BLOGGER

Sánchez had ambitions to be a journalist but studied Spanish philology at university. Having endured a decade of the Período Especial, in 2002 she emigrated to Switzerland, yet in a highly unusual U-turn in 2004 she decided to return to Cuba. Even before leaving for Switzerland Sánchez had been interested in new technology and had built herself a computer from spare parts. After her return, she has made a living (illegally) by teaching Spanish to foreign tourists and serving as a tour guide, and she has used the proceeds to finance her digital activities which started with her serving as webmaster for *Consenso* (2004–07), an online publication dedicated to independent journalism. In January 2007, prompted by the appearance on state television of some of the most vilified censors of the 1970s Quinquenio Gris [Grey Five Years],[10] the 'polémica intelectual' or 'email war' between Cuban intellectuals and the State raised hopes of greater freedom of expression. However, for Sánchez this 'debate' resulted only in more frustration when she was not allowed access to the 'polémica''s culmination in an official 'presentation' on the subject. As a result, in April 2007 Sánchez decided to start a blog where she could express both her hopes and her frustrations.[11]

Generación Y announces at the head of every page that it is 'un Blog inspirado en gente como yo, con nombres que comienzan o contienen una "i griega"' ['a blog inspired by people like me, with names that begin with or include a "Y"'], a particular phenomenon in the Soviet-influenced Cuba of the 1970s and 1980s.[12] She goes on to describe her generation as being composed of people who have been 'marcados por las escuelas al campo, los muñequitos rusos, las salidas ilegales y la frustración' ['marked by their experience of being sent to school in the countryside, Russian dolls, illegal emigration and frustration']. A keen sense of generational identities would appear to be a particular correlate to the official periodisations of revolutionary Cuban culture,[13] and Sánchez thus offers her voice as representative of those who experienced some of the years of greatest economic hardship and increasing disenchantment with the ideals of the 1959 revolution and the interpretation of those ideals by the regime in power since that point.[14] Nevertheless, Sánchez is at pains to make it clear that her work only represents her own opinions and experiences in contrast to the tendency of the State to speak for all Cubans (Henken 2010:208).

Accordingly the blog starts by offering vignettes of all the most absurd facets of Cuban daily life such as the scarcity of key foodstuffs, even fruits native to the tropics; the complications of working with two currencies and two forms of market (the state-controlled one versus the illegal, but very necessary, black market); the form-filling and queuing necessary to undertake even the most simple tasks; the declarations of political conformity required to access higher education or a good many jobs; the prohibition of ownership of new ICTs and the baroque means necessary to access the internet; the extreme subterfuge of farmers lying about the sex of their cattle in order to be able to drink milk (rather than having to sell it all to the State) or how illegal satellite dishes are concealed within false water tanks on people's roofs and the cabling hidden within related pipework. Small acts of civil disobedience as survival techniques are frequently the subject of her attentions. She also comments regularly on political events on the island and on their reporting (or lack thereof) in official media outlets, and, in contrast, she offers her own reports about the cases of political prisoners and/ or hunger-striking journalists, as well as those organising peaceful protests in their support such as the Damas de Blanco. The threads of this kind of report have increased in presence on her blog over time. At the other end of the spectrum she also includes less overtly politicised reports of concerts she has attended, book reviews or birthday wishes for close friends.

In the first year of its existence the blog entries typically consisted of an image, sometimes an ironic and/or iconic photograph of contemporary Cuba taken by Orlando Luis Pardo Lazo or others, sometimes simply an image downloaded from the internet illustrating the topic in hand, and a related text of some 500 words. Given the dates of individual posts, it is clear that Sánchez was uploading a couple of entries each time she managed to get online (on average once or twice a week). Given this lack of spontaneity Sánchez herself has claimed that *Generación Y* is not really a blog—the polished entries are at least as closely related to the Latin American literary-journalistic tradition of the *crónica* as they are to the more informal and provisional nature of the new genre as practiced in parts of the world where personal access to the internet and to freedom of expression is so much more easily had (Sánchez 2010:9).

Sánchez does not mention in her attempts to define her writing the even more complex relationship of these texts to the other media that illustrate them, and, on some occasions supplant them. Over time her work has increasingly experimented with the photo-essay format as well as incorporated YouTube footage of events in which she has been involved or of more studied podcasts. Images and videos are not simply used to illustrate her posts for aesthetic and/or ironic purposes—they also serve a denunciatory function of their own, providing evidence of protesters' physical abuse at the hands of the State or the organisation offline of illegal public gatherings. Since early 2008 Sánchez has also included links to other sites in her texts—these are increasingly prolific and complex. Furthermore, since late 2007 the blog has offered a space for readers to leave comments and it has clearly developed through a dialogue with its readers. All of this not only suggests the increasing facilities offered by blogging software and accessible to Sánchez, but the increasing importance of the international network of like-minded people that has galvanised around Sánchez. In 2008 and 2009 her blog received an average of 30,000 comments a month, with visits averaging out at 10 million a month since May 2008 (Henken 2010:217–18). Key posts were already being made available on a sister site in English by the end of 2007 and other translations of her work are also available.[15] Books of the blog have been appearing since the 2009 publication of an Italian translation, with versions now also available in Spanish, French, English, German and Polish,[16] and Sánchez has also recently published a handbook in Spanish on blogging (Sánchez 2011). Given this amount of international visibility and the strength of her network of supporters, Sánchez does not feel the need to hide her real identity online and has become increasingly emboldened in her criticism of the Castro regime.

The speed with which *Generación Y* has gathered momentum can only be described as viral. According to Henken, the blog started to take off after the addition of the reader comments facility and it was then propelled to world-wide notoriety by an article that appeared in *The Wall Street Journal* in late December 2007, after which a slew of other international news media picked it up and its fame grew with each successive article (Henken 2010:219–20). It has also received a number of prestigious awards such as the Spanish Ortega y Gasset prize for digital journalism in early 2008, while Sánchez herself was voted one of the top hundred most influential people in the world by *Time* magazine in the same year. In early 2008 the Cuban censors managed to limit access to Sánchez's blog on the island,[17] a fact which further increased her fame internationally, and since then she has been what she terms 'una bloguera a ciegas' ['a blind blogger'] (Sánchez

2010:14), managing to post to her blog by sending the entries via emails, texts and phone messages to friends abroad who maintain the blog for her. She can usually only access her own blog by using proxy servers. Sánchez has come to the attention not only of the Cuban (ex-)president Fidel Castro, who criticises her in his prologue to the Cuban edition of the book *Fidel, Bolivia y algo más* [*Fidel, Bolivia and Something More*] (2008), but also to that of the current US president, Barack Obama, who has read and commented on parts of her blog and who has responded to interview questions that Sánchez has sent him.[18]

The effects of censorship on Sánchez's blog are noticeable in the posts themselves which in Spring 2008 were more sporadic in publication, shorter than usual, and with much less illustration. Nevertheless, one must surmise that the challenges of censorship were quickly overcome given that her blog posts from 2009 onwards have been more prolific and more complex in design than ever. From that point on the question of censorship and blogging itself becomes a more frequent topic of the posts themselves. Many of her posts not only comment on the difficulties she encounters in terms of access to the internet, but convey through their form the compromised nature of their composition. Footnotes occasionally attest to pragmatic issues of how a post reached the blog and crossings-out with corrections in others signal the problems of redaction for those posting voice messages for her.

Since the blocking of Sánchez's blog for readers in Cuba there has also been a noticeable nuance in terms of intended audience. As she notes in various blog posts, she does continue to be read by those on the island who are in the know and who access the internet using the same ruses that she does or who circulate posts via memory sticks or read them over the phone to friends in the provinces or in prison. However, since the point at which her blog switched to being maintained largely by friends living abroad, Sánchez clearly starts to direct her entries at an audience that is international as well as national. As a result many entries contain information that would be self-evident to a national audience, particularly in the form of footnotes to gloss Cuban institutions, acronyms and idiosyncratic customs. Other posts offer instructions for interested, and presumably international, readers (although not political parties) with regard to how to make donations in order to help Sánchez sustain herself through independent journalism, and how to provide the hardware and software necessary to help both Sánchez and other bloggers record their experiences.

Nevertheless, her national audience is still the focus of a good number of posts. Particularly evident from 2009 onwards, Sánchez's blog becomes far more metatextual, focusing on blogging as a practice to achieve social change and encouraging others to join the movement via posts with information on how new technology may be harnessed to circumvent censorship. As such, increasing numbers of posts offer guides as to how to configure a mobile phone to send messages directly to a Twitter account or how to set up RSS feeds to one's blog.[19] In line with her increased focus on blogging as a means of achieving social change, Sánchez is also attentive to changes on the world scene that have been facilitated by the use of social media technologies such as the 2009 riots in Iran following the presidential elections and more recently the uprisings of the 2011 Arab Spring.

It is clear from this brief analysis of the development of Sánchez's blog over time that she is critical of the Cuban regime. In accordance with her training as a philologist, this is particularly evident in her criticism of the regime's use of language, especially its monopolisation of the whole lexicon of revolutionary discourse. Furthermore, where she quickly moves towards the promotion of blogging as an alternative form of revolutionary discourse—one which has the potential, in her view, to translate into real social change rather than become fossilised at the level of discourse—, her work also dialogues with the potential for the discourse of revolution to be resemanticised. The remainder of this case study focuses its attention on these aspects of Sánchez's work in more detail.

In official Cuban discourse the term 'revolution' refers not only to the events of the overthrow of Fulgencio Batista in 1959 but, perhaps more importantly, it refers to 'living the revolution' and working 'within' the framework laid out by the socialist regime in power ever since.[20] According to Sánchez, the term 'revolución' and its associated lexical field—terms such as 'la Patria', 'el Partido', 'el Máximo Líder', 'verde olivo', 'el hombre nuevo', 'virilidad', 'pionera/o', 'compañera/o' ['the Fatherland', 'the Party', 'the Supreme Leader', 'olive-green', 'the new man', 'virility', 'pioneer', 'comrade'], together with its diametrically opposed set of terms 'traición', 'muerte', 'gusano', 'imperialismo' ['treason', 'death', 'worm', 'imperialism'] and so on—are almost fetishised by the State and their incantatory use is omnipresent in Cuban daily life. Sánchez's standpoint with respect to the official discourse of the Cuban regime is to oppose what she sees as its unsubtle Manichaeism, its preference for obfuscation and euphemism, its bellicosity and associated machismo, its tendency to pomposity and overstatement, and above all, its monopolisation of language itself. In the introduction written to accompany the publication of her blog in book form, Sánchez identifies as a main aim of her work the desire to challenge binary thinking 'en un país donde las clasificaciones se expresan rígidas y los apelativos, contundentes' ['in a country where classifications are expressed in black-and-white terms and collective nouns are blunt tools'] (Sánchez 2010:9). She illustrates her point by listing some of the key binaries of revolutionary terminology: 'Aquí solo se puede ser «revolucionario» o «contrarrevolucionario», «escritor» o «ajeno a la cultura», pertenecer al «pueblo» o a un «grupúsculo»' ['Here you can only be a "revolutionary" or a "counterrevolutionary", a "writer [in support of the Regime]" or someone "who has no culture", a member of the "people" or of a "faction"'] (Sánchez 2010:9).

In the blog itself Sánchez comments on the government's binaristic advertising campaigns with slogans such as 'Revolución o muerte' ['Revolution or death'] or 'Socialismo o muerte' ['Socialism or death'] (see, for example,

'Cambiar el cartel' ['Time for a New Slogan'] 28/06/08). In other posts she focuses on the regime's preference for 'frase[s] triunfalista[s]' and 'cifra[s] engordada[s]' ['self-congratulatory expression[s]' and 'inflated figure[s]'] ('Periodismo o literatura' ['Journalism or Literature'] 08/07/08), and on its 'palabrería hueca' ['hot air'], offering her own translation of phrases such as 'inviabilidad sistémica del proyecto socialista cubano' ['systemic unviability of the Cuban socialist project'] as 'esto se jodió' ['this is screwed'] ('La trampa de las palabras' ['Verbal Trickery'] 03/09/07—all terms given in inverted commas in text). In other posts she pinpoints the discourse of 'el aburrido estatismo cubano' ['the boring Cuban State'] as more difficult to fathom than Egyptian hieroglyphs ('En busca de la piedra Rosetta' ['In Search of the Rosetta Stone', 25/02/08). And in still others she takes on the bellicosity of revolutionary discourse and its machista underpinnings—she identifies herself as among 'los que estamos hartos del lenguaje belicista' ['those who are fed up of the warmongering language'] of the regime and as 'cansada del macho enfundado en su uniforme verde olivo; del adjetivo "viril" asociado al valor; de los pelos en el pecho determinando más que las manos en la espumadera' ['tired of the macho man dressed in his olive-green uniform; of the adjective "virile" being associated with bravery; of hairy chests having more say than hands in sinks'] ('Un discurso bien macho' ['A Really Macho Form of Expression'] 01/03/09). On the subject of pomposity and overstatement Sánchez takes issue with the conceptualisation of the Revolution as something eternal in the post 'Los símiles, lo eterno y el poder' ['Similies, Eternity and Power'] (01/08/07) and challenges its monopolisation of the concept of utopia in entries such as 'La utopía impuesta' ['Compulsory Utopia'] (11/04/08). In these posts it is significant that Sánchez almost always identifies the terms of the regime's revolutionary discourse in inverted commas to signify both its monopolisation of the terms as well as to mark her own distance from them, highlighting their absurdity or caducity.

As a necessary counterbalance to so much 'revolutionary' discourse Sánchez also offers alternative suggestions. Thus she indicates a preference for terms such as '"efímero", "perecedero" y "transitorio"' ['"ephemeral", "perishable" and "transitory"'] over '"eterno", "siempre" y "jamás"' ['"eternal", "always", and "never"'] ('Los símiles, lo eterno y el poder'), and for 'frases como "prosperidad", "reconciliación", " armonía" y "convivencia"' ['expressions like "prosperity", "reconciliation", "harmony" and "coexistence"'] as opposed to the discourse of combativity and virility ('Un discurso bien macho'). While this antonymic methodology can become a reductive, repetitive and Manichaen exercise in itself, Sánchez also imagines possible scenarios where revolutionary discourse is seen to be defeated by its own tautologies and intransigencies. In 'Los hijos devoran a Saturno' ['Saturn Eaten by his Children'] (27/10/07) she argues that the lazy, hedonistic youth of Cuba with its MP3 players, low-slung jeans and *reggaetón* music (a Generación Z to her Generación Y) is incapable of aspiring to the ideals of 'el hombre nuevo' ['the new man'] and will manage quite simply to outwait the 'eternal' nature of the revolutionary regime (rather than directly overturn it). In another post she imagines herself as the grandmother of a child born to the current generation of Cuban youth and posits that her memories of socialism in Cuba will seem as distant a past to her grandchildren as the memories of youth have always seemed when conveyed from grandparent to grandchild ('Nietos descrídos' ['Sceptical Grandchildren'] 06/05/09). The eternity of the Cuban Revolution thus slips semantically from permanence (in its official revolutionary interpretation) to the fixed but finished status of all memories. Again, in 'En busca de la piedra Rosetta' she interprets Raúl Castro's references to a 'cese de gratuidades (. . .) insostenibles' ['an end to unsustainable free hand-outs'], by which he meant an end to state-subsidised food rations, in a literal fashion. She thus pretends that he must have wanted to indicate that all 'unsustainable gratuitous behaviour' would come to an end and, by means of an imaginary scene at her local market, she argues that she should now be able to use her ration book to obtain freedom of expression, association and choice.

Nevertheless, increasingly noticeable in Sánchez's work as the Cuban blogging movement gathers strength and as she takes a lead role in promoting it is the sense that her blogging activity really is seeking to 'revolutionise' social reality, rather than simply offer an analysis or critique of the regime and its discourse, and this entails a more complex dialogue with the discourse of the Revolution. Ironically perhaps, the prophetic, on occasion eulogistic, tone of blog posts auguring imminent social change increasingly offers parallels between Sánchez's writing and that of the 'poet of the Revolution', Nicolás Guillén. Sánchez's mockery of revolutionary discourse and in particular its use in official publications mirrors Guillén's mockery of the discourse of the bourgeoisie in *El diario que a diario* [*The Daily Daily*] (1972), and her claiming of rights echoes those rights so proudly announced in 'Tengo' ['I Have'] (1963).

Indeed, Sánchez's frequent focus on the right of Cuban citizens to have access to hotels previously reserved for foreign tourists (a reform announced in Raúl Castro's liberalising moves) echoes the assertion in 'Tengo' that a black person can no longer be stopped 'en la carpeta de un hotel' ['in a hotel lobby'] and denied even 'una mínima pieza' ['a tiny room'] (Guillén 1990:196). Sánchez also repeatedly focuses on reclaiming the right to the sea as part of the culmination of a new revolution in Cuba, reminding readers that since Cubans wanting to leave the island against the wishes of the regime have used the sea as a route, and since few Cubans have 'holidays' at the beach, the sea is seen as either an almost insurmountable barrier or simply out of bounds. This echoes Guillén's poem where he associates open access to the sea(shore) with the openness of the democratic process that lay at the base of the revolutionary project and the reclamation for the nation of its natural resources that had been reserved, until then, for private use by the rich. For Sánchez, then, the sea is still in need of the reclamation of which Guillén so eloquently wrote. And as a final and most compelling point of comparison in terms of poetics, even the frequent use of parentheses and other prosaic linguistic features in Sánchez's description of the leader she would like to have in 'De la casa a la Nación' ['From the Domestic to the National'] (07/02/08)—'No estoy esperando por un padre—omnipresente y omnipotente—sino por un Presidente, del que pueda quejarme—libremente—en público' ['I'm not hoping for a father—omnipresent and omnipotent—but for a President about whom I can complain—freely—in public']—echo the awkward, hesitant cadence of 'Tengo' where the narrator is just starting to describe the new society ushered in by the Revolution—'Tengo el gusto de ir / (es un ejemplo) / a un banco y hablar con el administrador, / no en inglés, / no en señor, / sino decirle compañero como se dice en español' ['I have the pleasure of going / (for example) / to a bank and speaking to the manager, / not in English, / not calling him Sir, / but calling him *compañero* as we do in Spanish'] (Guillén 1990:196).

Sánchez's blog, as it exists online at the time of writing (December 2011), makes no explicit mention of Guillén's significant legacy in contemporary Cuban culture; nor does it, therefore, make any acknowledgement of her rhetorical proximity to Guillén's revolutionary poetics.[21] It does, however, make occasional references to key singers of La Nueva Trova Cubana such as Pablo Milanés who were also responsible for putting to music key poems from Guillén's work. Thus Guillén's influence on Sánchez might be said to be as much filtered through Milanés's musical interpretations as it is direct. What is most significant in the attention paid to the cultural producers of the Revolution such as Milanés (and more implicitly Guillén) in Sánchez's work is her awareness of the seductiveness of early Cuban revolutionary discourse. The parallels drawn between her blog and the poetry of Nicolás Guillén are not therefore proof of the fact that Sánchez does not realise how close she comes to going 'full circle' in her critique of the discourse of the Revolution, but, taken in context, they reveal the hopes and aspirations of a new revolution; one not yet realised, but one that is nonetheless aware that it is, in essence, a revolutionary proposal. Sánchez's blog is not just descriptive or cathartic, as she claims it is—it proposes a methodology for achieving change to a more representative form of governance.

In her blog, Sánchez works to discredit the revolutionary discourse that is clearly associated with the way that the current regime expresses itself, reclaiming instead a more etymologically pure, original meaning for the term:

> El término 'revolucionario' tiene en la Cuba actual un significado bien distinto al que encontraríamos en cualquier diccionario de la lengua española. [. . .] Aquella palabra que una vez hizo pensar en rupturas y transformaciones ha involucionado hasta convertirse en un mero sinónimo de 'reaccionario'.

> [In contemporary Cuba the term 'revolutionary' means something quite different from what we would find in any Spanish dictionary. [. . .] That word that once made people think of rupture and transformation has inverted its meaning to the point where it has become no more than a

synonym for 'reactionary'.] ('La exclusión, la verdadera contrarrevolu-
ción' ['Exclusion, the Real Counter-revolution'] 15/07/10)

And if the concept of revolution can be stripped of its 'corrupting' association with the current Cuban regime, then Sánchez is happy to recycle it for
her own purposes and try to express it in less dogmatic, more participatory and pluralistic terms. In a significant post entitled 'Revolución.com'
(13/02/09), she demonstrates her conceptualisation of her activity in the
same kind of revolutionary terms that many supporters of the transformatory power of new and social media are using across the globe and in direct
contrast to the official rhetoric of revolution in Cuba where, as we have
seen, the internet is posited as an enemy of the Revolution:

> Una verdadera **revolución.com** ocurre paralela y contraria al raciona-
> miento que también nos quieren imponer en el mundo virtual. Esta no
> tiene barbudos, ni fusiles y mucho menos un líder gritando en la tribuna.
> Es lenta y aún focalizada, pero alcanzará a casi todos los cubanos.

> [A real **revolution.com** is happening, running alongside and in coun-
> terpoint to the rationing that the Government also wants to impose on
> us in the virtual world. This revolution doesn't have men with beards
> or rifles and certainly not a leader shouting from a platform. It's slow
> and still quite patchy, but soon enough it will reach almost all Cubans.]

Sánchez's revolution uses interactive technologies such as blogging and
other more fully fledged manifestations of social networking as its modus
operandi: As she notes in the same post 'Sus comandantes llevan raros nombres como Gmail, Wordpress, Skype o Facebook: no crean división, sino
que unen personas' ['Its leaders have strange names like Gmail, Wordpress,
Skype or Facebook: they don't create social rifts but instead bring people
together'].[22] It relies explicitly on the creation of an online/offline network of
civil society actors—Cubans living on the Caribbean island, those in the diaspora, and other sympathisers across the world—to protect those most out-
spoken in their demands for substantive change in Cuban politics. Sánchez
identifies this network as 'precaria' ['fragile'] but unstoppable ('"Habeas
data"'[23] 12/02/08) and even though she worries that Cubans do not have
enough real practice of democratic negotiations to be qualified to handle the
freedom afforded by virtual society ('Ciber-mutilados' ['Cyber-handicapped']
21/07/08), elsewhere she clearly hopes that they will succeed nonetheless and
be able to weave a robust civil society of their own: 'probemos hacer un
resistente tejido que nos trascienda' ['let's try to make a strong fabric that
can reach out to others'] ('La sociedad virtual' ['Virtual Society'] 01/04/08).[24]
   In another set of related metaphors that reveal the subtle positioning of
Sánchez's resemanticised revolutionary proposition, access to the internet is
described either as providing 'una balsa virtual' ['a virtual raft'] or as creating

'una isla virtual' ['a virtual island']. In the first case, the internet as 'balsa virtual' allows Cubans to escape the geopolitical confines of the island ('Tarde de textos y disgustos' ['An Afternoon of Books and Annoyances'] 15/02/08), and their ability to find ways to 'navegar' online [lit. 'to navigate'; fig. 'to surf the internet'] is seen to compensate the strict limitations placed on their ability to 'navegar' offline (to leave Cuba on a boat).[25] In 'Llévame a navegar, por el ancho mar' ['Take Me Sailing on the Big Wide Sea'][26] (21/02/09), Sánchez comments on the threat of a husband losing his job in the Cuban merchant navy as a result of his wife's blogging activities. As a couple they may manage to benefit from one or other form of escape, but not both. If in real life contemporary Cubans cannot embrace the Caribbean sea as part of their birth right, in the metaphorical terms of cyberspace they can do just that, thus nuancing Sánchez's recycling of Guillén's revolutionary reclamation of the sea.

These references to the internet as 'una balsa virtual' perhaps seem more appropriate a spatial conceptualisation than the other frequent analogy that circulates in Sánchez's work (and more widely in contemporary Cuba) that imagines Cuban cyberspace as 'una isla virtual'. Nevertheless, this choice of terms is predicated on its difference from other terms such as 'la blogosfera cubana' which encompasses blogs on the topic of Cuba written in exile and those written from the island itself. The desire to promote the development of 'una isla virtual' refers specifically to the question of direct access to the internet for all Cubans and thus to the creation of a space online for residents of the island itself where they can express themselves freely with a view to changing real island life if they want to. That virtual space, in contrast to the real island, is not cut-off or free-floating but part of a network of relationships and discussions that link Cubans on the island who are otherwise impeded from organising themselves as groups on the ground, and it is also embedded within a network that links it to the rest of the world. This is thus not a metaphor for a utopianist virtual Caribbean island. Instead it is much more grounded in online/offline dialogue. As Sánchez argues, 'En ausencia de utopías a las que aferrarse, la nuestra es una generación de plantas en el suelo, vacunada de antemano contra los ensueños sociales' ['In the absence of utopias to cling onto, ours is a generation with its feet firmly planted on the ground, immunised in advanced against social fantasies'] (Sánchez 2010:10), including those of virtual reality. It is this avoidance of utopianism that means that Sánchez's discourse of revolution avoids coming full circle, despite its acknowledgement of its revolutionary nature and despite the complexities of its relationship to the discourse of the Cuban Revolution.

FROM THE ZAPATISTA UPRISING TO DIGITAL ZAPATISMO

For others who live less in the shadow of a consecrated Latin American revolution and of the ubiquitous discourse of the still incumbent revolutionary regime, it is considerably easier to have recourse to a wide-ranging repertoire of (generally) appreciative references to historical revolutions and their iconic leaders and to link this with a (small-scale) utopianist project for a new social order online. This is the case of Fran Ilich's *possibleworlds. org* server which he originally conceived as a 'net-island'—an online space for like-minded individuals, set apart from what he saw as the globalising, neoliberal mainland of the internet. The *possibleworlds.org* project drew its inspiration directly from the Mexican Zapatistas and any analysis of the server and the various projects it hosts must therefore first deal with the discourse and practise of Zapatismo and its relationship to both older conceptualisations of revolution in Latin America, and the wider world, as well as its close association with networked digital technologies as a means of achieving its objectives, before going on to consider the precise relationship of Ilich's work to such a revolutionary genealogy.

In terms of its revolutionary credentials, the actions of the Ejército Zapatista de Liberación Nacional (EZLN), as it manifested itself to the wider world from January 1994 onwards, suggested a radical break with the traditional conceptualisation of revolution that had held sway across the world until that point. The uprising was described loosely by many prominent Left-wing commentators as the 'first *postmodern* revolution' or the first '*twenty-first century* revolution' (added emphasis).[27] Nevertheless, other more academic analysts would contest the Zapatista Uprising's status as a 'real' revolution at all (whether postmodern or 'avant-garde'), preferring to identify it as more of a 'politics of rebellion' (Holloway 2005:171). What was most strikingly different about the Zapatistas' approach (when compared with other twentieth-century revolutionary ideologies and, importantly, their historical praxis) was that the Zapatistas proposed non-hierarchical (networked) organisational structures and dialogue with all parties as a means of ensuring direct democratic process, accompanied by 'a strategy of "dissolution" rather than seizure of power' (Raby 2006:77). This refusal to become mired in the discourse or the structures of 'old forms of left-wing politics' is what, according to Holloway, has been most inspiring for other activists and social movements across the world (Holloway 2005:171).

Despite all this, the Zapatistas are not without a revolutionary genealogy, starting with their recourse to the figure of Emiliano Zapata, one of the most significant leaders to emerge in the early years of the 'Mexican Revolution' in support of the peasant and indigenous causes. In 'The Zapatistas: The Challenges of Revolution in a New Millennium', Mike González emphasises the aspects of Zapata's role that fit with traditional conceptualisations of revolution as well as indicates aspects that are more closely aligned with what is perceived to be different about the Zapatistas' approach, in particular Zapata's disinterest in consolidating his hold on power (González 2000). Nevertheless, Zapata's was to be an 'unfinished revolution' as he was hounded by the more power-hungry *caudillos* ['strong men'] who contrived to fossilise Mexican revolutionary discourse for the ensuing 70 years in the rule of what would become the Partido Revolucionario Institucional

[Institutional Revolutionary Party]. It is thus that the discourse of 'revolution' in Mexico must be problematised: Whose revolution are we talking about? Zapata's 'uncorrupted revolutionary ideal' or the revolution of what would become a rather more authoritarian and bureaucratic state?

While the above discussion situates the Zapatistas with respect to the traditional conceptualisation of social revolution within a specifically Mexican context and makes sense of their desire to reclaim Zapata as their hero, not that of the 'revolutionary' nation-state, it is also worth considering other, more international, aspects of their revolutionary heritage. According to González, the ideology behind the development of the EZLN has underpinnings that relate to a combination of (utopianist, peasant-focused) Maoism[28] and liberation theology, linked by 'an insistence on direct democracy and self activity', and conversely their politics demonstrate 'a clear reaction against the Stalinist variants of Communism' (González 2000). González also notes that the Cuban Revolution, and particularly the figure of Che Guevara who took his lead more from Mao than from Stalin, would have provided 'a beacon of revolutionary hope' to those who would later become Zapatistas, although its attraction waned for activists in Mexico subsequent to the Cuban Revolution's 'absorption into the Soviet bloc' (González 2000).

Zapatismo's relationship to the discourse of revolution is thus quite selective, preferring the aura of revolutionary heroes such as Emiliano Zapata and Che Guevara who died young and before their revolutionary projects had lost their utopianist shine. In this respect it is (perhaps naïvely) idealistic. However, it is arguable that what the Zapatistas have selected from historical revolutionary movements, regardless of their legacies, is the spirit of direct democracy, dialogue and permanent willingness to renegotiate the terms of that dialogue, and they have at least been successful in keeping their focus on these aspects.

Zapatismo, then, is about permanently questioning the way forward for society (cf. the 'caminamos preguntando' ['we keep asking questions as we go along'] maxim), and, perhaps most importantly, as the Zapatistas have done this, they have attempted to invent a new vocabulary, a new poetics, a new imaginary for this process. Even if they have not been without inspiration from the tradition of world revolutions, they have expressed themselves (and communicated their thoughts) very differently. Indeed, John Holloway sees the role of poetics as a crucial part of what Zapatista revolution is about:

> The poetry of the Zapatista uprising (of their communiqués and their actions) is not peripheral to their movement, not the external decoration of a fundamentally serious movement, but central to their whole struggle. [. . .] poetry not as pretty words but as struggle against the prosaic logic of the world, poetry as the call of a world that does not yet exist.
>
> (Holloway 2005:176)

The creation of such Zapatista-inspired 'possible worlds' and the poetics of revolution that they espouse are central to the project studied below.

What has come to be known as 'Digital Zapatismo' negotiates the transference of a Zapatista poetics of revolution into the digital sphere. 'Digital Zapatismo' has been defined as a form of digital 'performance' that 'combine[s] political protest with conceptual art in an act of social revelation' (Lane 2003:130). First articulated by Ricardo Domínguez and others working under the banner of the Electronic Disturbance Theatre (EDT), a group of four net.artists and net.activists formed in 1994 as a direct response to the Zapatista Uprising, Digital Zapatismo has typically consisted of acts of 'Electronic Civil Disobedience' that provide an online equivalent to such practices in the offline world. The EDT has developed and distributed software tools such as FloodNet (1998) and the Zapatista Tribal Port Scan (2001) which have enabled them to conduct ever more effective virtual sit-ins of key opponents' websites.

While the EDT's acts of Electronic Civil Disobedience are orchestrated in support of the ongoing Zapatista campaign, it has also released the Disturbance Developers Kit (1999) which has been credited with having a major influence on the development of hacktivist practices across the world (Lane 2003:132). Digital Zapatismo when used in the context of the latter loosens its reference to contemporary Mexican Zapatismo in particular, simply taking on the Zapatista ethos expressed in some of the more transferable maxims of the movement such as the pluri-culturalist 'un mundo donde quepan muchos mundos' ['a world that can accommodate many other worlds'] and the utopianist 'otro mundo es posible' ['another world is possible'], this latter a slogan much recycled by the antiglobalisation/anticapitalism protesters of recent years.

The practice of Digital Zapatismo may also take the form of creative work in digital media that proposes alternatives to mainstream immersion in the neoliberal world order, whether based on Zapatista-specific scenarios or not. In the opinion of Ricardo Domínguez, a key goal of the more creative examples of Digital Zapatista 'disruption' is not to effect physical/material or even syntactic (code-breaking) damage (the targets of more destructive hackers) but to provoke semantic disruption 'engaging and undermining the discursive norms and realities of the system as a whole' (gloss of Domínguez in Lane 2003:136). This is where Digital Zapatismo coincides most fully with the poetics of the Zapatista movement outlined above.

FRAN ILICH, ZAPATISTA ZORRO

A mercurial figure whose work frequently falls within the parameters of Digital Zapatismo is Fran Ilich, an itinerant Mexican writer, media artist, activist and (conceptual) entrepreneur.[29] Considered part of the Generation X of late twentieth-century Mexican literature (Conaculta en los Estados 2010), Ilich was active in the Mexican border cyberpunk/electronic scene in the early 1990s where he was co-founder of the multimedia Contra-Cultura (menor) collective that promoted 'techno-pacifist anarchy' as a response to the failure of '1960s revolution, feminism, the civil rights movements, [and] psychedelia'.[30] Ilich has subsequently continued building his reputation as a writer, with the publication of the critically acclaimed novels *Metro-Pop* (1997), *Tekno Guerrilla* (2007) and *Circa 94* (2010). Another significant string to Ilich's bow since the early 1990s has been scriptwriting and the creation of short video narratives, or 'net.films' in his later work.[31]

Ilich's career as a digital media artist and occasional hacktivist developed during the second half of the 1990s. He was the key organiser of Cinemátik 1.0 in 1998, reputedly the first Latin American cyberculture festival; from 2000 he was involved in the organisation of the Borderhack festivals in Tijuana[32] and he has also participated in other digital art events across Latin America and beyond. Ilich has had his own website—*de-lete.tv*, later *delete.tv*, now *sabotage.tv*—since 2001, and through these protean sites he promotes both his on- and offline creative work as well as designing the sites as forms of ludic digital media art themselves.

The inspiration underpinning a great many aspects of Ilich's work post–1994 has been the ethos and practice of Zapatismo, as well as its poetics. The influence of Zapatista poetics is clear to see in an essay penned in 2005 and finally published in 2011: *Otra narrativa es posible: la imaginación política en la era del internet* [*Another Narrative Is Possible: Political Imagination in the Internet Age*] dedicates a chapter to 'Digital Zapatismo' and, in its final published version, also has a foreword by Ricardo Domínguez. Ilich has also participated directly in a number of Zapatista marches and encounters, even sharing the podium with Subcomandante Marcos and other Zapatista commanders at the Primer Festival Mundial de la Digna Rabia [I World Festival of Dignified Rage] in 2009. In late 2005, following some of the ideas expressed in his *Otra narrativa es posible* essay to their logical conclusions, and inspired most immediately by discussions surrounding the release of the Sexta Declaración de la Selva Lacandona [Sixth Declaration of the Lacandon Jungle] which extended the spirit of Zapatismo to embrace all like-minded social movements (including the people of contemporary Cuba, if not explicitly the Castro regime itself),[33] Ilich set up the 'autonomous cooperative' server *possibleworlds.org*.[34] The server was intended to take up the Zapatista mantra that 'otro mundo es posible' by offering an alternative virtual space where the principles of the Sixth Declaration, and later the ethos of La Otra Campaña [The Other Campaign],[35] could be creatively explored.[36] Lest visitors be in any doubt about this, on its homepage the server makes its Zapatista affiliation very clear indeed:

> está usted en territorio autónomo zapatista en rebeldía.
> aquí manda el pueblo y el gobierno obedece.
> servidor ciberespacial adherido a la sexta declaración de la selva lacandona.
> online since 2005.

> [you are in autonomous zapatista territory in rebellion. /here the people rule and the government obeys. /cyberspatial server in support of the sixth declaration of the lacandon jungle. online since 2005.]

Furthermore, the server hosted a semi-official EZLN website—*La otra información* [*The Other Source of Information*]—from c.2006–07, and various other sites and materials that it hosts are explicit in their support of the Zapatistas (see, for example, issue 0 of the journal *Sabøt* (May 2007) which is dedicated to La Otra Campaña[37]). Many other sites/materials hosted by the server are not exclusively Zapatista in focus, but they relate to the spirit of the Sexta Declaración in their professed drive to be both 'autonomous' and 'cooperative', thus forming the accessible, public face of a small community of like-minded artists/activists (around 120 in total[38]) which aims to work together to at the very least *imagine*, and possibly start to create and deploy more widely, the principles of a world more suited to their aspirations. Thus the server and its contents set forth a utopian agenda of a generally more poetic than pragmatic nature.

The server's Zapatista affiliations are thus both clearly manifest and ostensibly earnest and we might reasonably expect any discourse of revolution apparent on the server to coincide with that of Zapatismo. Nevertheless, a more detailed study of the way in which a discourse of revolution is presented in the materials that the server hosts (the vast majority penned by Ilich himself), both endorses and complicates this assumption in a number of ways. A convenient snapshot of the discursive tendencies of Ilich's project is offered by a ludic (hypermedia) narrative that he created of the server's genesis, 'net-island: the blueprint of possible worlds' (2006–07), which was available on the server until 2008.

In this document Ilich claims that initially he and a small circle of idealistic friends daydreamed of trying to purchase or simply occupy a real island (in the Caribbean or South Pacific) to found their utopianist society of media artists and activists (a net.island). In the words of one of the group of friends (a conceptual artist) the basic idea was that 'bastaba con llegar a la isla y declarar una revolución y días después la independencia de Filipinas' ['all they needed to do was get to the island, declare a revolution and a few days later declare their independence from the Phillipines']. Impeded from doing so by a host of material factors, they then decided to transfer the same idea to cyberspace. The 'autonomous server' is thus described as a 'net-island' (now with a hyphen rather than a dot[39]) and the document is illustrated with a number of pictures of tropical paradises and ready-made *cabañas* taken from mainstream advertising, as well as images of readings that inspired Ilich and friends such as Bruce Sterling's post-cyberpunk novel *Islands in the Net* (1989) and Ross Norgrove's manual *Blueprint for Paradise: How to Live on a Tropic Island* (1983, sic).

In their virtual net-island, we are told, the 'dna' of the (guerrilla) cell (Rael Bernal, Sol-Ho, Ilich Sabotage and Adriana Segura) installed themselves by founding a bank (Spacebank—'a Latin American virtual community investment bank'), an advertising agency (Mundo Posible), a radio station (Radio Latina AM), an offline workshop (the Tijuana Media Lab) and sundry other initiatives. In 2007, a 'grupo de trabajo forzado' ['forced labour group'] or 'cuerpo de *elite*' ['*elite* corps'] consisting of Ilich, Ivan Monroy-López and Luisa Ungar, was brought in to replace the original 'dna' cell. The bank, trading in a virtual currency known as 'Digital Maoist Sunflowers' (later 'Digital Material Sunflowers'), was floated on the 'Brooklyn Stock Exchange' or 'BSEX'. In 2008, the server was subsumed by the 'cooperative media conglomerate' Diego de la Vega, s.a.de c.v. (a reference to the real name of the character Zorro, the masked Robin Hood figure of the US–Mexico borderlands, and a cultural icon that suggests clear parallels with the masked rebels of the EZLN). This latter umbrella organisation has continued with the proliferation of initiatives including a blog under the title *The World Street Journal*, the Collective Intelligence Agency think tank, an 'alternate reality game' entitled 'net.island',[40] and a digital media workshop franchise entitled Sweatshop.biz which has opened its first real branch at Plaza Revolución in Tijuana.

Clearly, there is a discourse of guerrilla tactics and revolutionary struggle to create a new society that pays homage to the Zapatista insurgency in the above narrative. Nevertheless, this discourse is almost inextricably entwined with one of 'discovery' and colonisation followed by the development of rampant corporate capitalism. Depending on one's reading, either the latter discourse quickly absorbs and redeploys the revolutionary impulse (appropriating the 'cool' revolutionary markers to advertise key features of the capitalist system, in, for example, the name of the cooperative media conglomerate or the virtual currency), or the revolutionary impulse contrives to work tactically from within the system (and thus corporate structures such as banks and media conglomerates may not be quite what they seem). The former reading would suggest that Ilich doubts the ability of Zapatismo to counter the system; the second is more clearly an example of Digital Zapatista 'semantic disruption'. Arguably, the second reading slightly outweighs the first, although ultimately the function of Ilich's 'possible worlds' is absolutely dependent on the (radical) ambivalence achieved by the need to 'navegar preguntando' ['keep asking questions as one surfs'], to appropriate the Zapatista maxim.

In the analysis that follows, the aim is not to explain away the interference of other readings, but to justify why the second reading, aligned with Zapatista politics and poetry, should be considered the more dominant one. In order to do this the treatment of the discourse of corporate capitalism on the server as a whole will be examined first, before going on to look at the discourse of revolution, since the treatment of the one affects our reading of the other. The analysis will then go on to consider the genealogy of the discourse of revolution present in Ilich's work and explore how he might be said to resemanticise this discourse in the light of the 'revolution' in new media technologies.

Given that the Zapatista inspiration of the server seems genuine and the server's homepage presents its relationship to Zapatista discourse quite earnestly (if somewhat playfully), it would seem reasonable to suppose that any references to capitalism, globalisation or neoliberalism will be critical. After all, the Zapatista Uprising was timed to coincide, by way of protest, with the signing of the North American Free Trade Agreement on 1 January 1994 between the USA, Canada and Mexico; an agreement which proposed to integrate Mexico (unequally) in the neoliberal projects of the other two First World economies. Thus, if references to these phenomena appear to endorse them, we might presume that they are parodic in intention. For example, Ilich describes Diego de la Vega s.a. de c.v. in ever-mutating combinations such as 'un conglomerado mediático cooperativo mexicano *coin-operated*' ['a *coin-operated* Mexican cooperative media conglomerate'] working within a 'nano-macro economy'.[41] These multiple permutations, the proliferation of adjectives and modifiers in the definitions themselves, and the increasingly evident mismatches in the combination of these, all work to encourage the viewer to read this as parody. Ilich also indicates in one or two places on the server that some key terminology used his work is intended to be read as 'un guiño' ['a playful reference'] rather than the adduction of a theoretically justifiable parallel, and the effect of just a few knowing 'guiños' is to spread a sense of ludic unreliability/instability throughout the work.[42] Thus the media conglomerate, the bank or any of the other sites on the server offering services to the general public appear to be spoofs, functioning in the same way as a media art project such as *Etoy.com* (1995–) that parodies the language, iconography and operations of big corporations and even engages in hacktivist actions against predatory corporations that would attempt to sue it (Tribe, Jana and Grosenick 2007:42).

Nevertheless, Ilich's server is not all parody designed to reveal the savagery of unbridled wealth creation or the vacuity of corporate capitalist discourse. Ilich notes that although 'the idea of the whole conglomerate is conceptual [...] it's more than just the "looks", [...] it does function like a corporation'.[43] The bank, the currency and the stock exchange might be virtual, but real (if modest) financial transactions bridge the gap between hard cash and the Digital Material Sunflower, and Ilich also reports the fact that real investment banks have shown an interest in investing in the commodities traded on the BSEX.[44] Spacebank's slogan on its homepage also suggests more (tactical?) acceptance than clear-cut parody, exhorting visitors to the site: 'don't hate banks become the banks' (sic). Furthermore, Ilich's server allows Google Adsense to place real corporate advertising on most of its pages in order to offset some of the equally real costs associated with running a server.[45]

In the light of all this, Ilich's project might be found to have rather more in common with the virtual world (and currency) of *Second Life* (2003–) which offers an immersive virtual experience—an almost complete alternative to the offline world—but one that is no more parodic, subversive or utopianist in its conceptualisation than the offline world itself. Indeed, recent developments might seem to confirm this similarity. In early 2012 the cooperative media conglomerate created an avatar and built a 'safehouse'

(Casa Dandelion) in *Second Life*, thus 'temporarily connecting the economies of the Digital Material Sunflower with the Linden Dollar'.[46] Nevertheless, what is important to note in this development is Ilich's preference for a
'non-immersive' approach to the virtual worlds offered by online Multi-User
Dungeons/Domains[47] and his permanent tacking back and forth between
different fora—offline interactions, social networking, the space of his own
server, and a presence in *Second Life* which is only seen as 'a complementary
activity'.[48] This constitutes a tactical and resistant approach to the potential
for absorption by the structures of the global system, be they corporate
capitalist enterprises or the facilities for imagined communities provided
by networked digital technologies. The parodic, critical approach to the
discourse of corporate capitalism thus prevails, just.

If the parody of corporate capitalism in Ilich's work is unstable, this also
impacts the way in which we read his very prominent discourse of revolution, which conversely tends to slip quickly from the earnestness which we
might reasonably read into his support for the Zapatista cause into a more
playful, and potentially parodic, or at least self-contradictory mode. In his
narrative of the possible revolutionary occupation of a real island Ilich
notes on several occasions that one of his peers inspiration comes from the
figure of Che Guevara and, tacitly, his role in the Granma expedition,[49]
and the references to cells, central committees and related 'subcomandan-
cias' ['command centres'] are, as noted earlier, all suggestive of the history
of guerrilla warfare and the installation of socialist regimes. In the 'net-
island' narrative, as well as in other materials located on the server, there
are also appreciative references to the leaders of Latin American independence movements such as Simón Bolívar, to the Cuban Revolution, to the
Nicaraguan Sandinistas, as well as a significant number of references to
Maoism, and even to the peasants of the French Revolution (and the origin
of the word 'sabotage').

By and large these references to revolutions and revolutionary heroes are
in consonance with the ideological underpinnings of Zapatismo examined
earlier and some of the idealism expressed by Ilich and friends will be derived
from that of the Zapatistas themselves. This perhaps accounts for the lack
of close attention paid to the history of Maoism in China or elsewhere in
the world, and a preference for (knowingly) 'romantic' references to figures such as Che Guevara and Mao Zedong. With respect to his attitude
to Maoism in particular, in personal communication Ilich simply asserted
that 'the ideas of collectivity behind 20th century maoist theory and their
aesthetics are a bit appealing.'[50] Accordingly, Ilich uses verbal and visual
references to Mao and Maoism in his work as an unproblematic shorthand
for 'revolution' understood in a positive light. This also extends to the use of
Chinese characters on the server and related cultural products to provide an
aesthetics of revolution. Examples include the Chinese calligraphy–styled Z
(for Zorro/Zapatista) on one side of the Digital Maoist/Material Sunflower
coin, with a pixelated hand-grenade icon on the other ('Digital Material

Sunflower' c.2011),[51] as well as an ideograph that Ilich originally believed was the symbol for revolution in the I-Ching and which appears in several places in Ilich's work, most notably as a constant feature in the often mutating art work at the top of the homepage of *possibleworlds.org* [see Fig. 6.1 for an example].[52]

But as with the discourse of corporate capitalism, there is an excess of references to all sorts of different revolutions in Ilich's work[53] with the result that what has been considered so different about Zapatista revolutionary principles is potentially lost in the mix. Furthermore, the impossible contiguity of the discourse of revolution to that of corporate capitalism inevitably compromises its ability to be read as sincere. In a virtual world where 'revolución' is aligned with the concept of the 'maquiladora' (Sweatshop.biz) and where equally 'ideologically correct' revolutionary products in Ilich's terms—beer from China, cigars from Cuba or coffee from Chiapas—have been bought and sold in Digital Maoist/Materialist Sunflowers (Ilich 2010), the discourse of revolution is not working as an antidote to neoliberalism. This confusion of discourses is clear in the self-description of Diego de la Vega s.a. de c.v. at the top of a drop-down menu of options on its homepage as 'Engaged in the business of NAFTA revolution'. While this might suggest a critical appreciation of NAFTA which will be revolutionised from within by conglomerates such as this, we should also be aware that it may mean carrying out NAFTA's 'revolutionary' neoliberal policies to the letter. Furthermore, as noted earlier in Ilich's narrative of the genesis of his net.island, the guerrillas/revolutionaries are also colonialists and capitalists and the discourse of their revolution even goes on to develop echoes of the 'forced labour camps' of the Soviet Gulag, the Chinese Cultural Revolution or the Holocaust.[54] There may thus be a deliberate parody of traditional revolutionary idealism in this parable of the creation and dissipation of a utopia condensed into a few short lines. Nevertheless, dismissing Ilich's discourse of revolution as parody is not so clear-cut and perhaps a better way of understanding this narrative is as a deliberate attempt to destabilise any coherent reading via the tactics of (Digital Zapatista) 'semantic disruption', a process in which terms mutate constantly such that parody is not on stable ground and the reader is kept asking questions.

Given the treatment of the discourse of revolution in Ilich's work outlined above, one is led to question whether there is anything new that Ilich's discourse of revolution has to suggest—an equivalent to Sánchez's 'revolución.com'—or whether this example of Digital Zapatista 'semantic disruption' will only rake over the coals of past revolutionary fires, and that in a radically ambivalent way? Will digital technologies and the virtual fora they enable allow Ilich to imagine a better kind of utopia rather than wallow in revolutionary nostalgia? Will he manage any better than Sánchez to resemanticise the discourse of revolution for a digital age?

Ilich conceives of digital technologies themselves as 'revolutionary', although not necessarily revolutionary in a way that can be endorsed unproblematically and instead he proposes to use these technologies 'de formas creativas, disruptivas, emancipatorias y de formas híbridas para que un mundo mejor sea posible' ['in creative, disruptive, emancipatory ways, and in hybrid ways that will help make a better world possible'] ('Partido CyberPunk' [CyberPunk Party], on *possibleworlds.org*). Furthermore, in line with his definition of 'digital materialism' as a closer appreciation of the imbrications of online and offline worlds, and as a development from his earlier more isolationist net-island concept, he argues, 'Maybe from our little corner of the Internet we can in fact collaborate, change the material reality by generating creative flows from experimental economics and finances, hacktivism, and narrative media'.[55] He is also aware of how difficult such a project might be: 'Cuando se piensa en una comunidad virtual se piensa en una utopía ideal, a pesar de que la experiencia demuestre una y otra vez que los caminos de la vida no son [. . .] los que creíamos' ['When we imagine a virtual community we imagine an ideal utopia, in spite of the fact that experience has shown time and again that the way life works is not the way we imagined it would'] (*World Street Journal*, 06/04/11).

Ilich's best conceptualisation of his aspirations with regard to a resemanticised discourse of revolution that proposes to harness the potential of new technologies but still very much in line with some of the more traditional revolutionary thought that inspires him is encapsulated in his (reworking of the) concept of 'digital Maoism'. It is evident that Ilich has been inspired to use the term 'digital Maoism' as a result of an article written by Jaron Lanier entitled 'Digital Maoism: The Hazards of the New Online Collectivism' (2006) in which Lanier critiques the 'hive mentality' promoted by key Web 2.0 applications through an (untheorised) association of this with the collectivist principles of Maoism (or communism more generally). Nevertheless, when Ilich makes specific reference to Lanier's essay, it may be understood that he has read 'digital Maoism' as a positive updating of the traditional Maoism he endorses: 'en honor a la colmena web 2.0, la realidad virtual y a Jaron Lanier decimos desde la Latinoamérica espiritual: !Que viva el maoísmo digital!' ['in honour of the web 2.0 hive, virtual reality and Jaron Lanier, from a Latin America of the spirit we say: Long live digital Maoism!'] (*World Street Journal* 08/04/11). Thus, Diego de la Vega s.a. de c.v. is described as having a 'política económica de insolvencia artificial y maoísmo digital' ['an artificially insolvent and digitally Maoist political economy'] and Sweatshop Revolución as being 'una verdadera pequeña sweatshop maoísta digital' ['a real little digital Maoist sweatshop'].[56] While elsewhere Ilich goes some way to acknowledging Lanier's approach to digital Maoism as a critique,[57] he generally chooses to resemanticise it to suit his own purposes, in the same way that he repurposes Chinese artist Ai Weiwei's porcelain sunflower seeds, as exhibited at the Tate Modern in London in 2010–11,[58] to become the key commodity on which his virtual currency, the Digital Maoist/Material Sunflower, is based, through what he terms a form of 'ideological hijack'.[59] This, then, is a resemanticised discourse of revolution that ostensibly recycles old dogma with digital modifiers, but it at least does so knowingly, and again, this semantic slipperiness may perhaps be recouped as simply part of the 'disruption' that digital Zapatismo proposes.

Mike González's description of Zapatismo and its poetics, as seen in the writings of Subcomandante Marcos, offers a particularly apposite depiction of the nature of Ilich's *possibleworlds.org* server:

> the paradoxes and internal contradictions [. . .] suggest a pluralistic vision, a notion of a political and imaginative space in which different views, visions and strategies for change can coexist without resolution. Aesthetically, it is pleasing and complex. Politically, it is paralysing.
>
> (González 2000)

Ilich and friends are neither revolutionary pragmatists nor hard-nosed ideologues. Instead, in the spirit of the poetry of Zapatista revolution, they are true romantics, more taken with the idea of revolution and its promise of utopia—hence the frequent references—than with the facts of history: 'Amor. vida evolución. siempre. ¡viva la revolución de los colores!' ['Love. life evolution. forever. long live the colour revolutions!'] (Ilich 2006–07), or even more simply put, '¡Viva la Revolution!' (*World Street Journal* 07/04/11, sic).

REVOLUCIÓN.SHOWBIZ?

If critics such as Jorge Castañeda have worried that 'the idea of revolution', conceived in traditional political terms, has 'withered and virtually died' in Latin America in the years since the Cold War ended, there is another significant factor that must be brought to bear when considering the more fluid circulation of ideas of Latin American-ness in these times of globalisation, cultural commodification and streamed media. That is the way in which the concept of revolution has been consciously redeployed as part of the (self-) marketing of Latin America through its popular cultural icons and outputs. Even though the consecrated icons of real Latin American revolutionary movements such as Che Guevara and his messianic image have long been part of the lexicon of popular culture,[60] willingly put into circulation in that context by photographers such as Korda who were very much influenced by the visual discourse of US advertising and fashion photography (Quiroga 2005:94–95), in contemporary Latin American popular culture, revolution is often freed from its reference to social movements and utopianism altogether, and repackaged as simply part of the highly marketable brand of titillatingly exotic, erotic, dangerous and unpredictable *latinidad*. Thus revolution is pure sex appeal in Ricky Martin's 'lovin' revolution'[61] or an edgy mix of sex and violence for smash-hit Puerto Rican *reggaetón* duo Wisin and Yandel.[62] Fran Ilich's parody of the appropriation of revolutionary discourse, both linguistic and visual, by media conglomerates runs a significant risk of being viewed as indistinguishable from this popular cultural repackaging of Latin American revolutionary discourse, despite its proposal of tactical resistance from within.

The seemingly more unequivocal and direct approach of blogging—in comparison with Ilich's use of parody—is also no guarantee of the assumption of a more contestatory position. Like Yoani Sánchez, pop-idols such as Shakira also blog in support of the Cuban Damas de Blanco and other good causes (Shakira 2010), and no matter how sincere Shakira's blogging activities, her incursions in this field clearly allow for the connection to be made in the popular imaginary between the sex appeal of the divas of mass culture and contestatory political discourse of a sort typically associated with 'revolution', regardless of whether it is actually for or against 'La Revolución [Cubana]' itself. Talking about politics—without getting too heavily into ideology—is thus made sexy. This aspect of the 'Latin American brand' has undoubtedly had some effect on the way Sánchez's work has circulated around the globe. In the unsigned article that appeared in *The Wall Street Journal* in December 2007 and that was responsible for drawing the world's attention to Sánchez's work, she was described in the first paragraphs in terms that emphasised her youth, body shape, dress sense and feminine charms—'the waif-like 32-year old', who 'flashed a wide smile' at guards and so on ('The Cuban Revolution' 2007). She is thus presented to the world as a feisty, feminine figure—very much on a par with Shakira and other Latin(a) American pop icons—before she is considered as a serious voice in the world of politics or independent journalism. Furthermore, while the title of the article itself—'The Cuban Revolution: Yoaní Sánchez Fights Tropical Totalitarianism, One Post at a Time'—does attempt to convey her political position, it 'sells itself' with a reference to 'The Cuban Revolution'. Although this gestures towards Sánchez's exploitation of the 'revolutionary' potential of new media, it also inevitably refers to the 1959 Cuban Revolution and the romantic appeal of a bygone era and its hopes of utopia. Thus, regardless of whether a cultural producer such as Sánchez seeks to resemanticise the discourse of revolution in her work, circulation online may militate against such change by catering to the mass tastes and conceptions of the West which are still predicated on the marketability of the discourse of good old (Latin American) revolution(s) and on sex, violence and the rest of the package.

It is arguable that, for better or for worse, the discourse of revolution is still closely bound up with Latin American-ness, in complex and ever-mutating configurations that draw on real contestatory political agendas working in counterpoint with powerful currents of desire no matter how stereotypical (for sexual encounters, for danger, for novelty, for that which has been prohibited in the striated, controlled spaces of European and North American cultural imaginaries). The 'revolution' in new media has not automatically guaranteed a reinvigoration of the discourse of revolution, or of the association of revolution with Latin American-ness—despite the early promise of the Zapatistas' use of the internet for contestatory purposes that put Latin America firmly on some people's maps of internet geography. To be effective, the discourse of revolution must be renegotiated at every turn, both with respect to the history of revolutions in the region and beyond, and with respect to its other associations and metaphorical deployments. It is this constant process of renegotiation in evidence in the work of both Sánchez and Ilich which is most valuable.

Conclusion: Latin American Cultural Practice Online

A Continuing Dialogue between Discourses

Throughout this volume, we have intended to show that online cultural products and practices are as central to the contemporary 'invention of Latin America' (Mignolo 2000) as predigital media were in the past, and we argue that, rather than online works proving to be the site of the radically new or the free-floating, Latin American online works interpellate (often critically) preexisting discourses of the region and beyond.

As we noted in our Introduction, the discourses of Latin American-ness we have covered in this volume are not meant to be exhaustive; rather, we elected to focus on a representative sample of some of the most prominent discourses that have been mobilised to represent Latin America over time, in particular, although not exclusively, from the birth of the incipient nations in the nineteenth century to the end of the twentieth century. Our intention has, therefore, been to trace how these discourses are renegotiated, reappropriated and, at times, challenged in the works of online cultural producers.

The discourses we selected started with the broad, overarching category of the cartographic imagination which maps out the entirety of Latin(o) America in Chapter One, and subsequently moved onto more discrete discourses which interrogate a particular facet of that Latin American-ness as mapped out in the cartographic approaches of this first chapter. In this respect, all the subsequent chapters, and their respective discourses, are, to an extent, subsets of this founding notion of the mapping of the region.

That said, it is important to note that by this we do not mean that our chapters are meant to be understood teleologically; while Chapter One does, indeed, provide a clear starting point for our discourses, this does not mean that Chapter Six, on which we end this volume, is posited as the final point in the trajectory. That is, it is not the intention of this volume, by ending on Chapter Six, to posit revolution as the necessary culmination of all the preceding discourses, and, indeed, we do not view the relationships between these discourses as a necessarily linear nor one-way process. Rather, what we have aimed to do across the chapters of this volume is to explore where appropriate the interconnections and the intricate dialogues between the discourses, as well as indicate how the practitioners whose work we selected are often in dialogue with each other. In the same way as the web-based works we analyse often rely on complex and constant track-backs, hyperlinks and multiple pathways, we envisage our chapters as speaking to each other, rather than coming to a full stop at the end of Chapter Six. For instance, maps, in the shape of participatory mapping, form part of the *Hiperbarrio* project as analysed in Chapter Two, and thus share some connections with our earlier comments on cartographies in Chapter One.

Indeed, part of our impulse in tracing the interconnections across these discourses comes from the fact that the 'original', predigital discourses did not, themselves, exist in a vacuum but were, instead, the product of intense debates and cross-fertilisations stretching across generations of thinkers in Latin America. The discourses of race and *mestizaje* that we explore in Chapter Five, for instance, often spoke back, in the predigital conceptualisations, to the discourses of civilisation and barbarism as discussed in Chapter Four. Here, for instance, leading forerunners in the debates on *mestizo* identity, such as Martí's famous declarations in the late nineteenth century regarding 'nuestra América mestiza' ['our mestizo America'], were in explicit dialogue with—and of course, directly challenging—Sarmiento's writings; Martí's writing evoked Sarmiento's binary as a formula against which the notion of 'nuestra América mestiza' must pit itself, with Martí declaring the 'batalla entre la civilización y la barbarie' ['battle between civilisation and barbarism'] to be no more than a smoke-screen for the struggle between 'la falsa erudición y la naturaleza' ['false erudition and nature'] (Martí 1994:67).[1] Similarly, regarding the development of the notion of the lettered city, of which we speak in Chapter Two, Rama cited both Sarmiento *and* Rodó (among many others) in his *Lettered City* as examples of the *letrado*. Rama's bringing together of these two writers under the same epithet is, of course, not without its own complexities,[2] yet it nevertheless indicates how Rama's own theorisations read from, and spoke back to, those who articulated the discourses located in other chapters of our volume. Meanwhile, regarding the discourses of revolution, with which we deal in Chapter Six, a significant amount of the rhetoric and communiqués of the Zapatistas—some of the most vocal advocates of revolutionary change in recent years—are remobilisations of, and responses to, discourses of raced identity, as explored in Chapter Five.[3] These discourses, thus, in their predigital formats were the product of dialogue, rather than existing in an intellectual vacuum. So too the cultural products we have chosen as our case studies in this volume, although located within a particular chapter and its corresponding discourse, speak to and share concerns with works located in other chapters.

In addition to these internal dialogues between discourses, we have also, throughout this volume, aimed to explore what happens to these predigital discourses when they come into contact (or conflict) with, the possibilities and limitations offered by new media technologies. Here, as we set out in our Introduction, and have aimed to exemplify in the subsequent chapters, the globalised tools offered by the digital era do not (always, necessarily) imply cultural homogenisation, nor are they (always, necessarily) the corollary of neoliberalism. Regarding the latter, our chapters have aimed to illustrate the vibrant online cultural practice of a variety of Latin(o) American artists, and trace how the various cultural producers play with the existing tools of digital technologies in an ambivalent fashion, at times playing along with the accepted uses of such tools, and at others, reformulating them in tactical and partially resistant ways in the interstices of the (global, capitalist) system.

Regarding the former, our chapters have aimed to address the question of embeddedness on the internet—a central issue that has been occupying scholars in internet studies over the past decade—and we hope to have illustrated how Latin American forms of identification and cultural practice still adhere online. This is not to say that we propose here a utopian picture in which all content creation by Latin Americans on the internet necessarily preserves the cultural specificity of the region; there are, clearly, a myriad of examples of Latin Americans blogging, tweeting and creating online works that make no immediate reference to their status as Latin Americans. Rather, we argue throughout this volume that some of the most vibrant work being undertaken by Latin Americans online involves active and knowing mobilisations of cultural specificity.

This brings us back to the notion of the 'postregional' which we sketched out in our Introduction. Throughout this volume, we have attempted to explore how the online works we analyse force a rethinking of conventional conceptualisations of Latin American identity as exemplified in the six discourses we have chosen. These rethinkings are also accompanied by rethinkings of broader conceptualisations such as territoriality, agency, citizenship, and local and global affiliations, among others. Many of these notions are central to conceptualisations of Latin America itself as a region, and to current debates in Latin Americanism, in particular those taking place in recent years over the potential demise of the area studies model. With this in mind we argue that, if the rise of the internet and other associated new media technologies has meant the waning of the nation-state, but at the same time the rise of the global *and* the local, then it may be precisely by studying the works of Latin American online cultural producers where we might find articulations of this emergent, postregional Latin American identity.

Notes

NOTES TO THE INTRODUCTION

1. See, for instance, Miller and Slater who critique the understanding of the internet as a 'monolithic or placeless "cyberspace"' and cyberspace as understood as 'an experience of extreme "disembedding" from an offline reality' (Miller and Slater 2000:1&4).

2. According to social media statistics published on the Fast Track Media website at the time of writing, there are more than 93 million users of Facebook in Latin America and over 55 million users of Twitter in the region (Fast Track Media 2011). Orkut, a rival social networking platform, has historically been the leading platform in Brazil; see Holmes (2009), who notes that Brazilians make up 49.7% of Orkut's users.

3. The *Cansei* movement (meaning, 'I'm fed up [of this]') was an elitist protest movement which began in 2007, led by a platform of groups in the Movimento Cívico pelo Direito dos Brasileros, and was catalysed around the aviation disaster in July of that year, although it protested more broadly against the policies of the Lula government.

4. The reference to the diary format and *testimonio* as nonfiction genres is not, of course, to deny the complex issues of self-construction, truth-value and self-reflexivity in diary writing (see Bunkers and Huff 1996). Nor is it to deny the heated debates regarding *testimonio* and truth claims, the most famous of which were generated by Stoll's controversial response (Stoll 1999) to *Me llamo Rigoberta Menchú y así me nació la conciencia* (1983), and which subsequently provoked heated academic debate on the genre (see Arias 2001 and Beverley 2004). Rather, we are here setting out a distinction between the format and purpose behind the blog, vis-à-vis hypertext fiction.

5. The notion of hypertext fiction strictly speaking would refer only to those works in this volume that have a narrative arc or have discernible characters, the two most commonly recognised features comprising fiction. The notion of the narrative arc as the backbone of a work of fiction was expressed as early as Aristotle's *Poetics* (c.335 BC), which set out *muthos* (plot) as the schema of action and one of the central structuring features of the poetic art (Aristotle 1997:71). Aristotle's ideas were revived in many formalist and structuralist theories of the mid-twentieth century, particularly in works such as Propp's *Morphology of the Folk Tale* (1968), and Barthes's *S/Z* (1970). While such formalist-structuralist notions fell out of favour with the rise of poststructuralism from the late 1970s onwards (and indeed, Barthes's *S/Z* itself marked out this transition), it is interesting to note that the concept of the narrative arc has resurfaced in much contemporary computer game

theory; see for instance Young and Riedl (2003), and chapters in Wardrip-Fruin and Harrigan (2006). Here, where we make reference to the narrative arc, we refer to the fact that there must be an underlying notion of narrative, regardless of whether that arc may be punctuated by flash-backs, loops, nonlinear structures or multiple pathways, among others.

6. Although the term 'the global village' is nowadays in common parlance taken to refer to the internet, it was first coined by Marshall McLuhan in 1964 to refer to the 'speed-up' of the contemporary age (McLuhan 1973:101).

7. For a historical overview of the development of cyberfeminism, see Daniels J. (2009) and Paasonen (2011).

8. The distinction is drawn in de Certeau's *The Practice of Everyday Life*, where a 'strategy' is defined as 'the calculus of force-relationship', while a 'tactic' 'insinuates itself into the other's place, fragmentarily, without taking it over in its entirety' (de Certeau 1984:xix).

9. For more analysis of 'Digital Zapatismo', see Chapter Six in this volume.

10. We are here acknowledging the fact that many of the leading figures in Latin American cultural studies stress its multidisciplinary nature; see, for instance, Beverley who argues that 'the point of cultural studies was not so much to create a dialogue between disciplines as to challenge the integrity of disciplinary boundaries per se' (Beverley 1993:20), and Trigo who goes even further, suggesting that, since 'multi- inter- or transdisciplinarity are deeply engrained in Latin American writing', a 'polygraphic practice' had already 'contaminated the disciplines', even before the appearance of Latin American cultural studies proper (Trigo 2004:9).

NOTES TO CHAPTER 1

1. See also Bethell (2010:457–60) for a good overview of this.

2. Elena Serrano, 'Día del guerrillero heróico (el Che continental)', silkscreen print, 1968, widely circulated by the Organización de Solidaridad con los Pueblos de Asia, África y América Latina (OSPAAAL) (reproduced in Cushing 2003:63). Other iconic OSPAAAL posters/magazine covers also made use of the Latin American map-as-logo, as well as those of other continents and countries in the global South.

3. The magazine *Wired*, first published in 1993, covers current and future trends in technology, and Barlow has contributed as a writer. While an important publication in terms of its coverage of new media, it has been criticised by some as promoting an overly conservative view of the internet whereby technology is 'the destiny of capitalism' (Stallabrass 2003:73), and for its perpetuation of gender stereotypes in its portrayal of the 'superior hypermacho' expert (Millar 1998).

4. It is worth noting that the campaign for the '.ct' (i.e. country top-level domain) failed, and that campaigners subsequently focussed on '.cat' (i.e. sponsored top-level domain) as a language-based cultural identifier. For more on *Associació puntCAT*'s campaign, see Gerrand (2006).

5. As Horst notes, works such as those of JODI play with the existence of two texts: what the user would conventionally see, or the 'smooth and commercially softened surface' of the phenotext; and the generating codes or 'technical foundation' making up the genotext. In JODI's work, it is the genotext that produces an image, whereas the phenotext is 'abstract chaos' (Horst 2008:95).

6. The use of green phosphor screen-display font as a shorthand for computer code was popularised in the *Matrix* films (dirs Andy and Larry Wachowski)

and associated franchises in the form of the 'digital rain' or 'green strings of data' making up the matrix (Monnet 2002:233), a technique that in itself drew on the 1995 film, *Ghost in the Shell* (dir. Mamoru Oshii). For more on *The Matrix* franchise's borrowings from *Ghost in the Shell*, see Monnet (2002).

7. For more on Cortázar and his relationship to hypertext, see Landow (1997:38&56); Bolter (1991:148); Douglas (2001:38, 44&56); and Gache (2006b:153).

8. The term 'net.art' in itself encapsulates this notion; the now mythical origins of the term purportedly stem from an email message received by Vuk Cosic in 1995 in which, due to the incompatibility of the software, the majority of the text was rendered as incomprehensible ASCII code, with the exception of a short part reading ': [...] J8~g#l\;Net. Art{-^s1 [...]' (Shulgin 1997). Thus the origins of the term 'net.art' itself lie in the productive (and unexpected) uses of codes to generate art, and to generate reflection on that same art.

9. See the chapters in Casares's edited companion volume, *netart latino "database"* (2009), particularly those by Pagola and Baigorri, for debates on the challenges posed by this notion of internet art 'located' in Latin America.

10. In a specifically Latin American context, it is worth noting Juan Ospina González's resistant and ironic reuses of predigital gaming formats such as Backgammon and Minesweeper in the context of Colombia's contemporary power struggles in his 2004 work, *Juegos de guerra colombiana: tácticas de guerra irregular* [*Colombian War Games: Irregular War Tactics*], or Coco Fusco and Ricardo Domínguez's invoking and reworking of the classic boardgame formats of *Monopoly* and *Turista Nacional* to critique the *maquiladora* economy in *Turista Fronterizo* [*Border Tourist*] (2005).

11. The resistant reuse of the 'join-the-dots' formula can also be seen in the work of other Hispanic net.artists, most notably in Spanish artist Cristina Buendía's *No-pasatiempo* [*Not-a-Pass-time*] (2004), in which users are encouraged to challenge the ludic system by 'rebelándose contra la numeración y el recorrido sugerido' ['rebelling against the numbering and the suggested order'] in order to critique the images of domestic violence traced by the dots (Zafra 2005).

12. For more on *wwwwwwwww.jodi.org*, see Green (2004:40–41).

13. A particular case in point would be Mackern's *Raw War* trilogy, which resemanticises ASCII code and programming conventions in the context of global inequalities, conflicts and local cultures being erased by imperialism.

14. Although there are by now several volumes drawing together the work of scholars and practitioners of net.art, precise and universally accepted definitions of net.art are conspicuous by their absence. Where scholars have sketched out overviews of the genre, these tend to be in the form of explorations of underlying 'typologies' (Daniels, D. 2009:44–46) or 'inclusive practices' (Corby 2006:2), rather than hard-and-fast rules of exactly what net.art 'is'. Indeed, disagreements over the exact terminology—with some, such as Stallabrass or Green opting for 'internet art' (Stallabrass 2003; Green 2004), or others such as Corby advocating the use of the term 'network art' (Corby 2006), and yet others proposing a broader umbrella categories such as 'new media art' (Tribe, Jana and Grosenick 2007) or 'art of the digital age' (Wands 2006)—are indicative of the fact that net.art as a genre and practice is still in the process of being defined.

15. Indeed, it is worth noting that many of the artists included in Mackern's database do not necessarily classify themselves as 'net.artists' as such.

16. Although the first graphical browsers were developed in 1992, it was the release of the Mosaic graphical web browser in 1993 which made the web widely accessible to nonspecialists and permitted access to multimedia content. For

more on the development of Mosaic, Netscape and other graphical browsers, and the subsequent explosion of internet use, see Abbate (2000:217).

17. Since courier font is a monospace font, where all characters are identical in width, it was one of the preferred fonts in ASCII-art, in which the characters' being of a fixed size and shape is of importance in the formation of the image.

18. *Rasquachismo* (*rascuachismo*) is a tactical and resistant Chicano aesthetic or sensibility based on the recycling and reappropriation of mainstream US cultural products and values, and on 'making do' with what is at hand given one's position within society. Allatson notes its significant deployment in performance art (Allatson 2007:200-01).

19. For more on the *Transborder Immigrant Tool*, see Cárdenas *et al.* (2009).

20. The original *Eloísa Cartonera* was founded in 2003 in Argentina in the wake of the 2001 peso crash and the *corralito* ['freezing of bank accounts'], and aimed to produce books in a collective, with the covers made from second-hand cardboard purchased from the *cartoneros* ['rubbish pickers'] of Buenos Aires (for more on postcrash Argentina and the *cartoneros*, see Chapter Two of this volume). The movement subsequently spread to other Latin American countries, including Bolivia, Brazil, Chile, Mexico, Paraguay and Peru. For more on *Eloísa Cartonera* and the subsequent *Cartonera* projects, see Bilbija and Carbajal (2009).

21. There are, of course, some exceptions: Stallabrass's volume dedicates some pages to the Zapatistas (2003:53, 82–83&99), to Mejor Vida Corp (53) and to Roberto Baggio's work in Brazilian *favelas* (84), although these are by no means the main focuses of his volume.

22. It has to be said that Mackern was largely successful in this aim; prior to his work, there was no one site pulling together the works of artists across the region, and chapters in the companion volume by prominent practitioners attest to its leading role in creating a sense of community. For instance, Argentine net.artist and video artist Gustavo Romano highlights the significance of the database in preserving the richness and variety of net.art in Latin America (Romano 2009), while curator Nilo Casares, in an intriguing piece tracing the varying formats of the work via use of the Internet Archive WayBack Machine, flags up the importance of the work in guiding the viewer on a journey through net.art (Casares 2009).

23. Guillermo Gómez-Peña, for example, is simply listed as Mexican.

24. Navas figures in Mackern's 'database' under .sv for El Salvador.

25. Given this trajectory, it is perhaps telling that Pilar does not figure in Mackern's 'database', although arguably his work never purported to be exhaustive.

26. See Taylor (2012a) for detailed critique of the *Goobalization* trilogy.

27. It should, however, be noted that Navas cuts the song off just before the reference to 'el barrio' and 'la esquina'.

28. While it directs itself to 'Latinos', and the reference to 'el barrio' might be interpreted as shorthand for Hispanic USA, the references in the song to 'modelos importados' and its roll-call of Spanish American nation-states would suggest that the song is not specifically embracing the Latino communities of the USA in its exhortations. Navas's shortened version of the song further abridges the possibility of this alternative interpretation.

29. *Info Please* first started as a radio quiz show in 1938, becoming an annual almanac in 1947. The online version dates from 1998.

30. It does omit Haiti, Jamaica and the Guyanas, which, according to Navas, 'are not considered culturally part of Latin American discourse', though this does problematise the inclusion of Suriname and Belize (Navas 2012). It is perhaps best to consider that Navas, like Colón and Blades, has taken some poetic license with his roll-call of nation-states.

31. In the data given US inhabitants of Hispanic origin are listed as the largest minority population and the 'sizeable Spanish-speaking minority' is listed alongside English as the only two languages spoken in the US (*Info Please*, data from c.2000).
32. The implication here is that local narratives, or discourses of identity, should be 'delocalised'; that is, made intelligible for other audiences.
33. Dodge and Kitchin describe CAIDA researcher Young Hyun's hyperbolic models of internet routing using the software tool Walrus with its interactive three-dimensional fish-eye lens as 'evocative images' that 'look like strange nebulous jellyfish with complex dense fronds, floating in a black sea' (Dodge and Kitchin 2001a:48; stills from the project on pages 48–49). The visualisation in this particular case shows the 'routing topology of the Internet as measured by a skitter monitor based in London' in 2000 (Dodge and Kitchin 2001a:48).
34. Eick and colleagues' arc map is actually a still image of 'a flat world map with country boundaries and traffic flows represented as looping arcs traversing the Earth' taken from an interactive visualisation tool called SeeNet3D (Dodge and Kitchin 2001a:58). See Praba Pilar's *Cyberlabia* print 8 which recycles this image [Fig. 1.3].
35. See Eick and colleagues' visualisations of internet traffic that use a globe (Dodge and Kitchin 2001b: plate 2b).
36. Though he does note that contestation is possible (Castells 2000:165) and that this may be achieved by using the internet to challenge social exclusion (Castells 2001b:241), nevertheless, Castells thinks largely in terms of social activism rather than the 'artivist' projects studied here.
37. The prints run 1–4 and 6–8; print 5 is missing from the series.
38. Available both as a pdf online and for purchase in hard copy from the artist herself.
39. For more on Los Cybrids see Chapter Five in this volume.
40. Though not the early blood-and-guts cyberfeminism of the Australian group VNS Matrix that coined the term (Fernández 2002).
41. For an early critical approach to cyberfeminism see Hawthorne and Klein (1999).
42. The title is reminiscent of Luce Irigaray's iconic feminist manifesto, 'When Our Lips Speak Together', in *This Sex Which Is Not One* of 1977 (Irigaray 1985:205–18).
43. This map is not as well known as others that Pilar has used and there is no indication given in her credits of the map's original purpose.
44. The sexworker is more or less opaque at various points allowing the viewer to see through her to the map behind. Indeed, in some places it looks as though she is emerging from the cuboid structure.
45. Indeed Margaret Anne Clarke's study of the Brazilian state's role in promoting Brazil and the global South more generally as active participants in the information society, and in terms of its development of domestic strategies to improve digital inclusion, including the creative and resistant recycling of items of high-tech waste, offers just one example of the ways in which a Latin American state can challenge the determinism implicit in a theory of different 'worlds' (Clarke 2012).

NOTES TO CHAPTER 2

1. For other examples of this trend, see Taylor's article on the resignification of the streets in Miranda Zúñiga's *Vagamundo* (Taylor 2011), and the resignification of the US-Mexico border in Fusco and Domínguez (Taylor 2012b).

2. See Bosco (2006) for an overview of the association, including its origins in 1977 and the 1986 split.
3. This last feature—the use of a nonintuitive interface—is also evident in Zerbarini's homepage itself, where, for example, features such as the predominantly black screen, the fact that the menus are hidden within flickering dots, and the deliberately small typeface, making the text virtually illegible at 100% resolution, all contribute to making the user's access to her site complicated and challenging.
4. Irene Coremberg's *Túneles de la memoria* [*Memory Tunnels*], also included within the exhibition, locates its resistant memory in the subterranean spaces beneath the fabric of the city.
5. H.I.J.O.S (Hijos por la Identidad y la Justicia contra el Olvido y el Silencio [Sons and Daughters for Identity and Justice against Oblivion and Silence]) is an organisation founded in 1995 by the sons and daughters of the disappeared, which carried out demonstrations outside the homes of perpetrators of human rights abuses in forms of protest termed *escraches*. The acronym plays on the term 'hijos', and speaks to the politics of the Madres de Plaza de Mayo in the overt signaling of familial relationships.
6. The term 'Guerra Sucia' refers to the Argentine military dictatorship of 1976–1983. The term 'escraches' is derived from the Argentine slang verb, '*escrachar*', meaning 'to uncover', and involves public demonstrations that aim to expose the identities of the torturers of the regime. See Kaiser's illuminating article on the *escraches*, where she argues that they must be considered 'within the context of the memory battles taking place in Argentina' since they involve bringing 'the past into the public sphere' (Kaiser 2002:505&511).
7. For more on *Los rubios*'s problematisation of memory, see Lazzara's 2009 article, which explores how this film 'destabilize[s] the notions of memory, identity, and the real', and 'pushes documentary's *failure to document* to its outer limits' (Lazzara 2009:150&154; original emphasis). On *Potestad*, see Page, who argues that this film's primary intent is not to testify, but instead to question 'the politics of the act of remembering itself' (Page 2005:15).
8. The *Nunca más* [*Never Again*] report of 1984, produced by CONADEP (Comisión Nacional sobre la Desaparición de Personas [National Commission on Disappeared People]), calculates a total of approximately 340 secret detention centres in Argentina.
9. Di Paolantonio sets the figure of those detained and tortured at ESMA at 5,000 (Di Paolantonio 2008:25). It is worthy of note that shortly after Zerbarini made *Tejido de memoria*, the ESMA was turned into an 'espacio de memoria' ['space of memory'] to commemorate the lives of those who were disappeared during the Guerra Sucia.
10. The Ley de punto final (law 23,492) was passed in December 1986 to put an end to prosecution of those accused of violence during the dictatorship, while the Ley de obediencia debida (law 23,521), passed in 1987, stated that neither officers nor subordinates could be legally punished for crimes committed during the dictatorship since they were acting out of 'due obedience'. Kirchner and the Argentine legislature took the first steps towards repealing both laws in 2003, leading to two years of legal debates, at the culmination of which, in 2005, the Argentine Supreme Court declared these amnesty laws unconstitutional, thus paving the way for future judicial proceedings. The repealing of these laws was largely seen as a victory for human rights, and led to the reopening of cases against the perpetrators of torture and other human rights abuses. For more on the repealing of these laws, see Roehrig (2009).
11. The image of Buenos Aires as a cosmopolitan port city has been the mainstay of much cultural production on and about Argentina, from Ernesto Sábato's

notion of the 'Babylonic' city to Rubén Darío's neologism 'cosmopolis'. For more on this and other literary representations of Buenos Aires, see Wilson (1999:2&6).

12. Carlos Menem, President of Argentina from 1989–1999, was famous for ushering in a raft of neoliberal reforms, including the wholesale privatisation of state-run companies such as *Entel*, *Aerolíneas Argentinas* and *Yacimientos Perolíferos Fiscales*, among many others, the mass dismissal of thousands of state employees, the slashing of billions of dollars off government social spending, and the opening of the Argentine economy to international markets. As Keen and Haynes note, this 'latest round of neoliberal orthodoxy' deepened national income inequality, gave rise to increasing poverty and social inequality, and led to the 'appearance of a class of "new poor"' (Keen and Haynes 2009:530).

13. The reference here is to the Argentine financial crisis of 2001, which culminated in the *corralito* [freeze on bank accounts] and the crash in December of that year.

14. While the exact number of *cartoneros* ['rubbish pickers'] is hard to specify, according to a survey cited in Schamber and Suárez, there were an estimated 10,800 *cartoneros* and street vendors in the city of Buenos Aires in 2002 (Schamber and Suárez 2002:6), while according to Chronopoulos, an estimated 100,000 people in Buenos Aires and Gran Buenos Aires rely on the income generated from this work (Chronopoulos 2006).

15. While the surge in numbers of the *cartoneros* took place after the 2001 crash, Chronopoulos argues that the seeds were sown in the Menem era, since, according to his research, the *cartoneros* are composed primarily of people who were 'displaced from the formal economy due to neo-liberal reforms in the 1990s' (Chronopoulos 2006:171).

16. The first *Siluetazo* protest took place in 1983 in the Plaza de Mayo, and involved the tracing of life-sized silhouettes onto paper, which were then pasted onto the city walls, in order to represent the 'presence of an absence' (Longoni 2007:176) of those who were disappeared during the dictatorship.

17. See Feitlowitz (1998), especially Chapter Six, for more on the 'death flights', in particular in the wake of the Scilingo revelations of 1995.

18. In 1986 the Madres split into two factions: the Madres de Plaza de Mayo-Línea Fundadora ['Founding Line'] and the Asociación Madres de Plaza de Mayo ['Association']. María del Carmen de Berrocal belongs to the latter of these two groups. As Bosco has shown, although the initial disagreements which led to the split were over leadership and organisational structure, the two groups now represent different political approaches: for the Línea Fundadora the main goal has remained 'finding truth and justice regarding the disappearances of the 1970s', whereas the Asociación 'increasingly positioned itself as a group working for social change more generally' and 'adopted a more revolutionary, anti-capitalist and anarchist stand' (Bosco 2004:388).

19. The fate and whereabouts of the estimated 500 babies who were born to women in captivity and subsequently abducted is an ongoing controversy in Argentina. The Abuelas de Plaza de Mayo ['grandmothers'] association was set up specifically to trace these missing children, and their work continues today (see Arditti 1999).

20. Indeed, it is significant that one of the video excerpts included in *Tejido de memoria* features Berrocal insisting on the importance of *habeas corpus* to the Madres' struggles.

21. The project's name is given differing forms of capitalisation in different locations on the site, including 'hiperbarrio', 'Hiperbarrio' and 'HiperBarrio'.

For reasons of clarity it has been standardised to 'Hiperbarrio' in this chapter, except where direct quotations from the site give a different variant.

22. Indeed, *Hiperbarrio* itself is a creative commons site, as indicated in the footer of each webpage.

23. Such a recuperation of popular forms of expression can also be noted in recent Colombian films and literature, such as Víctor Gaviria's 1990 film, *Rodrigo D., no futuro* [*Rodrigo D., no futuro*], and Alonso J. Salazar's *No nacimos pa' semilla* [*Born to Die*] (1990), both of which make use of *parlache* in their representation of their young, male, disenfranchised protagonists. It also has parallels with the use of urban slang in other contexts; see, for example, Sá's analysis of the online expression of urban youth from Capão Redondo, a poor neighbourhood on the south side of São Paulo in Brazil, in which she reveals how the 'characteristic traits of *paulista* oral language' are gaining 'a significant written register' through their use in online postings (Sá 2007:127).

24. YouTube statistics at the time of writing show a total of 24,802 views of *Historia de Suso* as at 27 April 2011.

25. We are here paraphrasing Rigoberta Menchú's famous statement in the opening paragraphs of her *testimonio* that her story is 'la vida de todos los guatamaltecos pobres' ['the story of all poor Guatemalans'] and that 'mi situación engloba toda la realidad de un pueblo' ['my situation encapsulates the reality of an entire people'] (Menchú 1992:21).

26. *Paisa* is a dialectal form of Spanish spoken by people in the North-West of Colombia, including Medellín, and is characterised by a high number of local and regional expressions, as well as by the use of *voseo* as the second-person singular form of address.

27. OpenStreetMap (OSM) is an organisation set up in 2004 which offers collaborative, editable maps of the world under a Creative Commons licence.

28. The Instituto Geográfico Agustín Codazzi is the Colombian state entity in charge of producing the official map of Colombia, and its website includes a searchable map of Colombia.

NOTES TO CHAPTER 3

1. Shortly after the publication of the 1996 anthology which brought together the work of Alberto Fuguet, Sergio Gómez and Edmundo Paz Soldán, among others, under the epithet 'McOndo', Fuguet's 1997 article 'I Am Not a Magic Realist!' set down some of the reasons for the McOndo generation's rejection of magical realism. Echoing the words of Reinaldo Arenas, Fuguet contended that 'Latin American magic realism has degenerated' and that it represents 'nothing more than a desire to pander to the magic-starved sensibilities of North American and European readers'. By contrast, Fuguet declared, 'unlike the ethereal world of García Márquez's imaginary Macondo, my own world is something much closer to what I call "McOndo"—a world of McDonald's, Macintoshes and condos' (Fuguet 1997).

2. Although the term 'Macon.doc' has appeared briefly in two recent publications, its use has not been fully theorised. Bisama's article used the term 'Macon.doc' to refer to a new relationship between subject, writing and urban space (Bisama 2002); Jaime Alejandro Rodríguez, one of the authors whose work is analysed in this chapter, uses the term in passing while referring to the McOndo generation, but does not expand on the meaning of 'Macon.doc' itself.

3. See Higgins (1990:148–53) for a detailed mapping out of the events of the novel onto Latin America's history.

4. Landow and Bolter's own subsequent publications, and revised editions of their earlier works, have themselves been more nuanced in this regard.

5. Hayles's point has been made by many other scholars of digital media; see, for instance, Aarseth's critique of the 'rhetoric of novelty, differentiation or freedom' which claims that 'digital technology enables readers to become authors' (Aarseth 1997:14): or Murray's reminder that 'activity alone is not agency' (Murray 1997:128).

6. The reader can access a 'map' by clicking on a link at the top of the main page which sets out the three basic divisions of the narrative, but there is no map or guidance as the reader goes along.

7. Although Rodríguez appears as lead author of the narrative, Carlos Roberto Torres Parra also appears under the 'authors' section of the website as being in charge of the digital design and interactivity. The 'credits' section, meanwhile, provides a longer list of contributors including Clara Inés Silva for the graphic design and illustrations, and Andrés López for the adaptation of texts.

8. We are here implicitly relying on Deleuze's notion of the 'society of control', as representing the workings of our contemporary, late capitalist era. Delezue argues that Foucault's original notion of disciplinary power has now given way to a new regime in which power is diffused throughout society and in which, drawing on Virilio, the 'ultra-rapid forms of free-floating control' are replacing 'the old disciplines operating in the time frame of a closed system' (Deleuze 1992:4). Within this new configuration, Deleuze argues, capitalism is now 'essentially dispersive' (Deleuze 1992:6), and its regime functions through the '*limitless postponements* of the societies of control' (Deleuze 1992:5; original emphasis).

9. Critics have frequently noted how Macondo, in its foundational period at least, represents an illusory, utopian locale; see, for instance, Fuentes (1969:60).

10. Indeed, it is striking how many of the reader responses to the question about location (currently standing at 75 postings) assume there is a direct correspondence between the futuristic Bogota depicted in the story and their contemporary experiences of the city.

11. On the death toll during the Bogotazo itself, Sharpless estimates that 'several thousand' died (Sharpless 1978:178), while Osquist puts a more exact figure on it, stating that at least 2,585 people died in Bogota (Osquist 1980:119). Braun, although arguing that the figures given in *El Espectador* and *El Tiempo*—substantially lower than those given by Sharpless and Osquist—are 'the best available', nevertheless concedes that these figures 'understate the reality', since many families clandestinely buried their dead (Braun 1985:171).

12. The reference here is to Lyotard's famous declarations regarding an 'incredulity towards meta-narratives' (Lyotard 1984:xxiv) and the concomitant rise of micro-narratives.

13. We do not here mean to dismiss potential readings against the grain, and take on board the scholarship which, from the 1980s, has problematised the notion of narrative suture; see, for instance Brown, who has argued that 'a spectator is in several places at once' (Browne 1975–76:12). Rather, we argue that access to the narrative is *predominantly* filtered through Gabriella.

14. Picasso painted 44 studies based on Velásquez's *Las Meninas*, the most famous of which was the large-scale version painted on 17 August 1957.

15. The question of Velázquez's perspective construction has generated heated debate among scholars as to the location of the mirror, the vanishing point of the painting, and the angle at which the artist stands, among others. See, for instance, Snyder and Cohen's response to Searle (both texts 1980).

16. It is worth noting that Barthes's 'Death of the Author' and *S/Z* (1970) were instrumental in informing Landow's seminal book on hypertext, with Landow drawing on Barthes's concepts such as networks and webs, and his distinction between readerly and writerly texts, in the development of his theory of hypertext.

17. Cortázar's theory as advanced vicariously through his 'surrogate author' (Vernon 1986:264) Morelli in *Rayuela* set up the *lector hembra* as a passive, nonintellectual reader who took a superficial approach to a text, as contrasted to the vitality, intellect and active mind of the *lector cómplice* ['complicit reader'] who would become 'copartícipe' ['coparticipant'] in the work of fiction (Cortázar 1963:561).

18. Early trends in cyberpunk fiction envisaged the 'console cowboy' as 'jacking into' cyberspace and leaving the 'meat' (that is, the body) behind. Such a conceptualisation has subsequently been much critiqued for its implicit gender politics; see for instance, Fernbach's illuminating analysis of the 'fantasized and fetishized technomasculinities' perpetuated by cyberpunk fiction (Fernbach 2000); or Balsamo, who denounces the 'gender conservatism' of cyberpunk writers (Balsamo 1996:130–31).

19. See, in particular, her 2006 volume, *Escrituras nomades* [*Nomadic Writings*].

20. Bell, for instance, argues that 'we experience cyberspace [. . .] by *mediating* the material and the symbolic' (Bell 2001:2); Lévy defines cyberspace as referring 'not only to the material infrastructure' but also to 'the human beings who navigate and nourish that infrastructure' (Lévy 2001:xvi); Nayar similarly defines cyberspace as encompassing 'the worlds and domains generated by digital information and communications technologies' as well as 'a set of relations and actions in electronic space' (Nayar 2010:2).

21. For more on the 'electronic frontier' and its critiques, see Chapter One in this volume.

22. See, for instance, Davies (2003:66–69).

23. Bemberg's *Camila* (1984) was released just after the return to democracy in 1983, and was seen by over 2 million viewers in Argentina, the largest audience ever for a national film. As scholars such as King have shown, the popularity of the film in large part lay in the fact that national audiences read it as an allegory for the recent dictatorship (King 2000:23).

24. Borges's fiction, in particular 'El jardín de los senderos que se birfucan' ['The Garden of Forking Paths'] and 'La biblioteca de Babel' ['The Library of Babel'], is often seen as prefiguring the multisequentiality of hypertext. See, for instance, discussions of Borges's fiction as anticipatory of electronic literature in Herbrechter and Callus (2009), Hayles (1999), Bolter (1991) and Sassón-Henry (2006), among others. Indeed, it is worth noting that Gache herself draws parallels between Borges's short stories and literary experimentation leading up to digital technologies, in her own theoretical writings, most notably in *Escrituras nómades* (Gache 2006b:32–33&162–64).

25. Cortázar gave the term 'capítulos prescindibles' to those chapters falling in the third section of *Rayuela*, subtitled 'De otros lados' ['Elsewhere']. They formed the backbone of the self-conscious literary play undertaken by *Rayuela*, and, in the words of Boldy, were characterised by 'generic incongruities, ironic foregrounding and critical *mises en abîme*' (Boldy 1990:130).

26. Of course, there is quite possibly a further layer of recursive author/*wreader* here: Given that 'Mariposas-libro' is based not only on quotations preloaded

by Gache, but also on those uploaded by users, the quotation could well have been submitted by a contributory *wreader* to this piece.

27. Indeed, Sierra has pointed out similarities between Gache's 'Mariposas-Libro' and *Rayuela*, given that 'the reader has to build a network of virtual connections in the text' (Sierra 2011).

28. For more on Gache and her extended dialogues with Surrealism, see her *Escrituras nómades*.

29. See in, particular, Sonvilla-Weiss (2010) for a detailed discussion of mash-up cultures.

30. See in this regard Pitman's analysis of how Blas Valdez disenabled the 'back' button in his stories, thus attempting to create an 'anti-hypertext' (Pitman 2007).

NOTES TO CHAPTER 4

1. As Martin has observed, 'like the Romans before them, the Spanish imperialists defined that which was other as barbarous, and themselves as civilized', and numerous studies have illustrated how colonial accounts of the Americas reproduced discourses of barbarism drawn from earlier contexts; see, for instance, Klein's illuminating study on the tendency of early sixteenth-century explorers and their illustrators to represent the native women as a type of female counterpart of the man-eating 'wild man' of European lore, and thus repeat preexisting European stereotypes (Klein 1995). See also Zea's excellent study of the origins of the term 'bárbaro', from the Greeks to present-day Latin America (Zea 1988).

2. As Rogers has observed, the *novela de la tierra* is often interpreted as a 'dramatization' of Sarmiento's binary (Rogers 2010:105). Examples of this include Gallegos's *Doña Bárbara* (1929), which pits the 'civilised' male hero against the 'barbarous' woman, and Güiraldes's *Don Segundo Sombra*, which engages with the civilisation/barbarism debates, although in its praise of the qualities of the *gaucho*, reverses some of Sarmiento's pronouncements.

3. See, for example, Nouzeilles's discussion of the perception of Patagonia as 'the last frontier' and as a 'chronotopical infinity stretching between modernity and barbarism' (Nouzeilles 1999:36&39).

4. Of course, nineteenth-century Argentine conceptualisations of the civilisation/barbarism divide as being mapped out spatially follow a history of such mappings, from the Greeks onwards; as Zea has observed, 'la dicotomía civilización/barbarie [funciona] como signos de poder y dependencia, de centro y periferia' [the dichotomy civilisation/barbarism [functions] as symbols of power and dependency, centre and periphery] (Zea 1988:21).

5. Harrison notes that the Greek idea of the '*barbaros*' was 'a term which seems originally to have designated those who could not speak Greek' (Harrison 2002:11), while Saïd notes that 'the Greeks often likened the incomprehensible languages of Barbarians to the twittering of birds' (Saïd 2002:100, n. 219).

6. *Borderismos* appear in Gómez-Peña's *The New World Border* (1996), while the figure of the Border Brujo is developed in the performance text of the same name published in *Warrior for Gringostroika* (1993), and has been described by Alaimo as performing 'Mexican/American subjectivities as sites of historical memory, political critique, language sorcery, and embedded, relational identities' (Alaimo 2000:174).

7. See, for instance, Kuhnheim's article (1998) which provides a critique of Gómez-Peña's use of the border metaphor as representative of hybrid identity in *The New World Border*, and also Chapter Five of this volume.

8. La Pocha Nostra is a 'transdisciplinary arts organization' set up in 1993 by Gómez-Peña, Roberto Sifuentes and Nola Mariano, whose name, according their manifesto, translates as 'the cartel of cultural bastards' (Gómez-Peña 2005a:78).

9. The images are taken from performances of the same name, coordinated by Gómez-Peña and Ali Dadgar, and performed by Gómez-Peña, Dadgar, Bella Warda, Roham Shaikhani, Isis Rodríguez, Mark Piñate, Liz Lerma and E. R. Lewis.

10. See, for instance, Spivak, who has called Said's volume *the* sourcebook in the discipline of postcolonial studies (Spivak, cited in Young 2003:8), or Huggan who describes it as 'one of the late twentieth century's few totemic critical works' (Huggan 2005:125).

11. Said comments, for instance, on the polarising representations which present the Orient as 'irrational, depraved, childlike, different', and the European, by contrast, as 'rational, virtuous, mature, "normal"' (Said 2003:40).

12. Visual representations of La Llorona have been popularised through the multiple filmic portrayals of this figure, most of which fall within Mexico's long-standing horror movie genre. The vast majority of these depict the eponymous protagonist as wearing a black cloak or a white veil; see, for instance, *La herencia de la Llorona* [*The Legacy of La Llorona*] (dir. Mauricio Magdeleno, 1947), *La Llorona* (dir. René Cardona 1960) and *La maldicion de la Llorona* [*The Curse of La Llorona*] (dir. Rafael Baledon, 1963) as a representative sample.

13. Although the scimitar is often used as a visual shorthand for Arab culture, as scholars have shown, the reality is somewhat more complex. As Peter Gottshalk and Gabriel Greenberg have noted, 'although Arab defenders in the Levant used straight-edged swords for the first two centuries of the Crusades, as was the norm amongst Crusaders, Western cultural memory forgets this. Instead, the sharply curved scimitar became a primary symbol of difference, marking the supposed chasm between Arab Muslims and the European Christians as seen in any number of Hollywood films' (Gottshalk and Greenberg 2008:46).

14. The more specifically racial aspects of Gómez-Peña's performance of ethnocyborg figures are analysed in the following chapter.

15. In his 2002 article, Foster comments on the 'long-standing technique of "reverse anthropology", in which Gómez-Peña and his collaborators generate performance personae by stylizing and exaggerating stereotypes of Mexicans' (Foster 2002:50–51).

16. Again, there are resonances here with many of Gómez-Peña's earlier works, particularly in the conjunction museum-ethnography-savages; there are similarities, for instance, with his performances with Coco Fusco of caged human exhibits which undertake, in the words of Alice Wexler, 'an ironic reversal of the five-century-old history of ethnographic exhibitions' within the framework of the 'demystification of the museum' (Wexler 2007:27–28).

17. The imbrication of anthropology in colonialism, and the danger that certain practices of anthropology might perpetuate imperialist stances, has often been debated within the discipline of anthropology itself from the late 1980s onwards. Comaroff has usefully summed up what he terms the 'colonial critique' of anthropology, which held that 'the entire theoretical scaffolding of anthropological knowledge was rotten to the core' and that its practices were 'corollaries of the racialization of difference, not to mention of the radical "othering" [. . .] at the dark heart of the discipline' (Comaroff 2010:525).

18. For more on these two movements, see Longoni's introduction to the edited work, *El siluetazo* (2008), and Wright's 2005 article on the *mujeres de negro*.

19. See, for instance, Restrepo, who notes that the 'erotic and dangerous figure of the Amazon' expressed European fears (Restrepo 2003:53).

20. The full list of terms in *Relational Border Map* is as follows: 1984; 7/7; 9/11; Alien; Blade Runner; Border Patrol; Bug; Contagion; Control; Corporation; Culture; Cyberspace; God; History; Information; Language; Metropolis; News; Noise; Oil; Order; Police; Race; Time; Window; World Border; World Trade. Here given in alpha-numerical order for ease of reference, when appearing in the work, the words occupy random and constantly shifting positions on the screen.

21. For more on *The Yes Men* and the Bhopal disaster, see Veldstra (2010).

22. US-based Union Carbide consistently denied responsibility for the Bhopal disaster, and instead pointed the finger of blame at Union Carbide India, notwithstanding the fact that this latter was in fact owned by Union Carbide. As Veldstra has put it, 'in other words, Union Carbide worked to deflect blame onto India itself' (Veldstra 2010:139). In this sense, Union Carbide makes use of world trade when it is to its own advantages, but then denies this same fact as a way of evading corporate responsibility for the disaster.

23. For more on the history of Indymedia, see Platon and Deuze (2003) and Pickard (2006).

24. For a brief overview of both of these projects, see Broeckmann (1997:49–50) and Stallabrass (2003:102–03).

25. The writ of *habeas corpus*, the safeguard by which citizens are protected against executive detentions in the absence of judicial trials, is granted in Article 1, Section 9, Clause 2 of the US Constitution. A series of legislations brought in by the Bush administration aimed to restrict the right to *habeas corpus*, in particular the Patriot Act of 2001 and the Detainee Treatment Act of 2005, both of which had serious implications over the right to *habeas corpus* for Guantánamo detainees. For more on the implications of these legislations for *habeas corpus* and human rights more broadly, see Buky (2006).

NOTES TO CHAPTER 5

1. For reasons of space, in this chapter, Latina/o will be used to refer to both Chicanas/os and other groups of Spanish American ancestry in the United States unless a distinction needs to be made.

2. For detailed studies of the *casta* system, see Vázquez (2007) and Martínez (2009).

3. For a useful account of the relationship of the term *raza* as used in Latin America to the concept of race in the English language, and in particular in US uses, see C. Rodríguez (2000). For conceptualisations of 'Latin looks' see C. Rodríguez (1997) and Dávila (2002).

4. Images may be performative and a naturalised performance may simply recycle stereotypes thus reinscribing reification. It is not the medium itself that is important so much as the way in which it works to convey its message.

5. For the purposes of this chapter, the 1991 version of the essay from *Simians, Cyborgs, and Women* has been used.

6. Hoeg's concept of 'a kind of "cybermestizaje"' refers to 'the possibility of transcending current embodied relations offered by the novel concept of virtual identities' (Hoeg 2000:95). For this he gives the example of the protagonist of Carmen Boullosa's *Duerme* (1994) whose 'performativity and material body are in constant flux, and therefore immune to rigid categorisation' (Hoeg 2000:99). His analysis, although brief, is highly suggestive in its gloss on (critical) *mestizaje* and cyborg subjectivity. Nevertheless, Hoeg's approach does not avoid the danger that *mestizaje* may be freed from a particular history and invoked as a modus operandi for all (of us) posthumans—he even cites Boullosa's argument that 'we should all be *mestizos*' (Hoeg 2000:99). This is potentially disempowering for *mestiza/o* and other subaltern subjectivities. As other critics have noted there is a tendency in mainstream US (and European) culture to appropriate the more appealing aspects of Latino culture such that 'we can all be Latin American now' (Beasely-Murray 2003:223).

7. See, for example, the hypermedia work available online produced by digital media artists Lucia Grossberger Morales [*Sangre boliviana*, 1994) and Jacalyn López García (*Glasshouses: A Tour of American Assimilation from a Mexican-American Perspective*, 1997).

8. The denaturalisation of the body and the focus on issues of power and violence in the representation of these cyborg figures points to this, although not unproblematically, as will be seen in the more detailed analysis of examples later in this chapter.

9. La Malinche was *conquistador* Hernán Cortés's indigenous translator, mistress and mother of his child—the first *mestizo*—and her name is typically associated with betrayal (of one's race) and lack of patriotism in Mexican popular culture. Feminist scholars such as Gloria Anzaldúa, Donna Haraway and many others besides have worked hard to resemanticise the meaning of her name and promote her as a figure of survival and resistance. (See also Alarcón 1982.)

10. The best of these critics are aware that in evoking '*la mestiza*' they are making reference to a *female* body from a specific ethnoracially defined group and they subsequently pay at least some attention to the relationship of real *mestizas* to digital technology (see, for example, Nakamura 2002:111–16). This is not always the case, however.

11. Nakamura also, suggestively, argues that the body of *la mestiza* functions prosthetically for Anglo-American academics—they use it to effect a 'reverse colonization' of cyberspace where the 'white computer-using liberal [. . .] insert[s] and reenvision[s] herself as other', as 'more . . . *colorful*' (Nakamura 2002:115; original emphasis).

12. Haraway's resistant cyborgs were also tacitly those that could be seen.

13. The most significant works that have been published on race and 'cyberspace', later digital culture more broadly conceived, include: Kolko, Nakamura and Rodman (2000), Nakamura (2002), chapters in Lee and Wong (2003b) and Silver and Massanari (2006), Nakamura (2008), McGahan (2008), Everett (2008; 2009), Chun (2006) and Chun and Joyrich (2009). Earlier, but still influential, essays by critics/cultural producers such as Nakamura, Ziauddin Sardar, Ananda Mitra, Jennifer González and Guillermo Gómez-Peña, among others, have also been reedited in the readers on cyberculture/new media edited by Trend (2001), Bell and Kennedy (2000) and Nayar (2010).

14. See, for example, Lykke and Braidotti (1996), Balsamo (1996), Wolmark (1999), and a number of articles in Green and Adams (2001).

15. In a later publication Ow also pursued a similar line of argument in a study of the representation of Asian cyborgs in the computer game *Shadow Warrior* (Ow 2000).

16. Gómez-Peña's work is referred to in passing in almost all the key monographs and anthologies on race and cyberculture/digital culture/new media (for example, Kolko, Nakamura and Rodman [2000], Nakamura [2002] or Everett [2009]). He has also received very thorough and perspicacious study with respect to the confluence in his work of issues of race and new technologies in the work of scholars such as Foster (2002), Miller (2004), and McGahan (2008), particularly with respect to his performance pieces from the 1990s (*Temple of Confessions* [1994–]; *The Mexterminator* [1995–]) and his publications (*The New World Border* [1996]; *Dangerous Border Crossers* [1999]). His writings on the subject of ethnoracial identity and the internet have also been included in several more wide-ranging anthologies and readers on digital culture (Hershmann Leeson [1996]; Trend [2001]). Quite tellingly, he has featured in the anglophone academy's coverage of world 'cybercultures' to the virtual exclusion of any other Latin(o) American online cultural producer or phenomenon bar the internet use of the Zapatistas and subsequent development of Digital Zapatismo. (For more detailed analysis of Digital Zapatismo, see Chapter Six in this volume.)

17. In the works studied in this chapter Gómez-Peña hyphenates the term 'ethno-cyborg'. In the materials referenced in Chapter Four, however, he wrote it as one word, 'ethnocyborg'. In this chapter, we have preferred to use the hyphenated version in consonance with the materials studied.

18. His use of the term 'poly-cultural cyborg' is a reference to the work of Allucquère Rosanne Stone, as he makes clear elsewhere in the same interview (González and Gómez-Peña 2009:249).

19. 'The Virtual Barrio' was first published in 1995 and in a final, revised form in 1997 (as reproduced in *Dangerous Border Crossers* [2000]). It is the latter version that has been consulted here. The article/manifesto has been subsequently reprinted in a number of different anthologies on digital culture: Trend (2001), for example, reproduces the text from a version published in Hershmann Leeson (1996).

20. *Coyote* is the name given to those who earn a living helping illegal immigrants to cross the US-Mexico border.

21. Although not evident in translation, in the statement 'el ciberespacio es café' Lozano-Hemmer and Gómez-Peña are referring playfully to the popularity of 'cibercafés' ['internet cafés'] in the 1990s/early 2000s.

22. See Beasley-Murray's conceptualisation of 'viral *latinidad*' and his anchoring of this concept in the origin of the SirCam virus in Latin America (Beasley-Murray 2003).

23. See also Harpold and Philip (2000) for a fascinating account of the discourse of 'cyber-cleanliness' and its relationship to race.

24. Some early performances using the material gathered from the questionnaire were also streamed live on the website (Dixon 2007:501).

25. See Chapter Four in this volume for detailed study of this last project.

26. A derogatory term for La Malinche.

27. For a definition of *rasquachismo* (*rascuachismo*) see Chapter One, note 18.

28. Both Roberto Sifuentes's Cyber-Vato and Gómez-Peña's El Mad Mex from the *Mexterminator* project are referred to as both cyborgs and as replicants (Gómez-Peña 2000:44).

29. In the photograph by Eugenio Castro labelled 'El Mad Mex' and displayed in 'Ethno-Techno: A Virtual Museum of Radical Latino Imagery and Fetishized Identities' (Gómez-Peña and La Pocha Nostra 1998–c.2000).

30. McGahan also finds Gómez-Peña's satirisation of the pseudo-scientific discourse of the opinion poll conveyed via the online questionnaire more radical than the resultant representation of ethno-cyborgs (McGahan 2008).

31. In the 'Virtual Museum of Radical Latino Imagery and Fetishized Identities' there are ironic glosses of what the images might mean. The essays and performance texts that appear on Gómez-Peña's websites and in published form also complement the images in a way that ensures a more critical appreciation of the artists' intentions.

32. Note that Pilar's self-description as 'New York/Colombian' in the context of her work with Los Cybrids is different from her self-description as a San Francisco 'Bay Area/Colombian' in the context of her work on her own *Cyberlabia* project studied in Chapter One.

33. Self-descriptions taken from the 'Artists' page on Los Cybrids' website. In terms of their relationship to Gómez-Peña, the group has worked with the Galería de la Raza in San Francisco, an institution with which Gómez-Peña is also intimately involved. At the time of Los Cybrids' involvement with the gallery it was being directed by Carolina Ponce de León, Gómez-Peña's partner. Garcia also undertook a year-long 'Master Residency in performance' with Gómez-Peña in 2000.

34. 'Manifesto', Los Cybrids' website.

35. The site was last updated in 2003 and was finally taken offline in late 2007. Dates for the group's offline existence given on Pilar's website. Dates for the existence of its website derived from the Internet Archive WayBack Machine. The group's last known performance took place at the 'Powering Up, Powering Down' event hosted by Teknika Radica at University of California–San Diego in early 2004 (Teknika Radica 2004). Present at the event were a number of figures from the academic establishment who have been closely involved in the elaboration of cyborg theory/posthumanism (Allucquère Rosanne Stone) and in work on race and cyberspace (Lisa Nakamura and Anna Everett).

36. Al Luján's 'Resist the Dot Con' mural (2000) did achieve substantial notoriety as a result of its appearance on the billboard and has been subsequently reproduced in numerous different media (Leaños c.2005).

37. 'Bios' from current version of *Alex Rivera.com* website.

38. Castillo (2011) also confirms this artistic genealogy.

39. The Bracero Program (1942–64) was an agreement between the US and Mexican governments that enabled the US to import temporary labourers from Mexico to make up for the loss of manpower occasioned by the Second World War and its aftermath, as well as the draconian repatriation of Mexican immigrants during the Great Depression of the 1930s (Snodgrass 2011).

40. Castillo (2011) also provides more data regarding the various different iterations of the short film and the website. The current version of the website is referenced in the bibliography to this volume (Rivera 2009–). Earlier versions may be accessed through the Internet Archive WayBack Machine.

41. The text accompanying each mural on the group's website makes its aims very clear.

42. Information given in the text accompanying the mural on Los Cybrids' website.

43. See Dawson's study of Black British artist Keith Piper's internet-based works for a similar approach to questions of race, representation, surveillance and new technologies (Dawson 2001).

44. Text accompanying the mural on Los Cybrids' website.

45. González also observes the ominous and dystopian imagery used in these murals (González, J. 2006:349–50).

46. 'Cybrid' is a scientific term from the field of stem cell research that refers to 'a cytoplasmic hybrid' (Knowles c.2010).

47. The changing self-portraits at the top of the 'Artists' page gesture towards the group members' identities as *mestiza/o* cyborgs in their combination of

anthropological images of racial 'specimens' mixed with the patterns and textures of digital material. This is particularly clear in the image of Pilar. The footer to its website also juxtaposes ASCII code with a strip of DNA, thus gesturing at the combination of cybernetics and implicitly 'raced' human beings as *mestiza/o* cyborgs.

48. '¡Órale!' is a Mexican Spanish exclamation which is the equivalent of 'Hey!'. The 'jota' in 'jotascript' refers to the J of Leaños's middle name, which he usually writes as 'Jota'. 'Te chingas' is Mexican Spanish for 'You're screwed'.

49. In fact they would switch repeatedly between the screen with a black background and the same screen with a light grey background.

50. This is the final 2003 version. Earlier versions of the pop-up warning simply said: 'WARNING! Cybrid Ideological Bacteria Downloading! WARNING!'.

51. Even small details such as its preference of the term 'bacteria' to 'virus' speak of its systematic desire to denaturalise language so as to better reveal the hidden alignment of race with infection.

52. Castillo compares the site at length with corporate labour outsourcing sites such as Cognizant, Bleum, Penske and Genpact (Castillo 2011).

NOTES TO CHAPTER 6

1. The Zapatistas were not the first Latin American group to engage in such practices, nor even necessarily themselves the original architects of their own web-presence. However, they have certainly become iconic in terms of the rest of the world's identification of Latin America's use of the internet. See Pitman (2007) for more detailed analysis.

2. While hacktivism refers to computer hacking for activist purposes and may include illegal activities, tactical media refers to the resistant use of different forms of mass media (including the internet) and generally restricts itself to what has been termed 'Electronic Civil Disobedience' but stops short of illegal acts. The difference between these two forms is, however, frequently far from clear. Both are also often considered as resistant art practices, given the high levels of creativity that are deployed in the name of resistance. For basic definitions, see Nayar (2010:100–03).

3. Voeux estimates that in 2008 there were c.150 independent journalists working in Cuba (Voeux 2008:2). See also Venegas (2010:168–71).

4. 'Internet: Mitos y realidades. Cuba en la Red', programme aired on *Televisión Cubana*, 22 January 2004 (quoted in Uxó 2010:12.4).

5. For more on the Cuban government's exploitation and policing of the internet see also Sullivan and Fernández (2000) and Venegas (2010). Ownership of key items of technology such as PCs and accessories, as well as video recorders, photocopiers and mobile phones, and the purchase of internet access accounts in Cuban pesos (although not in US dollars), were prohibited in Cuba during the 2000s (Uxó 2010:12.5). Some of these policies have been relaxed since the investiture of Raúl Castro in 2008.

6. Clearly, blogs can be written for many purposes, not all of which will be overtly political, and they may be considered more of a form of testimonial or life writing than of journalism; in a Latin American context, see Taylor (2007:244–45) for an analysis of the nature of the blog with respect to life writing, and Paz Soldán (2007:260–61) for an analysis of the relationship of the blog to the Latin American literary-journalistic *crónica* form. Individual blogs may of course choose to define their purpose quite clearly; however, significant numbers of blogs combine these features in different posts, identifying themselves more by the author's name than by a consistent theme or goal.

7. This title plays on the blogger's concerns about writing under her real name. Until mid-2008 she used the pseudonym Eva.
8. The portal also exists in a slightly different format under the title *Voces Cubanas* (2009–).
9. The launch of her blog predates by several months her husband's creation of the blog portal *Desde Cuba* and his own blog which he started in December 2007.
10. A five-year period of ideological 'retrenchment and intolerance' lasting from 1970 to 1975 (Kapcia 2008:41).
11. Much of the biographical information here, and in what follows, is synthesised from Sánchez's own blog posts, as well as her introduction to *Cuba libre* (2010:9–17), Porter's introduction to Sánchez's *Havana Real* (2011:ix–xv), and Henken's article (2010). Information on the 'polémica intelectual' is from Henken.
12. The letter 'Y' is relatively rarely used in Spanish.
13. See, for example, the awareness of strong generational identities evident in the writing of Leonardo Padura Fuentes. For allowing access to her work on this topic, thanks are due to University of Leeds doctoral student Diana Battaglia.
14. Sánchez's choice of title for her blog also undoubtedly makes reference to a more international understanding of recent generations, where she situates herself (spiritually at least) with Generation Y, or the 'Net Generation', with its familiarity with network society and its technologies, and its less dogmatic and more civic-minded characteristics (Cannon 2010).
15. Sites are now available (from the flag buttons at the top of the *Generación Y* logo) in nearly 20 different languages including Italian, French, German, Russian, Japanese and Chinese, but also Persian, Catalan and Finnish. These sites are selective and further study might be undertaken to consider the choices of which posts merit translation.
16. It is interesting to note how these books which are intended for an international market choose to sell Sánchez's blog on their front covers with reference to the typical iconography of the Cuban Revolution encapsulated in its flag (the colours, stripes and single star) and/or the faded glory of old Havana. All this is clearly in stark contrast to the nature of the blog itself. And while the design of the title bar of Sánchez's blog does employ some red, black and white, even the hint of some stripes, this is combined with the image of an open filing cabinet suggesting escape from the confines of revolutionary Cuba, and significantly, there are no stars in evidence.
17. Government censors have applied a filter that slows down the speed at which the blog loads onto a user's browser so as to make it virtually inaccessible (Henken 2010:220–21). The Cuban search engine Dos por Tres also fails to return any results for 'Yoani' (Uxó 2010:12.8).
18. Raúl Castro has not responded to a similar set of questions prepared for him.
19. See, for example, 'Móvil-activismo' ['Mobile Phone Activism'] (19/09/10) and 'Móvil-activismo 2' (22/09/10). In addition to her work in the development and maintenance of the blog portal *Desde Cuba*, Sánchez has also promoted blogging by running a blogging competition (La Isla Virtual, 2008) and workshops (the Café/Academia Blogger has been in operation since Spring 2009).
20. See Kapcia (2008) for an overview of the Cuban revolutionary process (Chapter 2:46–63) and a detailed analysis of popular mobilisation and other forms of participation in Cuba in the decades following the Revolution itself (Chapter 3:64–88).
21. In the published version in Spanish of Sánchez's blog, there is a post that does clearly acknowledge Guillén's work in its title which is a quotation from 'Tengo' ('abierto democrático: en fin, el mar' ['open and democratic: in short, the sea'] 09/11/07; in Sánchez 2010:73–74). It has been impossible to

establish whether this and one other contiguous post reproduced in the book have disappeared from the online blog archives by accident or as a deliberate sleight of hand intended to limit acknowledgement of Guillén's influence. The first reason seems, however, more probable than the second.

22. The growing use of smartphones and Twitter by Sánchez and others is also significant.

23. *Habeas data* is a writ whereby a person can request that s/he be provided with information held about him/her. Sánchez uses the term to insinuate that if Cubans are denied information of events, particularly domestic ones that concern them directly, by the official Cuban media, they will find ways to disseminate and access that information online.

24. This reference to weaving 'el deshilachado tapiz de nuestra sociedad civil' ['the frayed tapestry of our civil society'] and to net-weaving is recurrent in her work and specifically identified as a feminist approach in some posts ('Cosas de hombres' ['Matters for Men'] 18/06/08).

25. This is a relatively common metaphor to express the role that internet access plays in the opinion of many Cubans living on the island.

26. This is the title of a popular children's song in Cuba.

27. Commentators included Carlos Fuentes, John Berger and Roger Burbach (González, M. 2000; Radu 2004).

28. Although Maoism in China indulged in ideological excesses and caused great suffering to the Chinese people during the Cultural Revolution (1966–76), and although as it has spread internationally, it has also been the ideology underpinning of some of the most despotic regimes in twentieth-century history, for some it still has a positive ideological resonance that other forms of socialism and associated regimes do not. Particular features of the ideology (not necessarily the practice) that account for its appeal in Latin America, and particularly for the Zapatistas, may include its idealism, its rejection of the paternalistic role of the Party in favour of a more dialogic relationship between leaders and the masses, its focus on the rural rather than urban proletariat (agrarian socialism), and its advocation of People's War via guerrilla tactics (Rothwell 2010).

29. Unless otherwise indicated, the biographical information given here has been confirmed by Ilich himself (Ilich, personal email, 4 May 2012).

30. Contra-Cultura (menor) (1993:11), cited in Fallon (2007:164). See Fallon's article for more detailed analysis of Ilich's early work relating to the US-Mexican border region.

31. For more information on Ilich's video/net.film output, see Baugh (2008).

32. For a Mexican journalist's account of hacktivism, borderhacking and Ilich's role see Sandoval, H. (2006).

33. See Comité Clandestino Revolucionario Indígena, Comandancia General del Ejército Zapatista de Liberación Nacional (2005).

34. Nb. *possibleworlds.org* should not be confused with Possible Worlds (http://possibleworlds.com/), a prominent New York–based CGI design company.

35. The 'listening tour' of Mexico that Subcomandante Marcos and other Zapatistas undertook in 2006 as an alternative campaign to those waged by the candidates for the Mexican presidency that year.

36. Ilich, personal email, 7 February 2012.

37. Issue 1 (June 2005) is dedicated to 'media activismo, hacktivismo y net.culture subversiva' (sic) ['tactical media, hacktivism and subversive net.culture'].

38. Ilich, personal email, 23 December 2011.

39. Although this subtle difference is far from systematic in Ilich's writings.

40. The game was still under construction when this chapter was being researched in November/December 2011.

41. 'About Diego de la Vega', on *Diego de la Vega s.a. de c.v.* (2008–).
42. For example, the lexia on the 'grupo de trabajo forzado' in 'net-island: the blueprint of possible worlds' describes the use of the term 'grupo de trabajo forzado' ['forced labour group'] as 'un guiño' (Ilich 2006–07).
43. Ilich, personal email, 3 January 2012.
44. Ilich, personal email, 15 December 2011.
45. Regardless of the financial justification, this is a highly unusual decision in the field of Latin(o) American online cultural production.
46. Ilich, email circular to Spacebank account holders, 2 January 2012.
47. Ilich's 'net.island' game, that is intended to replace the hypermedia 'net-island' blueprint, describes itself in its development phase (November 2011) as a 'mundo virtual no-inmersivo' ['non-immersive virtual world'] or '*alternate reality game*' (added emphasis).
48. Ilich, email circular to Spacebank account holders, 2 January 2012.
49. Granma was the name of the yacht that Guevara, Castro and others sailed on to get from the USA to Cuba in 1956 in the run-up to the Revolution of 1959. It has since become an iconic reference for the Revolution and its ideology—as noted earlier, it is the title of the regime's official newspaper.
50. Ilich, personal email, 15 December 2011.
51. The symbol has no meaning in Chinese.
52. Ilich notes that he was subsequently informed that it is the symbol for 'abundance' in the I-Ching (Ilich, personal email, 15 December 2011); an error which he is happy to embrace.
53. Even the Industrial Revolution gets a mention ('Partido Cyberpunk', on *possibleworlds.org*).
54. There is a reference (albeit a question) as to whether 'el trabajo nos hará libres' ['work will set us free'], a clear echo of the maxim posted above the gates of many of the concentration camps of the Holocaust ('Grupo de trabajo forzado', Ilich 2006–07).
55. Ilich, email circular to Spacebank account holders, 2 January 2012.
56. 'About Diego de la Vega', on *Diego de la Vega s.a. de c.v.* (2008–) and *World Street Journal* 07/04/11, respectively.
57. Ilich, personal email, 16 December 2011.
58. Ilich has managed to buy some of the sunflower seeds from the same village that Ai Weiwei's seeds came from (Ilich, personal email, 15 December 2011). Ai Weiwei's work is critical of both contemporary neoliberal Chinese policies as well as of the legacy of Maoism. Ilich's association of Ai Weiwei's sunflower seeds with his own positive appreciation of Maoism constitutes the 'ideological hijack' to which Ilich refers.
59. Caption appearing in the first frame of the video loaded onto the Spacebank homepage.
60. Wickham-Crowley, for example, describes the growth in popular interest in Latin American guerrillas in the West in the 1960s (prompted by the success of the Cuban Revolution) and reminds his reader not to forget 'the number of posters adorning university walls throughout the world, graced with the quasi-beatific, black-bereted image of [Che] Guevara' (Wickham-Crowley 1993:4).
61. Ricky Martin has a track entitled 'Revolución' on his 1995 *A medio vivir* [*Half a Life*] album.
62. Wisin and Yandel's seventh album is entitled *La Revolución* (2009).

Bibliography

Aarseth, Espen J. 1997. *Cybertext: Perspectives on Ergodic Literature* (Baltimore: Johns Hopkins University Press).

Abbate, Janet. 2000. *Inventing the Internet* (Cambridge, MA: MIT Press).

Achugar, Hugo. 2003. 'Local/Global Latin Americanisms: "Theoretical Babbling" Apropos of Roberto Fernández Retamar', *Interventions*, 5:1, 125–41.

Agosín, Marjorie. 2008. *Tapestries of Hope, Threads of Love: The Arpillera Movement in Chile*, 2nd ed. (Lanham: Rowman and Littlefield).

Alaimo, Stacy. 2000. 'Multiculturalism and Epistemic Rupture: The Vanishing Acts of Guillermo Gómez-Peña and Alfredo Véa Jr.', *MELUS: Journal of the Society for the Study of the Multi-Ethnic Literature of the United States*, 25:2, 163–85.

Alarcón, Norma. 1982. 'Chicana's Feminist Literature: A Revision through Malintzin', in *This Bridge Called My Back: Writings by Radical Women of Color*, ed. Cherrie Moraga and Gloria Anzaldúa (Watertown: Persephone Press), pp. 182–90.

Alcaide, Carmen. 1997. 'El arte concreto en Argentina: Invencionismo—Madí—Perceptismo', *Arte, Individuo y Sociedad*, 9, 223–44.

Allatson, Paul. 2007. *Key Terms in Latino/a Cultural and Literary Studies* (Oxford: Blackwell).

Anderson, Benedict. 1991. *Imagined Communities*, revised ed. (London: Verso).

Appadurai, Arjun. 1996. *Modernity at Large: Cultural Dimensions of Globalization* (Minneapolis: University of Minnesota Press).

Ardao, Arturo. 1980. *Génesis de la idea y el nombre de América Latina* (Caracas: Centro de Estudios Latinoamericanos Rómulo Gallegas).

Arditti, Rita. 1999. *Searching for Life: The Grandmothers of the Plaza de Mayo and the Disappeared Children of Argentina* (Berkeley: University of California Press).

Arias, Arturo, ed. 2001. *The Rigoberta Menchú Controversy* (Minneapolis: University of Minnesota Press).

Aristotle. 1997. *Aristotle's Poetics*, trans. George Whalley (Montreal: McGill-Queens University Press).

Aronowitz, Stanley. 2009. 'Reflections on Seattle', *Dialectical Anthropology*, 33:2, 203–8.

Avelar, Idelber. 2000. 'Toward a Genealogy of Latin Americanism', *Dispositio/n*, 49, 121–33.

———. 2005. 'Xenophobia and Diasporic Latin Americanism: Mapping Antagonisms around the "Foreign"', in *Ideologies of Hispanism*, ed. Mabel Moraña (Nashville: Vanderbilt University Press), pp. 269–83.

Ayers, Jeffrey M. 1999. 'From the Streets to the Internet: The Cyber-Diffusion of Contention', *The Annals of the American Academy of Political and Social Science*, 566, 132–43.

Baigorri, Laura. 2009. '*netart latino database*: el mapeo emocional de la Red. Diálogo con Brian Mackern', in *netart latino "database"*, ed. Nilo Casares (Badajoz: MEIAC), pp. 69–84.

———. 2010. 'Game Art: nuevas interfaces para el arte y el juego', *Revista KEPES*, 6, 151–65.

Balsamo, Anne. 1996. *Technologies of the Gendered Body: Reading Cyborg Women* (Durham: Duke University Press).

Barlow, John Perry. 1996. 'A Declaration of the Independence of Cyberspace', https://projects.eff.org/~barlow/Declaration-Final.html. Accessed: 1 August 2010.

Barthes, Roland. 1970. *S/Z* (Paris: Editions du Seuil).

Barthes, Roland. 1977. 'The Death of the Author', in *Image, Music, Text*, trans. Stephen Heath (New York: Hill and Wang), pp. 142–48.

Bauer, Kenneth. 2009. 'On the Politics and the Possibilities of Participatory Mapping and GIS: Using Spatial Technologies to Study Common Property and Land Use Change among Pastoralists in Central Tibet', *Cultural Geographies*, 16:2, 229–52.

Baugh, Scott L. 2008. '*Hecho en México*, @cross "Digital Divides": Border Graffiti and Narrative-Cinema Codes in *Una Ciudad*'s City', in *Mediating Chicana/o Culture: Multicultural American Vernacular*, ed. Scott L. Baugh (Newcastle-upon-Tyne: Cambridge Scholars Publishing), pp. 140–64.

Baumgärtel, Tilman. 2001. *net.art 2.0: New Materials towards Net Art* (Nürnberg: Verlag für Moderne Kunst).

Beasley-Murray, Jon. 2003. 'Latin American Studies and the Global System', in *The Companion to Latin American Studies*, ed. Philip Swanson (London: Arnold), pp. 222–38.

Bell, David. 2001. *An Introduction to Cybercultures* (London: Routledge).

Bell, David, and Barbara M. Kennedy, eds. 2000. *The Cybercultures Reader* (London: Routledge).

Benegas, Diego. 2011. '"If There's No Justice . . . "': Trauma and Identity in Postdictatorship Argentina', *Performance Research: A Journal of the Performing Arts*, 16:1, 20–30.

Bermúdez, Silvia, Antonio Cortijo Ocaña and Timothy McGovern, eds. 2002. *From Stateless Nations to Postnational Spain* (Boulder: Society of Spanish and Spanish-American Studies).

Bethell, Leslie. 2010. 'Brazil and "Latin America"', *Journal of Latin American Studies*, 42:3, 457–85.

Beverley, John. 1993. *Against Literature* (Minneapolis: University of Minnesota Press).

———. 2004. *Testimonio: On the Politics of Truth* (Minneapolis: University of Minnesota Press).

Bhabha, Homi. 1990. *Nation and Narration* (New York: Routledge).

Bilbija, Ksenija. 2008. 'What Is Left in the World of Books: Washington Cucurto and the *Eloísa Cartonera* Project in Argentina', *Studies in Latin American Popular Culture*, 27, 85–102.

Bilbija, Ksenija, and Paloma Celis Carbajal, eds. 2009. *Akademia: A Primer of Latin American Cartonera Publishers* (Madison: Parallel Press).

Bilello, Suzanne. 1996. 'Cuba's Independent Journalists Struggle to Establish a Free Press', Report to the UN Human Rights Commission, Committee to Protect Journalists, http://www.cpj.org/attacks96/sreports/cuba.html. Accessed: 22 November 2011.

Bisama, Álvaro. 2002. 'Hipertextualizar la ciudad letrada', *Cyber Humanitatis*, 23, http://www.revistas.uchile.cl/index.php/RCH/article/view/5620/5488. Accessed: 20 April 2012.

Blais, Joline, and Jon Ippolito. 2006. *At the Edge of Art* (London: Thames and Hudson).

Boldy, Steven. 1990. 'Julio Cortázar: *Rayuela*', in *Landmarks in Modern Latin American Fiction*, ed. Philip Swanson (London: Routledge), pp. 118–40.

Bolter, Jay David. 1991. *Writing Space: The Computer, Hypertext, and the History of Writing* (Hillsdale: Lawrence Erlbaum).

Bookchin, Natalie. 2006. 'Grave Digging and Net Art: A Proposal for the Future', in *Network Art: Practices and Positions*, ed. Tom Corby (London: Routledge), pp. 68–73.

Bordwell, David, and Kristin Thompson. 2004. *Film Art: An Introduction* (New York: McGraw-Hill).

Borges, Jorge Luis. 1999. 'A New Refutation of Time', in *The Total Library: Nonfiction 1922–1986*, trans. Esther Allen, Suzanne Jill Levine and Eliot Weinberger (London: Penguin), pp. 317–32. [First published 1944.]

Bosco, Fernando J. 2004. 'Human Rights Politics and Scaled Performances of Memory: Conflicts among the *Madres de Plaza de Mayo* in Argentina', *Social and Cultural Geography*, 5:3, 381–402.

———. 2006. 'The Madres de Plaza de Mayo and Three Decades of Human Rights' Activism: Embeddedness, Emotions, and Social Movements', *Annals of the Association of American Geographers*, 96:2, 342–65.

Braun, Herbert. 1985. *The Assassination of Gaitán: Public Life and Urban Violence in Colombia* (Madison: University of Wisconsin Press).

Breton, André. 1962. *Manifestes du surréalisme* (Paris: Pauvert). [First published 1924.]

Briggs, Helen. 2003. 'Maybe We Are the Martians', *BBC News*, 30 May. http://news.bbc.co.uk/1/hi/sci/tech/3050209.stm. Accessed: 20 April 2012.

Broeckmann, Andreas. 1997. 'Towards an Aesthetics of Heterogenesis', *Convergence: The International Journal of Research into New Media Technologies*, 3:2, 48–58.

Brown, J. Andrew. 2010. *Cyborgs in Latin America* (New York: Palgrave Macmillan).

Brown, Jonathan, and Carmen Garrido. 1998. *Velázquez: The Technique of Genius* (New Haven: Yale University Press).

Browne, Nick. 1975–76. 'The Spectator in the Text: The Rhetoric of Stagecoach', *Film Quarterly*, 29:2, 26–38.

Buky, Michael. 2006. 'Patriot Games: Taking Liberties', *Social Alternatives*, 25:3, 32–37.

Bunkers, Suzanne L., and Cynthia Anne Huff, eds. 1996. *Inscribing the Daily: Critical Essays on Women's Diaries* (Amherst: University of Massachusetts Press).

Callahan, Manuel. 2005. 'Why Not Share a Dream? Zapatismo as Political and Cultural Practice', *Humboldt Journal of Social Relations*, 29:1, 6–37.

Calvino, Italo. 1974. *Invisible Cities*, trans. William Weaver (London: Harcourt Brace).

Calvo Peña, Beatriz, ed. 2010a. *Buena Vista Social Blog: Internet y libertad de expresión en Cuba* (Valencia: Advana Vieja).

———. 2010b. 'Internet, comunidad y democracia: la blogosfera cubana teje su propia "isla virtual"', in *Buena Vista Social Blog: Internet y libertad de expresión en Cuba*, ed. Beatriz Calvo Peña (Valencia: Advana Vieja), pp. 147–79.

Cannon, Stephen. 2010. 'When Gen Y Speaks, Boomers Must Listen', *Huffington Post*, 24 August, http://www.huffingtonpost.com/stephen-cannon/when-gen-y-speaks-boomers_b_692694.html. Accessed: 5 January 2012.

Cárdenas, Micha, Amy Sara Carroll, Ricardo Domínguez and Brett Stalbaum. 2009. 'The Transborder Immigrant Tool: Violence, Solidarity and Hope in Post-NAFTA Circuits of Bodies Electr(on)/ic', *Proceedings of the MobileHCI Conference 2009*, http://www.uni-siegen.de/locatingmedia/workshops/mobilehci/cardenas_the_transborder_immigrant_tool.pdf. Accessed: 28 March 2012.

Casares, Nilo, ed. 2009. *netart latino "database"* (Badajoz: MEIAC).

Castañeda, Jorge G. 1993. *Utopia Unarmed: The Latin American Left after the Cold War* (New York: Vintage).

Castañeda, Luz Stella. 2005. 'El parlache: resultados de una investigación lexicográfica', *Forma y función*, 18, 74–101.

Castells, Manuel. 2000. *The Information Age: Economy, Society and Culture*, vol. 3: *End of Millennium*. 2nd ed. (Oxford: Blackwell).

———. 2001a. 'Epilogue: Informationalism and the Network Society', in *The Hacker Ethic, and the Spirit of the Information Age*, ed. Pekka Himanen (London: Random House), pp. 155–78.

———. 2001b. *The Internet Galaxy: Reflections on the Internet, Business, and Society* (Oxford: Oxford University Press).

———. 2010. *The Rise of the Network Society*, 2nd ed. (Oxford: Blackwell).

Castillo, Debra A. 2005. *Redreaming America: Toward a Bilingual American Culture* (New York: State University of New York Press).

———. 2011. 'Rasquache Mockumentary: Alex Rivera's "Why Cybraceros?"', unpublished conference paper given at the International Conference on Latin American Cybercultural Studies, 19–20 May, University of Liverpool (supplied by the author).

Castillo, Debra A., and Edmundo Paz-Soldán, eds. 2001. *Latin American Literature and Mass Media* (New York: Garland).

Castro-Gómez, Santiago. 2003. 'Apogeo y decadencia de la teoría tradicional: una visión desde los intersticios', *Revista Iberoamericana*, 203, 343–353.

Cellini, Adelia. 2004. 'The Story behind Apple's "1984" TV Commercial: Big Brother at 20', *MacWorld*, 21:1, 18.

Chronopoulos, Themis. 2006. 'The *cartoneros* of Buenos Aires, 2001–2005', *City*, 10:2, 167–82.

Chun, Wendy Hui Kyong. 2006. *Control and Freedom: Power and Paranoia in the Age of Fiber Optics* (Cambridge, MA: MIT Press).

Chun, Wendy Hui Kyong, and Lynne Joyrich, eds. 2009. Special issue of *Camera Obscura 70: Feminism, Culture, and Media Studies*, dedicated to 'Race and/as Technology', 24:1.

Ciccoricco, David. 2007. *Reading Network Fiction* (Tuscaloosa: University of Alabama Press).

Civantos, Christina. 2006. *Between Argentines and Arabs: Argentine Orientalism, Arab Immigrants, and the Writing of Identity* (Albany: State University of New York Press).

Clark, John D. 2006. 'Linking the Web and the Street: Internet-Based "Dotcauses" and the "Anti-globalization" Movement', *World Development*, 34:1, 50–74.

Clarke, David B. and Marcus A. Doel. 2007. 'Shooting Space, Tracking Time: The City from Animated Photography to Vernacular Relativity', *Cultural Geographies*, 14:4, 589–609.

Clarke, Margaret Anne. 2012. 'Digital Brazil: Open Source Nation and the Meta-Recycling of Knowledge', in *The 'Noughties' in the Hispanic and Lusophone Worlds*, ed. Niamh Thornton and Kathy Bacon (Newcastle-upon-Tyne: Cambridge Scholars Publishing), pp. 203–17.

'CNYPG Welcomes Filmmaker Alex Rivera with his Film *Sleep Dealer* (2008)'. 2009. http://cinema.cornell.edu/cnypg/tours/alexrivera.html. Accessed: 29 January 2009.

Coleman, Sarah, and Nick Dyer-Witheford. 2007. 'Playing on the Digital Commons: Collectives, Capital and Contestation in Videogame Culture', *Media, Culture and Society*, 29:6, 934–53.

Comaroff, John. 2010. 'The End of Anthropology, Again: On the Future of an In/Discipline', *American Anthropologist*, 112:4, 524–38.

Comité Clandestino Revolucionario Indígena, Comandancia General del Ejército Zapatista de Liberación Nacional. 2005. 'Sexta Declaración de la Selva Lacandona', http://www.serazln-altos.org/sexta_declaracion.html. Accessed: 1 May 2012.

Committee on Internet Navigation and the Domain Name System, National Research Council. 2005. *Signposts in Cyberspace: The Domain Name System and Internet Navigation* (Washington, DC: National Academies Press).

Conaculta en los Estados, Dirección de Prensa. 2010. 'Gana Fran Ilich Morales Premio Binacional de Novela Joven Frontera de Palabras 2010', http://www.conaculta. gob.mx/estados/sala_prensa_detalle.php?id=4933. Accessed: 20 December 2011.

Corby, Tom, ed. 2006. *Network Art: Practices and Positions* (London: Routledge).

Cortázar, Julio. 1963. *Rayuela* (Madrid: Cátedra).

Crampton, Jeremy W. 2001. 'Maps as Social Constructions: Power, Communication, and Visualization', *Progress in Human Geography*, 25:2, 235–52.

———. 2009. 'Cartography: Performative, Participatory, Political', *Progress in Human Geography*, 33:6, 840–48.

Craven, David. 2002. 'Introduction: Revolving Definitions of the Word "Revolution"', in *Art and Revolution in Latin America, 1910–1990*, ed. David Craven (New Haven: Yale University Press), pp. 1–23.

Creeber, Glen, and Royston Martin, eds. 2008. *Digital Culture: Understanding New Media* (Maidenhead: Open University Press).

Critical Art Ensemble. 2001. *Digital Resistance: Explorations in Tactical Media* (New York: Autonomedia).

'The Cuban Revolution: Yoaní Sánchez Fights Tropical Totalitarianism, One Post at a Time', 2007. *The Wall Street Journal*, 22 December, http://online.wsj.com/public/ article/SB119829464027946687-2qWBoM9EpwF1S0_7hn6prJNeJqo_20080121. html?mod=tff_main_tff_top&apl=y&r=139874. Accessed: 6 January 2012.

Cushing, Lincoln. 2003. *¡Revolución! Cuban Poster Art* (San Francisco: Chronicle Books).

Cutting Edge: The Women's Research Group, ed. 2000. *Digital Desires: Language, Identity and New Technologies* (London: I. B. Tauris).

Dabove, Juan Pablo, and Carlos Jáuregui. 2003. 'Mapas heterotrópicos de América Latina', in *Heterotropías: narrativas de identidad y alteridad latinoamericana*, ed. Carlos Jáuregui and Juan Pablo Dabove (Pittsburgh: Instituto Internacional de Literatura Iberoamericana), pp. 7–35.

Daniels, Dieter. 2009. 'Historical Settings: Reverse Engineering Modernism with the Last Avant-Garde', in *Net Pioneers 1.0: Contextualizing Early Net-Based Art*, ed. Dieter Daniels and Gunther Reisinger (Berlin: Sternberg), pp. 15–62.

Daniels, Dieter, and Gunther Reisinger, eds. 2009. *Net Pioneers 1.0: Contextualizing Early Net-Based Art* (Berlin: Sternberg).

Daniels, Jesse. 2009. 'Rethinking Cyberfeminism(s): Race, Gender, and Embodiment', *Women's Studies Quarterly*, 37:1&2, 101–24.

Davies, Eryl W. 2003. *The Dissenting Reader: Feminist Approaches to the Hebrew Bible* (Aldershot: Ashgate).

Dávila, Arlene. 2002. 'Culture in the Ad World: Producing the Latin Look', in *Media Worlds: Anthropology in New Terrain*, ed. Faye D. Ginsburg, Lila Abu-Lughod and Brian Larkin (Berkeley: University of California Press), pp. 264–80.

Dawson, Ashley. 2001. 'Surveillance Sites: Digital Media and the Dual Society in Keith Piper's *Relocating the Remains*', *Postmodern Culture*, 12:1, http://pmc. iath.virginia.edu/text-only/issue.901/12.1dawson.txt. Accessed: 22 August 2011.

de Certeau, Michel. 1984. *The Practice of Everyday Life*, trans. Steven Rendall (Berkeley: University of California Press).

de la Campa, Ramón. 1999. *Latin Americanism* (Minneapolis: University of Minnesota Press).

———. 2005. 'Hispanism and Its Lines of Flight', in *Ideologies of Hispanism*, ed. Mabel Moraña (Nashville: Vanderbilt University Press), pp. 300–10.

Decena, Carlos Úlises, and Margaret Gray. 2006. 'Putting Transnationalism to Work: An Interview with Filmmaker Alex Rivera', *Social Text*, 24:3, 131–38.

Deleuze, Gilles. 1992. 'Post-Script on the Societies of Control', *October*, 59, 3–7.

Deleuze, Gilles, and Félix Guattari. 1977. *Anti-Oedipus: Capitalism and Schizophrenia*, trans. Robert Hurley, Mark Seem and Helen R. Lane (New York: Viking).

———. 2004. *A Thousand Plateaus: Capitalism and Schizophrenia*, trans. Brian Massumi (London: Continuum).

Deuze, Mark. 2006. 'Participation, Remediation, Bricolage: Considering Principal Components of a Digital Culture', *The Information Society: An International Journal*, 22:2, 63–75.

Di Paolantonio, Mario. 2008. 'A Site of Struggle, a Site of Conflicting Pedagogical Proposals: The Debates over Suitable Commemorative Form and Content for ESMA', *Journal of the Canadian Association for Curriculum Studies*, 6:2, 25–42.

'Digital Material Sunflower', c.2011, Eyebeam Art and Technology Centre, http://eyebeam.org/projects/digital-material-sunflower. Accessed: 15 June 2012.

Dixon, Steve. 2007. *Digital Performance: A History of New Media in Theater, Dance, Performance Art, and Installation*, with contributions by Barry Smith (Cambridge, MA: MIT Press).

Docuyanan, Faye. 2000. 'Governing Graffiti in Contested Urban Spaces', *PoLAR: Political and Legal Anthropology Review*, 23:1, 103–21.

Dodge, Martin, and Rob Kitchin. 2001a. *Atlas of Cyberspace* (Harlow: Addison-Wesley).

———. 2001b. *Mapping Cyberspace* (London: Routledge).

Douglas, Jane Yellowlees. 2001. *The End of Books—or Books without End? Reading Interactive Narratives* (Ann Arbor: University of Michigan Press).

Ebo, Bosah, ed. 2001. *Cyberimperialism?: Global Relations in the New Electronic Frontier* (Westport: Praeger).

Enteen, Jiliana. 2006. 'Spatial Conceptions of URLs: Tamil Eelam Networks on the World Wide Web', *New Media and Society*, 8:2, 229–49.

Esas voces que nos llegan. 2007–. http://esasvocesquenosllegan.wordpress.com/. Accessed: 2 July 2010.

Escobar, Arturo. 1999. 'Gender, Place and Networks: A Political Ecology of Cyberculture', in *Women@Internet: Creating New Cultures in Cyberspace*, ed. Wendy Harcourt (London: Zed Books), pp. 31–54.

Everett, Anna, ed. 2008. *Learning Race and Ethnicity: Youth and Digital Media* (Cambridge, MA: MIT Press).

———. 2009. *Digital Diaspora: A Race for Cyberspace* (Albany: State University of New York Press).

FACT (Foundation for Art and Creative Technology). 2004. *JODI: Computing 101B* (Liverpool: FACT).

Fallon, Paul. 2007. 'Negotiating a (Border Literary) Community Online *en la línea*', in *Latin American Cyberculture and Cyberliterature*, ed. Claire Taylor and Thea Pitman (Liverpool: Liverpool University Press), pp. 161–75.

Farris, Sara R. 2010. 'An "Ideal Type" Called Orientalism: Selective Affinities between Edward Said and Max Weber', *Interventions: The International Journal of Postcolonial Studies*, 12:2, 265–84.

Fast Track Media. 2011. 'Social Network Statistics for Latin America, 2011', *Fast Track Media*, 19 September, http://english.fastrackmedia.com/blog/post/social-network-statistics-for-latin-america-2011/. Accessed: 20 April 2012.

Feitlowitz, Marguerite. 1998. *A Lexicon of Terror: Argentina and the Legacies of Torture* (Oxford: Oxford University Press).

Fernández, María. 2002. 'Is Cyberfeminism Colorblind?', *Artwomen.org*, special issue on 'Cyberfeminism', http://www.artwomen.org/cyberfems/fernandez/fernandez1.htm. Accessed: 12 April 2012.

Fernández Retamar, Roberto. 1971. *Calibán: Apuntes sobre la cultura en nuestra América* (Mexico City: Diógenes).

———. 1975. *Para una teoría de la literatura hispanoamericana y otras aproximaciones* (Havana: Casa de las Américas).

Fernbach, Amanda. 2000. 'The Fetishization of Masculinity in Science Fiction: The Cyborg and the Console Cowboy', *Science Fiction Studies*, 27:2, 234–55.

Foster, Thomas. 1997. '"Trapped by the Body?" Telepresence Technologies and Transgendered Performance in Feminist and Lesbian Rewritings of Cyberpunk Fiction', *Modern Fiction Studies*, 43:3, 708–42.

———. 2002. 'Cyber-Aztecs and Cholo-Punks: Guillermo Gómez-Peña's Five-Worlds Theory', *Publications of the Modern Language Association*, 117:1, 43–67.

Fotopoulos, Takis. 2001. 'Globalisation, the Reformist Left and the Anti-Globalisation Movement', *Democracy and Nature: The International Journal of Inclusive Democracy*, 7:2, 233–80.

Franco, Jean. 1987. *Plotting Women: Gender and Representation in Mexico* (Chicago: University of Chicago Press).

———. 2002. *Decline and Fall of the Lettered City: Latin America in the Cold War* (Cambridge, MA: Harvard University Press).

Freire, Paulo. 1993. *Pegagogy of the Oppressed*, trans. Myra Bergman Ramos (New York: Continuum).

Friedman, Edward H. 1994. 'Executing the Will: The End of the Road in *Don Quijote*', *Indiana Journal of Hispanic Literature*, 5, 105–25.

Friedman, Elisabeth Jay. 2007. 'Lesbians in (Cyber)space: The Politics of the Internet in Latin American On- and Off-line Communities', *Media, Culture and Society*, 29:5, 790–811.

Friedman, Ted. 2005. *Electric Dreams: Computers in American Culture* (New York: New York University Press).

Fuchs, Christian. 2008. *Internet and Society: Social Theory in the Information Age* (New York: Routledge).

Fuentes, Carlos. 1969. *La nueva novela hispanoamericana* (Mexico City: Mortiz).

Fuguet, Alberto. 1997. 'I Am Not a Magic Realist!', *Salon*, June, http://www.salon.com/1997/06/11/magicalintro/. Accessed: 7 September 2012.

Fuguet, Alberto, and Sergio Gómez, eds. 1996. *McOndo* (Barcelona: Mondadori).

Fusco, Coco. 2003. 'On-Line Simulations/Real-Life Politics: A Discussion with Ricardo Domínguez on Staging Virtual Theatre', *The Drama Review*, 47:2, 151–62.

Gabilondo, Joseba. 1995. 'Postcolonial Cyborgs: Subjectivity in the Age of Cybernetic Reproduction', in *The Cyborg Handbook*, ed. Chris Hables Gray (New York: Routledge), pp. 423–32.

Gache, Belén. 2003. 'Literaturas nómades: Ciudades, textos y derivas', *Cuadernos del Limbo*, 1, http://www.findelmundo.com.ar/belengache/limb01.htm. Accessed: 14 May 2012.

———. 2006a. *Wordtoys*, http://www.findelmundo.com.ar/wordtoys/index.htm. Accessed: 14 May 2012.

———. 2006b. *Escrituras nómades: Del libro perdido al hipertexto* (Gijón: Ediciones Trea).

García Canclini, Néstor. 1989. *Culturas híbridas: Estrategias para entrar y salir de la modernidad* (Mexico City: Grijalbo).

García Márquez, Gabriel. 1978. *Cien años de soledad* (Bogotá: Oveja Negra). [First published 1967.]

Gerrand, Peter. 2006. 'A Short History of the Catalan Campaign to Win the *.cat* Internet Domain, with Implications for Other Minority Languages', *Digithum*, 8, http://www.uoc.edu/digithum/8/dt/eng/gerrand.pdf. Accessed: 28 March 2012.

Giges, Bob, and Edward C. Warbuton. 2010. 'From Router to Front Row: *Lubricious Transfer* and the Aesthetics of Telematic Performance', *Leonardo*, 14:1, 24–32.

Gómez-Peña, Guillermo. 1993. *Warrior for Gringostroika* (St Paul: Graywolf).

——. 1996. *The New World Border: Prophesies, Poems and Loqueras for the End of the Century* (San Francisco: City Lights).

——. 2000. *Dangerous Border Crossers: The Artist Talks Back* (London: Routledge).

——. 2003–. *Gómez-Peña's Pocha Nostra*, http://www.pochanostra.com/. Accessed: 22 March 2012.

——. 2005a. *Ethno-Techno: Writings on Performance, Activism, and Pedagogy* (New York: Routledge).

——. 2005b. *The Chica-Iranian Project: Orientalism Gone Wrong in Aztlán*, http://www.pochanostra.com/chica-iranian. Accessed: 27 March 2012.

——. 2008a. 'Border Hysteria and the War against Difference', *The Drama Review*, 51:2, 196–203.

——. 2008b. *The New Barbarians*, http://www.pochanostra.com/photo-performances/. Accessed: 27 March 2012.

Gómez-Peña, Guillermo, and La Pocha Nostra. 1998–c.2000. 'Ethno-Techno: A Virtual Museum of Radical Latino Imagery and Fetishized Identities', *La Pocha Nostra*, http://www.pochanostra.com/antes/rene/galeria/gallery.html. Accessed: 22 March 2012.

——. 1998–2003. *La Pocha Nostra*, http://www.pochanostra.com. Accessed: 28 June 2012.

——. 1998–c.2003. 'Pocha Nostra Photo Gallery', *La Pocha Nostra*, http://www.pochanostra.com/antes/pages/gallery/gallery.html. Accessed: 22 March 2012.

Gonzalez, Angel. 2001. 'A Disturbing, Latino View of Tech', *Wired*, 27 June, http://www.wired/com/culture/lifestyle/news/2001/06/44799. Accessed: 29 January 2009.

González, Jennifer. 2000a. 'The Appended Subject: Race and Identity as Digital Assemblage', in *Race in Cyberspace*, ed. Beth E. Kolko, Lisa Nakamura and Gilbert B. Rodman (New York: Routledge), pp. 27–50.

——. 2000b. 'Envisioning Cyborg Bodies: Notes from Current Research', in *The Cybercultures Reader*, ed. David Bell and Barbara M. Kennedy (London: Routledge), pp. 540–51. [First published 1995.]

——. 2006. 'Morphologies: Race as Visual Technology', in *re:skin*, ed. Mary Flanagan and Austin Booth (Cambridge, MA: MIT Press), pp. 339–53.

González, Jennifer, and Guillermo Gómez-Peña. 2009. 'Pose and Poseur: The Racial Politics of Guillermo Gómez-Peña's Photo-Performances', in *Race and Classification: The Case of Mexican America*, ed. Ilona Katzew and Susan Deans-Smith (Stanford: Stanford University Press), pp. 236–63.

González, Miguel. 2003. 'Cybracero: telepresencia de campesinos', *La Opinión*, Business Section, 27 April, pp. 1D–2D, http://www.cybracero.com/press/Cybracero_telepresencia_de_campesinos.pdf. Accessed: 27 June 2012.

González, Mike. 2000. 'The Zapatistas: The Challenges of Revolution in a New Millennium', *International Socialism Journal*, 89, http://pubs.socialistreviewindex.org.uk/isj89/gonzalez.htm. Accessed: 20 December 2011.

González Echevarría, Roberto. 1998. *Myth and Archive: A Theory of Latin American Narrative* (Durham, NC: Duke University Press).

Gottschalk, Peter and Gabriel Greenberg. 2008. *Islamophobia: Making Muslims the Enemy* (Lanham, MD: Rowman and Littlefield).

Gray, Chris Hables, ed. 1995. *The Cyborg Handbook* (New York: Routledge).

Green, Eileen, and Alison Adams, eds. 2001. *Virtual Gender: Technology, Consumption and Identity* (London: Routledge).

Green, Rachel. 2004. *Internet Art* (London: Thames and Hudson).

Groys, Boris. 2008. 'A Genealogy of Participatory Art', in *The Art of Participation: 1950 to Now*, ed. Rudolf Frieling *et al.* (New York: Thames and Hudson), pp. 18–31.

Guillén, Nicolás. 1990. *Summa poética*, ed. Luis Íñigo Madrigal, 7th ed. (Madrid: Cátedra).

Guzmán Bouvard, Marguerite. 1994. *Revolutionizing Motherhood: The Mothers of the Plaza de Mayo* (Oxford: SR Books).

Halberstam, Judith, and Ira Livingstone, eds. 1995. *Posthuman Bodies* (Bloomington: Indiana University Press).

Haraway, Donna J. 1991. *Simians, Cyborgs, and Women: The Reinvention of Nature* (London: Free Association Books).

Harley, J. B. 1989. 'Deconstructing the Map', *Cartographica: International Journal for Geographic Information and Geovisualization*, 26:2, 1–20.

Harpold, Terry. 1999. 'Dark Continents: A Critique of Internet Metageographies', *Postmodern Culture*, 9:2, http://pmc.iath.virginia.edu/text-only/issue.199/9.2harpold.txt. Accessed: 14 April 2011.

Harpold, Terry, and Kavita Philip. 2000. 'Of Bugs and Rats: Cyber-Cleanliness, Cyber-Squalor, and the Fantasy-Spaces of Informational Globalisation', *Postmodern Culture: An Electronic Journal of Interdisciplinary Criticism*, 11:1, http://pmc.iath.virginia.edu/text-only/issue.900/11.1harpoldphilip.txt. Accessed: 14 April 2011.

Harris, Enriqueta. 1982. *Velázquez* (Oxford: Phaidon).

Harrison, Thomas. 2002. 'General Introduction', in *Greeks and Barbarians*, ed. Thomas Harrison (New York: Routledge), pp. 1–16.

Harvey, David. 1990. *The Condition of Postmodernity* (Oxford: Blackwell).

Hawthorne, Susan, and Renate Klein. 1999. 'CyberFeminism: Introduction', in *CyberFeminism: Connectivity, Critique and Creativity*, ed. Susan Hawthorne and Renate Klein (Melbourne: Spinifex Press), pp. 1–16.

Hayles, N. Katherine. 1999. *How We Became Posthuman: Virtual Bodies in Cybernetics, Literature, and Informatics* (Chicago: University of Chicago Press).

———. 2008. *Electronic Literature: New Horizons for the Literary* (Notre Dame: University of Notre Dame Press).

Hearn, Gregory N., and Marcus Foth. 2007. 'Communicative Ecologies: Editorial Preface', *Electronic Journal of Communication*, 17:1–2, http://www.cios.org/www/ejc/v17n12.htm#introduction. Accessed: 28 June 2012.

Henken, Ted. 2010. 'En busca de la "Generación Y": Yoani Sánchez, la blogosfera emergente y el periodismo ciudadano de la Cuba de hoy', in *Buena Vista Social Blog: Internet y libertad de expresión en Cuba*, ed. Beatriz Calvo Peña (Valencia: Advana Vieja), pp. 201–42.

Herbrechter, Stefan, and Ivan Callus, eds. 2009. *Cy-Borges: Memories of the Posthuman in the Work of Jorge Luis Borges* (Cranbury: Associated University Presses).

Herlinghaus, Hermann. 2004. 'Literature and Revolution in Latin America', trans. Suzanne D. Stephens, in *Literary Cultures of Latin America: A Comparative History*, vol. 3, ed. Mario J. Valdés and Djelal Kadir (Oxford: Oxford University Press), pp. 563–93.

Hershmann Leeson, Lynn, ed. 1996. *Clicking In: Hot Links to a Digital Culture* (Seattle: Bay Press).

Hess, David J. 1995. 'On Low-Tech Cyborgs', in *The Cyborg Handbook*, ed. Chris Hables Gray (New York: Routledge), pp. 371–77.

Hicks, Alexander M., Thomas Janoski and Mildred A. Schwartz. 2005. 'Introduction: Political Sociology in the New Millennium', in *The Handbook of Political Sociology*, ed. Thomas Janoski *et al.* (Cambridge: Cambridge University Press), pp. 1–32.

Hicks, Emily D. 1991. *Border Writing: The Multidimensional Text* (Minneapolis: University of Minnesota Press).

Higgins, James. 1990. 'Gabriel García Márquez: *Cien años de soledad*', in *Landmarks in Modern Latin American Fiction*, ed. Philip Swanson (London: Routledge), pp. 141–60.

Hine, Christine. 2000. *Virtual Ethnography* (London: Sage).

Hiperbarrio. 2007–. http://hiperbarrio.org/. Accessed: 5 July 2010.

Hobson, Janell. 2007. 'Searching for Janet in Cyberspace: Race, Gender, and the Interface of Technology', in *Techknowledgies: New Imaginaries in the Humanities, Arts, and Technosciences*, ed. Mary Valentis, Tara P. Monastero and Paula Yablonsky (Newcastle: Cambridge Scholars Publishing), pp. 112–29.

Hoeg, Jerry. 2000. *Science, Technology, and Latin American Narrative in the Twentieth Century and Beyond* (Bethlehem: Lehigh University Press; London: Associated University Presses).

Holland, Eugene W. 1999. *Deleuze and Guattari's* Anti-Oedipus: *Introduction to Schizoanalysis* (London: Routledge).

Holloway, John. 2005. 'Zapatismo urbano', *Humboldt Journal of Social Relations*, 29:1, 168–78.

Holmes, Tori. 2009. 'Local Content in Brazil: Conceptual Framework and Methodological Implications', *Digithum*, 11, 12–19, http://digithum.uoc.edu/ojs/index.php/digithum/issue/view/11. Accessed: 20 April 2012.

———. 2012. 'The Travelling Texts of Local Content: Following Content Creation, Communication and Dissemination via Internet Platforms in a Brazilian Favela', *Hispanic Issues*, 9, 263–88.

Holton, Robert. 2000. 'Globalization's Cultural Consequences', *The Annals of the American Academy of Political and Social Science*, 570:1, 140–52.

Hongladarom, Soraj. 1999. 'Global Culture, Local Cultures and the Internet: The Thai Example', *AI and Society*, 13:4, 389–401.

Hooper, Kirsty. 2007. 'New Cartographies in Galician Studies: From Literary Nationalism to Postnational Readings', in *Reading Iberia*, ed. Helena Buffery, Stuart Davies and Kirsty Hooper (Oxford: Lang), pp. 122–39.

———. 2011. *Writing Galicia into the World: New Cartographies, New Poetics* (Liverpool: Liverpool University Press).

Horst, Philip. 2008. 'Code Poetry's Aesthetic (ww)web: Examples of Contemporary Intermedial Experiments', in *Another Language: Poetic Experiments in Britain and North America*, ed. Kornelia Freitag and Katherina Vester (Berlin: Lit Verlag), pp. 93–110.

Huggan, Graham. 2005. '(Not) Reading *Orientalism*', *Research in African Literatures*, 36:3, 124–36.

Ibold, Hans. 2010. 'Disjuncture 2.0: Youth, Internet Use and Cultural Identity in Bishek', *Central Asian Survey*, 29:4, 521–35.

Ilich, Fran. 2005–. *possibleworlds.org*, http://possibleworlds.org/. Accessed: 15 December 2011.

———. 2006–. *sabotage.tv*, http://sabotage.tv/. Accessed: 27 June 2012.

———. 2006–. *Spacebank*, http://spacebank.org/. Accessed: 15 December 2011.

———. 2006–07. 'net-island: the blueprint of possible worlds', *possibleworlds.org*, http://possibleworlds.org/net.island/blueprint.html. Accessed: 15 December 2011.

———. 2008–. *Diego de la Vega s.a. de c.v.*, http://diegodelavega.net/. Accessed: 15 December 2011.

———. 2010. 'Fragments. Diego de la Vega Corp. Annual Report, 2010', *The Red Specter*, http://www.espectrorojo.com/1/en/38/index.html. Accessed: 25 November 2011.

———. 2011a. *Otra narrativa es posible: imaginación política en la era de internet* (Córdoba, Argentina: Recovecos).

———. 2011b. *The World Street Journal*. April 5–November 27. http://diegodelavega.net/wsj/. Accessed: 15 December 2011.

———. 2011–12a. Personal emails to Thea Pitman, 25 November 2011–4 May 2012.

———. 2011–12b. Email circulars to Spacebank account holders, 26 November 2011–7 May 2012.

Indymedia. '1984 (Radio Play)', *Indy Media*, http://www.indymedia.org.uk/media/2005/03/307691.mp3. Accessed: 28 June 2012.

Info Please. 1998–. 'Company Overview', http://www.infoplease.com/aboutip.html. Accessed: 16 February 2012.

Irigaray, Luce. 1985. *This Sex Which Is Not One*, trans. Catherine Porter with Carolyn Burke (Ithaca: Cornell University Press). [First published 1977.]

Jáuregui, Carlos. 2001. 'Writing Communities on the Internet: Textual Authority and Territorialization', in *Latin American Literature and Mass Culture*, ed. Debra A. Castillo and Edmundo Paz-Soldán (New York: Garland), pp. 288–300.

JODI. 2001. *wwwwwwwww.jodi.org*, http://wwwwwwwww.jodi.org/. Accessed: 28 March 2012.

Kahn, Richard, and Douglas Kellner. 2004. 'New Media and Internet Activism: From the "Battle of Seattle" to Blogging', *New Media and Society*, 6:1, 87–95.

Kaiser, Susanna. 2002. 'Escraches: Demonstrations, Communication and Political Memory in Post-Dictatorial Argentina', *Media, Culture and Society*, 24, 499–516.

Kane, Stephanie C. 2009. 'Stencil Graffiti in Urban Waterscapes of Buenos Aires and Rosario, Argentina', *Crime, Media, Culture*, 5:1, 9–28.

Kantaris, Elia Geoffrey. 1998. 'Allegorical Cities: Bodies and Visions in Colombian Urban Cinema', *Estudios Interdisciplinarios de América Latina y el Caribe*, 9:2, http://www.tau.ac.il/eial/IX_2/kantaris.html. Accessed: 18 February 2010.

Kapcia, Antoni. 2008. *Cuba in Revolution: A History since the Fifties* (London: Reaktion).

Keating, Michael. 2001. *Plurinational Democracy: Stateless Nations in a Post-Sovereignty Era* (Oxford: Oxford University Press).

Keen, Benjamin, and Keith Haynes. 2009. *A History of Latin America*, 8th ed. (Boston: Houghton Mifflin Harcourt).

Kefala, Eleni. 2007. 'The Impossibility of *Hupar* in Borges and Bioy Casares', *Bulletin of Hispanic Studies*, 87:3, 367–84.

Kellner, Douglas. 2002. 'Theorizing Globalization', *Sociological Theory*, 20:3, 285–305.

King, John. 2000. 'María Luisa Bemberg and Argentine Culture', in *An Argentine Passion: María Luisa Bemberg and her Films*, ed. John King, Sheila Whitaker and Rosa Bosch (London: Verso), pp. 1–32.

Klein, Cecelia F. 1995. 'Wild Women in Colonial Mexico: An Encounter of European and Aztec Concepts of the Other', in *Reframing the Renaissance: Visual Culture in Europe and Latin America 1450–1650*, ed. Claire Farago (New Haven: Yale University Press), pp. 244–63.

Knowles, Lori P. c.2010. 'Ethics of Research Using Hybrids, Chimeras and Cytoplasmic Hybrids', http://www.stemcellschool.org/pdf/Ethics-of%20Research-Using-Hybrids.pdf. Accessed: 9 April 2012.

Kolko, Beth E., Lisa Nakamura and Gilbert B. Rodman, eds. 2000. *Race in Cyberspace* (New York: Routledge).

Korzybski, Alfred. 1994. *Science and Sanity: An Introduction to Non-Aristotelian Systems and General Semantics*, 5th ed. (New York: Institute of General Semantics). [First published 1931.]

Kraidy, Marwan M. 2001. 'From Imperialism to Globalization: A Theoretical Framework for the Information Age', in *Cyberimperialism? Global Relations in the New Electronic Frontier*, ed. Bosah Ebo (Westport: Praeger), pp. 27–42.

Kuhnheim, Jill S. 1998. 'The Economy of Performance: Gómez-Peña's *New World Border*', *Modern Fiction Studies*, 44:1, 24–35.

Kumar, Sangeet. 2010. 'Google Earth and the Nation State: Sovereignty in the Age of New Media', *Global Media and Communication*, 6:2, 154–76.

LaFarge, Antoinette, and Robert Allen. 2005. 'Media Conmedia: *The Roman Forum Project*', *Leonardo*, 38:3, 213–18.

Landow, George P. 1992. *Hypertext: The Convergence of Contemporary Critical Theory and Technology* (Baltimore: Johns Hopkins University Press).

———. 2009. 'Creative Nonfiction in Electronic Media: New Wine in New Bottles?' *Neohelicon*, 36, 439–50.

Lane, Jill. 2003. 'Digital Zapatistas', *The Drama Review*, 47:2, 129–44.

Lanier, Jaron. 2006. 'Digital Maoism: The Hazards of the New Online Collectivism', *Edge*, 30 May, 186, http://www.edge.org/3rd_culture/lanier06/lanier06_index.html. Accessed: 14 December 2011.

Larsen, Neil. 1995. *Reading North by South: On Latin American Literature, Culture, and Politics* (Minneapolis: University of Minnesota Press).

Latorre, Guisela. 2008. *Walls of Empowerment: Chicana/o Indigenist Murals of California* (Austin: University of Texas Press).

Lazzara, Michael J. 2009. 'Filming Loss: (Post-)Memory, Subjectivity, and the Performance of Failure in Recent Argentine Documentary Films', *Latin American Perspectives*, 36:5, 147–57.

Leaños, John Jota. c.2005. 'The (Postcolonial) Rules of Engagement: Cultural Activism, Advertising Zones and Xican@ Digital Muralism', http://www.leanos.net/Rules%20of%20Engagement.htm. Accessed: 22 August 2011.

Lee, Rachel C., and Sau-Ling Cynthia Wong. 2003a. 'Introduction', in *AsianAmerica.Net: Ethnicity, Nationalism, and Cyberspace*, ed. Rachel C. Lee and Sau-Ling Cynthia Wong (New York: Routledge), pp. xxiii–xxxv.

———, eds. 2003b. *AsianAmerica.Net: Ethnicity, Nationalism and Cyberspace* (New York: Routledge).

Lengel, Lauren B., and Patrick D. Murphy. 2001. 'Cultural Identity and Cyberimperalism: Computer-Mediated Explorations of Ethnicity, Nation, and Citizenship', in *Cyberimperialism? Global Relations in the New Electronic Frontier*, ed. Bosah Ebo (Westport: Praeger), pp. 187–204.

Lévy, Pierre. 2001. *Cyberculture*, trans. Robert Bononno (Minneapolis: University of Minnesota Press).

Loader, Brian D. 1997. 'The Governance of Cyberspace: Politics, Technology and Global Restructuring', in *The Governance of Cyberspace: Politics, Technology and Global Restructuring*, ed. Brian D. Loader (London: Routledge), pp. 1–19.

Longoni, Ana. 2007. '*El siluetazo* (The Silhouette): On the Border between Art and Politics', in *The Sarai Reader: Frontiers*, ed. Monica Nerula *et al.* (Delhi: Centre for the Study of Developing Societies), pp. 176–86.

———, ed. 2008. *El siluetazo* (Buenos Aires: Adriana Hidalgo Editora).

Los Cybrids (John Jota Leaños, René Garcia and Praba Pilar). 2001–07. *Los Cybrids: La Raza Techno-Crítica*, http://www.cybrids.com/, 2003 version available from http://prabapilar.com/pages/projects/los_cybrids/index.html. Accessed: 30 March 2012.

Lovink, Geert. 2002. *Dark Fiber: Tracking Internet Culture* (Cambridge, MA: MIT Press).

Lozano-Hemmer, Rafael, and Guillermo Gómez-Peña. 2001. 'Tech-illa Sunrise (.txt dot con Sangrita)', http://www.pochanostra.com/antes/jazz_pocha2/mainpages/techilla.htm. Accessed: 18 February 2008.

Lund, Joshua. 2006. *The Impure Imagination: Toward a Critical Hybridity in Latin American Writing* (Minneapolis: University of Minnesota Press).

Lykke, Nina, and Rosi Braidotti, eds. 1996. *Between Monsters, Goddesses and Cyborgs: Feminist Confrontations with Science, Medicine and Cyberspace* (London: Zed Books).

Lyotard, Jean-François. 1984. *The Postmodern Condition: A Report on Knowledge* (Manchester: Manchester University Press).

Mackern, Brian. 2000–2005. *netart latino database*, http://netart.org.uy/latino/. Accessed: 28 March 2012.

———. 2000. *JODI/web_o_matic [n]coder*, http://www.internet.com.uy/vibri/jwom/indexo.htm#. Accessed: 28 March 2012.

———. c.2002. *Cort_azar*, http://www.internet.com.uy/vibri/artefactos/cortazar/cortazar.htm. Accessed: 28 March 2012.

———. 2010. '*netart latino "database"*/Interface Map', *Proceedings of the 16th International Symposium on Electronic Art* (Berlin: Revolver Publishing), pp. 434–36.

Martí, José. 1994. 'Nuestra América', in *Páginas escogidas* (Barcelona: Norma), pp. 63–67. [First published 1891.]

Martin, Gerald. 1989. *Journeys through the Labyrinth: Latin American Fiction in the Twentieth Century* (London: Verso).

Martin, Ricky. 1995. 'Revolución', *A medio vivir* (Mexico: Sony Music Entertainment).

Martín-Barbero, Jesús. 1993. *Communication, Culture and Hegemony: From the Media to the Mediations*, trans. Elizabeth Fox and Robert A. White (London: Sage).

———. 2003. 'Identidad, tecnicidad, alteridad: Apuntes para re-trazar el *mapa nocturno* de nuestras culturas', *Revista Iberoamericana*, 69, 367–87.

———. 2009. 'Digital Convergence in Cultural Communication', *Popular Communication*, 7:3, 147–57.

Martínez, María Elena. 2009. 'The Language, Genealogy, and Classification of "Race" in Colonial Mexico', in *Race and Classification: The Case of Mexican America*, ed. Ilona Katzew and Susan Deans-Smith (Stanford: Stanford University Press), pp. 25–42.

Mato, Daniel. 2003. 'Prácticas intelectuales latinoamericanas en cultura y poder: Sobre la entrada en escena de la idea de "estudios culturales latinoamericanos" en un campo de prácticas más amplio, transdisciplinario, crítico y textualmente referido', *Revista Iberoamericana*, 69, 389–400.

McClintock, Anne. 1995. *Imperial Leather: Race, Gender and Sexuality in the Colonial Context* (London: Routledge).

McGahan, Christopher L. 2008. *Racing Cyberculture: Minoritarian Art and Cultural Politics on the Internet* (New York: Routledge).

McLuhan, Marshall. 1973. *Understanding Media: The Extensions of Man* (London: Abacus).

Mead, Rebecca. 2002. 'You've Got Blog: How to Put Your Business, Your Boyfriend, and Your Life Online', in Perseus Publishing, eds, *We've Got Blog: How Weblogs Are Changing Our Culture* (Cambridge MA: Perseus), pp. 47–56.

Melo, Jorge Orlando. 1997. 'Gaitán: el impacto y el síndrome del 9 de abril', *Revista Credencial*, December, http://www.lablaa.org/blaavirtual/revistas/credencial/diciembre1997/9602.htm. Accessed: 24 February 2010.

Menchú, Rigoberta, with Elisabeth Burgos-Debray. 1992. *Me llamo Rigoberta Menchú y así me nació la conciencia*, 2nd ed. (Barcelona: Seix Barral). [First published 1983.]

Mieszkowski, Katharine. 2000. 'Blow up the Internet!', *Salon Technology*, 24 July, http://archive.salon.com/tech/log/2000/07/24/los_cybrids/print.html. Accessed: 29 January 2009.

Mignolo, Walter D. 2000. *Local Histories/Global Designs: Coloniality, Subaltern Knowledges, and Border Thinking* (Princeton: Princeton University Press).

———. 2005. *The Idea of Latin America* (Oxford: Blackwell).

Miguélez-Carballeira, Helena. 2009. 'Alternative Values: From the National to the Sentimental in the Redrawing of Galician Literary History', *Bulletin of Hispanic Studies*, 86:2, 271–92.

Milberry, Kate, and Steve Anderson. 2009. 'Open Sourcing Our Way to an Online Commons: Contesting Corporate Impermeability in the New Media Ecology', *Journal of Communication Inquiry*, 33:4, 393–412.

Miller, Daniel, and Don Slater. 2000. *The Internet: An Ethnographic Approach* (Oxford: Berg).

———. 2002. 'Relationships', in *The Anthropology of Media: A Reader*, ed. Kelly Askew and Richard R. Wilk (Oxford: Blackwell), pp. 187–209.

Miller, Marilyn Grace. 2004. *Rise and Fall of the Cosmic Race: The Cult of Mestizaje in Latin America* (Austin: University of Texas Press).

Miller, Vincent. 2011. *Understanding Digital Culture* (London: Sage).

Monett, Dagmar. 2010. 'Estado de la blogosfera cubana: resultados de la primera encuesta realizada a sus bloggers', in *Buena Vista Social Blog: Internet y libertad de expresión en Cuba*, ed. Beatriz Calvo Peña (Valencia: Advana Vieja), pp. 59–83.

Monnet, Livia. 2002. 'Towards the Feminine Sublime, or the Story of "A Twinkling Monad, Shape-Shifting across Dimension": Intermediality, Fantasy and Special Effects in Cyberpunk Film and Animation', *Japan Forum*, 14:2, 225–68.

Montfort, Nick. 2003. *Twisty Little Passages: An Approach to Interactive Fiction* (Cambridge, MA: MIT Press).

Montrose, Louis. 1991. 'The Work of Gender in the Discourse of Discovery', *Representations*, 33, 1–41.

Moraña, Mabel. 2004. 'The Boom of the Subaltern', in *The Latin American Cultural Studies Reader*, ed. Ana del Sarto, Alicia Ríos and Abril Trigo (Durham: Duke University Press), pp. 643–54.

Moreiras, Alberto. 2001. *The Exhaustion of Difference: The Politics of Latin American Cultural Studies* (Durham: Duke University Press).

Moulthrop, Stuart. 1994. 'Rhizome and Resistance: Hypertext and the Dreams of a New Culture', in *Hyper/Text/Theory*, ed. George P. Landow (Baltimore: Johns Hopkins University Press), pp. 299–322.

Murray, Janet H. 1997. *Hamlet on the Holodeck: The Future of Narrative in Cyberspace* (Cambridge, MA: MIT Press).

Nakamura, Lisa. 2002. *Cybertypes: Race, Ethnicity, and Identity on the Internet* (New York: Routledge).

———. 2008. *Digitizing Race: Visual Cultures of the Internet* (Minneapolis: University of Minnesota Press).

Navas, Eduardo. 2000. 2002. *Plástico_2002_upDate*, http://navasse.net/plastico02/index.html. Accessed: 27 January 2012.

———. 2009–10. 'The Influence of Non-Places in the Concept of Latin America', curatorial essay for Transitio_MX 03 exhibition, Mérida, Yucatán, 1–10 October 2009, published in *Errata*, 3, December 2010, English version available at http://remixtheory.net/remixImages/ErrataImgWeb/Navas_Trans_Errata.pdf. Accessed: 16 April 2012.

———. 2010. 'Regressive and Reflexive Mashups in Sampling Culture', in *Mashup Cultures*, ed. Stefan Sonvilla-Weiss (Vienna: Springer), pp. 157–77.

———. 2012. Personal email communications with Thea Pitman, 11–12 April.

Nayar, Pramod. 2010. *An Introduction to New Media and Cybercultures* (Chichester: Wiley-Blackwell).

Niño, Martha Patricia. 2007. *Relational Border Map*, http://www.martha-patricia.net/relational-border-map.html. Accessed: 27 March 2012.

'No More Journalists Left in Cuban Prisons after Dissidents Flown to Spain'. 2011. *Reporters without Borders*, 8 April, http://en.rsf.org/cuba-no-more-journalists-left-in-cuban-08–04–2011,39987.html. Accessed: 4 January 2012.

Nouzeilles, Gabriela. 1999. 'Patagonia as Borderland: Nature, Culture, and the Idea of the State', *Journal of Latin American Cultural Studies*, 8:1, 35–48.

O'Bryen, Rory. 2008. *Literature, Testimony and Cinema in Contemporary Colombian Culture: Spectres of La Violencia* (London: Támesis).

Offen, Karl, and Jordana Dym. 2011. 'Introduction', in *Mapping Latin America: A Cartographic Reader*, ed. Jordana Dym and Karl Offen (Chicago: University of Chicago Press), pp. 1–18.

O'Gorman, Edmundo. 1961. *The Invention of America: An Inquiry into the Historical Nature of the New World and the Meaning of its History* (Bloomington: Indiana University Press).

Olney, James. 1998. *Memory and Narrative: The Weave of Life Writing* (Chicago: University of Chicago Press).

Olson, Kathleen K. 2005. 'Cyberspace as Place and the Limits of Metaphor', *Convergence: The Journal of Research into New Media Technologies*, 11:1, 10–18.

Ortega, Elena, ed. 2001. *Más allá de la ciudad letrada: escritoras de nuestra América* (Santiago de Chile: Isis Internacional).

Osquist, Paul. 1980. *Violence, Conflict, and Politics in Colombia* (New York: Academic Press).

Otra información, La. c.2006–2007. http://www.laotrainformacion.org. Accessed: 26 November 2006.

Ow, Jeffrey A. 2000. 'The Revenge of the Yellowfaced Cyborg: The Rape of Digital Geishas and the Colonization of Cyber-Coolies in 3D Realm's *Shadow Warrior*', in *Race in Cyberspace*, ed. Beth E. Kolko, Lisa Nakamura and Gilbert B. Rodman (New York: Routledge), pp. 51–68.

Paasonen, Susana. 2009. 'What Cyberspace? Traveling Concepts in Internet Research', in *Internationalizing Internet Studies: Beyond Anglophone Paradigms*, ed. Gerard Goggin and Mark McLelland (New York: Routledge), pp. 18–31.

———. 2011. 'Revisiting Cyberfeminism', *Communications: The European Journal of Communication Research*, 36:3, 335–52.

Pagden, Anthony. 1986. *The Fall of Natural Man: The American Indian and the Origins of Comparative Ethnology* (Cambridge: Cambridge University Press).

Page, Joanna. 2005. 'Memory and the Spectator in Postdictatorship Argentina: Misreading D'Angiolillo's *Potestad*', *Studies in Hispanic Cinemas*, 2:1, 15–27.

Pagola, Lila. '*netart latino database*: The Inverted Map of Latin American net.art [DOC]' in *netart latino "database"*, ed. Nilo Casares (Badajoz: MEIAC), pp. 31–65.

Partnoy, Raquel. 2003. *Women: Memory of Repression in Argentina*, http://argentina.engad.org/tango1.html. Accessed: 28 March 2012.

———. 2004. 'Women: Memories of the Repression in Argentina', http://downloads.nmartproject.net/Raquel_Partnoy_Lecture.pdf. Accessed: 14 May 2012.

Paz Soldán, Edmundo. 2007. 'Of Blogs and Other Matters', in *Latin American Cyberculture and Cyberliterature*, ed. Claire Taylor and Thea Pitman (Liverpool: Liverpool University Press), pp. 257–62.

Paz-Soldán, Edmundo, and Debra A. Castillo. 2001. 'Introduction: Beyond the Lettered City', in *Latin American Literature and Mass Media*, ed. Debra A. Castillo and Edmundo Paz-Soldán (New York: Garland), pp. 1–18.

Pécaut, Daniel, 2000. 'Configurations of Space, Time, and Subjectivity in a Context of Terror: The Colombian Example', *International Journal of Politics, Culture and Society*, 14:1, 129–50.

Peñaloza, Fernanda. 2010. 'On Skulls, Orgies, Virgins and the Making of Patagonia as a National Territory: Francisco Pascasio Moreno's Representations of Indigenous Tribes', *Bulletin of Hispanic Studies*, 87:4, 455–72.

Penteado, Cláudio, Marcelo dos Santos and Rafael Araújo. 2009. 'O movimento *Cansei* na blogosfera: o debate nos blogs de política', in *Blogs.com: estudos sobre blogs e comunicaçaõ*, ed. Adriana Amaral, Raquel Recuero and Sandra Montardo (São Paulo: Momento Editorial), pp. 135–59.

Pérez, Domino Renee. 2008. *There Was a Woman: La Llorona from Folklore to Popular Culture* (Austin: University of Texas Press).

Pérez-Torres, Rafael. 2006. *Mestizaje: Critical Uses of Race in Chicano Culture* (Minneapolis: University of Minnesota Press).

Pérez Valdés, Jesuhadín. 2009. 'El periodismo independiente cubano: anatomía de un suceso', *Convivencia*, 8 January, http://convivenciacuba.es/content/view/225/53/. Accessed: 22 November 2011.

Phadke, Roopali. 2010. 'Defending Place in the Google Earth Age', *Ethics, Place and Environment*, 13:3, 267–81.

Pickard, Victor. 2006. 'Assessing the Radical Democracy of Indymedia: Discursive, Technical, and Institutional Constructions', *Critical Studies in Media Communication*, 23:1, 19–38.

Pilar, Praba. 2003–. http://www.prabapilar.com/. Accessed: 17 February 2012.

———. 2005. *Cyberlabia: Gendered Thoughts and Conversations on Cyberspace* (Oakland: Tela Press). Also available at http://www.prabapilar.com/pages/projects/prabalibro.pdf. Accessed: 17 February 2012.

———.2012. Personal email to Thea Pitman. 29 March.

Pírez, Pedro. 2002. 'Buenos Aires: Fragmentation and Privatization of the Metropolitan City', *Environment and Urbanization*, 14:1, 145–58.

Pitman, Thea. 2007. 'Latin American Cyberprotest: Before and after the Zapatistas', in *Latin American Cyberculture and Cyberliterature*, ed. Claire Taylor and Thea Pitman (Liverpool: Liverpool University Press), pp. 86–110.

Plant, Sadie. 1999. 'The Future Looms: Weaving Women and Cybernetics', in *Cybersexualities: A Reader on Feminist Theory, Cyborgs and Cyberspace*, ed. Jenny Wolmark (Edinburgh: Edinburgh University Press), pp. 99–118.

Plate, Liedeke. 2007. 'Is Contemporary Women's Writing Computational? Unraveling Twenty-First Century Creativity with Penelope at her Loom', *Contemporary Women's Writing*, 1:1, 45–53.

Platon, Sara, and Mark Deuze. 2003. 'Indymedia Journalism: A Radical Way of Making, Selecting and Sharing News?', *Journalism*, 4, 336–55.

Postill, John. 2011. *Localizing the Internet: An Anthropological Account* (New York: Berghahn).

Pratt, Mary Louise. 1992. *Imperial Eyes: Travel Writing and Transculturation* (London: Routledge).

Propp, Vladimir. 1968. *Morphology of the Folk Tale*, trans. Laurence Scott (Austin: University of Texas Press).

Pula, Robert P. 1994. 'Preface to the Fifth Edition', in *Science and Sanity: An Introduction to Non-Aristotelian Systems and General Semantics*, Alfred Korzybski (New York: Institute of General Semantics), pp. xiii–xxii.

Quiroga, José. 2005. *Cuban Palimpsests* (Minneapolis: University of Minnesota Press).

Raby, D. L. 2006. *Democracy and Revolution: Latin America and Socialism Today* (London: Pluto Press; Toronto: Between the Lines).

Radu, Michael. 2004. 'Mexico's Zapatistas: Another Failed Revolution', *FrontPage Magazine*, 16 January, http://archive.frontpagemag.com/readArticle.aspx?ARTID=14649. Accessed: 20 December 2011.

Raley, Rita. 2009. *Tactical Media* (Minneapolis: University of Minnesota Press).

Rama, Ángel. 1984. *La ciudad letrada* (Hanover: Ediciones del Norte).

Ramos, Julio. 2001. *Culture and Politics in Nineteenth Century Latin America* (Durham: Duke University Press).

Ray, Audacia. 2007. *Naked on the Internet: Hookups, Downloads and Cashing in on Internet Sexploitation* (Emeryville: Seal Press).

Recuero, Raquel. 2008. 'Information Flows and Social Capital in Weblogs: A Case Study in the Brazilian Blogosphere', *ACM Conference on Hypertext and Hypermedia: Proceedings of Hypertext 2008*, pp. 1–11. http://pontomidia.com.br/raquel/ht08fp009recuerofinal.pdf. Accessed: 17 May 2012.

Restrepo, Luis Fernando. 2003. 'The Cultures of Colonialism', in *The Companion to Latin American Studies*, ed. Philip Swanson (London: Arnold), pp. 47–68.

Rheingold, Harold. 1993. *The Virtual Community: Homesteading on the Electronic Frontier*, (Reading: Addison-Wesley).

Richard, Nelly. 2003. 'El conflicto entre las disciplinas', *Revista Iberoamericana*, 69, 441–47.

Ríos, Alicia. 2004. 'Forerunners: Introduction', in *The Latin American Cultural Studies Reader*, ed. Ana del Sarto, Alicia Ríos and Abril Trigo (Durham: Duke University Press), pp. 15–34.

Rivera, Alex. 1997. *Why Cybraceros?*, http://www.invisibleamerica.com/whycybraceros.shtml. Accessed: 30 March 2012.

——. c.1998–. *AlexRivera.com*, http://alexrivera.com/. Accessed: 9 April 2012.

——. c.1998–. *Invisible Cinema*, http://www.invisibleamerica.com/movies.html. Accessed: 30 March 2012.

——. 2009–. *Cybracero Systems*, http://www.cybracero.com/. Accessed: 18 January 2011.

Roberts, Paul Craig. 2005. 'The Police State Is Closer than you Think', *Anti-War.com*, http://www.antiwar.com/roberts/?articleid=7556. Accessed: 17 May 2012.

Robertson, Roland, and Habib Haque Khondker. 1998. 'Discourses of Globalization: Preliminary Considerations', *International Sociology*, 13:1, 25–40.

Robinson, Ruth Adkins. 1999. 'Rap and Hip-Hop: Hip-Hop History', *Billboard*, 111:49, 38–41.

Rodríguez, Clara E. 2000. *Changing Race: Latinos, the Census, and the History of Ethnicity in the United States* (New York: New York University Press).

——, ed. 1997. *Latin Looks: Images of Latinos and Latinas in the U.S. Media* (Boulder: Westview Press).

Rodríguez Ruiz, Jaime Alejandro. 1999–. *Gabriella Infinita*, http://www.javeriana.edu.co/gabriella_infinita/portada.htm. Accessed: 13 December 2011.

——. 2004. *Trece motivos para hablar de cibercultura* (Bogota: Universidad Javeriana).

——. 2005. *Tecnocultura y comunicación* (Bogota: Universidad Javeriana).

——. 2006. *El relato digital: hacia un nuevo arte narrativo* (Bogota: Libros de Arena).

——. 2007. *Gabriella infinita: blog*, http://recursostic.javeriana.edu.co/multiblogs/cronicas.php. Accessed: 13 December 2011.

——. 2009. 'De Macondo a McOndo a macon.doc', *Cultura Popular y literatura en la narrativa colombiana*, http://recursostic.javeriana.edu.co/multiblogs2/culturapopular/2009/01/13/literatura-y-posmodernidad/. Accessed: 18 February 2010.

——, ed. 2011. *Narratopedia: reflexiones sobre narrativa digital, creación colectiva y cibercultura* (Bogota: Universidad Javeriana).

Roehrig, Terence. 2009. 'Executive Leadership and the Continuing Quest for Justice in Argentina', *Human Rights Quarterly*, 31:3, 721–47.

Rogers, Charlotte. 2010. 'Medicine, Madness and Writing in *La vorágine*', *Bulletin of Hispanic Studies*, 87:1, 89–108.

Rogala, Miroslaw. 2010. 'The Virtual and the Vivid: Reframing the Issues in Interactive Arts', *Technoetic Arts: A Journal of Speculative Research*, 8:3, 299–309.

Rojas, Hernado, and Eulalia Puig-i-Abril. 2009. 'Mobilizers Mobilized: Information, Expression, Mobilization and Participation in the Digital Age', *Journal of Computer-Mediated Communication*, 14:4, 902–27.

Roldán, Mary. 2003. 'Wounded Medellín: Narcotics Traffic against a Background of Industrial Decline', in *Wounded Cities: Destruction and Reconstruction in a Globalized World*, ed. Jane Schneider and Ida Susser (Oxford: Berg), pp. 129–48.

Romano, Gustavo. 2009. 'Madonna, Water Maps and Botanical Gardens', in *netart latino "database"*, ed. Nilo Casares (Badajoz: MEIAC), pp. 13–28.

Rothwell, Mathew D. 2010. 'The Chinese Revolution and Latin America: The Impact of Global Communist Networks on Latin American Social Movements and Guerilla Groups', *World History Connected*, 7:3, http://worldhistoryconnected.press.illinois.edu/7.3/rothwell.html. Accessed: 16 January 2012.

Rupert, Mark. 2005. 'In the Belly of the Beast: Resisting Globalization and War in a Neo-Imperial Moment', in *Critical Theories, International Relations, and 'the Anti-Globalization Movement': The Politics of Global Resistance*, ed. Catherine Eschle and Bice Maiguashca (London: Routledge), pp. 36–52.

Russell, Adrienne, and Nabil Echchaibi. 2009. *International Blogging: Identity, Politics, and Networked Publics* (New York: Lang).

Sá, Lúcia. 2007. 'Cyberspace Neighbourhood: The Virtual Construction of Capão Redondo', in *Latin American Cyberliterature and Cyberculture*, ed. Claire Taylor and Thea Pitman (Liverpool: Liverpool University Press), pp. 123–39.

Said, Edward. 2003. *Orientalism* (New York: Vintage). [First published 1978.]

Saïd, Suzanne. 2002. 'Greeks and Barbarians in Euripedes' Tragedies: The End of Differences?', in *Greeks and Barbarians*, ed. Thomas Harrison (New York: Routledge), pp. 62–100.

Saldaña-Portillo, Josefina. 2001. 'Who's the Indian in Aztlán? Re-Writing Mestizaje, Indianism, and Chicanismo from the Lacondón', in *The Latin American Subaltern Studies Reader*, ed. Ileana Rodríguez (Durham: Duke University Press), pp. 402–23.

Saldívar, José David. 1991. *The Dialectics of Our America: Genealogy, Cultural Critique, and Literary History* (Durham: Duke University Press).

Sánchez, Yoani. 2007–. *Generación Y*, http://desdecuba.com/generaciony/. Accessed: 25 October 2011.

———. 2010. *Cuba libre: vivir y escribir en La Habana* (Barcelona: Mondadori).

———. 2011. *Havana Real: One Woman Fights to Tell the Truth about Cuba Today*, trans. M. J. Porter (Brooklyn: Melville House).

Sandoval, Chela. 1999. 'New Sciences: Cyborg Feminism and the Methodology of the Oppressed', in *Cybersexualities: A Reader on Feminist Theory, Cyborgs and Cyberspace*, ed. Jenny Wolmark (Edinburgh: Edinburgh University Press), pp. 247–63. [First published 1995.]

———. 2000. *Methodology of the Oppressed* (Minneapolis: University of Minnesota Press).

Sandoval, Hugo. 2006. '"Hacktivismo": la protesta alcanza a internet', *El Universal*, 14 May, http://www.eluniversal.com.mx/nacion/138327.html. Accessed: 30 November 2006.

Sardar, Ziauddin. 1995. 'alt.civilizations.faq: Cyberspace as the Darker Side of the West', *Futures*, 27:2, 777–94.

Sarmiento, Domingo F. 1970. *Facundo: Civilización y barbarie* (Madrid: Alianza). [First published 1848.]

Sassón-Henry, Perla. 2006. 'Borges' "The Library of Babel" and Moulthrop's Cybertext "Reagan Library" Revisited', *Rocky Mountain Review of Language and Literature*, 60:2, 11–22.

Schamber, Pablo J., and Francisco M. Suárez. 2002. 'Actores sociales y cirujeo y gestión de residuos: una mirada sobre el circuito informal del reciclaje en el conurbano bonaerense', *Revista Realidad Económica Buenos Aires*, 190, 1–11, http://cdi.mecon.gov.ar/biblio/docelec/iade/RealEcon/190–2.pdf. Accessed: 17 May 2012.

Schiller, Herbert. 2001. 'The Global Information Highway: Project for an Ungovernable World', in *Reading Digital Culture*, ed. David Trend (Oxford: Blackwell), pp. 159–71.

Scott, Anne, Lesley Semmens and Lynette Willoughby. 2001. 'Women and the Internet: The Natural History of a Research Project', in *Virtual Gender: Technology, Consumption and Identity*, ed. Eileen Green and Alison Adam (London: Routledge), pp. 3–27.

Searle, John R. 1980. '"Las Meninas" and the Paradoxes of Pictorial Representation', *Critical Inquiry*, 6:3, 477–88.

Seed, David. 1999. *American Science Fiction and the Cold War: Literature and Film* (Edinburgh: Edinburgh University Press).

Shakira. 2010. 'The Ladies in White', *Shakira.com*, 25 March, http://www.shakira.com/news/title/the-ladies-in-white. Accessed: 7 January 2012.

Sharpless, Richard E. 1978. *Gaitán of Colombia: A Political Biography* (Pittsburgh: University of Pittsburgh Press).

Shklovski, Irina, and David M. Struthers. 2010. 'Of States and Borders on the Internet: The Role of Domain Name Extensions in Expressions of Nationalism Online in Kazakhstan', *Policy and Internet*, 2:4, http://www.psocommons.org/policyandinternet/vol2/iss4/art5. Accessed: 28 March 2012.

Shulgin, Alexei. 2007. 'net.art: The Origin', http://www.net-art.org/netart. Accessed: 28 March 2012.

Sierra, Marta. 2011. 'Global Patagonia: Belén Gache's Nomadic Writings', in *Transnational Borderlands in Women's Global Networks*, ed. Marta Sierra and Clara Román-Odio (Basingstoke: Palgrave Macmillan).

Silver, David. 2004. 'Internet/ Cyberculture/ Digital Culture/ New Media/ Fill-in-the-Blank Studies', *New Media and Society*, 6:1, 55–64.

———. 2006. 'Introduction: Where Is Internet Studies?', in *Critical Cyberculture Studies*, ed. David Silver and Adrienne Massanari (New York: New York University Press), pp. 1–14.

Silver, David, and Adrienne Massanari, eds. 2006. *Critical Cyberculture Studies* (New York: New York University Press).

Snodgrass, Michael. 2011. 'The Bracero Program, 1942–1964', in *Beyond the Border: The History of Mexican-U.S. Migration*, ed. Mark Overmyer-Velásquez (New York: Oxford University Press), pp. 79–102.

Snyder, Joel, and Ted Cohen. 1980. 'Reflexions on "Las Meninas": Paradox Lost', *Critical Inquiry*, 7:2, 429–47.

Soja, Edward. 1989. *Postmodern Geographies: The Reassertion of Space in Critical Social Theory* (London: Verso).

Sommer, Doris. 1991. *Foundational Fictions: The National Romances of Latin America* (Berkeley: University of California Press).

———, ed. 2006. *Cultural Agency in the Americas* (Durham: Duke University Press).

Sonvilla-Weiss, Stefan. 2010. 'Introduction: Mashups, Remix Practices and the Recombination of Existing Digital Content', in *Mashup Cultures*, ed. Stefan Sonvilla-Weiss (Vienna: Springer), pp. 8–23.

Stallabrass, Julian. 2003. *Internet Art: The Online Clash of Culture and Commerce* (London: Tate Publishing).

———. 2009. 'Can Art History Digest Net Art?', in *Net Pioneers 1.0: Contextualizing Early Net-Based Art*, ed. Dieter Daniels and Gunther Reisinger (Berlin: Sternberg), pp. 165–80.

Steinberg, Philip E., and Stephen D. McDowell. 2003. 'Mutiny on the Bandwidth: The Semiotics of Statehood in the Internet Domain Name Registries of Pitcairn Island and Nuie', *New Media and Society*, 5:1, 47–67.

Sterne, Jonathan. 2006. 'The Historiography of Cyberculture', in *Critical Cyberculture Studies*, ed. David Silver and Adrienne Massanari (New York: New York University Press), pp. 17–28.

Stewart Millar, Melanie. 1998. *Cracking the Gender Code: Who Rules the Wired World?* (Toronto: Second Story Press).

Stoll, David. 1999. *Rigoberta Menchú and the Story of All Poor Guatemalans* (Boulder: Westview).

Stone, Allucquère Rosanne. 1999. 'Will the Real Body Please Stand Up? Boundary Stories about Virtual Cultures', in *Cybersexualities: A Reader on Feminist*

Theory, Cyborgs and Cyberspace, ed. Jenny Wolmark (Edinburgh: Edinburgh University Press), pp. 69–98.

Strukov, Vlad. 2012. 'Spatial Imagining and the Ideology of Digital Commemoration: The Case of *Allods Online*', *Europe Asia Studies*, 64:8, pp. 1584–607.

Súarez-Villa, Luis. 2009. *Technocapitalism: A Critical Perspective on Technological Innovation and Corporatism* (Philadelphia: Temple University Press).

Sullivan, Laura, and Víctor Fernández. 2000. 'Cybercuba.com(munist): Electronic Literacy, Resistance, and Postrevolutionary Cuba', in *Global Literacies and the World-Wide Web*, ed. Gail E. Hawisher and Cynthia L. Selfe (London: Routledge), pp. 217–50.

Swanson, Philip. 2003. 'Civilization and Barbarism', in *The Companion to Latin American Studies*, ed. Philip Swanson (London: Arnold), pp. 69–85.

Taquini, Graciela. 2008. 'Transborges', *Cuaderno 27: Cuadernos del Centro de Estudios en Diseño y Comunicación*, 9, 63–72.

Taylor, Claire. 2007. 'Virtual Bodies in Cyberspace: Guzik Glantz's Weblog', in *Latin American Cyberculture and Cyberliterature*, ed. Claire Taylor and Thea Pitman (Liverpool: Liverpool University Press), pp. 244–56.

———. 2011. 'Resistant Gaming and Resignifying the Border Online: Ricardo Miranda Zúñiga's *Vagamundo, A Migrant's Tale*', *Journal of Latin American Cultural Studies*, 20:3, 301–19.

———. 2012a. 'Post-Digital Remixes and Carnivalesque Relinkings: Eduardo Navas's *Goobalization*', *Hispanic Issues*, 9, 192–213.

———. 2012b. 'Monopolies and *Maquiladoras*: The Resistant Re-encoding of Gaming in Coco Fusco and Ricardo Domínguez's *Turista Fronterizo*', *Journal of Iberian and Latin American Research*, forthcoming.

Taylor, Claire, and Thea Pitman, eds. 2007. *Latin American Cyberculture and Cyberliterature* (Liverpool: Liverpool University Press).

Taylor, Diana. 1997. *Disappearing Acts: Spectacles of Gender and Nationalism in Argentina's "Dirty War"* (Durham: Duke University Press).

———. 2003. *The Archive and the Repertoire: Performing Cultural Memory in the Americas* (Durham: Duke University Press).

———. 2006. 'DNA of Performance: Political Hauntology', in *Cultural Agency in the Americas*, ed. Doris Sommer (Durham: Duke University Press), pp. 52–81.

Teknika Radica. 2004. 'Powering Up, Powering Down' Conference, University of California–San Diego, 30 January–1 February, http://teknikariadica.cmagnus.com/teknikaradica/. Accessed: 29 March 2011.

Thier, Maike. 2011. 'The View from Paris: "Latinity", "Anglo-Saxonism", and the Americas, as Discussed in the *Revue des Races Latines*, 1857–64', *The International History Review*, 33:4, 627–44.

Thompson, Clive. 2002. 'Telepresence Mexican Labor', *Collision Detection*, 16 October, http://www.collisiondetection.net/mt/archives/2002/10/telepresence_me.php. Accessed: 17 April 2012.

Tickner, Arlene B. 2008. '*Aquí en el Ghetto*: Hip-hop in Colombia, Cuba, and Mexico', *Latin American Politics and Society*, 50:3, 121–46.

Torres García, Joaquín. 1984. *Universalismo constructivo* (Madrid: Alianza). [First published 1943.]

Tracy, James, ed. 2002. *The Civil Disobedience Handbook: A Brief History and Practical Advice for the Politically Disenchanted* (San Francisco: Manic D Press).

Tremayne, Mark, ed. 2006. *Blogging, Citizenship, and the Future of Media* (New York: Routledge).

Trend, David, ed.. 2001. *Reading Digital Culture* (Malden: Blackwell).

Tribe, Mark, Reena Jana and Uta Grosenick, eds. 2007. *New Media Art* (Berlin: Taschen).

Trigo, Abril. 2004. 'General Introduction', *The Latin American Cultural Studies Reader*, ed Ana del Sarto, Alicia Ríos, and Abril Trigo (Durham: Duke University Press), 1–14.

Trigo, Abril, Ana del Sarto and Alicia Ríos. 2003. 'Presentación', *Revista Iberoamericana*, 69, 323–31.

Trigo, Benigno. 2000. *Subjects of Crisis: Race and Gender as Disease in Latin America* (Hanover: Wesleyan University Press).

Turnbull, Giles. 2002. 'The State of the Blog Part 1: Blogger Past', in Perseus Publishing, eds, *We've Got Blog: How Weblogs Are Changing Our Culture* (Cambridge MA: Perseus), 78–85.

Uxó, Carlos. 2010. 'Internet Politics in Cuba', *Telecommunications Journal of Australia*, 60:1, 12.1–12.16.

Van Mourik Broekman, Pauline. 2003. 'Waste Net, Want Not: Art and New Media in 90s Britain', in *Shaping Technologies*, ed. Jeebesh Bagchi (Dehli/Amsterdam: Sarai), pp. 219–26.

Van Tomme, Niels. 2011. 'From Readymade to Readybought: JODI and the Ongoing History of Computer Art', *Art Papers*, 35:1, 30–35.

Vargas Llosa, Mario. 1995. 'Amadis in America', in *García Márquez*, ed. Robin Fiddian (London: Longman), pp. 56–62.

Vázquez, Óscar. 2007. 'Allegories of Race: Casta Paintings and Models for Theorizing Race', in *Early Modern Visual Allegory: Embodying Meaning*, ed. Cristelle Baskins and Lisa Rosenthal (Aldershot: Ashgate), pp. 57–74.

Veldstra, Carolyn. 2010. 'Patron Saint of Lost Causes, Live on the BBC: The Yes Men, Humour, and the Possibility of Politics', *Nordic Journal of English Studies*, 9:3, 139–53.

Venegas, Cristina. 2010. *Digital Dilemmas: The State, the Individual, and Digital Media in Cuba* (New Brunswick: Rutgers University Press).

Venter, David, and Ignatius Swart. 2002. 'Anti-Globalization Organization as a Fourth Generation People's Movement', *Society in Transition*, 33:1, 50–79.

Vernon, Kathleen M. 1986. 'Cortázar's 3 R's: Reading, Rhetoric and Revolution', in *Libro de Manuel*', *Modern Language Studies*, 16:3, 264–270.

Voeux, Claire. 2008. 'Cuba: No Surrender by Independent Journalists, Five Years on from "Black Spring"', with contributions by Benoît Hervieu, *Reporters without Borders*, http://www.rsf.org/IMG/pdf/Cuba_report.pdf. Accessed: 21 November 2011.

Wade, Peter. 2010. *Race and Ethnicity in Latin America*. 2nd ed. (London: Pluto).

Wands, Bruce. 2006. *Art of the Digital Age* (London: Thames and Hudson).

Ward, Thomas. 2007. 'From Sarmiento to Martí and Hostos: Extricating the Nation from Coloniality', *European Review of Latin American and Caribbean Studies*, 83, 83–104.

Wardrip-Fruin, Noah, and Pat Harrigan, eds. 2006. *First Person: New Media as Story, Performance and Genre* (Cambridge, MA: MIT Press).

Warschauer, Mark. 2000. 'Language, Identity, and the Internet', in *Race in Cyberspace*, ed. Beth E. Kolko, Lisa Nakamura and Gilbert B. Rodman (New York: Routledge), pp. 151–70.

Wexler, Alice. 2007. 'Museum Culture and the Inequities of Display and Representation', *Visual Arts Research*, 33:1, 25–33.

Wickham-Crowley, Timothy P. 1993. *Guerrillas and Revolution in Latin America: A Comparative Study of Insurgents and Regimes since 1956* (Princeton: Princeton University Press).

Wilson, Jason. 1999. *Buenos Aires: A Cultural and Literary Companion* (Oxford: Signal Books).

Wisin and Yandel. 2009. *La Revolución* (Puerto Rico: Machete Music).

Wolmark, Jenny, ed. 1999. *Cybersexualities: A Reader on Feminist Theory, Cyborgs and Cyberspace* (Edinburgh: Edinburgh University Press).

World Trade Organization, 'Mission Statement', http://www.wto.org/english/thewto_e/whatis_e/wto_dg_stat_e.htm. Accessed: 27 March 2012.

Wright, Melissa W. 2005. 'Paradoxes, Protests and the *Mujeres de Negro* of Northern Mexico', *Gender, Place and Culture*, 12:3, 277–92.

Young, Michael, and Mark Riedl. 2003. 'Towards an Architecture for Intelligent Control of Narrative in Interactive Virtual Worlds', *Proceedings of the 8th International Conference on Intelligent User Interfaces* (New York: ACM), pp. 310–12.

Young, Robert C. 2003. *Postcolonialism: An Historical Introduction*. (Oxford: Blackwell).

Yto.cl. 2007. 'Entrevista a Eduardo Navas: artista, historiador y crítico especializado en nuevos medios', *Escáner Cultural*, http://revista.escaner.cl/node/279. Accessed: 27 January 2012.

Zafra, Remedios. 2005. 'No pasatiempo, "Cárcel de Amor"', *Archivo de Creadores de Madrid* (Madrid: Ministerio de Cultura), p. 337. http://archivodecreadores.es/file/0/417/417.pdf

Zea, Leopoldo. 1988. *Discurso desde la marginación y la barbarie* (Barcelona: Anthropos).

Zerbarini, Marina. 2003. *Tejido de memoria*, http://www.marina-zerbarini.com.ar/tejido/dememoria.html. Accessed: 8 May 2012.

———. 2005. 'Subjetivo, íntimo y público', *Netart Review*, 68–79, http://www.netartreview.net/monthly/minima_marina.pdf. Accessed: 8 May 2012.

Žižek, Slavoj. 2006. 'Against the Populist Temptation', *Journal of Critical Inquiry*, 32, 551–74.

Index

A

Aarseth, Espen J. 86–7, 209n.5
Abril i Abril, Amadeu 33
Abuelas de Plaza de Mayo 207n.19
Abu Ghraib jail, Baghdad 129
Achugar, Hugo 118–19, 132
activism 6, 13–14, 74; *see also*
    antiglobalisation movements;
    hacktivism; tactical media
Agosín, Marjorie 61
Ai Weiwei 194, 220n.58
Alaimo, Stacy 120, 130, 131, 211n.6
Alarcón, Norma 123
Alcaide, Carmen 42
Allatson, Paul 204n.18
Allen, Robert 7
Allende, Isabel 84
Americanisation 9
Anderson, Benedict 30–1
Anderson, Steve 73
anthropology 128–9
antiglobalisation movements 12–13;
    Pilar 52; slogans 74, 187; World
    Trade Organization 133, 136;
    Yes Men 133
Anzaldúa, Gloria 147, 214n.9
Apollinaire, Guillaume 111
Appadurai, Arjun 11, 19–20, 21
Apple 135, 136
Arab Spring 179
Araújo, Rafael 6
Ardao, Arturo 30
area studies 18, 19, 22
Arenas, Reinaldo 208n.1
Argentina: Buenos Aires as cosmopolitan
    port city 63–4, 206–7n.11; Buenos
    Aires in Zerbarini's *Tejido de*
    memoria 60, 62–5, 66–71, 83;
    cartoneros 64–5, 207 nn.14–15;

civilisation and barbarism 115,
    116, 211n.4; *Eloísa Cartonera*
    204n.20; financial crash and crisis
    (2001–2) 64, 65, 207n.13; Gache's
    WordToys 104; *Guerra Sucia* 61,
    64, 206 nn.6, 9; *Ley de obediencia*
    debida 62, 71, 206n.10; *Ley*
    de punto final 62, 71, 206n.10;
    mapping 41; memory recuperation
    61–2; *siluetazo* movement 130
Arguedas, Alcides 15
Aristotle 108, 201n.5
Aronowitz, Stanley 133
arpillera movement 61
ArteUna interface, *30 Años de Golpe*
    Militar Argentina exhibition 36
ASCII-art 7, 204n.17; Mackern's *netart*
    latino database 39, 41, 42, 43, 45
Asociación de Periodistas
    Independientes de Cuba 172
Asociación Madres de Plaza de Mayo
    67–8, 70, 207n.18
Augé, Marc 50
author-god figure 86, 99; Gache's
    WordToys 111–12; Rodríguez's
    Gabriella infinita 98
author–reader dynamic, hypertext
    fiction 87, 114; Gache's
    WordToys 101; Rodríguez's
    Gabriella infinita 96–9
Autodefensas Unidas de Columbia
    (AUC) 77
Avelar, Idelber 18, 127
Avellaneda, Alfonso 112
Ayers, Jeffrey M. 12

B

Baggio, Roberto 204n.21
Baigorri, Laura 44, 137

Baledon, Rafael 212n.12
Balsamo, Anne 52, 53, 210n.18
barbarian theorising 116, 118–20, 139;
    Gómez-Peña 121, 139–40; Niño
    131–9, 140
barbarism *see* civilisation and
    barbarism
Barlow, John Perry 31, 103, 202n.3
Barthes, Roland 201n.5, 210n.16
Batista, Fulgencio 179
Baudelaire, Charles 111
Baudrillard, Jean 108
Bauer, Kenneth 81
Baumgärtel, Tilman 35
Beasley-Murray, Jon 17, 18, 215n.22
Bécquer, Gustavo Adolfo 111
Bell, David 210n.20
Bell Laboratories 50
Bello, Andrés 17
Bemberg, María Luisa 104, 210n.23
Benegas, Diego 65
Berger, John 219n.27
Berkeley, George 109
Bermúdez, Silvia 20
Berrocal, María del Carmen de 67, 68,
    207 nn.18, 20
Beverley, John 15, 202n.10
Bhabha, Homi 23
Bhopal disaster 134, 213n.23
Bichlbaum, Andy 133
Bilbija, Ksenija 43
Bisama, Álvaro 208n.2
Blade Runner (1982) 157
Blades, Rubén, 'Plástico' 47, 48–9
blogs 5–6, 14, 196; Cuba 171, 174–84;
    Gache 100; *Hiperbarrio* 74–5,
    80, 81, 82; Rodríguez, *Gabriella
    infinita* 88, 99; Sánchez 171,
    172, 175–84
Bolívar, Simón: Ilich's *possibleworlds.org*
    192; *mestizaje* 141, 142; 'Plástico'
    (Colón and Blades song) 48;
    revolution 169
Bolter, Jay David 6, 86, 209n.4
Bonanno, Mike 133
border *see* frontier/border
Borderhack festivals 188
Bordwell, David 95
Borges, Jorge Luis 46, 108–9, 112, 113,
    210n.24; *Ficciones* 86
Borsook, Paulina 52
Bosco, Fernando J. 66, 207n.18
Boullosa, Carmen, *Duerme* 214n.6
Bracero Program 162, 216n.39

Braun, Herbert 209n.11
Brazil: blogs 5, 14, 201 nn.2, 3;
    information society 205n.45;
    mapping Latin America 30;
    paulista oral language (São
    Paulo) 203n.23
Breton, André 110
Briggs, Helen 137
Brown, Andrew 145
Browne, Nick 209n.13
browser art 7, 34
Buendía, Cristina, *No-pasatiempo*
    203n.11
Burbach, Roger 219n.27
Bush, George W. 72, 125, 126, 138,
    213n.26

C
Caliban, School of 118
Calvino, Italo 111; *Le città invisibile*
    70, 71
Calvo Peña, Beatriz 6, 174, 175
Cameron, James 149
Camila (1984) 104, 210n.23
Canada 191
Cansei movement 201n.3
capitalism 9, 10, 200; Asociación
    Madres de Plaza de Mayo
    70; 'Cartografía colectiva'
    project (La Loma, Colombia)
    82; civilisation and barbarism
    117; deterritorialisation and
    reterritorialisation 59; Ilich's
    possibleworlds.org 190, 191,
    192, 193; lettered city 57, 59;
    Zerbarini's *Tejido de memoria*
    64; *see also* informational
    capitalism; late capitalism
Cardona, René 212n.12
Carri, Albertina, *Los rubios* 62, 206n.7
'Cartografía colectiva' project (La
    Loma, Colombia) 80–1, 82
cartography *see* mapping Latin America
cartonera publishing projects 43
Casares, Nilo 204n.22
Castañeda, Jorge 170, 195
Castañeda, Luz Stella 75
Castells, Manuel 11; informational
    capitalism 10, 51, 54, 55, 93
Castillo, Debra A. 2, 15, 57, 162, 166,
    216n.40, 217n.52
Castro, Eugenio 157, 159, 215n.29
Castro, Fidel 173, 178, 220n.49
Castro, Raúl 181, 217n.5, 218n.18

Castro-Gómez, Santiago 16
Catalan nationalists 33
Celaya, Miriam 175
Cervantes Saavedra, Miguel de, *Don Quijote* 46, 86, 112–13
Césaire, Aimé 138
characterisation in hypertext fiction 106
Chiappe, Doménico, *La huella de Cosmos* 99
Chile 41, 61
China 192, 219n.28, 220n.58
Chingada, La 156
Chonta (Mauricio Rodríguez) 79
Chronopoulos, Themis 65, 207 nn.14–15
Chuang-Tzu 108, 109
Ciccoricco, David 6
Cinemátik 1.0 festival 188
citizen journalism 6
citizenship 6; postnational 20
Civantos, Christina 127
civilisation and barbarism 25, 115–20, 139–40, 199; Gómez-Peña 120–31, 151; *mestizaje* 143, 151; Niño 131–9
Clark, John 12–13
Clarke, David 70
Clarke, Margaret Anne 205n.45
Cold War 30, 169, 170
Coleman, Sarah 73
Colombia: Bogota in Rodríguez's *Gabriella infinita* 89–90, 91–2, 93; *Bogotazo*/*La Violencia* 90–2, 93; cityscape in films 92–3; *Hiperbarrio* 6, 72–82; net. art 203n.10; Rodríguez 87–8, 89–90, 91–2, 93
Colón, Willie, 'Plástico' 47, 48–9
colonialism and imperialism: cartography 30, 31, 39, 42, 45, 51, 55; civilisation and barbarism 115, 122, 123; colonial gaze 131; La Llorona image 123; *mestiza/o* cyborgs 159; *mestizaje* 141, 153; Orientalism 122; problematisation of Latin American studies 17–19, 22, 28
Comaroff, John 212–13n.18
Comisión Nacional sobre la Desaparición de Personas (CONADEP) 206n.8
computer game theory 201–2n.5
conceptual art works 8
Consenso 175

construction of Latin America 22–7; Posse's *Los perros del paraíso* 110
Contra-Cultura (menor) 187
Convergence: The International Journal of Research into New Media Technologies 3
ConVerGentes blog 80, 81
Cooperative Association for Internet Data Analysis (CAIDA) 50, 53, 205n.33
copyleft 73
Corby, Tom 43, 203n.14
Coremberg, Irene, *Túneles de la memoria* 206n.4
Cortázar, Julio 34–5, 99; *Rayuela* 35, 109, 210 nn.17, 25, 211n.27; 62; *modelo para armar* 112
Cortés, Hernán 214n.9
Cosic, Vuk 203n.8
Crampton, Jeremy W. 29, 31, 55, 80
Craven, David 169, 170, 171
Critical Art Ensemble 13–14, 134
critical regionalism 21, 22; Mackern's *netart latino database* 45
crónica 6, 177
Cuba: independent journalism and the blogosphere 5, 171, 172–5, 196; mapping 31; Revolution 92, 169, 171–3, 176, 179–84, 186, 196, 220 nn.49, 60; Sánchez's *Generación Y* 171, 172, 175–84
cultural homogeneity 9, 10, 11, 12, 199
cultural specificity 4, 58, 200
cultural studies 15–22
cybercultural theory 3–4
cyberfeminism 10; critical 52; cyborg consciousness 147, 148; Pilar 52; weaving 68
cyberimperialism 52
cybermestizaje 145, 214n.6
cyberpunk fiction 99, 210n.18
cyborgs: consciousness 144–50; Los Cybrids 160–1, 163–6; Gómez-Peña 151–60; *mestizaje* 26, 149–68; Rivera 161–3, 166–7
Cybrids, Los: La Raza Techno-Crítica 8, 26; *mestiza/o* cyborgs 151, 160–1, 163–5, 167; Pilar 52

D

Dabove, Juan Pablo 42
Dadgar, Ali 212n.9
Damas de Blanco 176, 196

D'Angiolillo, Luis César, *Potestad* 62, 206n.7
Daniels, Dieter 35, 37, 43, 203n.14
Darío, Rubén 111, 207n.11
Davis, Sheila 52
Dawson, Ashley 216n.43
de Certeau, Michel 13, 202n.8
de la Campa, Ramón 15, 20–1, 57–8
Deleuze, Gilles 88, 209n.8
del Sarto, Ana 16–17
depth cues 95
Desde Cuba 175, 218 nn.9, 19
deterritorialisation 59
Deuze, Mark 4
diary format 6, 201n.4
digital commons 73
digital culture studies 4–5
digital performance 7
Digital Zapatismo 171, 187, 215n.16;
     Ilich 188, 190–1, 195
Di Paolantonio, Mario 62, 206n.9
Dixon, Steve 7, 144, 145, 148
Docuyanan, Faye 77
Dodge, Martin 31, 205n.33
Doel, Marcus 70
domain names: Mackern's *netart latino
     database* 40–1, 45; mapping the
     internet 32–3, 34, 40–1
Domínguez, Ricardo 14, 187, 188,
     205n.1; *Transborder Immigrant
     Tool* 42; *Turista Fronterizo*
     203n.10
Dos por Tres search engine 173,
     218n.18
dos Santos, Marcelo 6
Dyer-Witheford, Nick 73
Dym, Jordana 30

E
Ebo, Bosah 9
Eick, Stephen 50, 53, 54, 205 nn.34–5
Ejército Zapatista de Liberación
     Nacional (EZLN) 169, 185, 186,
     189, 190; *see also* Zapatistas
Electronic Disturbance Theater (EDT)
     14, 42, 187
Eloísa Cartonera 43
embeddedness: internet ethnography
     4, 14; Zerbarini's *Tejido de
     memoria* 66
Enteen, Jiliana 40
Esas voces que nos llegan blog 74–5
Escobar, Arturo 74
Escobar, Reinaldo 175, 218n.9

escraches 61, 65, 206 nn.5, 6
Escuela Superior de Mecánica de la
     Armada (ESMA) 62
Esquivel, Laura 84
ethnicity 143; *see also mestizaje*; race
ethnography, internet 4
Etoy.com 191
Europe: mapping Latin America 30, 31,
     39, 45; *mestizaje* 141, 214n.6
Everett, Anna 216n.35

F
Facebook 5, 201n.2
Fajardo, Sergio 74
Fallon, Paul 6
Farris, Sara R. 122
Fernbach, Amanda 210n.18
Fin del mundo 100
Flickr 6
FloodNet 14, 187
Foster, Thomas 125, 128, 152, 156,
     212n.16
Foucault, Michel 209n.8
France 30, 192
Franco, Jean 15, 57, 58
Free (Libre) and Open Source Software
     (FOSS/FLOSS) 37, 73
Freire, Paulo 138
Freud, Sigmund 108
Friedman, Edward H. 112, 136
Friedman, Elisabeth Jay 6
frontier/border: civilisation and
     barbarism 115, 116–17, 119,
     120–1, 131–9; conceptualisation
     of the internet 31–2; metaphor
     for cyberspace 103
Fry, Ben 53
Fuchs, Christian 10, 11, 93
Fuentes, Carlos 219n.27
Fuguet, Alberto 208n.1
Fusco, Coco 205n.1, 212n.17; *Turista
     Fronterizo* 203n.10
Futurism 7

G
Gabilondo, Joseba 148, 149, 152
Gache, Belén 14, 100; *Escrituras
     nómades* 210 nn.19, 24, 211n.28;
     WordToys 6, 25, 84, 100–13
Gaitán, Jorge Eliécer 90
Gallegos, Rómulo, *Doña Bárbara* 211n.2
Garcia, René 52, 216n.33; *mestiza/o
     cyborgs* 160
García Canclini, Néstor 15, 17

García Márquez, Gabriel 208n.1; *Cien años de soledad* 84–5, 86, 89, 92, 101
Garrin, Paul: *Border Patrol* 137, 138, 139; *MediaFilter* 137; *Name-Space* 137
Gaviria, Victor 208n.23
gender: cyberpunk fiction 210n.18; and globalisation 9–10; Gómez-Peña's work 123, 124, 130–1; lettered city 57, 72; 'madres' 68; Pilar 52; Rodríguez's *Gabriella infinita* 98–9; Zerbarini's *Tejido de memoria* 69, 72, 83
Ghost in the Shell (1995) 203n.6
Giges, Bob 7
globalisation 8–13; area studies 18; and barbarian theorising 119; digital tools 199; Electronic Disturbance Theater 14; Ilich's *possibleworlds. org* 191; Latin American cultural studies 17; lettered city 58; mapping Latin America 56; Navas's work 46, 47, 49
global network capitalism 93
'global village' metaphor 8, 202n.6
Gómez, Sergio 208n.1
Gomez-Peña, Guillermo 8, 42, 151, 215n.16; *The Chica-Iranian Project* 121–5, 126–7, 128, 139–40, 155; civilisation and barbarism 25, 116, 120–31, 132, 139–40, 151; and Los Cybrids 216n.33; *Dangerous Border Crossers* 120, 215 nn.16, 19; 'Ethno-cyborgs and Genetically Engineered Mexicans' 215n.28; influence 162; Mackern's *netart latino database* 204n.23; *mestiza/o* cyborgs 26, 150–60; *The Mexterminator* 155, 156, 215n.16; *The New Barbarians* 121, 128–30, 131; *The New World Border* 120, 130–1, 156, 211 nn.6, 7, 215n.16; 'Tech-illa Sunrise' 153–4; *The Temple of Confessions/The Ethno-Cyberpunk Trading Post and Curio Shop on the Electronic Frontier* 155, 215n.16; 'The Virtual Barrio @ The Other Frontier' 151, 154, 215n.19; *El Warrior for Gringostroika* 125, 211n.6

González, Jennifer 143, 148–9, 152, 163, 168, 216n.45
González, Juan Ospina, *Juegos de guerra colombiana* 203n.10
González, Mike 185, 186, 195
González Echevarría, Roberto 85
Google 81–2, 191
Gottshalk, Peter 212n.13
governance of cyberspace 9
graffiti 77–9, 80
Granma 173, 220n.49
graphical browsers 39, 203–4n.16
Gray, Chris Hables 144
Green, Rachel 203n.14
Greenberg, Gabriel 212n.13
Greek language 118, 211n.5
Grosenick, Uta 203n.14
Grossberger Morales, Lucia 214n.7
Groys, Boris 7
Grupo Arte Callejero 65
Guantánamo Bay 213n.26
Guattari, Félix 88
Guevara, Ernesto 'Che' 31, 186, 192, 195, 220 nn.49, 60
Guillén, Nicolás 181, 182, 184, 218–19n.21
Guiraldes, Ricardo, *Don Segundo Sombra* 211n.2
Guzmán Bouvard, Marguerite 67, 68

H
habeas corpus 71, 138, 207n.20, 213n.26
habeas data 219n.23
hacker ethics 37
hacktivism 8, 217n.2; Electronic Disturbance Theater 187; *Etoy. com* 191; Ilich 188, 194; Niño's *Relational Border Map* 133, 134; revolution 171
Halberstam, Judith 145
Haraway, Donna 144, 146–7, 148, 158, 165, 214 nn.9, 12
Harley, J.B. 29, 31
Haro, Jorge 100
Harpold, Terry 33, 51, 55, 215n.23
Harris, Enriqueta 96
Harrison, Thomas 211n.5
Harvey, David 102
Hawaii 11
Hayles, N.Katherine 6, 87, 145, 209n.5
Haynes, Keith 207n.12
Heemskerk, Joan 34; *see also* JODI
Henken, Ted 177

Herencia de la Llorona, La (1947)
    212n.12
Herlinghaus, Hermann 169
Hess, David J. 149
Hexterminators: SuperHeroes of the
    Biozoid Era 52
Hicks, Alexander 74
Hicks, Emily 86
Higgins, James 92
H.I.J.O.S. 61, 65, 206n.5
Hine, Christine 4
Hiperbarrio 6, 24, 58–9, 72–82, 83, 199
hip-hop culture 79–80
Hispanism 15, 20–1, 48
Historia de Suso 75–7
Hoeg, Jerry 145, 214n.6
Holloway, John 185, 186
Holmes, Tori 6, 14
Holton, Robert 9, 11
homogenisation: cultural 9, 10, 11, 12,
    199; and globalisation 9, 10,
    11, 12
Hongladarom, Soraj 12
Hooper, Kirsty 20
Horst, Philip 202n.5
Huggan, Graham 212n.10
Hume, David 109
hypertext fiction 6, 14, 84–7, 113–14;
    Cortázar, *Rayuela* 35; Gache,
    WordToys 100–13; Rodríguez,
    Gabriella infinita 87–100
Hyun, Young 205n.33

I
IBM 135
Ibold, Hans 12
ICANN 33
Ilich, Fran 8, 13, 26–7, 171, 187–8,
    197; *possibleworlds.org* 171,
    185, 188–96
imperialism *see* colonialism and
    imperialism
Indymedia 135, 136
Info Please website 47, 48, 204n.29
informational capitalism 10, 33;
    Argentina 69; Castells 10, 51,
    54, 55, 93; Gache's *WordToys*
    103; hypertext fiction 93;
    lettered city 59; Navas's
    Plástico_2002_upDate 50;
    Pilar 50, 51–2, 55; Rodríguez's
    Gabriella infinita 93; *see also*
    late capitalism
Infomed website (Cuba) 173

Instituto Geográfico Agustín Codazzi 81,
    208n.28
International Monetary Fund (IMF) 72
Internet Archive WayBack Machine
    204n.22, 216 nn.35, 40
Internet Corporation for Assigned
    Names and Numbers (ICANN)
    33
internet geography 33, 50–1, 197; Pilar's
    Cyberlabia 51–2, 53, 54, 55
internet studies 3–5
Iranian riots (2009) 179
Iraq War 124–5
Irigaray, Luce 205n.42

J
Jana, Reena 203n.14
Janoski, Thomas 74
Jáuregui, Carlos 42, 58
JODI 34, 36; *wwwwwwwww.jodi.org*
    37
Joyce, James, 'Eveline' 60

K
Kac, Eduardo 145, 146
Kaiser, Susanna 65, 206n.6
Kane, Stephanie C. 78
Kantaris, Geoffrey 92–3
Kazakhstan 40
Keating, Michael 33
Keen, Benjamin 207n.12
Kefala, Eleni 109
Kellner, Douglas 10, 11
King, John 210n.23
Kirchner, Néstor 62, 206n.10
Kitchin, Rob 31, 205n.33
Klein, Cecelia F. 211n.1
Korda, Alberto 195
Korzybski, Alfred 132
Kraidy, Marwan 9
Kuhnheim, Jill S. 120, 130–1, 211n.7
Kumar, Sangeet 82
Kyrgyzstan 12

L
LaFarge, Antoinette 7
Landow, George P. 6, 35, 86, 87, 109,
    209n.4, 210n.16
Lane, Jill 187
language issues: blogs 75; civilisation and
    barbarism 118; code, language
    as 111; Cuban revolutionary
    discourse 179–80, 182–3; domain
    names 32; *parlache* (Colombia)

75, 77, 208n.23; *paulista* (São
  Paulo) 208n.23
Lanier, Jaron 194
Larsen, Neil 17–18, 23
late capitalism 9, 10; hypertext
  fiction 93, 113; lettered city
  58; mapping Latin America
  42; media manipulation 136;
  Rodríguez's *Gabriella infinita*
  92, 93, 103; society of control
  209n.8; systemic violence 138;
  see also informational capitalism
Latin American (cultural) studies 15–22
latinidad: Gómez-Peña 151–2, 159;
  Navas 46, 49–50; revolution
  195; Rivera 166; viral 168,
  215n.22
Latorre, Guisela 164
Lazzara, Michael J. 206n.7
Leaños, John Jota 52; *mestiza/o* cyborgs
  160, 161, 164, 217n.48
Lefebvre, Henri 902
Lerman, Liz 124, 212n.9
'lettered city' 24–5, 57–9, 82–3, 199;
  Hiperbarrio 72–82; Zerbarini
  59–72
Lévy, Pierre 4, 8, 210n.20
Lewis, Emiko R. 124, 212n.9
Livingstone, Ira 145
Llorona, La 123–4, 212n.12
Llorona, La (1960) 212n.12
Loader, Brian D. 9, 31
local identities 11–12
localisation of the internet 4
locality, and internet ethnography 4
locatedness 2, 59; Gache's *WordToys*
  101; hypertext fiction 89, 101
location, and Latin American (cultural)
  studies 19
logo-maps 30–1, 33, 50–1, 55
Longoni, Ana 213n.19
López, Andrés 209n.7
López García, Jacalyn 214n.7
Lovink, Geert 13
Lozano-Hemmer, Rafael 153–4, 158
Luján, Al 216n.36
Lula da Silva, Luiz Inácio 201n.3
Lund, Joshua 142
Lyotard, Jean-François 92

M

Mackern, Brian 24, 34–46, 132;
  Cort_azar 34–5; *JODI/web_o_
  matic [n]coder* 34; *netart latino*

database 7, 28, 35–41, 42–5, 47,
  204 nn.24–5; *Raw War* 203n.13
Macondo 25, 84–7, 113–14; Gache
  100–13; Rodríguez 87–100
Madres de Plaza de Mayo 14, 24, 65,
  66, 206n.5; Zerbarini's *Tejido
  de memoria* 58, 59, 60, 62, 63,
  67–8, 71
Madres de Plaza de Mayo-Línea
  Fundadora 207n.18
Magdaleno, Mauricio 212n.12
magical realism 25, 84–7, 113–14; Gache
  100–13; Rodríguez 87–100
Maldicion de la Llorona, La (1963)
  212n.12
Malinche, La 147, 156, 214n.9,
  215n.26
Maoism 186, 192, 219n.28, 220n.58;
  digital 194
Mao Zedong 106, 107, 192
map-as-logo 30–1, 33, 50–1, 55
mapping Latin America 24, 28–34,
  55–6, 198, 199; 'Cartografía
  colectiva' project (Colombia)
  80–1, 82; Gache's *WordToys*
  101–2, 105; Mackern 34–46;
  Navas 46–50; Niño's *Relational
  Border Map* 132–9; Pilar 50–5
Mariano, Nola 212n.8
Martí, José 16, 23, 30, 33; *mestizaje*
  141, 199
Martin, Gerald 211n.1
Martin, Ricky 195, 220n.61
Martín-Barbero, Jesús 15–16, 17, 58,
  85, 105
Mato, Daniel 17, 18
Matrix films 202–3n.6
McClintock, Anne 131
McDowell, Stephen D. 32, 40
McGahan, Christopher L. 159, 215n.30
McGee, Art 52
McLuhan, Marshall 202n.6
McOndo movement 84, 208 nn.1, 2
media conmedia performance works 7
Mejor Vida Corp 204n.21
Melo, Jorge Orlando 91
memory; Calvino's *Le città invisibile*
  70, 71; *Hiperbarrio* 73, 82; and
  weaving 60–1, 68; Zerbarini's
  Tejido de memoria 60, 61, 68, 69,
  71–2
Menchú, Rigoberta 208n.25
Menem, Carlos 64, 65, 66, 69, 207
  nn.12, 15

Mercator projection 30, 50
mestizaje 26, 141–4, 168, 199; cyborg consciousness 144–50; cyborgs 150–68; Los Cybrids 160–1, 163–6; Gómez-Peña's work 151–60; Rivera 161–3, 166–7
Mexico: Bracero Program 216n.39; Ciudad Júarez/Chihuahua killings 130; Gómez-Peña's *Chica-Iranian Project* 123-5; Gómez-Peña's *mestiza/o* cyborgs 152, 158; Ilich 187–8; La Llorona image 123–4, 212n.12; La Malinche 214n.9; North American Free Trade Agreement 191; Revolution 141, 169, 185–7, 188; Tijuana Bloguita Front 14, 22; US–Mexico relations 13–14, 123–4, 127, 129, 205n.1
Michelangelo, *La Pietà* 130
Mignolo, Walter 17, 18, 23; civilisation and barbarism 116, 117, 119, 127, 132, 212n.15; mapping the Americas 29–30
Miguélez-Carballeira, Helena 20
Milanés, Pablo 182
Milberry, Kate 73
Miller, Daniel 4, 11–12, 14, 201n.1
Miller, Marilyn Grace 141–2
Miller, Vincent 4
Monroy-López, Ivan 190
Montfort, Nick 87
Moraña, Mabel 115
Moreiras, Alberto 18–19, 20, 21
Mosaic browser 203–4n.16
Moulthrop, Stuart 88
Movimento Cívico pelo Direito dos Brasileros 201n.3
multinational corporations 10, 12, 13; and the media 135, 136; *Yes Men* 134
Murray, Janet H. 87, 106, 209n.5

N
Nakamura, Lisa 149, 154, 162–3, 166, 214n.11, 216n.35
narrative arc: computer game theory 201–2n.5; hypertext fiction 6, 201–2n.5
national cultures 9
nation-state 9, 10; 'Cartografía colectiva' project (La Loma, Colombia) 82; civilisation and barbarism 115; consolidation 23;

cultural studies 16; *Hiperbarrio* 82, 83; Mackern's *netart latino database* 41, 44, 45; mapping the internet 32, 33, 51; multinational media giants 136; Navas's *Plástico_2002_upDate* 47, 48, 49; Pilar's *Cyberlabia* 54; and the postnational 19, 20–1
Navas, Eduardo 7, 24, 46–50, 55; Mackern's *netart latino database* 204n.24; *P2P[iece]* online exhibition 36; *Plastico_2002_upDate* 28, 47–9, 50
Nayar, Pramod 210n.20
neo-imperialism/-colonialism: anthropology 129; Gache's *WordToys* 103; García Márquez's *Cien años de soledad* 92; Gómez-Peña's *Chica-Iranian Project* 123–4, 125; mapping Latin America 45, 55; mapping the internet 32, 33; Niño's *Relational Border Map* 133; World Trade Organization 133, 136
neoliberalism: Argentina 64, 65, 67, 207 nn.12, 15; 'Cartografia colectiva' project (La Loma, Colombia) 82; digital tools 185, 200; Digital Zapatismo 187; First World 51; globalisation 8, 10–11, 12–13, 14; Ilich's *possibleworlds.org* 191, 193; *mestiza/o* cyborgs 160; Rodriguez's *Gabriella infinita* 92; *Yes Men* 134
Neruda, Pablo: in Gache's *WordToys* 109
net.art 6–7, 14; borders and frontiers 117; civilisation and barbarism 117, 120, 132–9; cyborgs 149; defining 38, 203n.14; European and North American works on 43–4; *Fin del mundo* 100; Mackern 28, 34–46, 47; mapping Latin America 34–46; Navas 46–9; Niño's *Relational Border Map* 132–9; Zerbarini 58–72
netartreview 46
networked digital culture studies 4–5
Next Five Minutes (N5M) 13
Nicaragua 169, 192
Niño, Marta Patricia 25, 116, 131–2, 139, 140; *Relational Border Map* 7, 131, 132–9, 140
Niven, David 135

No nacimos pa' semilla (1990) 208n.23
Norgrove, Ross 189
North American Free Trade Agreement
    (NAFTA) 191, 193
Nouzeilles, Gabriela 211n.3
novela de la tierra 116, 211n.2
Nueva Trova Cubana, La 182

O
Obama, Barack 178
O'Bryen, Rory 91, 92
Offen, Karl 30
O'Gorman, Edmundo 22–3
Olney, James 61
Olson, Kathleen K. 32
online performance art 7–8; civilisation
    and barbarism 120–31; Gómez-
    Peña 120–31
OpenStreetMap (OSM) 6, 80, 82,
    208n.27
Ortega, Elena 57, 58
Organización de Solidaridad con los
    Pueblos de Asia, África y América
    Latina (OSPAAAL) 202n.2
Orientalism 122–3, 125, 128
Orkut 5, 201n.2
Orwell, George, *1984* 135, 136
Orwell Rolls in his Grave (2003) 135
Oshii, Mamora 203n.6
Osquist, Paul 209n.11
Otra Campaña, La 188
Ow, Jeffrey A. 214n.15
Oxford Internet Institute 3

P
Paasonen, Susana 31
Pacific Islands 40
Pacific Northwest National Laboratory
    53
Padura Fuentes, Leonardo 218n.13
Paesmans, Dirk 34; *see also* JODI
Pagden, Anthony 118
Page, Joanna 206n.7
Pappas, Robert Kane 135
Parche, El (blog) 75
Pardo Lazo, Orlando Luis 175, 176
participatory art 7
participatory democracy 170
participatory mapping 80–1, 199
Partido Revolucionario Institucional
    185–6
Partnoy, Raquel 36, 60
Paz-Soldán, Edmundo 15, 57, 208n.1
Pécaut, Daniel 91, 92

Peñaloza, Fernanda 131
Penteado, Cláudio 6
Perez, Domino Renee 123
Pérez-Torres, Rafael 142–3, 144, 152
performance art 50; cyborgs 145, 150–68;
    online 7–8, 120–31
Phadke, Roopali 82
Philip, Kavita 215n.23
Picasso, Pablo, *Las Meninas* 96, 97,
    209n.14
Pilar, Praba 7, 24, 46, 50–5, 216n.32;
    'Computers Are a Girl's Best
    Friend' 53; *Cyberlabia* 28, 51–5,
    205n.34, 216n.32; Mackern's
    netart latino database 204n.25;
    mestiza/o cyborgs 160, 165–6,
    217n.47
Piñate, Mark 212n.9
Pinochet regime 61
Piper, Keith 216n.43
Pirez, Pedro 65
Pitman, Thea 211n.30
Plant, Sadie 68
Pocha Nostra, La 121, 212n.8; *mestiza/o*
    cyborgs 150, 155, 159, 160
Poe, Edgar Allan 111
Ponce de Léon, Carolina 216n.33
Posse, Abel: in Gache's *WordToys* 109,
    110; *Los perros del paraíso* 110
postcolonialism: civilisation and
    barbarism 122, 123, 125,
    130, 138, 212n.10; cyborg
    consciousness 148, 149; Pilar
    53, 54
posthumanism 145; *mestiza/o* cyborgs
    163, 164
Postill, John 4, 12
postnationalism 19–21
postregionalism 21, 22, 200; Navas 46,
    50; Pilar 46, 55
Pratt, Mary Louise 39
Primer Festival Mundial de la Digna
    Rabia 188
procedural authorship 106–7
Propp, Vladimir, *Morphology of the
    Folk Tale* 201n.5
Puenzo, Luis, *La historia oficial* 61
Puig-i-Abril, Eulalia 6
Pula, Robert P. 132
Pyra 5

R
Raby, D. L. 169, 185
race 143; Pilar 52; *see also mestizaje*

Raley, Rita 13
Rama, Ángel 70; *La ciudad letrada* 24,
    57–8, 199
rasquachismo 156, 204n.18; Gómez-Peña
    42; Rivera 162
Rayones 77–80
Recuero, Raquel 5
regionalism 21, 30; tactical 22
Reisinger, Gunther 44
Rembrandt 112
Remix Theory 46
Restano, Yndamiro 172
Restrepo, Luis Fernando 213n.20
Retamar, Fernández 118; *Calibán* 116
reterritorialisation 59
revolution 26–7, 169–71, 195–6, 198,
    199; García Márquez's *Cien años
    de soledad* 92; Ilich 187–95;
    independent journalism and
    the Cuban blogosphere 172–5;
    Rodríguez's *Gabriella infinita*
    92; Sánchez 175–84; Zapatistas
    184–7
Richard, Nelly 16
Ríos, Alicia 16–17, 116
Risch, John 53
Rivera, Alex 8, 151, 161–2, 164;
    Cybracero Systems 26, 151,
    162–3, 166–7; *Sleep Dealer* 162,
    167
Roberts, Paul Craig 138
Robinson, Ruth Adkins 79
Rodó, José Enrique 23; *Ariel* 116
Rodrigo D., no futuro (1990) 208n.23
Rodríguez, Isis 212n.9
Rodríguez, Jaime Alejandro 87–8;
    Gabriella infinita 6, 25, 84,
    87–100, 101, 103, 105, 106,
    107; Macon.doc 208n.2
Rodríguez, Mauricio (Chonta) 79
Rogala, Miroslaw 7
Rogers, Charlotte 211n.2
Rojas, Hernando 6
Rokeby, David 137
Roldán, Mary 72, 76
Romano, Gustavo 100, 204n.22
Rosas, Juan Manuel de 104
Russian domain names 32

S
Sá, Lúcia 208n.23
Sábato, Ernesto 206–7n.11
Sabøt 189
Said, Edward 125; *Orientalism* 122

Saïd, Suzanne 211n.5
Salazar, Alonso J. 208n.23
Saldívar, José David 118
Sánchez, Yoani 6, 26–7, 175, 193, 196,
    197; *Generación Y* 171, 172,
    175–84
Sandinistas 192
Sandoval, Chela 104, 147–8
Saper, Craig 43
Sardar, Ziauddin 31–2
Sarlo, Beatriz 15
Sarmiento, Domingo Faustino 17, 25,
    115–16, 127, 128, 199, 211n.2,
    212n.15
Schamber, Pablo J. 207n.14
Schiller, Herbert 9
Schwartz, Mildred 74
Scott, Anne 9–10
Scott, Ridley 135, 157
Second Life 191–2
Seed, David 90
SeeNet3D 205n.34
Semmens, Lesley 9–10
Serrano, Elena 202n.2
Servin, Jacques 133
Sexta Declaración de la Selva
    Lacandona 188, 189
Shadow Warrior 214n.15
Shaikhani, Roham 212n.9
Shakira 196
Sharpless, Richard E. 209n.11
Shelton-Mann, Sara 156
Shiva, Vandana 53
Shklovski, Irina 40
Sierra, Marta 211n.27
Sifuentes, Roberto 156, 212n.8, 215n.28
Silicon Graphics 53
Siluetazo movement 65, 207n.16
Silva, Clara Inés 209n.7
Silver, David 3, 4
SirCam virus 215n.22
slang 75, 77, 208n.23
Slater, Don 4, 11–12, 14, 201n.1
Soja, Edward 92
Sommer, Doris 15, 23
Sonvilla-Weiss, Stefan 211n.29
South Park 137, 139
Spain 141
Spivak, Gayatri Chakravorty 212n.10
Stalinism 186
Stallabrass, Julian 35, 43, 203n.14,
    204n.21
Steinberg, Philip E. 32, 40
Stelarc 145, 158

stereotypes: Gómez-Peña's works
122–3, 124, 126, 130, 131,
139; *mestiza/o* cyborgs 159;
revolution 169
Sterling, Bruce, *Islands in the Net* 189
Stoll, David 201n.4
Stone, Allucquère Rosanne 158,
215n.18, 216n.35
Struthers, David M. 40
Suárez, Francisco M. 207n.14
Suárez-Villa, Luis 10
Surrealism 101, 110, 162
Swanson, Philip 117, 120
Swart, Ignatius 133

T
tactical media 8, 13–14, 37, 93, 217n.2;
Los Cybrids 164; definition 13,
134; Niño's *Relational Border
Map* 134–5; revolution 171
tactical regionalism 22
Tamil Eelam websites 40
Taylor, Diana 2, 67
technocapitalism 10
Teknika Radica 216n.35
telematic performance 7
Terminator films 149, 155
testimonio 6, 57, 76, 201n.4
Thailand 12
30 Años de Golpe Militar Argentina
exhibition 36
Thompson, Kristin 95
Tibet 81
Tickner, Arlene 79
Tijuana Bloguita Front 14, 22
Torres García, Joaquin 31, 56; *América
invertida* 41–2
Torres Parra, Carlos Roberto 209n.7
Transborder Immigrant Tool 14, 42
translational network capitalism 10
Tribe, Mark 203n.14
Tricontinental 31
Trigo, Abril 16–17, 202n.10
Triknick, Carlos 100
Trinidad 11
Twitter 5, 201n.2

U
Unamuno, Miguel de, *Niebla* 86
Ungar, Luisa 190
Union Carbide 134, 213n.23
United Farm Workers Union 52
United States of America: Abu
Ghraib jail, Baghdad

129; Americanisation 9;
antiglobalisation movements 133;
Bracero Program 162, 216n.39;
civilisation and barbarism 117,
121, 123–5, 126–7, 138–9;
Cuban connectivity 173; cyborg
consciousness 149; Detainee
Treatment Act (2005) 213n.26;
habeas corpus 138, 213n.26;
immigrants 117, 24, 129, 137,
139, 162, 163; Iraq War 124–5;
mapping Latin America 30, 31,
41, 45; mapping the internet
32, 40; media as impediment to
democracy 135; *mestiza/o* cyborgs
164, 166, 168; *mestizaje* 141,
142, 146, 154, 158, 160, 214n.26;
Navas's *Plástico_2002_upDate*
48, 49; new technologies in the art
world 156; North American Free
Trade Agreement 191; Patriot Act
(2001) 213n.26; photography
195; Pilar's *Cyberlabia* 53, 54,
55; 'Plástico' (Colón and Blades
song) 48, 49; *rasquache* aesthetic
204n.18; third world feminism
147, 148; US–Mexico relations
13–14, 123–4, 127, 129, 205n.1
urbanisation 92
Uruguay 103–4
Uxó, Carlos 173

V
Valdez, Blas 211n.30
Vamos, Igor 133
van der Straet, Jan, *America* 115
Vanegas Montoya, Jaime Gabriel 75
Vargas Llosa, Mario 85
Vasconcelos, José 141
Velázquez, Diego, *Las Meninas* 96, 97,
209–10 nn.14–15
Veldstra, Carolyn 213n.23
Venezuelan Revolution 169
Venter, David 133
Videobarrio 75–80
Virilio, Paul 209n.8
viruses, computer 154, 155, 165–6, 167
VNS Matrix 205n.40
Voeux, Claire 217n.3

W
Wachowski, Andy and Larry 202n.6
Wade, Peter 143
Walrus 53, 205n.33

Wands, Bruce 203n.14
Warburton, Edward C. 7
Warda, Bella 212n.9
Warhol, Andy 112
war on terror 126, 127
Warschauer, Mark 11
weaving 61–2, 68–9
Wexler, Alice 212n.17
Wickham-Crowley, Timothy P.
    220n.60
Willoughby, Lynette 9–10
Wired 31, 144, 202n.3
Wisin and Yandel 195, 220n.61
*Women: Memory of Repression in
    Argentina* exhibition (2003) 36,
    60
World Trade Organization (WTO) 133,
    134, 135, 136
wreader 87, 114; Gache's *WordToys*
    105–6, 107, 109, 111, 112,
    113, 210–11n.26; Rodríguez's
    Gabriella infinita 98, 99
Wright, Melissa W. 213n.19

Y
Ybarra, Juan 160
Yes Men 133–4, 135
YouTube 75, 177

Z
Zapata, Emiliano 185–6
Zapatistas 22, 170, 174, 185–7,
    197, 199, 204n.21, 215n.16;
    Electronic Disturbance Theater
    14, 187; Ilich's *possibleworlds.
    org* 188–9, 190–1, 192, 193;
    influence 171, 185, 188; *see also*
    Digital Zapatismo
Zapatista Tribal Port Scan 187
Zea, Leopoldo 118, 211n.1, 211n.4
Zerbarini, Marina 14; *La borra* 60;
    *Eveline, fragmentos de una
    respuesta* 60; *Gemelos* 60;
    Tejido de memoria 72, 24, 58–9,
    60–1, 62–72, 73, 74, 82–3
Žižek, Slavoj 138
Zúñiga, Miranda, *Vagamundo* 205n.1

For Product Safety Concerns and Information please contact our EU
representative GPSR@taylorandfrancis.com
Taylor & Francis Verlag GmbH, Kaufingerstraße 24, 80331 München, Germany